Global History & Geography

Cover Image: Mohandas Gandhi (1869–1948) was one of the most admired figures of the 20th century. His commitment to nonviolent civil disobedience in India's effort to win independence from Great Britain inspired civil rights leaders around the world, including Martin Luther King Jr. This sculpture honoring him was created by D. P. Roy Choudhury and completed in 1959. It stands in Chennai, a city on the southeast coast of India. **Source:** Thinkstock

AMSCO SCHOOL PUBLICATIONS, INC.,

a division of Perfection Learning®

Reviewers and Consultants

Jay Corcoran
Social Studies Chair
Walt Whitman High School
Huntington Station, New York

Greg Roos
Social Studies Teacher
Remsen Central School District
Remsen, New York

Doreen Gordon
Director of Social Studies and Business
Hauppauge Public Schools
Hauppauge, New York

Gloria Sesso
Director of Humanities
Patchogue Medford Schools
Patchogue, New York

Rich Pyszczek
Coordinator of Social Studies
Buffalo Public Schools
Buffalo, New York

Nick Stamoulacatos
Supervisor for Social Studies
Syracuse City School District
Syracuse, New York

© 2020 by Perfection Learning®
Please visit our website at: ***www.perfectionlearning.com***

When ordering this book, please specify:
ISBN: 978-1-5311-2189-1 or **R609701**

All rights reserved. No part of this book may be reproduced, stored in a retrieval system, or transmitted in any form or by any means, electronic, mechanical, photocopying, recording, or otherwise, without the prior permission of the publisher. For information regarding permissions, write to: Permissions Department, Perfection Learning, 2680 Berkshire Parkway, Des Moines, Iowa 50325.

Printed in the United States of America

8 9 10 11 12 13 BB 24 23 22 21 20 19

Contents

Source: Thinkstock

Source: Shutterstock

Source: Shutterstock

Introduction

Preparing for the Global History and Geography II Exam

This book prepares students for the New York Regents exam that they will take at the end of 10th grade. The exam covers the course Global History and Geography II: 1750–present. It emphasizes the history practices and reasoning skills used by historians, with a strong focus on:

- interpreting and using evidence
- chronological reasoning and causation
- comparison and contextualization

Overview of the Exam

The exam is designed to test the knowledge and skills identified in the New York Social Studies Framework.

Types of Questions

All questions on the Global History and Geography Regents exam will refer to a stimulus, such as an excerpt from a written document, a map, a photo, or a chart. The exam will be divided into three parts based on question type.

Format of the Exam	
Part and Question Type	**Number of Questions**
I. Multiple Choice	28 questions
II. Constructed Response	Two sets of three questions
III. Extended Essay	One set of five documents used to write one essay

Multiple-Choice Questions

Each question will be based on a stimulus. Each stimulus will be used to answer two questions. Students will need to both interpret the stimulus and use their knowledge of global history and geography to identify the best answer.

Constructed-Response Questions

This part will consist of two sets of questions. Each set will include three questions based on two documents. Each question will ask students to write a short answer. The questions will always follow this pattern:

Question 1 will include a document and ask about the **context** in which it was created. It will ask about either:

- the historical context, the circumstances in time in which a historical development occurred
- the geographic context, the location in which the development took place

Question 2 will include a document and ask about the **source** that created it. Students should:

- identify the bias, point of view, audience, or purpose of the person (or people) who created the document

Question 3 will ask about the relationship between the documents used in the first two questions. The relationship will be one of three types. Students will:

- identify and explain a cause-and-effect relationship between the events or ideas in the documents
- identify a turning point—a significant idea or historical event that brings about a change—associated with the events or ideas in the documents and explain why it is a turning point
- identify a similarity or difference between the ideas presented in the two documents

Extended Essay

Students will write a long essay about an enduring issue, which is a challenge or problem that one society has faced across time or one that many distinct societies have faced. The exam will provide students with five documents. In their essays, students should:

- identify and define an enduring issue that appears in at least three of the five documents
- argue that the issue has affected or been affected by people in different periods or places, and how the issue has continued to exist or has changed over time
- use both evidence from the documents and their outside knowledge of social studies

Content Coverage

The exam focuses on the period from 1750 to the present. However, the inclusion of some earlier events and facts is necessary to supply proper historical context. Likewise, while the exam focuses on events and ideas in Europe, it reflects the growing importance of European interaction with the rest of the world.

Thinking Skills

The exam questions use a number of action verbs that indicate what the student is supposed to do. Some of the most common are listed in the following chart.

Responding to Verbs Used in Questions		
Action Verb	**Definition**	**Expectation**
Compare	To consider or describe as similar or equal	Provide and explain the ways in which two or more things are similar
Contrast	To set in opposition to show or emphasize difference	Provide and explain the ways in which two or more things differ from each other
Define	To give the precise meaning or the basic qualities of something	Provide a concrete, real-world example to strengthen a definition
Describe	To provide a representation in words	Note the attributes or characteristics of a place, idea, or person
Discuss	To offer a considered review	Give factors, definitions, descriptions, explanations, examples, etc. of something
Explain	To give an account or add details	Offer reasons or examples to make an idea plainly understood
Identify	To state a clear, concise, specific answer	Often, a single, well-written sentence is sufficient, but you can add clarifying details. However, do not contradict or add confusion to your original answer

Features of This Book

This book presents the core knowledge and skills that students need to learn in Global History and Geography II. The features of the book are described below.

Introduction

In the Introduction, students will be introduced to the following:

- **Elements of the New York Regents Exam** Types of questions, the number of each type of question, time allotment, and how questions are structured
- **Features of New York Global History and Geography** Explains the elements of the book such as the Introduction, the Chapter Openers, Lessons, Chapter Reviews, Period Reviews, and Practice Exams
- **New York Social Studies Framework** Summarizes the New York Social Studies Practices, Common Core Reading Standards for Literacy in History/Social Studies, Unifying Themes, and Course Content for Global History and Geography II
- Scoring Rubrics for Extended Essays

Period Openers

Like the New York Social Studies Framework for Global History and Geography II, *New York Global History and Geography* is divided into four periods. Each period begins with a two-page world map. Each map has callout boxes describing important historical events or developments that are linked to specific regions on the map. These provide students with a quick overview of key points they will be studying in the period.

Chapter Openers

In *New York Global History and Geography*, each chapter begins with a two-page chapter feature. These openers are divided into four sections.

- **Chapter Overview** This provides a short introduction to the chapter content by examining its overarching themes.
- **New York Framework Standard Key Idea** Each chapter is organized around a single Key Idea from the New York Framework, beginning with a snapshot of the world in 1750 and continuing chronologically through to the modern issues of globalization and the movement for human rights.
- **Identify Enduring Issues** This activity helps students practice their skill of identifying enduring issues from text, a key skill in writing the extended essay on the Regents Exam.
- **Key Terms and Names** The chapter's Key Terms and Names are listed thematically, with page numbers included.

Lessons

Each lesson has a number of elements that help students learn important content and practice skills.

- **Conceptual Understanding** Lessons begin with a more focused standard from the New York Framework, indicating to students specifically what they will learn in the pages to come.
- **Analyze a Primary Source** Before students dig into the lesson narrative, they begin with instruction on reading a primary source. A source related directly to the key content for the lesson is accompanied by several marginal notes that provide tips to help students interpret the source.
- **Narrative** The core content described in the New York Framework is presented in clear, concise language.
- **Read Closely** Throughout the narrative, notes in the margin help students develop their skill at reading history. Each note includes a question for students to answer so they can immediately apply that skill to the text they are reading.
- **Application** Finally, each lesson ends with another primary source for students to read and interpret.

Chapter Review

Chapters end with a series of activities to help students analyze the chapter content and practice the sort of questions they will face on the Regents Exam. Tips for answering questions are offered where appropriate.

- **Multiple-Choice Questions** Students answer several sets of multiple-choice questions, each of which is based on one or more pieces of stimulus.
- **Short-Answer Questions** Students write short-answer responses to questions that refer to one or more documents.
- **Speaking and Listening Activity** In groups or individually, students engage in activities that address New York Speaking and Listening standards, such as:
    - initiating and participating in collaborative discussions with diverse partners
    - presenting information, findings, and supporting evidence clearly, concisely, and logically
    - adapting speech to a variety of contexts and tasks, demonstrating a command of formal English when indicated or appropriate

Extended Essay

Each period ends with one or two sets of documents for students to use in writing an extended essay about an enduring issue.

Practice Exam

This book concludes with a practice exam modeled after the Regents exam.

New York Social Studies Framework

The state of New York provides guidance in what content and skills students should study. Some of this guidance is described below.

Social Studies Practices

Students are expected to learn a number of approaches, or practices, that will help them to think like historians.

1. **Gathering, Interpreting, and Using Evidence** Students should learn to:
    - use evidence to create and answer questions but they should also learn to consider alternative hypotheses and answers
    - gather evidence from a wide range of sources and analyze it in terms of point of view, bias, purpose, and other important criteria
    - analyze the arguments of others, effectively make inferences and draw conclusions, and use disparate sources of evidence to create meaningful understandings of the past

2. **Chronological Reasoning and Causation** Students should learn:
   - how events are related in time—that earlier ideas and events can influence those that come later
   - that events and ideas can have short- or long-term effects
   - the importance of historical continuity and change
   - to relate patterns of continuity and change to larger historical processes and themes
3. **Comparison and Contextualization** Students should learn to:
   - compare multiple aspects of historical periods and/or events and geographic regions
   - analyze multiple historical developments within, across, and between societies and in a range of times and places
   - recognize the relationships between geography, economics, and history and see how these relationships function as a context for events and movements
4. **Geographic Reasoning** Students should learn to:
   - ask geographic questions about the importance of place and use geographic tools to assess the relationships between people, places, and environments
   - assess the relationship between human activities and the environment
   - recognize how societies are influenced by place and region
5. **Economics and Economic Systems** Students should understand the impacts of such economic concepts as:
   - marginal benefits/marginal costs, incentives, competition
   - property rights and the rule of law in a market economy
   - how government economic policies affect the economy
6. **Civic Participation** Students should learn to:
   - interact respectfully with others when participating in activities with their communities
   - get involved, when necessary, in social and political issues both as an individual and with groups
   - recognize that the protection of peoples' freedoms and rights in a democratic society depends on their taking responsibility to work to influence those in positions of power

Common Core Reading Standards for Literacy in History/Social Studies

Key Ideas and Details When analyzing sources, students should learn to cite textual evidence, determine central ideas and provide an accurate summary, and determine the difference between correlation and causation in a series of events.

Craft and Structure Students should learn to determine the meanings of history/social studies-focused words and phrases and analyze how key points in a text are highlighted by differing text structures.

Integration of Knowledge and Ideas Students should be able to use charts and graphs in conjunction with text, as well as analyze the extent to which text supports an author's claim.

Range of Reading and Level of Text Complexity By the end of grade 10, students should be able to read and comprehend history/social studies texts in the grades 9–10 text complexity band.

Common Core Writing Standards for Literacy in History/Social Studies

Text Types and Purposes Students should learn to:

- write arguments that focus on discipline-specific content, introducing claims and counterclaims fairly and supporting each with data and evidence
- use linking words and phrases to create a cohesive text and provide a concluding section that supports the argument presented by:
    - introducing a topic and organizing ideas using headings, tables and charts, and multimedia, when appropriate
    - developing the topic using solid and relevant facts, details, quotations, and other appropriate information
    - using precise, domain-specific language and discipline-appropriate style, while maintaining an objective tone

Production and Distribution of Writing Students should be able to improve their writing during the process through revision, editing, rewriting, or refocusing their approach to suit a specific audience or purpose. They should also be able to use technology to publish, update, and distribute writing projects.

Research to Build and Present Knowledge Students should learn to conduct short and extended research projects, gathering and synthesizing information from multiple authoritative sources while avoiding plagiarism and using a standard citation format.

Range of Writing Students should be able to write over extended and shorter time frames for a variety of tasks, purposes, and audiences.

Unifying Themes

The ten Unifying Themes for social studies represent different viewpoints that teachers and students can use when approaching the Key Ideas and Conceptual Understandings found in the New York Social Studies Framework.

1. **Individual Development and Cultural Identity (ID)** The development of personal and cultural identity occurs within the broader framework of a person's geography, era, social and economic class, experiences, politics, and more.
2. **Development, Movement, and Interaction of Cultures (MOV)** Cultural elements such as politics, religion, and race strongly affect things like literature, film, and music. Cultural diffusion and change over time strongly affect these and other cultural elements.
3. **Time, Continuity, and Change (TCC)** The formal research methods that historians apply help them reconstruct and interpret events, analyze historical cause and effect, and weigh the validity of competing theories of events.
4. **Geography, Humans, and the Environment (GEO)** Human populations and their activities have a profound effect on the natural environment. Interactions between people, places, regions, and environments are important aspects of history.
5. **Development and Transformation of Social Structures (SOC)** Social structures, such as economic and social classes and political and social institutions, are affected and often defined by gender, race, ethnicity, age, and other similar factors. This fact can promote social and political inequalities.
6. **Power, Authority, and Governance (GOV)** Different forms of government have differing characteristics and functions. In each form, power has different origins and is used in different ways (and sometimes abused). Diplomacy, conflict, and war are major aspects of governmental power and authority and major subjects of historical study.
7. **Civic Ideas and Practices (CIV)** In a democratic republic, citizens have certain freedoms, rights, and responsibilities (including civic participation and engagement). But in the modern, globalized world, do people have certain responsibilities toward the global community? In nondemocratic countries, people often struggle to achieve and keep basic freedoms and rights.
8. **Creation, Expansion, and Interaction of Economic Systems (ECO)** The study of history includes such economic topics as production, consumption, resource scarcity, supply and demand, trade, globalization, and the role of the government in the economy.
9. **Science, Technology, and Innovation (TECH)** Scientific, technological, and intellectual theories and discoveries directly influence social, economic, and cultural change.
10. **Global Connections and Exchange (EXCH)** Human societies have interacted from the very beginning, exchanging goods, ideas, and technologies. This has accelerated over time as technology has facilitated even greater cultural diffusion. Globalization has many social, political, and economic benefits and consequences.

Course Content

The New York Framework is divided into four periods. The first three are chronological, with the final one focused on contemporary concerns.

1. **The World in 1750** This period exists to give students a sense of historical context at the outset of their studies. In order to understand interactions, ideas, events, and movements in the world after 1750, it is crucial to know what the world was like in the years leading up to that moment in time. This is the shortest period, composed of a single Key Idea.
2. **1750–1914: An Age of Revolutions, Industrialization, and Empires** Period Two covers the largest time span. It was a tumultuous period that began with mostly preindustrial societies ruled by royal families to something approaching the society people know today, with modern nation-states and rapidly evolving technologies. Period Two sees the world at the edge of the explosion of political and social upheaval and violence that shook the world for the following 30 years.
3. **1914–Present: Crisis and Achievement in the 20th Century** Period Three covers World War I and World War II, and it also examines the crucial interwar period where a worldwide economic depression and ongoing resentment over World War I led to extreme political movements mired in hate and bent on conquest. The Cold War dominated the second half of the 20th century, with nuclear tensions and proxy wars in different areas of the globe.
4. **Contemporary Issues** The 21st century has seen its own achievements and challenges. Technological advances have promoted globalization, increasing communication, trade, and opportunity in many parts of the world. But tensions between traditional ways and modernization persist, and environmental degradation and human rights issues remain central issues.

Ten Key Ideas

Each Key Idea in the New York Framework is the starting point for one chapter in *New York Global History and Geography*. That Key Idea is stated on the first page of the chapter. Within each Key Idea are Conceptual Understandings, and each of these is the starting point for a lesson within the ten chapters.

1. **The World in 1750**
2. **Enlightenment, Revolution, and Nationalism**
3. **Causes and Effects of the Industrial Revolution**
4. **Imperialism**
5. **Unresolved Global Conflict (1914–1945)**
6. **Unresolved Global Conflict (1945–1991)**
7. **Decolonization and Nationalism**
8. **Tensions Between Traditional Cultures and Modernization**
9. **Globalization and a Changing Global Environment**
10. **Human Rights Violations**

Enduring Issues

Many of the most important challenges in history appear repeatedly in societies throughout the world. Because they are concerns that people have confronted over long periods they are called *enduring issues*. The chart below lists several enduring issues, along with a few examples of each.

Examples of Enduring Issues

Enduring Issue	Examples from History
Conflict	1. Voltaire challenged religious discrimination in the Enlightenment. 2. Vietnam fought for independence against France. 3. The United States confronted the Soviet Union in the Cold War.
Cooperation	1. European states negotiated to divide Africa for colonization. 2. Countries agreed to create the United Nations. 3. Public health agencies worked together to fight polio.
Power	1. Enslaved Haitians abolished slavery successfully. 2. Nazis seized control of Germany. 3. Terrorists attacked the United States on September 11, 2001.
Inequality	1. Women argued for equality at the time of the French Revolution. 2. Whites had more rights than did blacks during apartheid in South Africa. 3. Western Europe was wealthier than East Asia during the 20th century.
Innovation	1. Manufacturers developed new machines during the Industrial Revolution. 2. Militaries used tanks and planes in World War I. 3. Farmers planted new varieties of grain in the Green Revolution.
Interconnectedness	1. The European Enlightenment influenced revolutions in the Americas. 2. Many ethnic groups lived together in the Ottoman Empire. 3. The Internet linked people globally as never before.
Ideas and Beliefs	1. Adam Smith developed the concept of the invisible hand. 2. The United Nations supported universal human rights. 3. Hindus and Muslims fought during the partition of India.
Environmental Impact	1. Enclosure reduced the amount of land available for common use. 2. Factory emissions caused air and water pollution. 3. Deforestation and economic development led to desertification.
Scarcity	1. Industrialized countries desired resources from their colonies. 2. Great Britain rationed goods during World War II. 3. The OPEC oil embargo led to a gasoline shortage in the United States.

Applying the Task Models

1. Best Use for a Source

Historians rely on primary sources to understand the past. Primary sources include any firsthand account of an event. They can be either a written or an artistic account by either participants or observers. However, each type of source has both strengths and weaknesses that influence how historians can use them best. The chart below lists some of the common types of primary sources and their strengths and weaknesses.

Evaluating Types of Primary Sources		
Type	**Strengths**	**Weaknesses**
Diary	Often reflects insight into how a person felt	Sometimes lacks context of how others thought or felt
Memoir	Often expresses an insider's view of events	Sometimes written to flatter a leader or attack an opponent
Speech	Often indicates what a leader believes or what the leader thinks listeners want to hear	Sometimes deliberately misleading in order to make the speaker popular
Newspaper reports	Often provides objective information	Sometimes sensationalized to sell copies
Government report	Often presents detailed, neutral, information	Sometimes reflects a government's bias
Religious artifacts	Often shows what people believed and held valuable	Sometimes open to several interpretations

For each source listed below, write a question that it could help answer.

1. The diary of a British Empire official writing about the Christians and Hindus

____

____

2. A letter home from an English merchant living in the Ottoman Empire

____

____

3. A mask used in a religious ceremony in Benin

____

____

4. Ship records listing cargo on voyages between Lisbon and Beijing in 1700

____

____

2. Identify the Author's Intention

Interpreting a source accurately requires understanding why the author wrote it. The table below summarizes issues to identify in order to recognize what an author is trying to communicate.

Influences Shaping an Author's Intention		
Type of Influence	**Description**	**Examples**
Point of View	The author's role in an event	• The author's level of wealth or race
Purpose	The reason the source was created	• A desire to persuade or to entertain
Context	The general historical conditions	• A time of economic prosperity or religious conflict
Bias	The values of the author	• A supporter of gender equality or slavery
Form of the Source	The nature of the source	• A long book or a short newspaper advertisement
Time the Source Was Created	The chronological period	• During the Romantic era or World War II
Place the Source Was Created	The geographic location	• A large coastal city or a small village in the mountains
Intended Audience	The people the author created the source for	• A few experts or all potential voters

For each source listed below, identify two influences that might shape how the author might write the item identified.

1. The diary of a French university professor commenting on the influence of the Enlightenment in the 1790s

____

____

2. A journalist writing in 1815 in a British newspaper describing the demands by women for more rights

____

____

3. A letter from a Prussian diplomat to his supervisor reporting on a meeting with Catherine the Great in 1790

____

____

4. A speech by Louis Kossuth on the relationship between Hungarians and Austrians

____

____

3. Identifying Support for a Claim

A claim is a statement asserted to be true. A well-written claim is not simply a personal preference. Rather, it can be supported—or opposed—with facts, reasons, or informed opinions.

Statement	Is this a good example of a claim?
I like Adam Smith's idea, expressed in 1776, of the "invisible hand" because it explains a complex idea simply.	No: it is a personal preference. Other people cannot use evidence to prove or disprove it.
Smith's idea of the "invisible hand" is useful because it describes how a market economy actually works.	Yes: people can provide facts and informed opinions to support or oppose it.

The table below evaluates how well statements support a claim about the usefulness of Smith's idea of the "invisible hand."

Statement	Is this a good example of support?
The "invisible hand" explains how consumers and producers coordinate their decisions.	No: it simply rewords the claim.
Smith was from Scotland.	No: it is not relevant to whether his idea was useful.
If consumers will pay higher prices for milk, this sends a message to dairy farmers to increase their herds.	Yes: it provides a concrete example to support the general statement.

Evaluate whether each sentence is a good example of a well-written claim.

1. I believe history is my favorite subject to study in school.

____

____

2. The ideas of Adam Smith still influence how people think about the economy today.

____

____

Evaluate whether each sentence is a good example of support for a claim that learning history is valuable.

3. Studying global history prepares people to understand current events.

____

____

4. History classes usually require more reading than do biology courses.

____

____

4. Select a Plausible Claim

Historians build an interpretation about the past based on primary sources. Based on the sources, they make plausible claims that they think logically follow from the source. However, not all claims based on a primary source are equally plausible. Following is a primary source written by Reverend James Mulligan describing the diet of farmers in Ireland in 1845. Read it and consider the claims stated in the table after it.

> The small farmers live on potatoes and milk. It is considered that he is a very fortunate man if he has milk for his family. He sells his butter and never uses oatmeal in his house. It is thus obvious that oatmeal plays a quite secondary role in the household economy of the poorer classes, and that the primary meal consists of potatoes.
>
> **Source:** Rev. James Mulligan, "Description of Carrickmacross, Co. Monaghan," (1845). Oliver J. Thatcher, ed., *The Library of Original Sources* (Milwaukee: University Research Extension Co., 1907).

Claims and Plausibility

Claim	How plausible or logical is the claim?
Farmers ate the same food every day.	Very plausible: Mulligan states it clearly.
Farmers in Ireland rarely bought food.	Plausible: Mulligan refers to the "poorer classes." This is also a logical claim based on the lack of variety in their diet.
Most farmers kept cows for milk.	Somewhat: Farmers lived on milk, which implies they had cows, but Mulligan then says that only the "fortunate" farmers had milk.
Farmers preferred to eat oatmeal rather than potatoes.	Not logical: Mulligan says nothing about what farmers prefer, so this claim does not flow logically from the source.

Evaluate the plausibility of each claim listed below.

1. All European farmers were eager to use new technology in the early 1800s.

____

____

2. Developments in Meiji Japan and Victorian England in the 1800s proved that industrialization required democratization.

____

____

3. Without reforms such as the growth of labor unions in the 1800s, Europe would have exploded in revolution.

____

____

4. Urbanization and industrialization often occurred together.

____

____

5. Identify Turning Points in History

A **turning point** is an event in history that led to lasting change. For example, the following excerpt demonstrates how a single telegram can lead to crucial and lasting change in historical events. In 1917, most of Europe was involved in World War I, but the United States and Mexico were not. The German foreign secretary, Arthur Zimmermann, sent a telegram to the German minister in Mexico proposing that, if the United States declared war on Germany, Mexico should declare war on the United States. However, the telegram was intercepted by British intelligence and passed along to the United States. People in the United States were furious that Germany was trying to start a war between the United States and Mexico. One month later, the United States declared war on Germany. Just over a year later, Germany was defeated.

> We make Mexico a proposal of alliance on the following basis: make war together, make peace together, generous financial support and an understanding on our part that Mexico is to reconquer the lost territory in Texas, New Mexico, and Arizona [in 1848]. The settlement in detail is left to you.

Understanding the Zimmermann Telegram	
What was Zimmermann proposing to Mexico?	He proposed a Mexico-Germany alliance if the United States declared war on Germany.
Why did the telegram affect the U.S. public so strongly?	Germany offered to help Mexico take territory that had be-longed to the United States for about 70 years.
How does the telegram represent a turning point in history?	It influenced the opinions of war-wary people in the United States and changed the course of World War I.

Describe how each of the following represented a turning point.

1. the Treaty of Versailles, 1919

____

____

2. Battle of Stalingrad, 1942–1943

____

____

3. the U.N. Charter, 1945

____

____

4. the formation of Israel, 1948

____

____

6. *Identify Change and Continuity in History*

Change and continuity, or an uninterrupted succession, are vital lenses through which historians attempt to analyze historical events and trends. Change is different than a turning point, in that it is much less sudden. Historians often identify change by comparing two distinct historical moments to see how circumstances differ between them—for example, Tokugawa Japan in the mid 1600s and Meiji Japan in the latter half of the 1800s. However, it is usually the case that when comparing two points in time such as these, while change is often apparent, there is also continuity. The following chart identifies examples of both change and continuity between the aforementioned points in Japanese history.

Japan Before and After the Meiji Restoration	
Change	**Continuity**
Japan opened to contact with the outside world	Country never colonized
Samurai stripped of their positions; new military based on Western model instituted	Unique, traditional Japanese culture survived
Emperor became head of a constitutional democracy	The emperor still a figurehead for government, society
Power of shoguns eliminated	Society still peasant based

Select an important event from history. Write the name of it in the top bar. Then list three changes from before and after the event, and three continuities.

Name	
Changes	**Continuities**
1.	1.
2.	2.
3.	3.

7. Identify Central Causes

In order to explain and understand historical events more accurately, historians try to determine their central causes. Most historical events do not have a single, central cause. Rather, events take place in a framework with many variables. For example, some causes arise from long-term circumstances and some arise from short-term circumstances. Most arise from a combination of both. The chart below lists multiple causes of World War I.

Short-Term and Long-Term Causes of World War I	
Long-Term Causes	• Repeated invasions of Russia from the west over several centuries • The advent of Communist control in Russia in 1917
Short-Term Causes	• Invasion of Russia by Nazi Germany in 1941 • The Soviet defeat of German forces and occupation of most of Eastern Europe at the end of World War II

Label each phrase as a long-term cause or a short-term cause of World War I and briefly describe its signficance.

1. The assassination of Archduke Ferdinand in Sarajevo

2. Imperialist competition between European nations

3. Germany's seizure of Alsace and Lorraine after the Franco-Prussian War

4. Serbian nationalism

8. Identify Central Effects

In their attempts to make sense of historical events, historians also try to determine their central effects. As is true with the causes of historical events, most do not have a single, central effect, and the effects manifest themselves over a continuum, with some being short term and others being long term. The chart below shows a number of effects of World War II.

Short-Term and Long-Term Effects of World War II	
Long-Term Effects	▪ The devastation of a large number of Europe's cities ▪ The Berlin blockade and airlift ▪ The installation of Communist regimes in countries behind the Iron Curtain
Short-Term Effects	▪ The creation of NATO, an alliance of Western democracies ▪ The creation of the Warsaw Pact, an alliance of Soviet-controlled nations ▪ The Cold War struggle for power and influence worldwide between the Soviet Union and the United States

Label each phrase as a short-term or a long-term effect of World War I and briefly describe its significance.

1. World War II

____

____

____

2. Runaway inflation postwar Germany

____

____

____

3. The development of the Nazi Party

____

____

____

4. The destruction of the towns and cities of northwestern France

____

____

____

9. *Identify the Impact of Time and Place*

Where and when a historical event occurred affects why it occured. As a result, historians think about the importance of time and place on events and issues.

- What people or movements had impacts on other people or movements?
- Did an area's topography play a role?
- Did the involvement of another actor contribute to the outcome?

In the timeline below, note how time and place shaped events in Indochina.

Date	Events
1887	The French establish full control of Indochina (Vietnam, Laos, and Cambodia).
1940	During World War II, Germany defeats France in Europe. Germany's ally, Japan, takes possession of Indochina.
1941	Vietnamese Communist leader Ho Chi Minh forms a nationalist alliance, the Viet Minh, to resist Japanese control.
August 1945	Japan surrenders and the communist-led Viet Minh takes control.
1946	British and Indian troops help the French retake part of Vietnam.
November 1946	War between Viet Minh and French forces begins.
1946–1954	Viet Minh fighters win a guerrilla war against the French, using Vietnam's dense jungles for cover and with aid from Communists who won power in China in 1949.
1954	Viet Minh victory at Dien Bien Phu marks France's defeat.

Explain how either time or place influenced each event.

1. In World War II, Nazi Germany overran France, but failed to conquer Britain.

____

____

2. Chiang Kai-Shek established a Chinese government in Taiwan in 1949.

____

____

3. Jordan, Syria, Lebanon, and Egypt attacked Israel in 1948.

____

____

4. In the 1950s, more French had settled in Algeria than in Indochina.

____

____

10. Identify a Similarity

Historians closely study different documents or other evidence to make note of similarities and differences between them. Similarities in sources can help historians notice where a consensus exists or realize the strength of a certain theory. Differences can help show where bias might exist in a certain source or where further research is necessary. The following chart offers examples of ways that certain pieces of evidence might show similarities.

Types of Sources	Similarities
Two news reports of the same event	Statements that appear in both reports are more likely to be accurate.
Two maps of the same region but from different periods	Boundaries that are the same show continuity in history.
Memoirs by two participants in an event	Recollections that are shared might suggest similarities in the outlook of the two writers.

Identify three similarities stated in the following passage.

Some projections for Uganda suggest it will not change much by 2060. The average number of births per female will remain far higher than the global average. Population will continue to be centered in the southeastern part of the country. Women will continue to be about 48 percent of the labor force. However, projections are also that the infant death rates will drop sharply, that people will live longer, and that the total population of the country will almost triple.

Source: Based on information from http://www.ifs.du.edu/ifs/frm_CountryProfile.aspx?Country=UG

Similarities
1.
2.
3.

11. Identify a Difference

Historians study documents and other evidence to locate and analyze differences. Differences often indicate turning points or change over time. The following chart offers examples of ways that certain pieces of evidence might show differences.

Types of Sources	Differences
Two news reports of the same event	Statements that appear in only one report reflect the reporter's point of view.
Two maps of the same region but from different periods	Elements that differ might show changes in population distribution or boundaries.
Memoirs by two participants in an event	Recollections that differ might reflect the participants' differing roles or viewpoints.

After reading these two sources on globalization, summarize the differences.

Benefits of Globalization

Libertarians have traditionally promoted globalization because of its liberating effects on people's lives. Globalization is an international extension of free markets and open societies. In effect, it is capitalism without borders. . . . Globalization permits us to interact with whomever we choose, and to buy from, to work for, or to borrow from others than the local employers and suppliers.

Source: https://www.libertarianism.org/encyclopedia/globalization.

Costs of Globalization

The free movement of labor also has its downsides. When workers can move freely from one nation to the next, countries that have a dearth of job opportunities often struggle. Skilled employees do not often stay in countries without a strong job market, which can cause a labor drain. . . . The environment impact of globalization is considered to be negative by most experienced observers. The increased consumption of a wide variety of products leads to increased production which causes an uptick in pollution. Simply put, the environment is under added strain, which can have devastating long-term effects on the planet's environmental stability.

Source: https://occupytheory.org/globalization-pros-and-cons-list/.

1. ______________________________

12. Identify an Informed Action

The process of taking an informed action begins with education. In a democratic society, it is critical for citizens—individually or as part of a group or organization—to seek out and use important information about issues that affect their lives and the lives of their fellow citizens. (This highlights the absolutely crucial role that a free and independent media plays in a democratic society.) Once a citizen or group of citizens has identified an issue and formulated a viewpoint based on accurate information, one result can be civic activism—activities designed to improve people's communities, environments, and/or governments. A wide range of activities falls under the umbrella of civic activism:

- helping clean up a neighborhood park
- volunteering at a school or community center
- advocating for poor or homeless citizens
- raising money for a local library
- running for public office

Read the following article and answer the questions that follow it.

Hannah Testa is a fifteen-year-old activist from Georgia who founded the environmental advocacy organization Hannah4Change in 2014. By working together with Georgia state senators, she was able to have February 15th proclaimed as Plastic Pollution Awareness Day (PPAD) in the state. . . . "The purpose of PPAD is education. I wanted to educate Georgians about the growing crisis of plastic pollution, and as more and more people become aware of the issue, they'll eventually change their ways. Hopefully we'll be able to pass a bill to ban single-use plastics. . . . The shocking truths revealed in Plastic Paradise [a documentary about the Great Pacific Garbage Patch] drove her to start doing whatever she could to make a difference. . . . "You have to realize that you are never too young or too old to make a difference," she said. . . . "With the Internet and social media, there are many effective ways to make your voice heard. . . . We just need to care enough to act."

Source: http://www.onegreenplanet.org/environment/activist-fighting-end-plastic-pollution/

1. Explain how Testa informed herself about an issue.

2. Describe the informed action she took.

13. Answer Questions about Visuals

In the study of history, visual evidence, such as maps, graphs and charts, timelines, cartoons, and photographs, can be a source of critical evidence. Sources such as these need to be analyzed thoroughly. The following chart gives some suggestions on how to effectively analyze visual sources.

Types	Methods for Analyzing
Maps	• Study the map legend to understand what each dot, line, shading, color, etc. represents. • Use the map's compass and scale. • Note when the map was made, who made it, and for whom it was made to understand the point of view it represents.
Graphs and Charts	• Use the title to identify the graph's or chart's main idea. • Note how the headings, axes, and any types of lines or shading help organize the information. • Identify details that support the main idea.
Timelines	• Determine the time period covered in the timeline. • Identify how the timeline has been divided and why it was done in this way. • Identify patterns, such as cause and effect, continuity, and change.
Cartoons	• Look for signs of the cartoonist's political leanings and cultural background that might represent bias. • Evaluate the cartoon in the context of the era it was created.
Photographs	• Analyze the details in the photograph. • Consider whether the photograph became a symbol of a historical era or event.

Find an example of a visual used in a recent news story. Answer the following questions about it.

1. What is the main point of the visual?

____

____

2. What important details does the visual provide?

____

____

3. What is the point of view of the person who created the visual?

____

____

14. Identify Stakeholders and Issues

A stakeholder is anyone who has a share or an interest in an issue or enterprise. A stakeholder issue is the issue or enterprise in which the stakeholder is engaged. For example, imagine that in a state, a group wanted to pass a law by referendum removing an animal from a protected list and allowing people to hunt the animal in limited amounts. This would be the stakeholder issue. The stakeholders in this scenario are, broadly, the voters of the state and the legislators who introduced the referendum. But there are also more specific stakeholders, including:

- members of conservation groups dedicated to wildlife preservation
- members of groups that support the right to hunt
- lobbying groups on both sides
- people who run outdoor-related tourism businesses such as hunting lodges

Read the following article and answer the questions that follow.

Is Eminent Domain Being Abused?

Just about everyone knows that under a process called eminent domain, the government can (and does) seize private property for public use—to build a road, a school or a courthouse.

But did you know the government can also seize your land for private use if they can prove that doing it will serve what's called "the public good"? . . .

Jim and Joanne Saleet are refusing to sell the home they've lived in for 38 years. They live in a quiet neighborhood of single-family houses in Lakewood, Ohio, just outside Cleveland. The City of Lakewood is trying to use eminent domain to force the Saleets out to make way for more expensive condominiums. . . .

But Lakewood's mayor, Madeleine Cain . . . wants to tear down the Saleets' home, plus 55 homes around it, along with four apartment buildings and more than a dozen businesses. Why? So that private developers can build high-priced condos, and a high-end shopping mall, and thus raise Lakewood's property tax base. . . .

Dana Berliner and Scott Bullock are attorneys at a libertarian non-profit group called The Institute for Justice, which has filed suit on behalf of the Saleets against the City of Lakewood. They claim that taking private property this way is unconstitutional. "This is a nationwide epidemic," says Berliner. "We have documented more than 10,000 instances of government taking property from one person to give it to another in just the last five years."

Source: https://www.cbsnews.com/news/eminent-domain-being-abused

1. What is the issue being debated in this passage?

____

____

2. Who are the stakeholders in the issue described in the passage?

____

____

15. Identify a Course of Action

Throughout history, issues have presented themselves, and a course of action is needed to address the issue. In some instances, a course of action is recommended by a historical figure, a group, or a government.

Read the following historical news article from 1900. Then answer the questions that follow.

Mark Twain on Imperialism

Samuel L. Clemens (Mark Twain), who arrived here from Europe tonight, was asked: "Have you given any thought to the grave question of imperialism?"

"It is most too grave a question for one of my temperament," was the reply, "but I have taken a try at it, and it has got the better of me.

"I left these shores at Vancouver a red-hot imperialist. I wanted the American eagle to go screaming into the Pacific. It seemed tiresome and tame for it to content itself with the Rockies. Why not spread its wings over the Philippines? I asked myself, and I thought it would be a real good thing to do.

"I said to myself: Here are a people who have suffered for three centuries. We can make them as free as ourselves, give them a government and country of their own, put a miniature of the American constitution afloat in the Pacific, start a brand new republic to take its place among the free nations of the world. It seemed to me a great task to which we had addressed ourselves.

"But I have thought some more, since that time, and I have read carefully the treaty of Paris. I have seen that we do not intend to free, but to subjugate, the people of the Philippines. We have gone there to conquer, not to redeem. We have also pledged the power of this country to maintain and protect the abominable system established in the Philippines by the friars.

"It seems to me that it should be our pleasure and duty to make those people free and let them deal with their own domestic questions in their own way. And so I am an anti-imperialist. I am opposed to having the eagle put its talons on any other land."

Source: http://uwch-4.humanities.washington.edu/Texts/twain/Mark%20Twain%20on%20Imperialism.htm.

1. What is the issue being debated in this passage?

____

____

2. Who is recommending a course of action?

____

____

3. Describe the course of action recommended.

____

____

16. Identify Relationships in Time

Historians note the chronological order in which events happen. This can help them identify how one event might have caused a later one. Creating a timeline is one effective way of organizing historical events chronologically. The following timeline lists events in 1945, near the end of World War II.

Date	Event
April 16	Soviet troops surround Berlin.
April 30	Hitler kills himself in his bunker in Berlin.
May 7–9	Germany surrenders.
August 6	United States drops an atomic bomb on Hiroshima.
August 9	United States drops an atomic bomb on Nagasaki.
September 2	Japan surrenders.
October 24	The United Nations is founded.
November 20	The Nuremberg War Crimes Tribunal begins to work.

Historians are cautious about making claims of causation. To make a claim that one event caused another, historians need to do more than simply show that one event happened before another. The Soviet attack on Berlin probably contributed to Hitler's decision to commit suicide. However, whether Japan's surrender led to the founding of the United Nations is not clear.

Number these events in chronological order. Then explain a likely cause-and-effect relationship between two or more of them.

Event	1. Order
A. Massive unemployment in Germany.	
B. Germany invades Poland.	
C. The Allies win World War I.	
D. World War II begins.	
E. The Treaty of Versailles cripples Germany's economy.	
F. Hitler seizes control of the German government.	

1. ____

____

____

____

17. Identify a Problem

In history, a problem is a condition or event that causes difficulties for people. However, problems for some people are often opportunities for others. For example, weak regulations on air pollution might lead to problems such as lung disease for some people, but benefit those who own or work in factories.

The following chart shows the annual rate of inflation, how much prices increased, in the world between 2003 and 2009. Healthy economies often have low inflation. It encourages people to invest and to borrow money to buy homes. However, high inflation is usually considered a problem. For example, retired persons living on fixed incomes have trouble affording higher prices for food and housing. People with large debts can benefit from high inflation, as long as wages increase with prices. In the data below, the largest problem for some people occurred in 2003. For others, the largest problem was in 2008.

	2003	2004	2005	2006	2007	2008	2009
Inflation	3.3%	3.6%	4.2%	4.5%	5.1%	9.0%	2.9%

Source: https://data.worldbank.org/indicator/FP.CPI.TOTL.ZG

Identify the opportunities and problems that arose from the changes in the political situation in the Balkans between 1988 and 2018.

Balkan Countries in 1988 and 2018		
1988	**2018**	
Albania	Albania	Macedonia
Bulgaria	Bulgaria	Montenegro
Greece	Bosnia and Herzegovina	Romania
Romania	Croatia	Serbia
Yugoslavia	Greece	Slovenia
	Kosovo	

1. Opportunities

____

____

____

____

____

2. Problems

____

____

____

____

____

18. Identify a Response to a Problem

When a problem exists, how can people respond? The following article describes a problem. This problem and a response to it are listed in the chart below.

Guatemala's Democracy, June 4, 1994

President Jorge Serrano Elias . . . last week suspended constitutional government, dissolved the Supreme Court and Congress, censored the press, restricted freedom of assembly, and allowed arrests without warrants. . . .

In response to the move, Japan announced June 1 that it was restricting future aid to Guatemala to emergency and humanitarian aid. . . . European governments have suspended another $100 million. The United States froze much of a $50 million aid package.

Source: https://www.csmonitor.com/1993/0604/04181.html

Problem	Response
Guatemalan President Jorge Serrano Elias assumed dictatorial powers in the nominally democratic state of Guatemala.	Japan, European governments, and the United States enacted strong economic sanctions against Guatemala.

Read the following excerpt. Identify the problem and the response outlined in it.

The Ebola Crisis, May 29, 2018

The international medical humanitarian organization Doctors Without Borders/ Médecins Sans Frontières (MSF) started vaccinating Ebola frontline workers yesterday in . . . [the] Democratic Republic of Congo (DRC). The vaccination, which is being conducted with Epicentre—MSF's research arm—will also be offered to contacts of patients. . . .

The vaccination trial—which is only one element of the larger strategy to control the spread of Ebola—will be administered using a "ring" approach. This involves identifying newly diagnosed and laboratory-confirmed Ebola patients, locating the people they have been in contact with—often family members, neighbors, colleagues, and friends—and vaccinating them. This type of approach aims to help contain and prevent the spread of infection.

Source: https://www.doctorswithoutborders.org

Problem	Response
1.	2.

Period 1

Chapter 1

A Snapshot of the World, 1750

The World in 1750

Since the earth is a sphere, no printed map shows both shapes and distances exactly. Some maps show one of these well but the other poorly. This map shows both fairly accurately.

Map Notes

This map includes notes around its edges that describe important historical events. To make clear what place on the map is the setting for the information in the note, the note and the place are labeled with a letter.

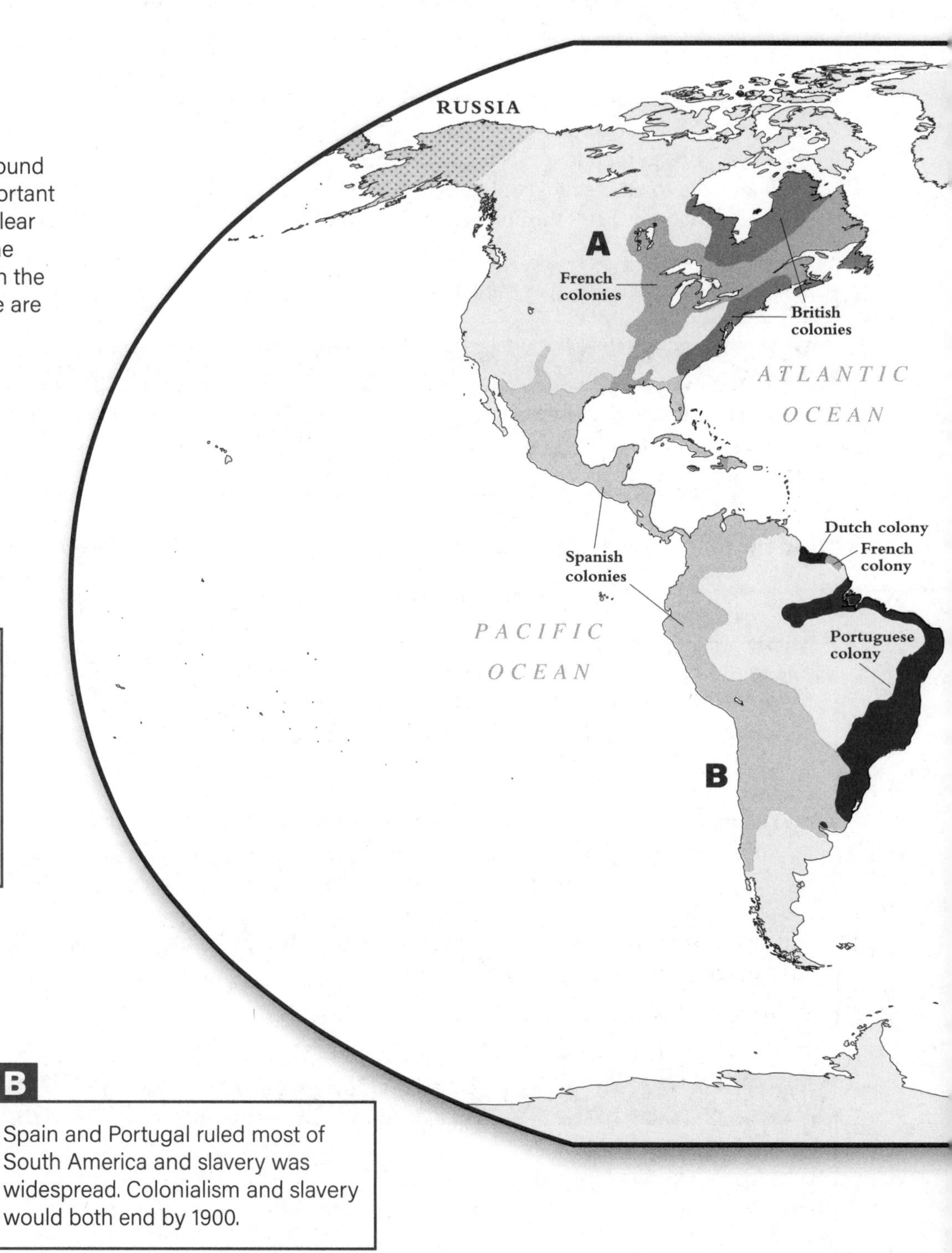

A

Great Britain, France, Spain, and a variety of Native Americans controlled most of North America. Both France and Great Britain lost most of their American empires by 1800.

B

Spain and Portugal ruled most of South America and slavery was widespread. Colonialism and slavery would both end by 1900.

C

Africa suffered as people were captured, enslaved, and sold to slave owners in the Americas, the Middle East, and India. Powerful states did emerge in West Africa.

D

The widespread use of machinery began in Great Britain in the mid-18th century. This change revolutionized world history.

E

The Russian Empire was expanding across Asia as Europeans and Americans were expanding westward in North America. Both would reach the Pacific Ocean.

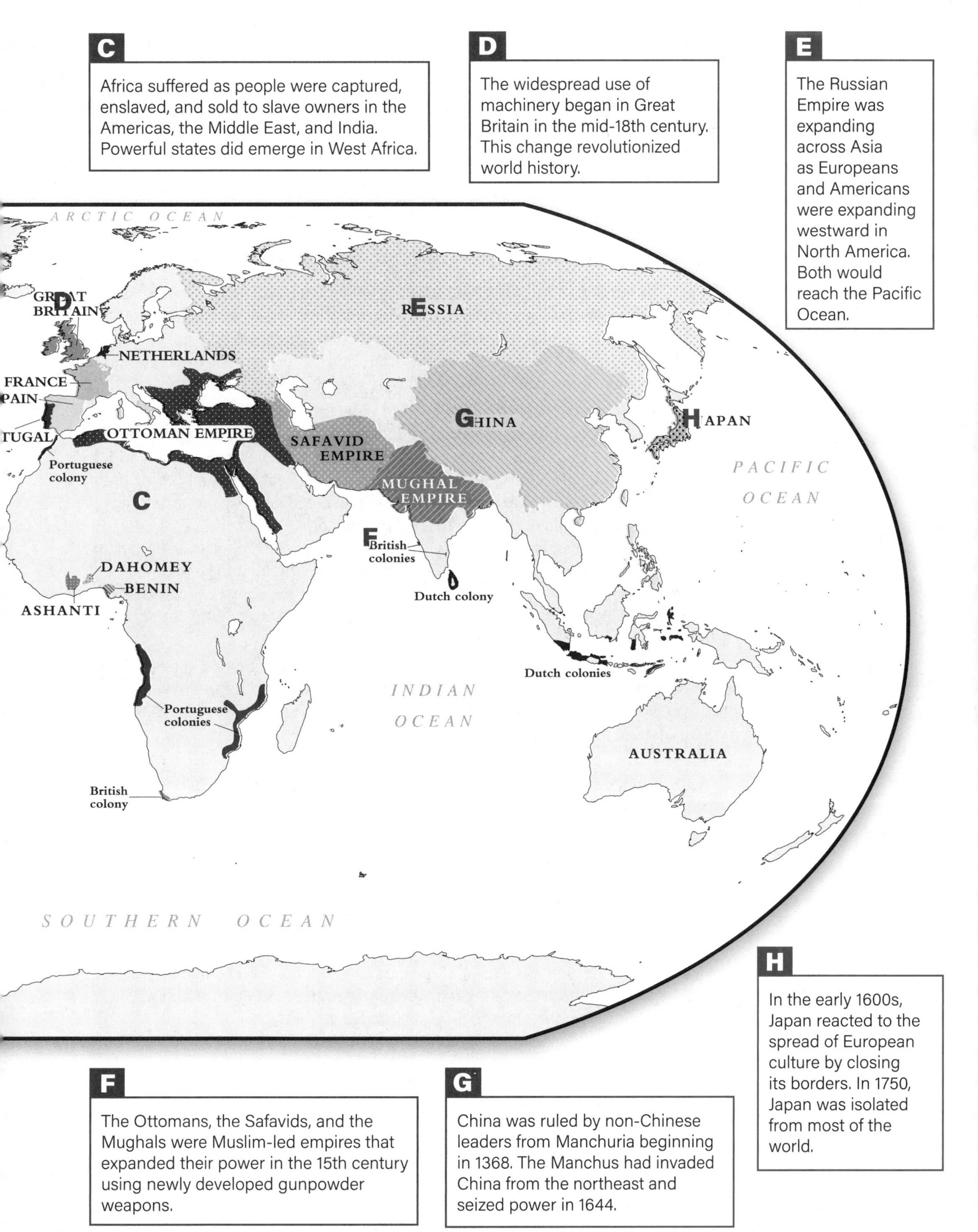

H

In the early 1600s, Japan reacted to the spread of European culture by closing its borders. In 1750, Japan was isolated from most of the world.

F

The Ottomans, the Safavids, and the Mughals were Muslim-led empires that expanded their power in the 15th century using newly developed gunpowder weapons.

G

China was ruled by non-Chinese leaders from Manchuria beginning in 1368. The Manchus had invaded China from the northeast and seized power in 1644.

CHAPTER 1

A Snapshot of the World, 1750

Chapter Overview

Around 1750, Eurasia's major powers were Great Britain, France, Russia, the Ottoman Empire based in Turkey, and the Mughal Empire based in India. Each responded to major challenges based on its particular heritage and situation.

The Ottomans and the Mughals The Ottoman Empire and the Mughal Empire had existed for centuries. Each was led by Muslim rulers and often practiced religious and ethnic tolerance, had a centralized political system, and profited from extensive trade. The development of all-water routes from Europe to East Asia undercut the overland trade the Ottomans relied upon for prosperity.

Japan and France Japan was not a world power in 1750. This was by choice. Since the early 1600s, Japan's government had feared that European Christians would undercut its traditional culture, so it limited contact with the outside world. In contrast to the Mughal Empire, which lost power to Europeans, Japan became highly centralized and peaceful. However, its isolation prevented advances in technology and thought that were developing in the rest of the world.

In some ways, Japan was similar to France. Under Japan's Tokugawa shogunate and France's Bourbon dynasty, the central government struggled to control the large landowners who had been the traditional leaders in the country. Each created a national bureaucracy that could collect taxes and administer government services without relying on the regional leaders.

Responses from China and Africa Other empires tried other responses to growing Western power. In China, the Qing dynasty allowed trade to grow, a strategy that would prove costly for China in the 1800s. In West Africa, three states—Ashanti, Benin, and Dahomey—increased their power by selling enslaved people to Europeans.

An Enduring Issue: Connections One enduring issue in this chapter is the significance of interconnectedness among people in various regions. The Ottomans and the Mughals were highly connected with others through land-based trade. China and West Africa were shaped by their contacts with Europeans. In contrast, Japan was shaped by its lack of ties with other cultures.

***New York Social Studies Framework:* Key Idea 10.1**

The world in 1750 was marked by powerful Eurasian states and empires, coastal African kingdoms, and growing European maritime empires. The interactions of these states, empires, and kingdoms disrupted regional trade networks and influenced the development of new global trade networks.

Source: *New York State Grades 9–12 Social Studies Framework.*

1. Rewrite Key Idea 10.1 in your own words.

____

____

Identify Enduring Issues

Many topics that historians study are ones that people in cultures around the world have faced over decades or centuries. These topics are enduring issues. The excerpt below is from observations made by Arthur Young. In the 1780s, he traveled from his home in England to France to study how people farmed and lived there.

> The poor people seem poor indeed; the children terribly ragged . . . shoes and stockings they are luxuries. A beautiful girl of six or seven years playing with a stick, and smiling under such a bundle of rags as made my heart ache to see her; they did not beg and when I gave them any thing seemed more suprised than obliged. One-third of what I have seen of this province seems uncultivated [not used for farming], and nearly all of it in misery. What have king, and ministers, and parliaments, and states, to answer for their prejudices, seeing millions of hands that would be industrious, idle and starving.

Source: Arthur Young, *Travels in France during the Years 1787, 1788, 1789* (1889).

Young was concerned about at least two issues that people continue to debate. One is poverty. The other is government's role in promoting prosperity. List five issues that you think people in the past faced and that still endure today.

1. ______________________________

2. ______________________________

3. ______________________________

4. ______________________________

5. ______________________________

Key Terms by Theme

Movement

missionaries (p. 7)

Geography

Edo (p. 10)
Paris (p. 11)
Versailles (p. 11)
Nagasaki (p. 15)

Social Structures

devshirme (p. 8)
janissaries (p. 8)

Governance

Ottoman Empire (p.7)
Mughal Empire (p. 7)
Tokugawa Shogunate (p. 7)
Bourbon Dynasty (p. 7)
Akbar (p. 8)
Aurangzeb (p. 9)
shoguns (p. 9)
Tokugawa Ieyasu (p. 10)
Louis XIV (p. 11)
Louis XV (p. 12)
Pax Tokugawa (p. 15)
Peter the Great (p. 17)
Manchu (p. 17)
Qing Dynasty (p. 17)
Ashanti (p. 18)
Dahomey (p. 18)
Benin (p. 18)

Exchange

East India Company (p. 16)

Lesson 1 States and Empires

Smallpox was one of the most feared diseases in 18th-century Europe, killing hundreds of thousands of people each year. About 30 percent of those who caught the disease died from it. However, in the Middle East and Asia, people had developed procedures to protect themselves from smallpox. In the following letter to a friend written in 1717, Lady Mary Wortley Montagu, wife of the English ambassador to the Turkish Ottoman Empire, describes what the Turks did. Montagu became a leading advocate of the procedure in England. After she persuaded the Royal Family to use it, it became widely adopted. Among those who were treated, less than 2 percent of those who caught smallpox died from the disease.

In the late 18th century, an English doctor, Edward Jenner, developed a similar but even safer procedure. In the 20th century, the disease continued to kill millions of people per year. However, it was finally eradicated in 1979, the first infectious disease ever eliminated globally.

Conceptual Understanding 10.1a Powerful Eurasian states and empires faced and responded to challenges ca. 1750.

Source: *New York State Grades 9–12 Social Studies Framework.*

Analyze a Primary Source

Mary Wortley Montagu, letter to Sarah Chiswell, April 7, 1717

I am going to tell you a thing that I am sure will make you wish yourself here. The smallpox, so fatal and so general amongst us, is here entirely harmless by the invention of engrafting (which is the term they give it). There is a set of old women who make it their business to perform the operation. . . . They make parties for this purpose, and when they are met (commonly fifteen or sixteen together) the old woman comes with a nutshell full of the matter of the best sort of smallpox and asks what veins you please to have opened. She immediately rips open that you offer to her with a large needle (which gives you no more pain than a common scratch) and puts into the vein as much venom as can lie upon the head of her needle. . . .

The children or young people play together all the rest of the day and are in perfect health till the eighth. Then the fever begins to seize 'em and they keep their beds two days, very seldom three. . . . Ever year thousands undergo this operation. . . .There is no example of any one that has died in it, and you may believe I am very well satisfied of the safety of the experiment since I intend to try it on my dear little son. I am patriot enough to take pains to bring this useful invention into fashion in England, and I should not fail to write to some of our doctors very particularly about it if I knew any one of 'em that I thought had virtue enough to destroy such a considerable branch of their revenue for the good of mankind.

Source: Adapted from Mary Wortley Montagu, letter to Sarah Chiswell, April 7, 1717. Reprinted at pyramid.spd.louisville.edu.

Read Closely: Point of View
Look for signs that reflect a person's perspective. Underline the phrases that indicate that Montagu wants to describe something she found unusual in Turkey.

Read Closely: Purpose
Readers can infer Montagu's purpose when she notes that smallpox is "so fatal" elsewhere but "entirely harmless" in Turkey. She wants the English to learn from the Turks.
Underline the steps that Montagu claims are used to make the illness harmless.

Read Closely: Context
Montagu is writing during a period known as the Scientific Revolution. Europeans were more willing to experiment with new ideas than in the previous 1,500 years.

Read Closely: Intended Audience
Montagu's letter is written to one friend, but her audience is much larger.
Circle the passage where Montagu indicates her primary intended audience.

Comparing Powerful Empires

In 1750, people throughout the world interacted extensively. Traders, travelers, and **missionaries** carried goods and ideas from their home countries to other lands. Often, the introduction of new ideas—or the threat of attack—created challenges for countries to respond to. The **Ottoman Empire** in southwest Asia, the **Mughal Empire** in south Asia, the **Tokugawa Shogunate** in Japan, and the **Bourbon Dynasty** in France show four ways people responded to these challenges.

Read Closely: Identify Related Change
One way to understand the significance of a development is to note how it is connected to changes elsewhere. Describe the connection between changes in the Ottoman Empire and in the Byzantine Empire.

The Ottoman Empire

The **Ottoman Empire** began as a small dominion in northwest Anatolia (modern Turkey) just before 1300. Its first ruler was Osman I. Over the 400 years, he and his successors built a massive empire spanning large parts of southwestern Asia, southeastern Europe, and North Africa.

The Empire Expands The Ottoman Empire's founder and his immediate successors gained modest amounts of territory to both the east and the west up until 1450. (This was in spite of a crushing defeat at the hands of the central Asian warlord Tamerlane in 1402.) The territory to the west came at the expense of the Byzantine Empire, which was steadily deteriorating.

During this period, many local European rulers were defeated militarily, but some, seeing the power of the Ottomans, simply submitted to Ottoman control. Those who did this were left to rule their own territories as long as they paid tribute and provided soldiers for battles upon demand. In this way, the Ottomans could rule areas with a minimum of investment and bureaucracy while the local people were allowed to go about their lives much as before.

In 1453, after repeated attempts, the Ottomans managed to conquer the city of Constantinople, effectively taking control of the Byzantine Empire. This further opened southeastern Europe to Ottoman power. By the end of the 17th century, the empire stretched from the Persian Gulf and the Caspian Sea in the east to past Algiers in North Africa and to the walls of Vienna in the west.

Read Closely: Turning Point
A phrase such as "repeated attempts" indicates a trend or phase in history. Inserting "after," as in "after repeated attempts," suggests a shift from one phase to another. What significant shift occurred in 1453?

THE OTTOMAN EMPIRE

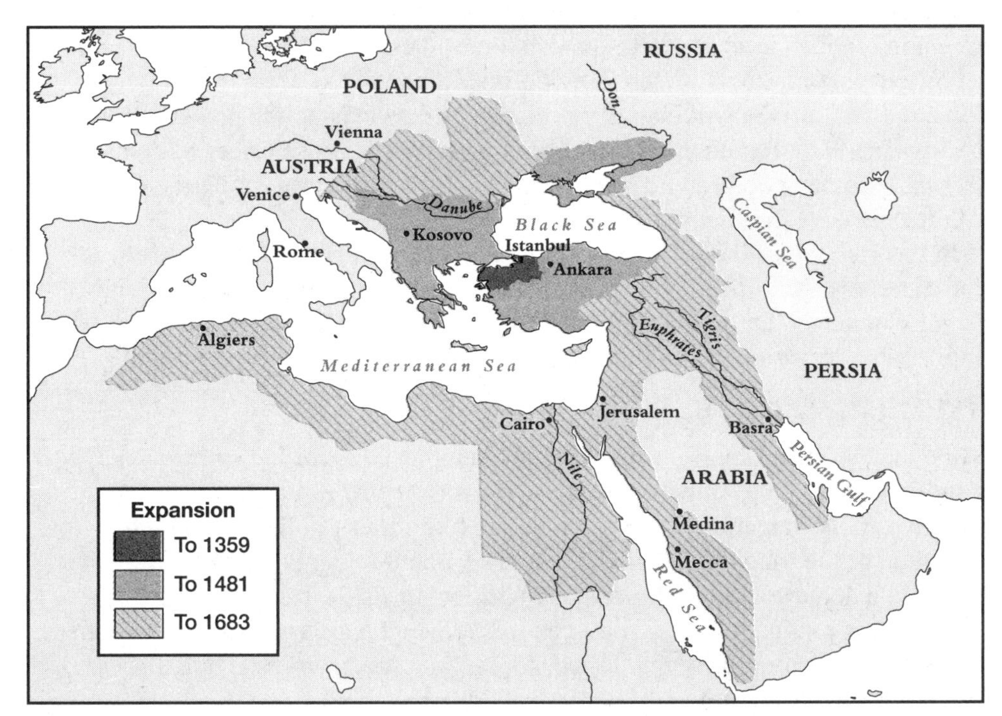

The Ottoman Empire conquered through its military might. But it kept its empire through effective administration and an ever-improving legal system. To staff their military and government, the Ottoman sultans used a selection system called the ***devshirme.*** Through it, the empire recruited, by force, Christian boys who lived within the empire to serve in the government. Boys aged 8 to 20 were taken each year from conquered Christian lands in Europe. After converting to Islam, they were taught various skills in politics, the arts, and the military. Some became elite soldiers, the **janissaries,** while others became administrators—scribes, tax collectors, diplomats, and so on—throughout conquered lands.

The Ottoman Economy As the territory of the Ottoman Empire expanded, so did the size and variety of its economy. Taxes collected from people in the conquered territory made the government prosperous. Much of the wealth of the empire, and an important source of tax revenue, was from trade:

> **Read Closely: Distinguish Terms**
> A sentence that begins "However" often describes a contrast with an idea expressed previously, such as distinguishing between two similar words. What is the difference between *persecuted* and *discriminated against?*

- The empire controlled the North African coast of the Mediterranean Sea, which had a profitable trade in gold and slaves that originated in West Africa and were transported north across the Sahara.
- Ottoman merchants vied for control of seaborne trade in the Mediterranean and beyond with merchants from the cities of Venice and Genoa as well as the various kingdoms of Spain.
- Luxury goods from India, China, and islands in the Pacific flowed in overland through the empire's eastern provinces, particularly silk and spices.
- Artisans with the empire created distinctive tiles, pottery, and rugs, for example.

One reason for the success of trade in the Ottoman Empire was that sultans generally allowed Christian and Jewish merchants to prosper as long as they paid taxes. In particular, after Spain expelled Jews in 1492, the Ottomans welcomed the Jews to settle in their empire. Jews and Christians were not persecuted for their faith by the threat of prison or torture. However, Jews and Christians were discriminated against—they did not have the same legal and political rights as Muslims.

However, by the end of the 17th century, the Ottomans faced economic decline. One cause was new technology, particularly improvements in ships and navigation tools. These allowed Spanish, Portuguese, British, and Dutch seafarers to transport luxury items by sea more cheaply than the Ottomans could overland. Corruption within the Ottoman upper classes had weakened the power of the sultans. The flow of gold and silver from the Americas cause prices to go up. As a result, Ottoman goods could not be produced at a price low enough to compete with inexpensive European imports.

> **Read Closely: Identify a Problem**
> New technology often brings both progress for some and problems for others. How did European progress in shipbuilding and navigation result in problems for the Ottoman Empire?

In the first half of the 18th century, the decline of the Ottoman Empire was well under way. European powers such as the Habsburg Empire, Russia, and Venice challenged Ottoman supremacy in southeastern Europe, pushing the empire's borders back to their locations in the 1500s.

The Mughal Empire

While the Ottoman Empire was at its peak, another Muslim-led empire emerged in India. In the 1520s, a time in which India was in political disarray, Babur, a descendant of Tamerlane, conquered much of northern India, marking the beginning of the Mughal Empire. It would be Babur's grandson Akbar, however, who would achieve grand religious and political goals. Ruling from 1556 to 1605, **Akbar** proved to be the most capable of Mughal rulers, installing practices and establishing prosperity that lasted, for the most part, until the mid-1700s.

Akbar In his first 40 years in power, Akbar defeated Hindu armies and extended his empire to the south and west. From his capital in Delhi, he established an effective ruling system. It consisted of strong central government, some local control for governors, an efficient civil service, and a system of fairly administered laws. For example, all of his people had the right to appeal to him for final judgment in any lawsuit. As Akbar's fame spread, capable men from many parts of Central Asia came to serve him.

Akbar was tolerant of the many religions that existed in his empire. He allocated grants of money or land to Hindus and Muslims alike. He gave money for a Catholic church in Goa, where Portuguese traders had a base on the southwest coast of India. He provided land grants for the relatively new religion of Sikhism. He tried to mediate the conflict between Hindus and Muslims, in part by exempting Hindus from the poll taxes paid by all non-Muslims in the empire.

The Mughal Empire under Akbar was wealthy, well governed, and generally peaceful. Overseas trade, carried out mostly by Arab traders, flourished. Traded goods included wool, silk and cotton cloth, sugar, salt, spices, precious stones, indigo, and more—all of which were traded, for the most part, for gold and silver. In later years when direct trade with Europe increased, this demand for payment in precious metals irked European traders. However, the demand for Indian goods was so great that they paid the requested prices.

The Mughals Beyond Akbar The Mughal Empire mostly flourished up through most of the 17th century. But under the ruler **Aurangzeb,** the empire began to falter. He attempted to increase the size of the empire and bring all of India under Muslim rule. Additionally, he wanted to rid the empire of its Hindu influences. His military expeditions drained the treasury, and peasant uprisings, sparked by Aurangzeb's insistence on an austere and pious Islamic lifestyle, spread and intensified. Both Hindu and Islamic princes began to revolt.

Following Aurangzeb's death in 1707, a series of competitions for leadership weakened the empire. So, too, did invasions from the west, which further emboldened regional leaders to challenge central Mughal authority. By 1750, the Mughals were weak and getting weaker. Their weakness allowed for a new power to arise in the region: Great Britain. Before long, British power would become preeminent in India.

An Enduring Issue: Human Rights
Akbar is famous for practicing religious toleration. This is one response to the challenge faced by people in many cultures where people with different beliefs live together.

Read Closely: Propose a Course of Action
To understand an individual's actions, see them in the context of actions by others. For example, Akbar and Aurangzeb followed very different policies. Based on their different policies, what advice might Akbar have given to Aurangzeb?

Comparing the Ottoman and Mughal Empires

Ottoman Empire Only	Both the Ottoman and Mughal Empires	Mughal Empire Only
• Defeated the Byzantine Empire • Required some Christian boys to become devshirme • Collapsed partly because of corruption	• Ruled by Muslim leaders • Showed toleration to Jews and Christians • Prospered because of trade • Benefitted from a strong, stable central government	• Traded silk, spices, and gems to Europe in exchange for gold • Allowed a new religion, Sikhism, to develop • Collapsed partly because of an overzealous ruler and regional uprisings

The Tokugawa Shogunate

Read Closely: Stakeholders
Read to understand the motives of people. One way to motivate people to be loyal is to give them a stake in the stability of the government. Explain how the Tokugawa Shogunate created stakeholders among the daimyo.

Military leaders known as **shoguns** ruled Japan in the emperor's name from the 12th to the 15th centuries. But then conflicts between landholding aristocrats called *daimyo* left Japan in disarray. Each daimyo ruled his own territory as he saw fit and used his personal army of warriors, known as samurai, to try to conquer more territory. One result of this was ongoing warfare. A second result was that the samurai developed a tradition of loyalty and obedience to their daimyo that became an important part of Japanese culture.

The fighting among the daimyo finally ended over a 35-year period because of the efforts of a series of three leaders. With the help of gunpowder weapons, these leaders united Japan under a central government strong enough to impose peace. These leaders were:

- Oda Nobunaga, a daimyo from central Japan. Armed with muskets purchased from Portuguese traders, he took over Kyoto in 1568. Before his assassination in 1582, he controlled about one-third of Japan.
- Toyotomi Hideyoshi was born a peasant, but he rose to become a military leader under Nobunaga. He took Nobunaga's place and continued to force other daimyo to submit to his power. By 1598, he controlled most of Japan.
- **Tokugawa Ieyasu** shifted the center of power from Kyoto to the city of **Edo,** renamed Tokyo in 1868. He was declared shogun in 1603. His successors ruled Japan into the mid-19th century, in an era known as the Period of Great Peace. The lack of conflict allowed the economy and the culture to flourish.

Tokugawa Government When Tokugawa Ieyasu took power, Japan was divided into 250 hans, or territories. Each was controlled by a daimyo who had his own army. The Tokugawa Shogunate replaced this feudal system with a more centralized government.

Read Closely: Impact of Time
Noticing changes in context time will help you see the influence of time on ideas such as social class. For example, explain whether you think merchants in the United States today are treated differently than were merchants in Tokugawa Japan.

One way the Tokugawa government controlled the daimyo was that it required each one to maintain residences in both their home territory and the capital. When a daimyo was residing in his home territory, his family was required to stay in Edo—essentially as hostages. This system gave the shogunate great power and reduced the daimyo to weak landlords who managed the hans.

Samurai Status As civil wars ended in Japan, the samurai warrior class had fewer wars to fight. Many became unemployed. Some wandered the countryside acting as samurai without masters, while others became bandits. The government urged samurai to become bureaucrats in the restructured government. However, work as a bureaucrat did not pay as well as being a samurai had in the past.

Despite their falling fortunes, the traditional warrior class of the daimyo and samurai remained highly respected. They were near the top of the social pyramid in Japan—below only the emperor and the court. Below the warrior class were peasants and farmers, who labored to produce the food people depended upon. Artisans and merchants ranked below the peasants and farmers.

This structure reflected the influence of the ancient Chinese philosopher Confucius. People viewed merchants as parasites because they did not make anything. Rather, they profited using products created by others. Their low rank notwithstanding, some merchants became quite wealthy, even wealthier than some daimyo. These merchants were able to build lavish houses in Edo, right alongside those of highly respected daimyo.

Economic Growth Under the stability of the centralized Tokugawa government, silk production flourished. The silver mine in Iwami Ginzan, one of the largest in the world, provided a desired metal for trade. The use of banking and paper money also spurred commercial development. Agricultural production increased dramatically during the period, resulting in surplus crops of rice and cotton. Although the government restricted foreign trade, Chinese, Korean, and Dutch traders did have some access to Japan.

Fear of Foreigners However, by the 1630s, Japan's leaders began to see foreigners and especially Europeans, who brought new technology and the religions of Christianity, as a threat. As a result, Japan expelled nearly all foreigners from the country and banned foreign books.

Read Closely: Actions
Historians try to explain what information, reasons, or values led people to act as they did. These explanations are particularly important when later generations might disagree with those actions. What beliefs informed the decision of the Japanese to expel foreigners in the 17th century?

Comparison: Edo and Versailles/Paris

At the beginning of the 18th century, the capital cities of Edo, Japan, and **Paris,** France, were half a world apart, but they had some important similarities. Both were centers of prosperous states.

Bourbon Versailles

Paris had long been France's capital and seat of government. But in the century leading up to 1750, successive kings from the house of Bourbon had begun to move their personal and public lives to a new palace complex at **Versailles,** about ten miles southwest of Paris.

King **Louis XIV** (ruled 1643–1715) inherited a relatively modest complex at Versailles. However, during his reign he built it into a huge and sumptuous palace complex. He spent enormous amounts of money on the construction and moved the seat of government there from Paris in 1682.

The development of Versailles was, in part, an effort to subdue the country's

Source: Wikimedia Commons

Aerial view of the Palace of Versailles, France.

nobles, who had long resisted domination by the kings. A noble who wanted to have influence and status in France during Louis's rule wanted to attend court at Versailles. But at Versailles, Louis was firmly in charge and was able to control and minimize the nobles' power. The power and domination of the Versailles court continued under the king's successor, **Louis XV** (ruled 1715–1774).

Read Closely: Importance of Place To understand the importance of geography in history, notice why events happen in one place rather than another. How did Louis XIV and Louis XV use the location of Versailles to centralize power over France?

When Versailles was the center of court activity, the arts flourished there and in Paris. The great writers Molière and Racine blossomed under Louis XIV's patronage. Academies of the sciences, music, and architecture were founded. During the reign of Louis XV, the king was a generous patron of the sciences, taking a particular interest in botany. The Trianon Botanical Gardens at Versailles featured a vast range of plants that had been brought by French explorers from the far corners of the world.

In spite of the architectural, scientific, and cultural high points of Versailles, the palace complex was a cause of numerous, serious issues for France. It was expensive to build and maintain, so it contributed to the tax burden on French peasants. It also isolated the French royalty and nobility, both geographically and culturally, from the people of France. Both as a drain on the treasury and as an isolating factor, Versailles helped prepare France for a revolution that began in 1789.

Edo

As noted earlier, Edo became the Tokugawa period's capital around 1600. During the following 150 years, Edo grew into a large urban center with a prospering economy and flourishing artistic culture. As in the court at Versailles, attendance by provincial lords at the seat of government was basically required. This enabled the shogun to control the nobles' power and activities, which further strengthened the central government. After the banishment of foreign influences in Japan, another tactic to strengthen the power of the shogun, the Japanese economy experienced growth, and the culture of Edo and Japan began to change.

Read Closely: Recognize Differences
Words such as "unlike" indicate that the text is describing a difference between two places, trends, or events. How did funding for the arts differ in France and in Japan in the 18th century?

The Arts in Japan Unlike in France, achievements in the arts were not a direct result of royal patronage. It was the increasingly more powerful and wealthy merchants and artisans of Edo who patronized and developed the arts. The great poet and prose writer Bashõ lived and worked in Edo, helping to further the development of haiku and other literary styles. Kabuki theater, a dramatic form using singing, dancing, and highly stylized costumes and sets, developed largely in Edo during this period as well.

Diversity in Japan After 1720, some foreign influences, including books, were allowed in Japan once again. Western literature, known as "Dutch learning," became popular among the merchant class—especially the subjects of Western culture and technology.

Another foreign influence in Japan in the 18th century came from China. Chinese thought spurred a movement among some in Japan known as neo-Confucianism. Like traditional Confucianism, this movement emphasized the importance of obeying one's parents and practicing rituals. However, it was new in its emphasis on reason and rational thinking.

The Dutch learning and the new Confucianism reflected the cultural diversity found within Japan. A third sign of this diversity appeared in language. Variations in speech were so strong that people from opposite ends of the country could not understand each other. While they all shared an identity as Japanese, their country was a collection of local regions rather than a strongly united single state.

Application

Read the excerpt and answer the questions that follow it.

Toyotomi Hideyoshi, Edict on the Collection of Swords, 1588

a. The farmers of all provinces are strictly forbidden to have in their possession any swords, short swords, bows, spears/firearms or other types of weapons. If unnecessary implements of war are kept, the collection of annual rent may become more difficult, and without provocation uprisings can be fomented [started]. Therefore those who perpetrate improper acts against samurai who receive a grant of land, must be brought to trial and punished . . . Therefore, the heads of provinces, samurais who receive a grant of land, and deputies must collect all the weapons described above and submit them to Hideyoshi's government.

b. The swords and short swords collected in the above manner will not be wasted. They will be used as nails and bolts in the construction of the Great Image of Buddha [at the Hokoji Temple]. In this way, the farmers will benefit not only in this life but also in the lives to come.

c. If farmers possess only agricultural implements and devote themselves exclusively to cultivating the fields, they and their descendants will prosper. This compassionate concern for the well-being of the farmers is the reason for the issuance of this edict, and such a concern is the foundation for the peace and security of the country and the joy and happiness of all the people.

Sources: Hitomi Tonomura, *Community and Commerce in Late Medieval Japan* (Stanford UP, 1992).

1. Specify the point of view of the writer of this edict, Toyotomi Hideyoshi.

___

___

2. Select a phrase and explain how it demonstrates Toyotomi's purpose in issuing this edict.

___

___

3. Describe the context of Japan in the 16th century that is useful in understanding why Toyotomi issued this edict.

___

___

4. Explain if bias is shown or not by Toyotomi.

___

___

Lesson 2 *Interactions in Eurasia*

Conceptual Understanding
10.1b Perceptions of outsiders and interactions with them varied across Eurasia.

Source: *New York State Grades 9–12 Social Studies Framework.*

The European missionaries who visited China in the late 17th century ignited an exchange of knowledge between the western and eastern ends of Eurasia. In the following account, a Catholic priest describes the reaction of the Chinese emperor to the European system of writing musical notes.

Analyze a Primary Source

A Catholic Priest Listens to Music in China, 1679

Read Closely: Accuracy
The Chinese had been using written musical notation for over 1,500 years to describe the tones made by bells, though not for entire songs.

Read Closely: Motivation
The passage describes the emperor's reaction to the music. It might reflect his honest feelings. Or it might show his desire to be polite to his guests.
Underline the portions of the passage where the emperor seems to show delight at the skill of the Europeans.

Read Closely: Variations
Note that secondary sources can reflect varied interpretations. At one point in the excerpt, the emperor's reaction might be seen as skepticism of the Europeans, enjoyment at seeing a surprising skill, or a desire to be sure he was correct.
Circle the statement from the account where skepticism could be attributed to the emperor.

Read Closely: Generalization
One claim that flows logically from the phrase "It must be owned" is a general trait of the emperor: he was eager to learn from Europeans. This claim could be supported or rejected based on other statements.

They [the Chinese] have no musical notes, nor any sign to denote the diversity of tones, the raising or falling of the voice, and the rest of the variations that constitute harmony. The airs which they sing or play upon their instruments are got only by rote and are learnt [learned] by the ear. Nevertheless, they make new ones from time to time. . . .

The ease wherewith we retain an air after the first hearing, by the assistance of notes, extremely surprised the late Emperor Kangxi. In the year 1679, he sent for Père [Father, a title for a Catholic priest] Grimaldi and Père Pereira to play upon an organ and a harpsichord that they had formerly presented him; he liked our European airs and seemed to take great pleasure in them; then ordered his musicians to play a Chinese air upon their instruments, and played likewise himself in a very graceful manner.

Père Pereira took his pocketbook and pricked down all the tune while the musicians were playing, and when they had made an end repeated it without missing one note, which the emperor could scarcely believe, his surprise was so great. . . . He admired, above all, that the Father had learned in so short a time an air which had been so troublesome to him and his musicians, and that by the assistance of characters he could recollect it at any time with pleasure.

To be more certain of this, he put him to the trial several times, and sung several different airs, which the Father took down in his book, and then repeated exactly with the greatest justness [accuracy]. "It must be owned," cried the emperor, "the European music is incomparable, and this Father [speaking of Padre Pereira] has not his equal in all the empire." This prince afterwards established an academy of music, and made the most skillful persons in that science members of it, and committed it to the care of his third son, a man of letters and who had read much.

Source: Jean-Baptiste Du Halde, *The General History of China,* Volume 3 (London: John Watts, 1734), pages 68–69. books.google.com

Europeans and Asians

In two regions of Asia, well-established governments came into direct contact with Europeans during the 16th century. They were the Mughal Empire in southern Asia and the island of Japan in far eastern Asia.

Portuguese and Japan

The first Europeans to land in Japan were shipwrecked Portuguese sailors who ran aground on Japan's southern coast in 1543. The local daimyo was interested in the guns they had and thus began trading with the Portuguese. From this small beginning, Japanese history would move in new directions.

Read Closely: Turning Point
Phrases such as "From this small beginning" imply that what is coming next will mark a turning point in history, when something new is developing. Describe the turning point in European-Japanese relations that happened in 1543.

Christianity in Japan

Over the following 50 years, traders and then missionaries arrived from Portugal and later from Spain, England, and the Netherlands. The Europeans traded guns and products from their other Asian holdings, particularly spices, for Japanese silver and other products. The Catholic missionaries from Portugal and Spain were relatively successful, converting about 300,000 Japanese to Christianity.

Japan's leaders knew Spain had taken control of the Philippines, partly through spreading Christianity. They feared a similar fate for Japan. In the 1590s, some daimyo began to limit Christian missionary activity. Within a few decades, these limits evolved into jailing, beating, and killing Japanese Christians.

Japanese Seclusion

By the mid-1630s, the Tokugawa shogun had barred nearly all contact with foreigners. Not only were all foreigners banned from travel to Japan, but no Japanese were able to travel abroad. The shogun allowed one exception to this policy of seclusion. On an island in the harbor of the port city of **Nagasaki,** Chinese, Korean, and Dutch merchants were allowed to continue limited trading.

Japan's seclusion lasted for about 250 years. Geography explains one reason Japan was able to isolate itself. As an island country, Japan had greater control over the entry of foreigners than did countries with land borders. In addition, Japan could more easily control which aspects of foreign culture to borrow or reject.

Seclusion ended when American warships arrived in 1853 and forced Japan to accept more foreign trade. However, Japan continued its tradition of selecting which foreign influences to accept. In the late 1800s, Japan adopted only what it considered the best of Western practices in government, education, and technology. So, even as Japan modernized, it maintained its distinctive heritage.

Read Closely: Recognize Cause
Historical events usually have many causes. One way historians show causes is through examples. What example caused Japanese leaders to be fearful of Europeans?

Results of Japan's Isolation

Topic	Result
Independence	Japan avoided Western domination, a fate that China, India, and the Philippines suffered.
Culture	Japan protected its distinctive traditions, such as the role of the samurai, and its writers, actors, and painters flourished.
Social Structure	Japan maintained a feudal system until after many countries had abandoned it.
Technology	Japan was slow to adopt new technology developed in other countries until the 1860s.
Peace	Japan had a long period of peace, the **Pax Tokugawa.**

Mughal Interactions with Outsiders

Read Closely: Recognize the Impact of Place
When words such as "unlike" are used to describe a place, they often suggest how one place differs from another. How did the geographic positions of India and Japan influence their trade with Africa and other parts of Asia?

From the beginning of the Mughal Empire, contacts between people in India and outsiders were important. Unlike the island nation of Japan, Mughal territory lay along a much-used overland route between southeast Asia and western Asia, where it connected to routes into Europe. By sea, India was connected with east Africa, the Persian Gulf, and the Red Sea.

New Trade Routes

When the Portuguese discovered the sea route to Asia around the southern tip of Africa, Europeans were able arrange trade in Asian goods without need of land-based traders in western Asia. They established a base at Goa in southwestern India and several others along the route through the Indian Ocean and more still in the islands of southeast Asia. After 1600, direct contact and trade with Europeans increased as the English East India and Dutch **East India companies** became more heavily involved.

The British in South Asia

But it was interaction with the English that would prove to be most consequential for South Asia. By the late 17th century, the English were supplying Mughal Indian textiles to Europe. The English held fortified posts in the port cities of Madras (modern Chennai) and Calcutta (modern Kolkata) and ran a profitable trade out of Bombay (modern Mumbai). The mutual profitability of this trade helped maintain an uneasy peace between the British and the Mughals.

Read Closely: Identify Continuity
A trend consists of several events that can be described in the same way. List one or more phrases that describe continuity in Britain's role in India between the 17th century and the 19th century.

The British strongholds in India, supported by its powerful navy and firearms, eventually produced dire consequences for the Mughals. British generals increasingly played the role of king-maker, installing local leaders whom they could control. Despite ongoing resistance, the 100 years following 1750 saw the strengthening of British power in India. What territory they did not seize they dominated by controlling local princes through a mixture of threats and payoffs.

Unlike the Tokugawa in Japan who reponded to Europeans with isolation, the Mughals in India fostered trade with Europeans. As a result, Japan kept its independence, but India was entirely colonized by Great Britain. British domination of India finally ended in 1947.

World Empires and Kingdoms, c. 1750

Two of the most successful European empires were created by small countries, Great Britain and the Netherlands. They grew through a combination of ambition, naval power, and effective political maneuvering.

European Maritime Empires

Britain is the best example of a small land that became immensely powerful. By 1750, this island nation was among the world's preeminent naval powers. It controlled extensive territories across the globe. Besides India, Great Britain ruled Ireland, Canada, the 13 colonies that would become the United States, and several profitable suger-producing islands in the Caribbean (such as Jamaica and Barbados), as well as scattered colonies in West Africa and South America.

The Netherlands, whose people are often referred to collectively as "the Dutch," was another small state that ruled over a vast and wealthy empire. In 1750, its colonial holdings included lands in the Caribbean, South America, and southern Africa. Its most valuable possessions were in Asia. They included

Ceylon (an island south of India), Formosa (an island east of China), and several islands off the coast of southeast Asia, including Sumatra, Java, and Borneo.

Portugal got a head start on the other European maritime empires when its navigators first rounded Africa and sailed into the Indian Ocean in 1487, reaching India for the first time in 1498. Over the following 200 years, it became a colonial and trading powerhouse, with territories around Africa and throughout the Indian Ocean. However, by 1750, many of its overseas territories had been lost to competitors such as Britain and the Netherlands. At that time, it still held the city of Goa on the southwest coast of India, the Atlantic island groups of Madeira and the Azores, and territory on both coasts of Southern Africa (in what are today Angola and Mozambique). Portugal's prize colony was the huge and economically important Brazil in South America.

Read Closely: Note Differences
A country can experience opposing trends over time. For example, new technology might create new jobs and wealth but over time create hardships for those who lose their jobs. How was the relationship between the Ottomans and the Byzantines the opposite of the relationship between the Ottomans and the Habsburgs?

The Ottoman Empire

At its height, the Ottoman Empire was one of the largest empires the world had ever seen. In addition, it remained enormously influential and greatly feared for a long period, most of four centuries. The beginning of its decline came in 1683, when it laid siege to the Austrian capital of Vienna but was eventually defeated. Between 1750 and 1800, it lost much of its territory in southwestern Europe to the strengthening Austrian Habsburgs and the Russian Empire. As such, its power was on the wane. Though it still controlled a relatively large territory, its influence was decreasing.

The Russian Empire

In the century before 1750, the Moscow-based Russian Empire acquired substantial new territory. Much of this expansion occurred under **Peter the Great,** who ruled from 1682 to 1725. One motive for expanding was geographic. To prosper from foreign trade, Russia needed seaports it could use year-round. Before its expansion, Russia's ports were all along its northern coast, and they were blocked by ice during winter. By 1750, Russia extended about 4,000 miles, from the Baltic Sea in the west to the Pacific Ocean in the east. It was by far the largest country in the world.

In the following century, Russia would continue to expand under Catherine the Great, who ruled from 1762 to 1796. Continuing its search for warm-water ports, Russia drove south until it reached the Black Sea. From there, Russian ships could sail into the Mediterranean Sea and on to the oceans of the world.

Read Closely: Similarity
Identifying similar incidents in various places or time periods shows an understanding of larger trends and patterns in history. For example, how was the impact of China's expensive but failed military campaigns similar to events in India under Aurangzeb around the same time?

China Under the Qing Dynasty

During a famine in 1644, a peasant revolt led by a minor court official overthrew the Ming Dynasty. The fall of the Ming allowed the **Manchu,** a non-Chinese people from the region northeast of China called Manchuria, to seize power. The Manchu, ruling as the **Qing Dynasty,** pacified all of China within 40 years. Though always resented by many Chinese as foreigners, the Manchu held power for 267 years, until 1911.

Between the 1660s and 1750, Qing emperors expanded Chinese territory through military conquest. They spread north into Mongolia and west into Central Asia. To the south, they established a protectorate over Tibet and took control of Nepal. However, military campaigns against Burma and Vietnam were unsuccessful. In addition, the failed efforts were so costly that China decided to raise money by granting trading privileges to European powers. This decision would later prove very costly in another way—a reduction of Chinese sovereignty.

Three West African Kingdoms

In the century leading up to 1750, powerful states developed in West Africa. They exercised regional power and prospered through trade, including the sale of enslaved people.

Read Closely: Plausible Claim
Historical evidence can usually support a variety of claims. For example, the text provides information about the slave trade, guns, and empires in West Africa. Write a plausible claim that explains the relationship between at least two of these three topics.

The Ashanti One of these was the **Ashanti.** They began to strengthen and expand after 1670 when a new king defeated his opposition and established a new capital at Kumasi. In the early 1700s, the Ashanti traded slaves with the Dutch and British. One trade good they received was guns, which they used to expand their territory at their neighbors' expense. By 1750, the Ashanti kingdom had reached its greatest extent, stretching from its coastal trading centers well into the continent's interior.

Dahomey To the east of the Ashanti, the kingdom of **Dahomey** flourished at about this time. It carried on a slave trade through the port at Ouidah. Slaves taken in raids on neighboring societies were also kept in Dahomey to work in the king's fields, supplying food for the royals and the army. Dahomey had an intense rivalry with its neighbor to the northwest, Oyo, to which it was forced to pay tribute beginning in the 1730s.

Benin To the east of the Ashanti, in what is today southern Nigeria, lay the kingdom of **Benin.** It was founded as early as the 13th century. Over time, the kingdom became highly organized, eventually trading goods such as palm oil and pepper with Europeans. But during the 18th century, the power of the oba, or king, of Benin began to wane.

An Enduring Issue: Trade
The rise of powerful states in West Africa reflected the importance of trade. Many states have built their economic and political power through trade.

WEST AFRICA IN 1750

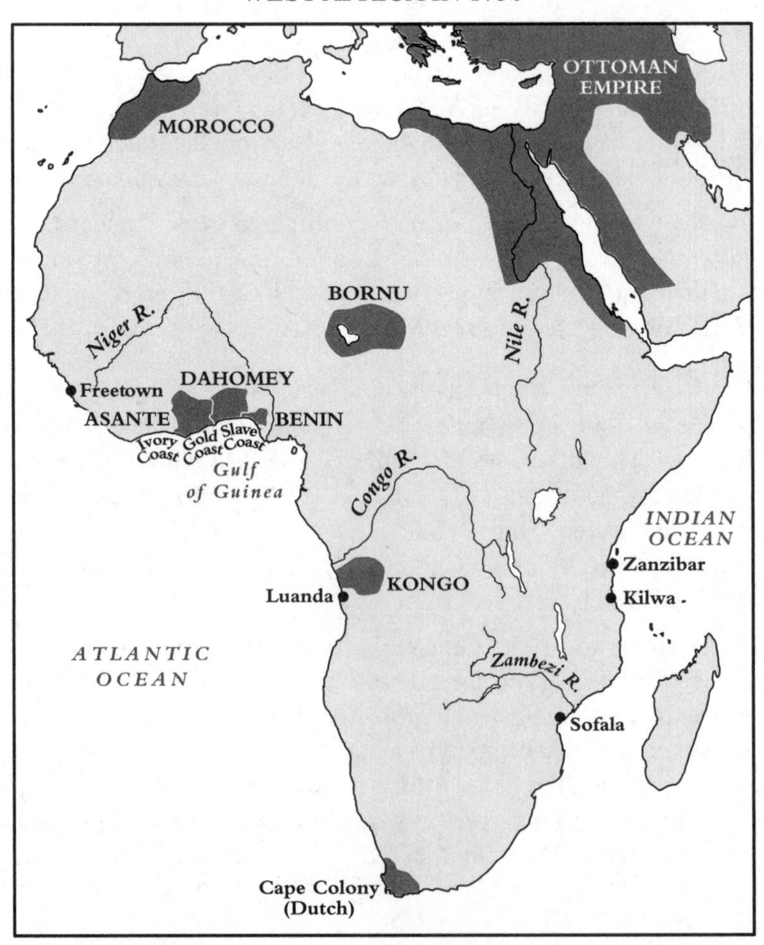

Application

Read the excerpt and answer the questions that follow it.

Wang Youpu, Lecture on Ceremony

> Were I now to speak of the details of rituals and ceremonies, you soldiers and common people probably would have difficulty learning them because they are so numerous. But you all possess the basic elements of ceremonial behavior. For example, you know that there should be filial piety towards parents, honor and respect for superiors, harmony between husband and wife, affection among brothers, honesty among friends, and mutual responsibility among those of the same lineage. This proves that internally you already possess the basic elements of ceremony and deference.
>
> Why then make a fuss about the externals? If you could really, in dealing with others, be extremely cooperative, in conducting yourselves be extremely obliging, in the family express the affection appropriate between parents and children, elder and younger brothers, in your villages maintain accord between the old and the young, the great and the small, then those habits of struggling over minor differences and getting into noisy disputes would be reformed and the tendency toward indulgent and degenerate conduct would be restrained. . . .
>
> Let all of you—scholars, farmers, artisans, merchants, and soldiers—take care in practicing ceremonial deference. If one place becomes good, then many places will become so, and finally the entire realm will be in excellent harmony. Won't we then have a world in perfect concord?
>
> **Source:** *Chinese Civilization: A Sourcebook,* edited by Patricia Buckley Ebrey, 2nd ed. (New York: The Free Press, 1993), pages 298–300. ©1993 The Free Press.

1. Based on the first sentence, identify a logical inference about how the writer viewed the rules of rituals.

____

____

2. Interpret if the writer placed a high value on equality among all people.

____

____

3. Based on the last sentence of the first paragraph ("This proves . . ."), explain which statement is the best logical inference about the writer's beliefs.

   a. People are naturally moral, and society should help them live that way.

   b. People are naturally immoral, and society must force them to act properly.

____

____

Chapter 1 *Review*

Multiple-Choice Questions

Directions (1–6): For each statement or question, choose the number of the word or expression that, of those given, best completes the statement or answers the question.

Base your answers to questions 1 and 2 on the passage below and your knowledge of social studies.

> When the Japan of our day astonished the world by abolishing feudalism, adopting the civilization of Christendom, creating a constitutional government, and becoming in most outward features a modern state, there were many who said that "the Japanese had reached in twenty years what it took other countries centuries to acquire."
>
> The statement is no more true than to say that a nation is born in a day, or that the acorn planted this morning will be an oak tomorrow evening.
>
> Such talk seems very foolish to the student of Japanese history. He knows that for two hundred years the Dutch seed of European civilization was growing secretly. He sees, also, other great forces, both inwardly and outwardly, undermining the systems of Iyeyasu and preparing for the New Japan.
>
> **Source:** William Elliot Griffis, *Japan in History Folklore and Art* (Boston: Houghton Mifflin, 1892), page 203.

1. Which statement best describes the point of view of the author?

   (1) European influences were undermining Japanese traditions for centuries.
   (2) The United States was primarily responsible for the Meiji Restoration.
   (3) Tokugawa Iyeyasu tried to open up Japan to greater foreign trade.
   (4) Japan's industrialization occurred incredibly rapidly.

2. This passage could be best used to support a claim that focused on

   (1) continuity and change over time
   (2) comparison and contrast
   (3) contextualization
   (4) generalization

Tips for Answering Multiple-Choice Questions

Most questions are short and clearly written. However, if you are unsure of what a question is asking, try to rephrase it in your head. Imagine you are rewording it to ask a younger student. Or break it into phrases and consider what each phrase means by itself.

Base your answers to questions 3 and 4 on the map below and on your knowledge of social studies.

INDIA IN THE MUGHAL PERIOD

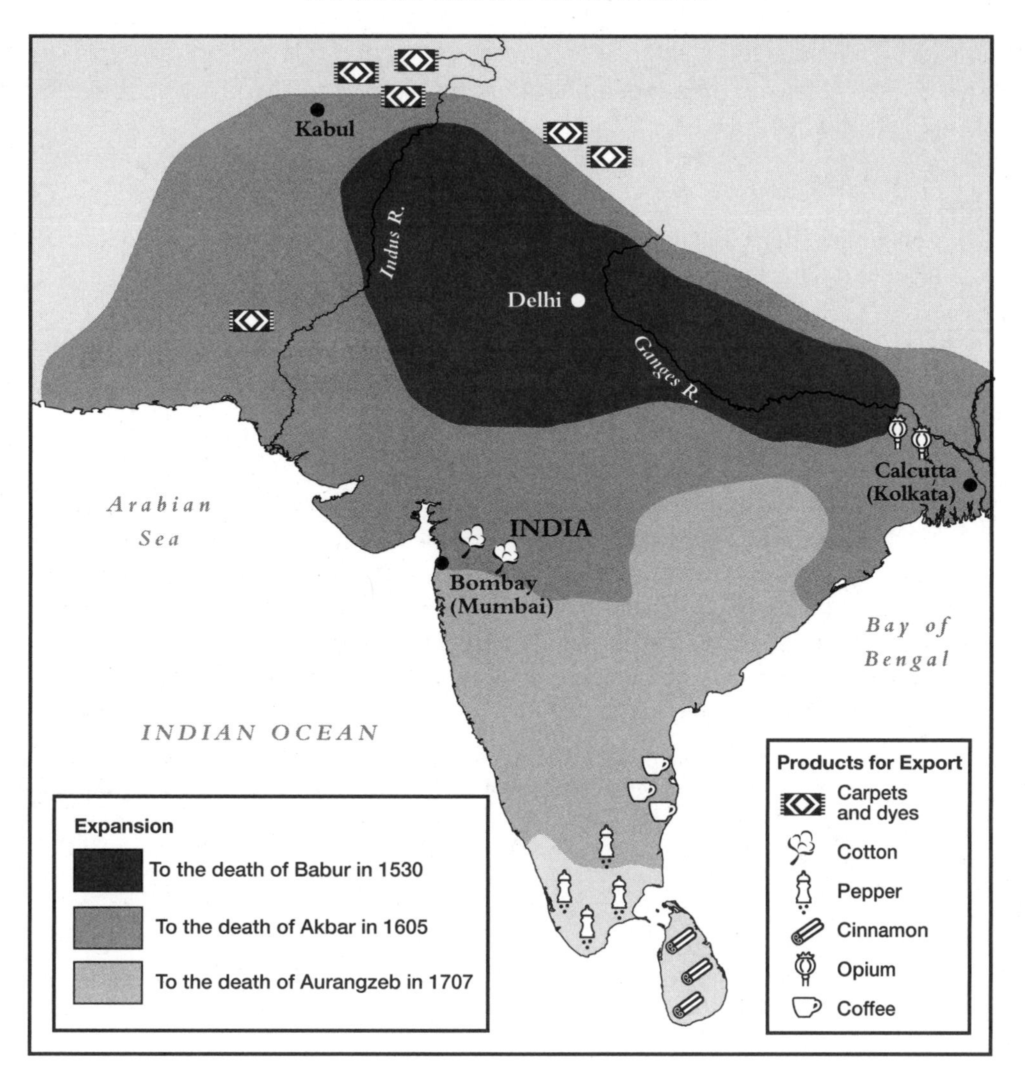

3. Which cities shown on this map were most typical of places where Europeans settled during this period?

   (1) Kabul and Bombay because they were on the eastern side of regions
   (2) Delhi and Calcutta because they were places where exports were produced
   (3) Bombay and Calcutta because they were along coasts
   (4) Kabul and Delhi because they were far inland

4. Which statement best describes the purpose of this map?

   (1) to demonstrate why unifying India under a central government was difficult
   (2) to explain why Europeans were interested in trade with India
   (3) to suggest geographic reasons for changes in religion in India
   (4) to show how India differed from Russia or China in this period

Tips for Answering Multiple-Choice Questions

When you read a multiple-choice question, try to answer it before reading the answers. If you know the content well, this will help you identify the answer quickly. It will also avoid the danger that you might get persuaded by an answer that sounds right but is not. For example, if the question is about the location of European trading posts, recall what you know about trade and European interests in India.

Base your answers to questions 5 and 6 on the passage below and your knowledge of social studies.

> The original formation of the body of Janissaries is described, and praise bestowed on their subordination and gallantry, and on the glorious exploits that marked their career, as long as they retained their original virtue, as long as they were the foremost band under . . . Islamism, for defense or for conquest. This they had long ceased to be; and it is shown how, from dutiful subjects, they had become turbulent traitors, how the Odas or Barracks, which they were bound to live in, by their law, were deserted for their private shops and houses, and the resorts of the idle and vicious; how from soldiers they had become mere . . . trucksters, keepers of coffee-houses, porters, and boatmen; and how they had been brought to consider the only part of military duty an attendance on pay-days. . . .
>
> **Source:** Charles MacFarlane, *Constantinople in 1828: A Residence of Sixteen Months in the Turkish Capital and Provinces* (London: Saunders and Otley, 1829), Vol. II, pages 17–18.

5. At their peak of power, the people described in the excerpt made the Ottoman Empire strong in the mid-1700s because they maintained control of
   (1) trade routes through the eastern Mediterranean Sea
   (2) the wealthiest regions in Europe
   (3) caravan routes in West African
   (4) lands in Africa, Europe, and Asia

6. Which technology aided the success of the people described in the passage?
   (1) wheelbarrow
   (2) gunpowder
   (3) woodblock printing
   (4) steam engine

Short-Answer Questions

CRQ Directions (7-9): Analyze the documents and answer the short-answer questions that follow each document in the space provided.

Base your answer to question 7 on Document 1 below and on your knowledge of social studies.

Document 1

The People of the Ottoman Empire				
Group	**Europe**	**Asia**	**Africa**	**Total**
Turks	1,000,000	10,700,000	0	11,700,000
Greeks	900,000	1,000,000	0	1,900,000
Armenians	200,000	2,000,000	0	2,200,000
Jews	70,000	80,000	0	150,000
Slavonians	4,000,000	0	0	4,000,000
Albanians	820,000	0	0	820,000
Arabs	0	885,000	3,800,000	4,685,000
Syrians and Chaldeans	0	200,000	0	200,000
Roma	214,000	0	0	214,000
Other	11,000	285,000	0	296,000
Total	7,215,000	15,150,000	3,800,000	26,165,000

Source: Adapted from Sutherland Menzies, *History of the Ottoman Empire in Europe* (London: William Collins, Sons, & Co., 1877), page 300.

7. Explain what this table shows about the geographic context of the Ottoman Empire.

____

____

____

____

Tips for Answering Short-Answer Questions

When you read a table of data, you can get the main theme and organization of it by looking at:

- the title
- the subheads at the top of each column
- the subheads in the left column of each row

In the table above, the writer organized people into groups by their nationality rather than their religion, language group, or some other trait. This choice might reflects what is important to the writer. However, it might also reflect what information is available.

Base your answer to question 8 on Document 2 below and on your knowledge of social studies

Document 2

This excerpt is from Akbar the Great, leader of the Mughal Empire. Akbar requested that priests journey to his empire to teach him about Christianity. One was Portuguese priest, Antonio Monserrate.

> Know, O chief Fathers of the Order of St. Paul, that we are very well disposed unto you. We are sending unto you Ebadulla our envoy, and Dominicus Petrius, that they may communicate to you in our own words our desire that two learned priests should be sent unto us, to bring the chief books of the Law and the Gospel, in order that we may learn the Law and its full meaning and perfect truths in every respect. For I earnestly desire thoroughly to learn that Law. Let them not hesitate therefore to be sent out with the same envoys when they leave Goa on the return journey; and let them bring the books of the Law with them. Let the priests understand that I shall receive them with all possible kindness and honor. Their arrival will be a great delight to me: and when I have learnt what I long to know about the law and its perfection and the salvation it offers, they shall be allowed to return as soon as they like.
>
> **Source:** Antonio Monserrate, *The Commentary of Father Monserrate, S. J., on His Journey to the Court of Akbar* (London: Milford, 1922), page 2.

8. Using this excerpt, identify the bias of Akbar about learning.

____

____

____

____

Base your answer to question 9 on both Documents 1 and 2 and on your knowledge of social studies.

> **Cause**—refers to something that contributes to the occurrence of an event, the rise of an idea, or the bringing about of a development.
>
> **Effect**—refers to what happens as a consequence (result, impact, outcome) of an event, an idea, or a development.

9. Identify and explain a cause-and-effect relationship associated with the historical developments in Documents 1 and 2. Be sure to use evidence from both Documents 1 and 2 in your response.

Speaking and Listening: Reflect on the Key Idea

Working with a partner or a small group, identify at least five ways that the European states interacted with people in other regions of the world.

1.
2.
3.
4.
5.

Period 1 *Enduring Issue Extended Essay*

Directions

An enduring issue is an issue that exists across time. It is one that many societies have attempted to address with varying degrees of success. Read the following documents and take notes in the margin identifying at least two themes in each one. Then use these notes and the Planning Page to prepare to write the essay. Finally, on a separate sheet of paper or on a computer, write your extended essay.

In your essay:

Identify the issue based on a historically accurate interpretation of **three** documents.

Define the issue using evidence from three documents.

Argue that this is a significant issue that has endured by showing:

- How the issue has affected people or been affected by people.
- How the issue has continued to be an issue or changed over time.

Include outside information from your knowledge of social studies and evidence from the documents.

Keep in mind these terms:

Identify—means to put a name or to name

Define—means to explain features of a thing or concept so that it can be understood

Argue—means to provide a series of statements that provide evidence and reasons to support a conclusion

Topics to consider for your essay: (See page xvii.)

- Conflict
- Coperation
- Power
- Inequality
- Innovation
- Interconnectedness
- Ideas and Beliefs
- Environmental Issues
- Scarcity

Document 1

Japan's edict closing the country to foreigners, 1635

Provision 1.	Japanese ships are strictly forbidden to leave for foreign countries.
Provision 2.	No Japanese is permitted to go abroad. If there is anyone who attempts to do so secretly, he must be executed. The ship so involved must be impounded and its owner arrested, and the matter must be reported to the higher authority.
Provision 3.	If any Japanese returns from overseas after residing there, he must be put to death.
Provision 4.	If there is any place where the teachings of padres (Christianity) is practiced, the two of you [officials in Nagasaki] must order a thorough investigation. . . .
Provision 10.	Samurai are not permitted to purchase any goods originating from foreign ships directly from Chinese merchants in Nagasaki.

Source: Japan: *A Documentary History,* Volume 1, edited by David John Lu. (Armonk, New York: M. E. Sharpe), 2005.

Document 2

Robert Clive, British officer in India, letter to the East India Company about the Battle of Plassey, 1757

The subject of this address is . . . no less than the entire overthrow of Nabob Suraj-u-Dowlah [the leader of the Bengal kingdom in eastern India], and the placing of Meer Jaffier [another Indian leader] on the throne. I intimated, in my last [letter], how dilatory [slow] Suraj-u-Dowlah appeared in fulfilling the articles of the treaty. This disposition [attitude] not only continued but increased, and we discovered that he was designing our [the British] ruin, by a conjunction [alliance] with the French. . . .

About this time some of his [Suraj-u-Dowlah's] principal officers made overtures to us for dethroning him. At the head of these was Meer Jaffier, then *Bukhshee* [paymaster] to the army, a man as generally esteemed as the other [Suraj-u-Dowlah] was detested. As we had reason to believe this disaffection pretty general, we soon entered into engagements with Meer Jaffier to put the crown on his head.

Source: *Selections from the Sources of English History,* edited by Charles William Colby, (London: Longmans, Green and Company, 1913).

Document 3

Peter the Great, decrees on relationships with foreigners, 1701

Economics
We have always tried to maintain internal order, to defend the state against invasion, and in every possible way to improve to extend trade. With this purpose we have been compelled to make some necessary and salutary changes in the administration, in order that our subjects might more easily gain a knowledge of matters of which they were before ignorant, and become more skillful in their commercial relations. We have therefore given orders, made dispositions, and founded institutions indispensable for increasing our trade with foreigners, and shall do the same in the future. . . . To attain these worthy aims, we have endeavored to improve our military forces, which are the protection of our State, so that our troops may consist of well-drilled men, maintained in perfect order and discipline. In order to obtain greater improvement in this respect, and to encourage foreigners, who are able to assist us in this way, as well as artisans profitable to the State, to come in numbers to our country, we have issued this manifesto. . . .

Clothing
Western dress shall be worn by all the boyars, members of our councils and of our court . . . gentry of Moscow, secretaries . . . provincial gentry, gosti [merchants], government officials, streltsy [armed guards], members of the guilds purveying for our household, citizens of Moscow of all ranks, and residents of provincial cities . . . excepting the clergy. . . and peasant tillers of the soil. The upper dress shall be of French or Saxon [Saxony is a German region] cut, and the lower dress . . . —waistcoat, trousers, boots, shoes, and hats—shall be of the German type. They shall also ride German saddles. Likewise the womenfolk of all ranks . . . shall wear Western dresses, hats, jackets, and underwear . . . and shoes. From now on no one [of the above-mentioned] is to wear Russian dress or Circassian [Circassia is a region near the Black Sea] coats, sheepskin coats, or Russian peasant coats, trousers, boots, and shoes. It is also forbidden to ride Russian saddles, and the craftsmen shall not manufacture them or sell them at the marketplaces.

Source: http://college.cengage.com/history/primary_sources/world/edicts_and_decrees.htm.

Prepare to Write an Extended Essay

MY ENDURING ISSUE IS: ____

You may use the Enduring Issues Planning Page organizer to prepare to write your essay. Writing on this Planning Page will NOT count toward your final score.

You may also choose to prepare to write the Enduring Issues Essay by creating an outline or graphic organizer on your own sheet of paper.

ENDURING ISSUES PLANNING PAGE

Essay Requirements	Yes	Circle documents that apply	One or two possible ideas for outside info
Is this an issue supported by at least three documents? Which documents support this issue?		1 2 3 4 5	
Which documents can be used to develop the definition for this issue?		1 2 3 4 5	
Has this issue significantly affected people or been affected by people?		1 2 3 4 5	
Has this issue endured across time or changed over time? In which document or documents do you see this?		1 2 3 4 5	

Period 2 Revolutions, Industrialization, and Empires, 1750—1914

Chapter 2

Enlightenment, Revolution, and Nationalism

Chapter 3

The Industrial Revolution

Chapter 4

Imperialism

Map Notes

A

Between 1750 and 1914, the United States won independence from Great Britain, seized land from Native Americans, and became a global industrial power.

B

In the 19th century, many countries in South America won independence from Spain or Brazil. However, several suffered from destructive civil wars that slowed economic development.

C

In Europe, political and cultural boundaries were becoming more similar. Tiny states that shared cultures were unified to create the larger states of Germany and Italy.

D

Chinese efforts to limit the influence of Great Britain and other foreigners in their country resulted in clashes known as the Opium Wars and the Boxer Rebellion.

E

Japan feared that Europeans would dominate it as they had China. To protect itself, Japan's government forced rapid industrialization and became a military power.

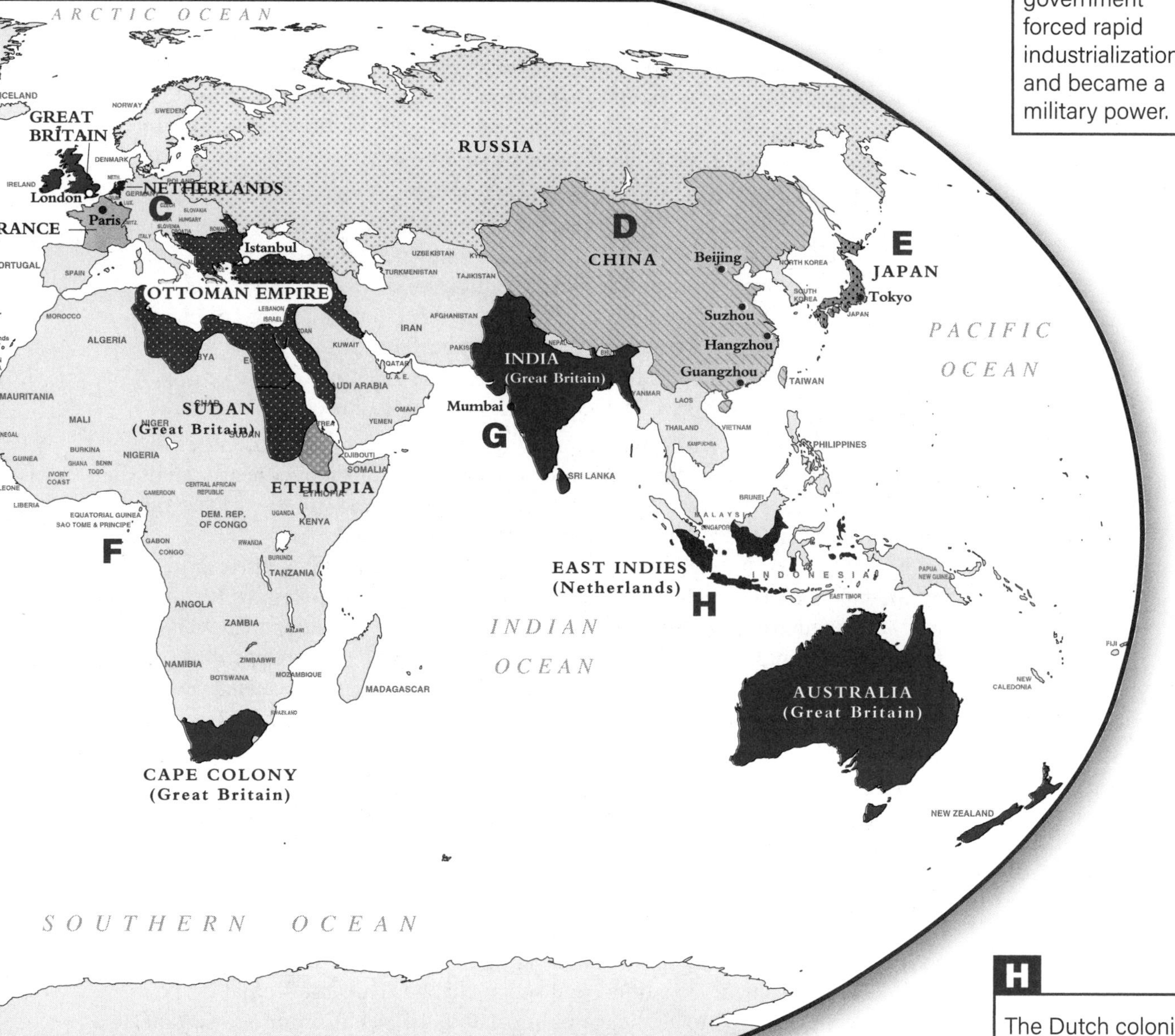

H

The Dutch colonies on islands that today are part of Indonesia were among the most valuable possessions in the world for the spices they produced.

F

The transatlantic slave trade mostly ended in the 1800s. However, by 1914, Europeans claimed control of nearly all of Africa. Anti-colonial forces were strongest in South Africa, Ethiopia, and Sudan.

G

Mumbai was one of the ten largest cities in the world. Urbanization was occurring throughout Asia in the 19th century.

CHAPTER 2

Enlightenment, Revolution, and Nationalism

Chapter Overview

Between 1750 and 1914, people around the world changed how they thought about the basic political questions: What rights do individuals have? Should all people be treated equally? Which groups had the right to form their own country? The answers created revolutionary changes, eventually throughout the world.

Rights and Equality In 1750, people commonly accepted that rights came from the government. Usually, this meant that they had only the freedom granted them by the king or queen. The idea that all people had natural, inalienable rights that every legitimate government should respect was just emerging. Still, supporters of equality, democracy, or religious toleration were criticized. However, by 1914, these concepts were widely accepted. Most governments acknowledged rights such as freedom of speech and freedom of religion. Even though many governments violated these rights, they had become the ideal.

Colonies, Slavery, and Nationalism In 1750, four European countries—Great Britain, France, Spain, and Portugal—claimed control over nearly all of the Americas, and slavery was legal everywhere. By 1914, the Americas were filled with independent countries and slavery had been abolished.

In 1750, many people in Europe and Southwest Asia lived in either large, multiethnic empires, such as the **Austrian Empire** and the **Ottoman Empire,** or in small kingdoms and independent cities. People did not assume that everyone in their state should speak the same language and practice the same culture. By 1914, people commonly accepted that people should. This shift caused wars that split the Austrian Empire into many countries, combined hundreds of German states into one German empire, and united several states into one country of Italy.

An Enduring Issue: Ideas One enduring issue in this chapter is the importance of ideas. Debates about the ideas underlying government, slavery, and nations shaped the most important events between 1750 and 1914.

> ***New York Social Studies Framework:*** **Key Idea 10.2**
>
> The Enlightenment called into question traditional beliefs and inspired widespread political, economic, and social change. This intellectual movement was used to challenge political authorities in Europe and colonial rule in the Americas. These ideals inspired political and social movements.
>
> **Source:** *New York State Grades 9–12 Social Studies Framework.*

1. Rewrite Key Idea 10.2 in your own words.

____

____

Identify Enduring Issues

To prepare to write an extended essay about an enduring issue, practice seeing how specific statements are connected to broad concerns. Reread the Chapter Overview on the previous page. For each of paragraphs 3, 4, and 5, identify one key statement and one or more enduring issues that it addresses.

Chapter Overview	Key Statement	Enduring Issues
Paragraph 2	"all people had natural, inalienable rights"	▪ The source of political rights ▪ The specific rights that individuals have
Paragraph 3		
Paragraph 4		
Paragraph 5		

Key Terms by Theme

Identity

Deist (p. 37)
nationalism (p. 55)

Geography

Paris (p. 48)
colony (p. 51)
Balkans (p. 57)

Governance

Austrian Empire (p. 32)
Ottoman Empire (p. 32)
William Wilberforce (p. 41)
Catherine the Great (p. 43)
American Revolution (p. 47)
French Revolution (p. 48)
Maximilien Robespierre (p. 50)
Olympe de Gouges (p. 50)
Haitian Revolution (p. 51)
Napoleon Bonaparte (p. 51)
Toussaint L'Ouverture (p. 51)
Simón Bolívar (p. 52)
Otto von Bismarck (p. 55)
German Unification (p. 56)
Giuseppe Garibaldi (p. 57)
Italian unification (p. 57)

Civic Ideals

democracy (p. 32)
divine monarchy (p. 35)
John Locke, *Two Treatises on Government* (p. 35)
Baron de Montesquieu (p. 36)
checks and balances (p. 36)
separation of powers (p. 36)
Voltaire (p. 36)
Jean-Jacques Rousseau, *The Social Contract* (p. 39)
Mary Wollstonecraft (p. 41)
William Wilberforce (p. 41)
enlightened despots (p. 42)
Declaration of Independence, 1776 (p. 49)
Declaration of the Rights of Man and of the Citizen, 1789 (p. 49)
Declaration of the Rights of Woman and of the Female Citizen, 1791 (p. 50)

Lesson 1 *The Rights of Citizens*

Conceptual Understanding
10.2a Enlightenment thinkers developed political philosophies based on natural laws, which included the concepts of social contract, consent of the governed, and the rights of citizens.

Source: *New York State Grades 9–12 Social Studies Framework.*

People have long debated what gives a government the right to rule over individuals. In the 17th century, most Europeans believed that a government's authority came came directly from God. Late in the century, an English philosopher, John Locke, argued that the right to rule came from the consent of the people being governed.

Analyze a Primary Source

John Locke, *Second Treatise on Government,* 1691

Read Closely: Key Point
Writers commonly express their main point or points early in a document.
Underline the main point made by Locke regarding the source government power.

Read Closely: Logical Order
As you read, look for a flow in the ideas. For example, after Locke states that people give up some freedom, he addresses the logical question: Why would people do this?

Read Closely: Repetition
Note when a writer repeats a word for emphasis. Locke wants to emphasize that individuals should be willing to follow decisions supported by most people in their community.
Circle the repeated word that Locke uses to show his desire for people to support their community.

Read Closely: Conclusion
The last paragraph of a section of writing often summarizes what has been written before. In this paragraph, Locke reviews his main points before going on to others.

Men being, as has been said, by nature, all free, equal, and independent, no one can be . . . subjected to the political power of another, without his own consent.

The only way, whereby any one divests [gives up] himself of his natural liberty, and puts on the bonds of civil society, is by agreeing with other men to join and unite into a community, for their comfortable, safe, and peaceable living one amongst another, in a secure enjoyment of their properties, and a greater security against any, that are not of it.

This any number of men may do, because it injures not the freedom of the rest; they are left as they were in the liberty of the state of nature. When any number of men have so consented to make one community or government, they are thereby presently incorporated, and make one body politic, wherein the majority have a right to act and conclude the rest.

For when any number of men have, by the consent of every individual, made a community, they have thereby made that community one body, with a power to act as one body, which is only by the will and determination of the majority: or else it is impossible it should act or continue one body, one community, which the consent of every individual that united into it, agreed that it should; and so every one is bound by that consent to be concluded by the majority. . . .

And thus every man, by consenting with others to make one body politic under one government, puts himself under an obligation, to every one of that society, to submit to the determination of the majority, and to be concluded [act according to its decisions] by it.

Source: John Locke, *Two Treatises of Government,* 1691. Reprinted in ***The Works of John Locke***, Vol. 4 (London: Rivington. 1824). Online Library of Liberty.

Enlightenment and Rights

The European intellectual movement known as the Enlightenment began in the early 17th century and flourished for nearly 150 years. Like Renaissance humanists, Enlightenment thinkers revered the philosophy, history, and poetry of the classical Greeks and Romans. Like those in the Scientific Revolution, Enlightenment thinkers were devoted to experimentation, observation, analysis, and reason. The Enlightenment was challenged by new schools of thought after the French Revolution in 1789. However, its influence remained strong.

English Political Philosophy

Before the Enlightenment, most Europeans believed in **divine monarchy,** that a king's or queen's authority came from God. As a result of this belief, monarchs argued no one should limit their power. Enlightenment political philosophers challenged these ideas. They argued that people had natural rights that limited the power of rulers. Authority might ultimately come from God, but it was expressed through the people of a state. This formed the basis of modern democracy.

Thomas Hobbes The English political philosopher Thomas Hobbes (1588–1679) rejected the belief God gave authority to a government. Rather, he believed this authority came from the people. He also argued that people were naturally selfish and combative. Without a strong a government to keep order, their lives would be "nasty, brutish, and short." For self-protection, people created a government by making a deal that he called a social contract. They gave up some of their freedom in exchange for security. One freedom they sacrificed was the right to criticize or influence the ruler. Even religious leaders had to bow to the will of the monarch. Hobbes believed that only an absolute monarch with unquestioned power would have enough power to maintain peace.

John Locke Thomas Hobbes was soon overshadowed by another English political philosopher: **John Locke** (1632–1704). Like Hobbes, Locke based government authority on a social contract rather than divine will.

However, Hobbes and Locke the viewed human nature very differently. Hobbes agreed with the common belief that each individual's personality was set before birth—by nature. People could be controlled, but not changed. In contrast, Locke thought that humans were born with no particular way of thinking or acting. In his work *An Essay Concerning Human Understanding* (1689), Locke represented a newborn baby's mind as a *tabula rasa,* Latin for "blank slate." People were shaped by how they were treated—by nurture. As a result, Locke thought education was very important in shaping how a child would act as an adult. In addition, political freedom was important in producing a moral, productive person.

Locke was heavily influenced by the scientists of his day, including his friend Isaac Newton. Just as scientists were searching for natural laws that governed the physical world, Locke searched for natural laws that governed the human world. He thought that one of these laws was that people naturally desired to pursue good and to avoid pain. What made this law distinctive was how Locke thought people could recognize what was truly good for them. Rather than rely upon feelings or instincts that they had naturally, or by traditions they were taught by others, they could use reason. Like the scientists of his day, Locke trusted reason even when it led to conclusions that were not obvious or not widely accepted..

Reason also allowed people to decide to enter into a social contract with other humans for the benefit of themselves and others. In order to obey natural laws, humans must recognize that they have certain natural rights—the rights to life,

Read Closely: Concepts
Recognizing contrast makes distinctions clear. Give examples of how nature and nurture can each shape someone.

Read Closely: Examples
Identify fundamental issues about which people disagree, such as the role of reason. Identify one example of an attitude or behavior that is not based on reason.

liberty, and property. In *Two Treatises of Government* (1689), Locke argued that the function of government is to protect these rights and that these right belong naturally to individuals. This was a contrast to earlier philosophers who believed that government should enforce religious teachings or should maintain traditions that kept a community close together.

An Enduring Issue: Security
The idea of a social contract is one example of how people could improve security in their lives. In all societies, people develop some response to the dangers facing them.

Locke's emphasis on the natural rights of individuals led to another disagreement with Hobbes. While Hobbes feared dissent, Locke believed in the right of people to disagree with and influence a government. Further, if the government continued to violate the natural rights of individuals, citizens had a duty to overthrow the government.

Locke's ideas about government and natural rights became very influential, first in Europe and the Americas. They helped inspire the colonists who rebelled against Great Britain to found the United States in 1776, as well as other colonial rebellions in Latin America. Locke's ideas expressed in *Two Treatises of Government* now shape how people around the world think about government.

French Political Philosophy

Hobbes and Locke, the most influential European political philosophers in the 17th century, were both English. In the 18th century, the most influential European thinkers were French.

Montesquieu The **Baron de Montesquieu** (1689–1755) published *Reflections on the Causes of the Rise and Fall of the Roman Empire* (1734). In it, Montesquieu advanced the unusual idea that the strengths of the Roman Empire, such as its wealth, power, and territorial expansion, resulted in its weaknesses. Rome's real strength was its citizens' civic virtue, which weakened as the empire expanded and became more affluent and complacent.

But it was *The Spirit of the Laws* (1750) that made Montesquieu among the best-known philosophers in Europe. Montesquieu admired the English method of dividing political power among the monarch, the Parliament, and the English courts. He suggested that all governments should split powers among three separate, equally powerful branches:

- executive
- legislative
- judicial

Read Closely: Connections
Composers in the 18th century such as Franz Joseph Haydn and Wolfgang Mozart wrote music that emphasized balance and order. How was the music similar to philosophy of Montesquieu?

Like Locke, Montesquieu strongly influenced the United States. The U.S. Constitution shows his ideas about the **separation of powers** among distinct branches of government as well as creating **checks and balances** among these branches.

Voltaire Writing under the pen name Voltaire, François-Marie Arouet (1694–1778) was the most famous man in Europe of his time. He wrote books and essays about government, religion, and philosophy, as well as popular plays. In some ways he built upon the ideas of Hobbes and Locke:

- Like Hobbes, he was pessimistic about human nature. He felt that few people were capable of governing themselves.
- Like Locke, he believed that people have natural rights. No government could take these away. In particular, he supported free speech. He reportedly claimed, "I disagree with what you said but I will defend to the death your right to say it."

Voltaire advocated for a government led by a wise monarch. He particularly admired England's system. In his *Letters Concerning the English Nation* (1734), he praised England for its freedom in religion and commerce.

Along with many other Enlightenment thinkers, Voltaire was a **deist.** Like other deists, Voltaire believed in God, but not in the traditional Christian conceptions. He saw God as similar to a clockmaker. God made the universe and then let it operate on its own. God did not intervene in human affairs. Further, the universe ran according to basic laws, and humans could understand these laws using reason rather than faith.

Voltaire's beliefs in natural rights and religion combined to make him a strong defender of **religious tolerance,** the idea that people should be allowed to follow their chosen beliefs without fear of exile, jail, or other punishment. Voltaire's views were controversial. To call someone "tolerant" was a criticism that they lacked strong religious beliefs. Even in Great Britain, the country Voltaire admired, Roman Catholics could not serve in Parliament or attend the most prestigious universities. However, over the following century, Voltaire's progressive ideas on tolerance would slowly become common.

Read Closely: Context
Keep in mind the era in which a writer lived. Rousseau was writing in a time of rapid change in how people made goods. How is this context significant to understanding his writing?

Jean-Jacques Rousseau Another major French philosopher of the Enlightenment, **Jean-Jacques Rousseau** (1712–1778) felt that both reason and civilization destroyed the best in human beings. While many felt that society was improving, Rousseau believed that people had been better off living in what he called a state of nature: in small, agricultural communities without elaborate institutions of government, religion, and industry. There, people's inherent, or inborn, goodness was not spoiled. He described people in societies without elaborate civilizations as "noble savages." Rousseau believed the noble savage was generous, free, spontaneous, and sincere.

Rousseau realized that it was impossible for people to return to this pre-existing state of nature. However, he believed that the basic goodness of the noble savage survived and that children demonstrated it. Therefore, adults should strive to educate children in such a way as to preserve their unspoiled state. Children should be allowed to develop naturally rather than be tightly controlled.

Landmarks of the Enlightenment

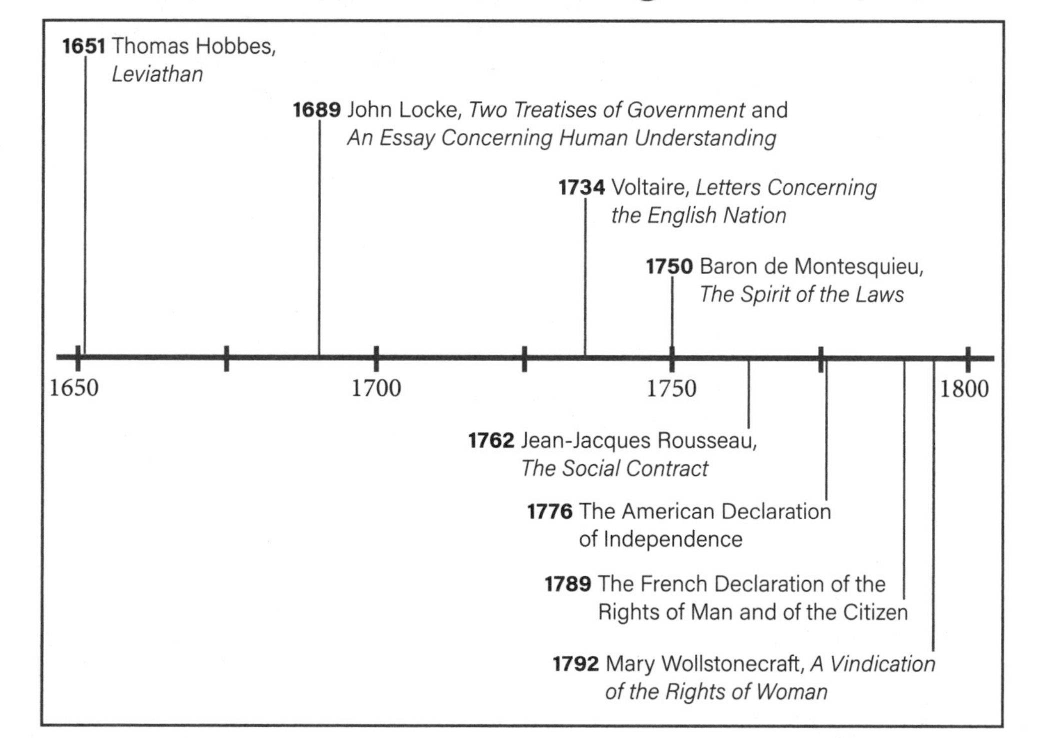

Read Closely: Patterns
Identify two patterns regarding the authors and works listed on this timeline. Examples of patterns include topics, chronology, and the gender or nationality of the writers.

Quotations from French Philosophers

Montesquieu

- The tyranny of a prince in an oligarchy is not so dangerous to the public welfare as the apathy of a citizen in a democracy.
- A nation may lose its liberties in a day and not miss them in a century.
- Laws undertake to punish only overt acts.

Voltaire

- Those who can make you believe absurdities can make you commit atrocities.
- Judge a man by his questions rather than his answers.
- Common sense is not so common.

Rousseau

- Man was born free, and he is everywhere in chains.
- Nature never deceives us; it is we who deceive ourselves.
- We should not teach children the sciences; but give them a taste for them.

Read Closely: Connections
Practice connecting specific examples or anecdotes with more general ideas. Explain how one quotation listed in the box expresses an idea described in the text.

Rousseau recognized that modern society cannot function without some form of government. His goal was to make that government as least oppressive as possible. In his book *The Social Contract* (1762), Rousseau described his ideal society. Like early philosophers, he agreed that members of a society agreed to give up some of their freedom in order to serve the common interests of all the people in the society.

However, philophers disagreed with how to identify the common interest. Rousseau called the expression of the common interest the **general will**. He did not think the general will was always the view of the majority of people. The majority could be mistaken about what actions were in their best interest. Rousseau believed that sometimes a small group of well-informed people would be best able to determine what would serve society overall. Further, he argued that those who disagreed with the general will must obey it so that society would operate smoothly.

Read Closely: Evidence
Look for evidence to support concepts. What evidence supports the criticism of Rousseau that he was not clear on how to identify the general will?

Rousseau's theories inspired many later leaders. Among these were the writers of the U.S. Constitution in 1787, the radicals of the French Revolution that began in 1789, and communists who ruled China and Russia in the 20th century. Readers of Rousseau disagreed sharply on how to determine the general will:

- Supporters of republican or democratic government argued that voting was the clearest way to discover the general will. In Rousseau's time, very few people could vote, but today many countries allow nearly all adults to cast ballots.
- Supporters of dictators trusted a single leader to express the general will. They emphasized that a highly educated ruler might make better decisions than a mass of poorly educated peasants and workers.
- Opponents of government in general thought that it was the wrong way to determine the general will. They cited Rousseau's belief in the noble savage to justify their skepticism about all forms of public authority.

Application

Read the excerpt and answer the questions that follow it.

Jean-Jacques Rousseau, *The Social Contract,* 1762

> So long as men remained content with their rustic huts, so long as they were satisfied with clothes made of the skins of animals and sewn together with thorns and fish-bones, adorned themselves only with feathers and shells, and continued to paint their bodies different colors, to improve and beautify their bows and arrows and to make with short-edged stones fishing boats or clumsy musical instruments; in a word, so long as they undertook only what a single person could accomplish, and confined themselves to such arts as did not require the joint labor of several hands, they lived free, healthy, honest and happy lives, so long as their nature allowed, and as they continued to enjoy the pleasures of mutual and independent intercourse. But from the moment one man began to stand in need of the help of another; from the moment it appeared advantageous to any one man to have enough provisions for two, equality disappeared, property was introduced, work became indispensable, and vast forests became smiling fields, which men had to water with the sweat of his brow, and where slavery and misery were soon seen to germinate and grow up with the crops.
>
> **Source:** Jean-Jacques Rousseau, *The Social Contract*, 1762.

1. In the first line of *The Social Contract,* Rousseau claimed that "man is born free; and he is everywhere in chains." Determine if the document supports this claim.

____

____

____

____

2. Compare and contrast the views of Rousseau and Hobbes about the state of nature.

____

____

____

____

3. Describe the general historical context in which Rousseau wrote this document.

____

____

____

____

Lesson 2 *Challenges to Traditional Beliefs*

Conceptual Understanding 10.2b Individuals used Enlightenment ideals to challenge traditional beliefs and secure people's rights in reform movements, such as women's rights and abolition; some leaders may be considered enlightened despots.

Source: *New York State Grades 9–12 Social Studies Framework.*

Mary Wollstonecraft (1759–1797) was considered a radical for her time. She was a strong advocate for equality between men and women at a time when traditional gender roles were changing.

Analyze a Primary Source

Mary Wollstonecraft, *A Vindication of the Rights of Woman,* 1792

Read Closely: Claims
To gain support, Wollstonecraft makes a claim that might be agreeable to some readers but that she wants to refute. *Circle the claim that Wollstonecraft makes that does not agree with her position.*

Read Closely: Specifics
Authors sometimes make a general claim and go on to support it with specific details. *Underline the specific details that Wollstonecraft uses to support her claim.*

Read Closely: Key Phrases
A phrase such as "in fact" suggests that the writer is showing a contradiction between an act that people do and its significance.

Read Closely: Main Point
Wollstonecraft's overall point is to criticize the general attitude of men toward women. She supports this point with a common and simple example.

That woman is naturally weak, or degraded by a concurrence of circumstances, is, I think, clear. But this position I shall simply contrast with a conclusion, which I have frequently heard fall from sensible men in favor of an aristocracy: that the mass of mankind cannot be anything, or the obsequious slaves, who patiently allow themselves to be driven forward, would feel their own consequence, and spurn their chains. Men, they further observe, submit everywhere to oppression, when they have only to lift up their heads to throw off the yoke; yet, instead of asserting their birthright, they quietly lick the dust, and say, Let us eat and drink, for tomorrow we die. Women, I argue from analogy, are degraded by the same propensity to enjoy the present moment; and, at last, despise the freedom which they have not sufficient virtue to struggle to attain. But I must be more explicit. . . .

I lament that women are systematically degraded by receiving the trivial attentions, which men think it manly to pay to the sex, when, in fact, they are insultingly supporting their own superiority. It is not condescension to bow to an inferior. So ludicrous, in fact, do these ceremonies appear to me, that I scarcely am able to govern my muscles, when I see a man start with eager, and serious solicitude to lift a handkerchief, or shut a door, when the *lady* could have done it herself, had she only moved a pace or two.

Source: Mary Wollstonecraft, *A Vindication of the Rights of Woman*, 3rd edition (London, J. Johnson, 1796), pages 119–121. books.google.com.

New Ideas About Rights

As Enlightenment thought developed, the ideas of natural laws and natural rights emerged as central themes. Natural laws governed human behavior just as they did the physical world. They allowed people to establish a social contract and give their consent to a government. Natural rights were controversial. Did they apply only to white, European men? Or did they apply to everyone? Further, how were the established rulers of Europe to incorporate them, if at all, into systems that were already quite beneficial to them?

Read Closely: Claims
Synthesizing multiple facts into a claim is crucial to understanding and defending an argument. What facts support the claim that many women wanted to change their place in society during the Enlightenment?

Rights of Women

Enlightenment thinkers discussed natural law and natural rights in broad terms. They referred to "all men," a phrase often used to mean all humans. But in practice, free, white men had many rights that slaves, people of color, and women did not. Inspired by Enlightenment ideals, reformers fought to secure rights for more people.

Mary Wollstonecraft did not receive a formal education in schools as a child. Few women did in her time. Unmarried women without money of their own could find work as a governess or teacher, but not in many other fields. However, Wollstonecraft's informal education and intelligence gave her opportunities few women had. She became a translator, reviewer, and editor for a London publisher. Early in her career, she wrote a treatise on female education, *Thoughts on the Education of Daughters* (1787), and a novel, *Mary: A Fiction* (1788).

But it was her 1792 work *A Vindication of the Rights of Woman* that had the greatest impact. It was one of the first expressions of feminism. One reason men treated women as uneducated, frivolous, and superficial was that women were not permitted to study philosophy, theology, science, and other topics. Wollstonecraft argued for universal public education. Males and females should get equivalent instruction. Equal education, she believed, would help women in many ways:

- It would give women a sense of self worth based on their intellectual abilities rather than their appearance.
- It would prepare women to participate in political and professional society.
- It would enable women to support themselves financially rather than relying on men.

Wollstonecraft's ultimate goal was for women to gain the same rights and abilities as men through the application of reason.

Read Closely: Place
A major event in one country often affects neighboring and allied countries. How do you think outlawing the slave trade in the United States and Europe changed the way Great Britain perceived slavery?

Rights of Enslaved People

One basic natural right was the right to liberty. It made citizenship, social contracts, and opportunity possible. But enslaved people had no liberty. Africans kidnapped from their homes and transported to the Americas, often on English ships to English colonies, lived and died in bondage.

William Wilberforce (1759–1833) led the battle to end first the slave trade and then slavery. He won election to the House of Commons in 1780, at the age of 21. Although young, he was a superb Parliamentary speaker. A devout Christian and reformer, Wilberforce supported public education, parliamentary reform, and religious freedom. However, he is best known for his dedication to abolitionism.

Wilberforce introduced his first anti-slavery motion in the House of Commons in 1788, but it was defeated. He reintroduced the motion every year for the next 18 years and worked with reformers in the United States and Europe to

> **Read Closely: Stakeholders**
> Major shifts in society always have stakeholders who benefit or lose as a result. Who are people who benefited from Wilberforce's anti-slavery campaign? Who are people who lost?

also end the slave trade. Finally on March 25, 1807, Great Britain outlawed the participation of British subjects in the importation and sale of slaves in its empire.

However, ownership of enslaved people remained legal, and other countries continued the slave trade. In response, the British Royal Navy—by far the most powerful navy in the world—began to intercept slave ships attempting to transport slaves across the Atlantic. The British warships searched the seas off West Africa, South America, and Cuba for slave ships, capturing more than 100 suspected slavers by 1861.

Wilberforce's triumph in Parliament brought him great prestige. Stopping the slave trade helped him to pursue other goals—improving the quality and morality of life in Great Britain. He continued his campaign against the institution of slavery. On July 26, 1833, Great Britain abolished slavery at home and in its colonies. Wilberforce died three days later.

British Reformers

Individual	Goal	Accomplishments
Mary Wollstonecraft	To achieve equality between men and women	▪ Wrote *Thoughts on the Education of Daughters* ▪ Wrote *A Vindication of the Rights of Woman*
William Wilberforce	To abolish slavery	▪ Persuaded Parliament to ban the slave trade in 1807 ▪ Persuaded Parliament to abolish slavery in the empire in 1833

Enlightened Despots

Enlightenment thinkers generally agreed on the importance of natural rights, reason, and liberty. However, they disagreed on how to achieve these goals. Some trusted citizens to support them. They supported efforts to expand participation in politics. For example, they wanted to shift power over taxation from the monarch to the legislative body.

Others advocates for the Enlightenment had no faith in people, even when wealthy and educated, to govern wisely. Further, they realized that strong monarchs would not allow others to become politically powerful. To reach the Enlightenment goals, they relied on strong monarchs to force political change.

> **Read Closely: Identify Bias**
> Many people are biased, prepared to think a certain way based on their position or upbringing, and it affects their judgment. How do you think enlightened despots might be biased?

Several monarchs agreed. They were **enlightened despots**, monarchs who wished to follow the most advanced ideas of their time but also to rule with absolute power. They were also shrewd politicians who realized that some of the reforms promoted by philosophers would strengthen their states.

Frederick the Great

At age 28, Frederick II (ruled 1740–1786) became ruler of his Berlin-based family's kingdom. It consisted of a handful of disconnected regions in central and eastern Europe. The largest of these was called Prussia. It was not a powerful kingdom. However, his father, fearing the powerful neighbors on each side—France, Russia, and Austria—had built a large, well-trained military. Frederick II immediately put it to use. He became known as "the Great" for his conquests of surrounding territories. When he died after ruling for 46 years, Prussia was one of Europe's leading powers.

Despite his battlefield successes, Frederick the Great's primary interests were not military. They were the arts and humanities. He loved philosophy and literature, wrote poetry and music, and left a legacy of great architecture in Berlin. As a young man, he greatly admired French Enlightenment figures. He corresponded with Voltaire for years before the two finally met. Frederick invited Voltaire to be a member of his court.

Read Closely: Central Cause
Look closely to see how a person's actions reveal their true thoughts. Frederick the Great was mainly concerned with social reforms in Prussia. Why do you think he focused on conquering surrounding territories as soon as he gained power?

Frederick the Great made many reforms that reflected Enlightenment ideals. Describing himself as "only the first servant of the state," he took many measures to make his subjects happy and well educated. Adopting Voltaire's principle of tolerance, he allowed his subjects to worship as they saw fit. He also improved Prussian schools, made the legal system more fair and easier to understand, and outlawed the practice of torture.

Like other enlightened despots, his reforms were important but limited. He disapproved of serfdom, but did not abolish it. Nor did he change the structure of Prussian society. It remained dominated by wealthy landowners and military leaders.

Catherine the Great of Russia

Catherine the Great (ruled 1762–1796) also corresponded with Voltaire. Influenced by him and other thinkers, she attempted several reforms. She wanted to organize and simplify Russia's laws. She was unable to complete this task, but she did make Russia's legal system more just and merciful. For example, she prohibited torture and religious persecution. (These laws, however, were frequently broken.) She also made some improvements in Russian schools.

Read Closely: Change
Notice when a text describes a gap between a ruler's policy and the government's actions. By focusing on just the policy or just the action, a source can portray the ruler either positively or negatively. How might a writer who disliked Catherine the Great describe her policy on torture?

Source: Shutterstock

This statue of Catherine the Great was erected in St. Petersburg in 1873. The scepter she holds in her right hand symbolizes her power. The people shown below her include several generals and political leaders. As a reflection of her Enlightenment attitudes, they also include a famous poet, Gavrila Derzhavin, and a leader of the Russian Academy of Sciences, a woman named Ekaterina Dashkova.

Read Closely: Actions
Pay attention to repeated events. Throughout history, uprisings have failed because people did not fully consider their situation. What would you have recommended the serfs do?

As Russia's leader, Catherine owned about 500,000 serfs. Yet she considered measures to improve the lives of serfs, even freeing them. Before she acted on this, an army of serfs launched what became the largest serf uprising in Russian history. Her army subdued them, but maybe 20,000 people were killed.

After this, Catherine began to see the serfs as a danger. She sided more with the nobles, whose support she needed to rule. By the end of her reign, the nobles had more power over serfs than before. She gave the landlords absolute power over them.

Catherine's fame, like that of Frederick II, came from conquest. Under her, Russia added territory, mostly in Poland and the region north of the Black Sea.

Maria Theresa and Joseph II of Austria

Maria Theresa (ruled 1740–1780) and her son, Joseph II (ruled 1780–1790), made more sweeping reforms than did Frederick and Catherine. Maria Theresa began by weakening the control that the Catholic Church had over her subjects, making Austria's tax system more just and giving the serfs more freedom.

Joseph, who was also the Holy Roman Emperor (ruled 1765–1790), tried to carry these reforms further. He gave Protestants and Jews civil rights and passed laws against their persecution. He abolished serfdom entirely. He also passed a law requiring landlords to pay the peasants cash in exchange for their labor.

Not all reforms worked well. In particular, the law requiring cash payments from landords to peasants was unpopular. Landlords resented having to use their cash this way. Peasants did not want the cash. They bought and sold things through the barter system (by trade rather than with cash). Joseph's successor, Leopold II (ruled 1790–1792), reversed this reform. Landlords could once again force their peasants to work for them.

An Enduring Issue: Modernization
Catherine's attempt to modify serfdom and Joseph II's support for a cash-based economy met strong resistance. Advocates of change and defenders of tradition often clash.

Policies of Enlightened Despots

Reforms	Frederick the Great (Prussia)	Catherine the Great (Russia)	Maria Theresa and Joseph II (Austria)
Religion	Tolerated deists, Catholics, and other religious groups	Prohibited religious persecution	Ended the persecution of Protestants and Jews and gave them civil rights
Laws	Made the legal system more fair and easier to understand	Prohibited torture and made the legal system more just and merciful	Revised the tax system to make it more just
Serfdom	Disapproved of serfdom but did nothing about it	Tried to end serfdom, but eventually gave landlords even greater power over serfs	Forced landlords to pay serfs, but the law was reversed
Foreign Policy	Seized Silesia fom Austria, part of Poland, and other territories to unite Prussia lands	Supported aggressive expansion into the Crimea region	Lost Silesia to Prussia but otherwise defended Habsburg lands

Application

Read the excerpt and answer the questions that follow it.

A Petition from Peasants in Southern Russia to Tsar Peter

1. We your slaves have, by the grace of God, heard that Your Imperial Majesty, coming from the southern lands in Orenburg Province, has taken on great strength. We praised God that our beautiful sun of old, after having hidden beneath the ground, now rises in the East and in its mercy wishes to warm us, Your humble and loyal slaves, with its grace, so we peasants with one accord bow our heads to the very ground.

2. We [your] slaves, all the peasants of the aforementioned ward, most humbly request the tsar's mercy from the officers and do not wish to oppose them in any way. Your Majesty did not declare His anger and punishment towards us, so we ask the lords His officers to spare us from the fatal sword and [ask them] to obey His [Majesty's] orders.

3. We also have a great hope that His Tsarist Majesty will mercifully spare us from the vicious, wild poisonous animals, the boyars and officers, and break off their sharp claws--for example, Mikhailo Ivanovich Bashmakov at the Iugov State Factories . . . .

4. To this end, we slaves, all the peasants, have sent reliable people to discover the truth about Your Majesty . . . . If you please, give them encouragement so that we slaves may know of Your Tsarist Majesty's health, for which we slaves would have great jubilation.

5. May the humble petition of us slaves receive the gracious attention of Your Majesty, so that we humble folk shall not suffer any harm at the hands of your troops.

Source: academic.shu.edu/russianhistory/index.php/The_Pugachev_Rebellion. Translated by Daniel Fields.

1. Explain the peasants' view of the tsar based on the excerpt.

____

____

2. Identify a passage(s) that shows what the peasants thought their best course of action was in communicating with the tsar.

____

____

3. Write a claim that logically flows from this excerpt.

____

____

4. Describe the context of life in Russia in which this document was written.

____

____

Lesson 3 *Upheavals in France and the Americas*

Conceptual Understanding 10.2c Individuals and groups drew upon principles of the Enlightenment to spread rebellions and call for revolutions in France and the Americas.

Source: *New York State Grades 9–12 Social Studies Framework.*

In France in 1789, one of the most important revolutions in world history began. The symbolic beginning occurred on July 14, when a mob seized control of a prison, the Bastille. Among the leaders was Camille Desmoulins, whose speech identified the problem that the outraged crowd wanted to address.

Analyze a Primary Source

Camille Desmoulins, Speech at the Bastille, July 14, 1789

Read Closely: The Problem
Desmoulins identifies the problem as the conflict between monarchy and republican government.
Underline the phrase in which he indicates that he knows that overthrowing the king could lead to bloody war.

Read Closely: Claims
Note how Desmoulins provides support for his claim by quoting a defender of the monarchy.

Read Closely: Solutions
To fix the problems of a monarchy, Desmoulins states that the people need to be enlightened. In this excerpt, he does not explain what he means, but it supports his idea that monarchies rely on corruption, while republics rely on honesty.

Read Closely: Examples
When writers support a claim by citing examples from history, readers should evaluate whether the history is used accurately.
Circle one case in which Desmoulins cites history.

There is one difference between a monarchy and a republic, which alone should suffice to make people reject with horror all monarchical rule and prefer a republic regardless of the cost of its establishment. In a democracy, though the people may be deceived, yet they at least love virtue.

It is merit which they believe they put in power as substitutes for the rascals who are the very essence of monarchies. The vices, concealments, and crimes which are the diseases of republics are the very health and existence of monarchies. Cardinal Richelieu [a prominent leader and supporter of the French monarchy] avowed openly in his political principles, that "kings should always avoid using the talents of thoroughly honest men."

Long before him Sallust said: "Kings can not get along without rascals; on the contrary, they should fear to trust the honest and upright." It is, therefore, only under a democracy that the good citizen can reasonably hope to see a cessation [end] of the triumphs of intrigue and crime; and to this end the people need only to be enlightened.

There is yet this difference between a monarchy and a republic: the reigns of Tiberius, Claudius, Nero, Caligula and Domitian [these were five rulers in Classical Rome whose reigns ended in conflict] all had happy beginnings. In fact, all reigns make a joyous entry, but this is only a delusion.

Source: Williams Jennings Bryan, *The World's Famous Orations: Volume VII, Continental Europe (380–1906)* (New York: Wallachia Publishers, 2015). First published 1906.

An Era of Revolution

The Atlantic world was reshaped by a series of violent political changes in a fifty-year period centered on the year 1800. These changes challenged both they sytems of feudalism and monarchy that had existed for centuries in Europe.

The French Revolution

In the late 1700s, France faced difficult times. Some of the problems were short-term. It had lost a war and colonies to Great Britain. The war resulted in large debts for the monarchy. Several bad harvests resulted in widespread hunger and the threat of famine. People needed help from their government. In short, the king needed more money. The only way to get it seemed to be by raising taxes. This proved to be very unpopular and helped spark political upheaval that was grounded partially in principles of the Enlightenment.

Precondition France also faced long-term problems in the late 18th century. These problems were systemic. That is, they were based on the way society was organized and rather than simply the debts from one war or hunger from one bad harvest or chaos from one weak ruler. They were ongoing problems:

- The many wars fought by Louis XIV against Great Britain and other countries had drained the country's treasury. One of these costly wars was the **American Revolution.** However, the nobles and clergy refused to pay higher taxes or give up any of their privileges to solve the government's economic problems. As a result the government was always short of money.
- France did not have one set of courts and laws that applied to everyone. The king or his representatives could imprison anyone for any reason for any period of time. A person could be put in jail for the remainder of his or her life without ever being tried for a crime. The inequality in the judicial system had existed for centuries.
- French society was divided into three groups called estates. The clergy made up the First Estate. The nobles constituted the Second Estate. The Third Estate included nearly all the population and paid nearly all of the taxes. However, they owned only about 65 percent of the land. This inequality was ongoing.

Read Closely: Central Cause
When you are reading, take note of all the causes for a major event. One may be more important than the others. Between the failing economy, a broken legal system, and social inequality, which problem was most responsible for France's decline?

France's Estates in the 18th Century

Estate	Population	Land Ownership	Taxation
First: Clergy	Less than 1%	About 10%	Less than 1%
Second: Nobility	Less than 2%	About 25%	Less than 1%
Third: Commoners	More than 97%	About 65%	More than 98%

The Beginning of the Revolution In 1789, the financial crisis forced King Louis XVI to act. He called a session of the Estates General, a body that included representatives of all three estates, to raise money to pay government expenses. Though the Estates General was France's lawmaking body, but it had not met in 175 years.

At the meeting, half of the representatives were from the Third Estate. However, voting was done by estate. Each of the three estates received one vote. So the First and Second Estates could outvote the Third, two to one.

An Enduring Issue: Power
In France before the Revolution, power was distributed among the three estates, regardless of how many people belonged to each one. Fights over how to distribute power are common in history.

The National Assembly The Third Estate felt that each representative should have a vote. When the First and Second Estates disagreed, the Third Estate withdrew from the Estates General and formed a new body, the National Assembly. Members of the assembly took an oath to provide France with a constitution that would limit the power of the king and give more rights to the common people.

Source: Bettmann Archives

The figures in this political cartoon represent the three estates in France in the late 18thcentury: the clergy, the nobility, and the commoners.

Read Closely: Course of Action
When reading, put yourself in the place of historical figures. It will help you understand their mistakes. King Louis XVI's threats caused riots. After the withdrawal of the Third Estate, what would you have done in his place?

Most French people supported the aims of the National Assembly. When the king threatened to arrest its leaders, riots broke out across the country. On July 14, 1789, an angry crowd in Paris captured the Bastille, a fortress in Paris where the government imprisoned political opponents. Though it held only a handful of prisoners, it symbolized the oppressive power of the government.

At the same time in **Paris,** leaders of the revolutionary movement set up a government to replace the existing one. The **French Revolution** had begun.

In the countryside, the peasants rose up against the nobles and burned manor houses on some estates. Peasants sought to find and destroy grain and tax records. These records determined how much money or grain the peasants owed the Church or the landowning noble. When the people stopped paying taxes and the royal officials fled to keep from being killed, the government broke down. The king was forced to accept the revolutionary government led by the National Assembly.

Causes and Effects of the French Revolution	
Cause	**Effect**
The Enlightenment spread ideas about freedom and equality.	Lower-class French citizens began to question their socioeconomic positions.
Harvests were poor and the government reacted weakly.	Hunger, angry citizens wanted reforms to make the government more responsive to suffering.
King Louis XVI raised taxes on the poor.	Many French citizens were outraged by higher taxes on them instead of the wealthy upper class.
The governing system failed to represent the French people equally.	The Third Estate withdrew from the Estates General to form the National Assembly.
King Louis XVI threatened to arrest leaders of the National Assembly.	French citizens captured the Bastille, a prison that symbolized the government's power.

New Rights and a Constitution The National Assembly changed France in many ways. In August 1789, it adopted the **Declaration of the Rights of Man and of the Citizen.** This document, like the American **Declaration of Independence** (1776), was inspired by the Enlightenment ideas of Locke, Voltaire, and Rousseau. Its first article declared that "all men are born free and equal in rights." The declaration provided the people of France with such basic rights as freedom of speech, religion, and the press. It also guaranteed the right of the people to participate in the government of France.

The National Assembly continued to rule while a new constitution was being developed. For example, the National Assembly reformed the legal system to provide for elected judges, trial by jury, and an end to brutal punishments. Nobles could no longer purchase judicial and high military positions.

The National Assembly took power as a revolutionary but temporary government. In 1791, it approved a new constitution with three key features:

- It replaced the National Assembly with a new law-making body called the Legislative Assembly.
- It gave the new legislature ways to check the power of the king.
- It placed the land of the Catholic Church under the control of the national government.

Under pressure, Louis XVI accepted the new constitution.

Read Closely: Similarity
Look for similarities in historical events. New revolutionary governments generally had comparable goals. How did the French Declaration of the Rights of Man share values with the American Declaration of Independence?

The French Republic

The passage of a new constitution and creation of the Legislative Assembly did not end the turmoil in France. Rather, turmoil increased. Between 1791 and 1815, the French would usually be at war with each other or with other countries.

Jacobins Leading the Legislative Assembly was a political faction known as the Jacobins. However, they were sharply divided over how to deal with France's German-speaking neighbors, Austria and Prussia. These two countries feared the spread of revolutionary ideas. They prepared to invade France to restore the power of the king. Some Jacobins were cautious. They wanted to rebuild France before entering a war. Others charged that King Louis XVI had plotted with Austria and Prussia. They argued that France should to to war in order to protect the revolution. In 1791, France declared war on Austria and Prussia.

The split among the Jacobins caused the National Assembly to call for new elections to choose representatives who would write a new constitution. These representatives met in the National Convention, then drew up a new constitution that radically changed France's government. It abolished the monarchy and made France into a republic.

Execution of the King The National Convention then held a trial for the powerless king. By a wide margin, they found the ex-king guilty of various crimes against the people of France. However, the convention was closely divided on the proper punishment. The Jacobin leader of the Paris delegation to the National Convention was **Maximilien Robespierre,** a believer in the idea of the general will as described by Rousseau. Robespierre argued for execution. Others argued for moderation. Executing a monarch was rare. No European monarch had been executed since 1649, when the English beheaded Charles I. Robespierre won. On January 21, 1793, Louis XVI was taken to the guillotine.

Read Closely: Central Effect
To fully understand an important event, look for indirect results, not just big changes. How did the Reign of Terror probably affect France's neighboring countries?

The Reign of Terror In July 1793, Robespierre became leader of the 12-man Committee of Public Safety, which allowed him to control the French government during the country's growing financial and military crisis. The committee enacted measures to stabilize the economy and further the formation of a large army to combat the foreign powers attacking France's borders. Counterrevolutionary uprisings, especially in the south and west of France, also had to be put down. This action began the Reign of Terror.

During this period, special courts ordered the execution of many thousands of people whom Robespierre and his allies considered "enemies of the republic." Victims of the Terror included aristocrats, clergy, and even ordinary people suspected of treason, even if no actual proof existed. Their deaths at the guillotine were public spectacles.

For Robespierre and other members of the Committee of Public Safety, the Reign of Terror was necessary. They believed that only an authoritarian, violent government could defend the gains made by the French Revolution. They had to eliminate all those who might oppose or even criticize the National Convention. (It governed France during this stage of the revolution.)

Read Closely: Problem
Look for differences between what leaders say and what they do. New governments may quickly abandon their original principals. In what way(s) did the Committee of Public Safety oppose the reasons that started the French Revolution?

One victim of the Terror was writer and social reformer **Olympe de Gouges.** She is best known for her **Declaration of the Rights of Woman and of the Female Citizen** (1791), a rebuttal to the Declaration of the Rights of Man and of the Citizen. It argued, among other things, that women should be given the same rights as men. Late in 1793, she fell afoul of the Committee of Public Safety for her moderate views concerning the king and other subjects. She went to the guillotine on November 4.

As the Terror claimed more victims and Robespierre became more aggressive, members of the National Convention began to fear for their lives. Moderates and extremists joined together to overthrow him. In July 1794, his opponents had Robespierre arrested and he and his allies went to the guillotine in short order. His death ended the Reign of Terror. Between 15,000 and 30,000 had died.

The End of the Revolution In 1795, another constitution placed France under the control of the Directory, a five-member committee. The Directory proved to be corrupt and inefficient. It could not solve the country's serious financial issues. Furthermore, in 1798, France's enemies gained new strength. Britain, in control of the seas, persuaded other countries to join the fight against France. In 1799, French armies lost land battles in Italy, Switzerland, and the Netherlands. The future looked dark.

In that same year, an able, 30-year-old general named **Napoleon Bonaparte** returned to France after a victory in Egypt. With broad support from the French people, he tried to overthrow the Directory. He succeeded.

Napoleon ended the French Revolution. Voters approved a new constitution that gave him ruling power as First Consul. In effect, he was a military dictator. In 1804, Napoleon proclaimed an end to the republic. France became an empire. Its first ruler was Napoleon I. Many French hoped that the successful military leader could bring some stability to their country. However, ten years of brutal warfare, known as the Napoleonic Wars, followed.

Read Closely: Informed Action
When reading, pay attention to how people respond to extreme circumstances. Just years after the French Revolution ended a king's reign, France's people unified behind a military dictator. What do you think their reasoning was for doing this?

Colonial Revolutions in the Americas

As the French Revolution was causing upheaval in Europe, colonial revolutions were spreading through the Americas. Thirteen British colonies had already declared their independence in 1776, forming the United States. French and Spanish colonies soon followed.

Saint-Domingue (Haiti) In the wake of the French Revolution, enslaved Africans in the French Caribbean **colony** of Saint-Domingue rose in rebellion. The colony was on the island that contains the present-day countries of Haiti and the Dominican Republic.

The sugar plantations of what is today Haiti provided France with great wealth. The enslaved Africans who worked on the plantations greatly outnumbered the French colonists. As the slaves' anger at their harsh treatment built up, some began to look for opportunities to revolt. When the slaves heard of the French Revolution, they felt that the French government would be too busy dealing with the turmoil at home to send troops across the sea.

In 1791, **Toussaint L'Ouverture,** a freed slave, led a successful uprising against the colonists. L'Ouverture remained in control until Napoleon sent an army to retake the island in 1802. As L'Ouverture resisted this attack, he was captured and put in prison, where he died in 1803. L'Ouverture's successor, Jean-Jacques Dessalines, drove off the French. Saint-Domingue became independent in 1804.

Read Closely: Turning Point
Pay attention to the order of major events to understand how each affected the others. How do you believe the Saint-Domingue rebellion marks a turning point in Western history?

The **Haitian Revolution** was the largest successful slave rebellion in history. It spread fear among slave-owners throughout the Americas, who reacted with new laws to repress slaves in their own countries.

Source: Shutterstock

The bronze statue *The Unknown Slave* was erected in Port-au-Prince, Haiti, in 1967. It was designed by a Haitian artist, Albert Mangonès, to honor the successful slave rebellion in Saint-Domingue in 1791. It has become an international symbol of the fight against slavery.

> **Read Closely: Stakes**
> People usually have more than one reason for their actions. While Simón Bolívar was working for the welfare of his people, what other motivations might he have had for South American revolutions to succeed?

South America In the Spanish Empire, a free and relatively wealthy class of people drove the colonial revolution for independence. **Creoles,** colonists who were born in Latin America to Spanish parents, wanted to be free of the heavy hand of Spain's economic and political dominance. They tended to be wealthy owners of land, mines, and businesses. They were also well educated and aware of the Enlightenment ideas behind the revolutions in North America and Europe. In 1808, when the armies of Napoleon Bonaparte conquered Spain, the Latin American colonists took their opportunity to revolt.

The struggle to free Venezuela began about 1808 under the leadership of Francisco de Miranda and **Simón Bolívar.** Miranda had fought in the French Revolution. He had also tried to get help for his revolutionary causes from the English government and Catherine the Great of Russia. The Venezuelans won their independence in 1811, but a year later, Spanish forces retook the country. Miranda was captured and died in prison.

However, Bolívar escaped to Colombia. He continued the struggle for independence. Finally, between 1819 and 1825, the rebels drove the Spanish out of Colombia, Venezuela, Ecuador, and Peru. Bolívar was honored throughout the region:

- People referred to him as The Liberator.
- He served as president of Colombia.
- The new country of Bolivia named was after him.

Source: Shutterstock.

The influence of the French Revolution on Latin American independence was recognized by the country of Nicaragua when it issued this stamp showing the storming of the Bastille.

Application

Read the excerpt and answer the questions that follow it.

Simón Bolívar, Letter to the Governor of the English Colony of Jamaica, September 6, 1815

The role of the inhabitants of the American hemisphere has for centuries been purely passive. Politically they were nonexistent. We are still in a position lower than slavery, and therefore it is more difficult for us to rise to the enjoyment of freedom....States are slaves because of either the nature or the misuse of their constitutions; a people are therefore enslaved when the government, by its nature or its vices, infringes on and usurps the rights of the citizen or subject. . . .

We have been harassed by a conduct which has not only deprived us of our rights but has kept us in a sort of permanent infancy with regard to public affairs. If we could at least have managed our domestic affairs and our internal administration, we could have acquainted ourselves with the processes and mechanics of public affairs. . . .

Despite the convictions of history, South Americans have made efforts to obtain liberal, even perfect, institutions, doubtless out of that instinct to aspire to the greatest possible happiness, which, common to all men, is bound to follow in civil societies founded on the principles of justice, liberty, and equality. But are we capable of maintaining in proper balance the difficult charge of a republic? Is it conceivable that a newly emancipated people can soar to the heights of liberty, and, unlike Icarus [a character in Greek mythology who flew close to the sun and fell to his death when his wings melted], neither have its wings melt nor fall into an abyss? Such a marvel is inconceivable and without precedent. There is no reasonable probability to bolster our hopes.

Source: https://library.brown.edu/create/modernlatinamerica/chapters/chapter-2-the-colonial-foundations/primary-documents-with-accompanying-discussion-questions/document-2-simon-bolivar-letter-from-jamaica-september-6-1815/.

1. Detail the context in which Bolívar's explanation is given as to why South Americans were unable to enjoy freedom.

____

____

2. Identify what changes in the past, as identified by Bolívar, would have better prepared South Americans to "obtain liberal, even perfect, institutions."

____

____

3. Explain how Bolívar used the legend about Icarus to support his claim.

____

____

4. Quote a phrase or sentence that indicates how optimistic Bolívar was that South Americans could solve their problems quickly.

____

____

Lesson 4 The Emergence of Nations

Conceptual Understanding
10.2d Cultural identity and nationalism inspired political movements that attempted to unify people into new nation-states and posed challenges to multinational states.

Source: *New York State Grades 9–12 Social Studies Framework.*

When Otto von Bismarck was born in 1815, Germany did not exist as a unified country as it does today. Germans were divided into many dozens of small kingdoms, dukedoms, etc. Bismarck united them, creating a powerful nation in the middle of Europe.

Analyze a Primary Source

Otto von Bismarck, Interview with a French Journalist, 1869

Read Closely: Contrasts
One way to recognize what a person values is by recognizing what he or she does not value. *Underline the phrase that indicates that Bismarck does not value popularity.*

Read Closely: Comparison
Bismarck tries to strengthen support for his claim by contrasting Germans with their neighbors. He believes others have more of a stake in government than do Germans.

Read Closely: Generalizations
Writers sometimes make broad statements such as this one as a way to surprise readers. *Circle one generalization used by Bismarck to surprise readers and grab their attention.*

Read Closely: Self-Interest
The closing sentence reflects where Bismarck sees his interests: in the success of his prince and the unification of Germany.

I know I enjoy the same unpopularity in France as I do in Germany. Everywhere I alone am held responsible for a situation I did not make, but which was imposed upon me as upon you. I am the scapegoat of public opinion, but I torment myself little about that.

With a perfectly tranquil conscience, I pursue a goal which I believe useful to my country and to Germany. As for the means, for want of others, I make use of those that are offered to me. There are many things to say about the Prussian domestic situation. In order to judge it impartially, it is necessary to study and to know thoroughly the special character of the men of this country. While today France and Italy each form a great social body animated by a common spirit and a common feeling, in Germany, on the contrary, it is individualism which dominates. Here each one lives apart in his little corner, with his own opinion, among his wife and children, always distrusting the government as well as his neighbor, judging everything from his personal point of view, but never from the viewpoint of all.

The feeling of individualism and the need of contradiction are developed in the German to an inconceivable degree. Show him an open door—rather than going through it, he is bent upon wanting to open a hole in the wall beside it. Also, whatever it does, no government will ever be popular in Prussia. . . .

And I told the Crown Prince, who, in his education and inclinations, is by preference a man of parliamentary government: "What does it matter if I am hanged, provided that my hangman's rope binds your throne solidly to Germany!"

Source: Frederick Hollyday, ed., *Bismarck: Great Lives Observed* (Englewood Cliffs, N.J.: Prentice-Hall, 1970), pages 27–31.

Uniting Divided Cultural Groups

The newly free nations of the Americas, such as Haiti, Colombia, and Ecuador, were not the only territories to see changes in their status in the 19th century. New nations came into being in Europe in the 19th and early 20th centuries as well. The leaders demanding creation of a new nation were fuelled, in part, by a sense of cultural identity and by the wave of **nationalism** that spread during the era.

The Unification of Germany

In the 18th century, the region known as Germany was a collection of over 300 independent states. By 1848, these states had consolidated into a confederation of 38 states ruled by princes or kings. Prussia was the largest and most powerful of the states, and many Prussians believed they should be the core of a newly united German nation. King Wilhelm I of Prussia shared this belief.

Blood and Iron To help Wilhelm I achieve his goal, he appointed Otto von Bismarck to be his chief minister in 1862. Bismarck believed in practical rather than idealistic policies to achieve his goals, a viewpoint known as realpolitik. The world, he said, could be changed only by "blood and iron." He intended to use the Prussian military to unify Germans under Prussian leadership.

France, Austria (the other large German state), and many smaller German states opposed creation of a powerful Prussia. To overcome this opposition, Bismarck use warfare. The 1866 Austro-Prussian War (also known as the Seven Weeks' War) involved the two German powers' dispute over the administration of two small northern German states: Schleswig and Holstein. Bismarck persuaded France and Russia not to aid Austria in the war, and Prussia was quickly victorious. The easy defeat of Austria demonstrated Prussia's military strength. It also ended Austria's influence over the future of a German state.

Read Closely: Difference
Comparing major historical figures will help you understand why they made certain choices. What are some differences between Napoleon's command of the French military and Bismarck's command of the Prussian military?

North German Confederation To extend Prussia's political power, Bismarck organized the North German Confederation in 1867. It brought together many small northern German states under Prussia's leadership. However, four major states in southern Germany chose not to be part of the confederation. Mainly Roman Catholic, the south Germans feared domination by the Protestant north Germans. The south Germans also did not want to upset France by joining with Prussia.

Franco-Prussian War To encourage the southern states to join with the northern ones, Bismarck started another war—this time with France. He stirred up anti-French feeling in both northern and southern Germany. Emperor Napoleon III of France was also eager for a war. He wanted to stop Prussia from gaining more power. In addition, the emperor hoped that a military victory over Prussia would make him more popular in his own country.

To bring about the war, Bismarck stirred up hostile feelings between the French and the Prussians by playing on their national pride. Through the use of a misleading telegram, Bismarck made it seem as though the two countries had insulted each other. As a result, newspapers in France and Prussia demanded war.

Read Closely: Continuity
Examining the context of an event will help you clarify its importance. Individual wars are just part of a larger military history. How did the Franco-Prussian war fit in with other major conflicts in Europe?

France declared war in July 1870. The south German states blamed France for the situation and came to the aid of the North German Confederation. The Franco-Prussian War, therefore, was really a war between France and all of Germany. German armies invaded France. They defeated a large French army under the personal command of Napoleon III and took the emperor prisoner in September 1870. The Germans moved on to Paris, and in January 1871, the French capital surrendered. The Germans had achieved a quick and total victory.

German Unification The Treaty of Frankfort (May 1871) ended the war. Under its terms, France gave up the province of Alsace and part of Lorraine. These areas that bordered the southern German states were rich in coal and iron. France also had to pay a large sum of money to Germany, and troops remained in France until all of the money was collected.

Read Closely: Turning Point
Study the order of events to understand how a great leader can shape the course of history. How was Bismarck's appointment a turning point in Germany's history?

Following the great victory of 1871, Bismarck met with the leaders of all the German states at the French palace of Versailles outside Paris. There, with much ceremony, the south German states joined with the North German Confederation to form the German Empire, or Reich. King William I of Prussia became the kaiser, or emperor, of all Germany, and Bismarck was named the chancellor, or prime minister. The formation of a power German state in the middle of Europe, and the fear it caused in other countries were one factor that would lead to a major war, World War I four decades later.

The Unification of Italy

Since the Middle Ages, the region of Italy had been divided into several provinces, small kingdoms, and city-states. In the early 1800s, some were independent, some were ruled by Austria, and some by the pope.

Mazzini and Garibaldi In the 1830s, the voice of a young nationalist leader, Giuseppe (Joseph) Mazzini, began to be heard. He founded Young Italy, a secret society that called for the unification of Italy under a representative government. Mazzini stirred up revolts in several cities, but they were quickly put down by the authorities. Mazzini was forced into exile.

An Enduring Issue: Nationalism
Nationalism helped unify both Germany and Italy. The force of nationalism has unified or divided many states over the past two centuries.

ITALY BEFORE UNIFICATION IN 1871

A second great figure unifying Italy was **Giuseppe (Joseph) Garibaldi.** In 1848, he led troops in the northern Italian states in a failed revolt against Austrian rule. The following year, he attempted to replace the pope's rule over Rome with a more liberal government. The effort failed when French troops sent by Napoleon III arrived to back the pope. As a result, Garibaldi, too, was exiled.

Read Closely: Claim
Examine the text to understand people's motivations. Despite being repeatedly defeated, Mazzini and then Garibaldi continued to rebel against their government. What is a plausible claim about their reasons for trying so many times?

Cavour In 1852, the **Italian unification** movement gained new life under Camillo di Cavour. This period, called the Risorgimento, or reawakening, saw King Victor Emmanuel II of Sardinia and Piedmont name Cavour prime minister. Cavour believed in constitutional monarchy and in industrial growth. He strengthened the economy of Piedmont, which bordered France and Switzerland in the northwest of Italy, so that it had the power to win Italian territory from Austria.

Cavour's first move was to arrange a secret alliance with France and then provoke a war with Austria. When Austrian troops invaded Piedmont, the French aided the Italians. The 1859 treaty that ended the war ceded the northern Italian state of Lombardy to Piedmont. The Austrian invasion increased nationalist feelings across northern Italy. Rebellions broke out as Tuscany, Parma, and Modena demanded freedom from Austrian control and unification with Piedmont. Austria agreed. The foundation for the Italian nation had been built.

Garibaldi's Return In May 1860, Garibaldi landed on the island of Sicily with an army of about 1,000 soldiers called Red Shirts. His fiercely nationalistic soldiers defeated the larger, professional army of the island's Bourbon rulers. Then Garibaldi and his army crossed over to mainland Italy, taking control of the southern third of the peninsula. Cavour sent the Piedmontese army to aid Garibaldi, helping him capture the Papal States in central Italy (but not Rome). Garibaldi and his Red Shirts transferred their conquered territory to Victor Emmanuel, who became King of Italy in March 1861.

In 1866, Prussia's victory over Austria in the Seven Weeks' War ended Austria's control over Venetia in Italy's northeast. Then, in 1870 during the Franco-Prussian War, the French withdrew their troops from Rome and Italian troops moved in. In 1871, for the first time in many centuries, the entire peninsula was part of the same state. The leaders of unification were honored: Mazzini as the soul, Cavour as the brains, and Garibaldi as the sword.

Read Closely: Impact of Place
Paying attention to every aspect of an event will make it easier to understand. It is crucial to consider the surroundings of a moment in history. How was the Italian rebellion affected by other conflicts in Europe at the time?

Dissolving Multinational States

The upsurge of nationalism felt by the peoples of Europe had differing effects in different regions and situations. In the cases of Germany and Italy, it brought smaller, culturally similar entities together to form unitary states. But in the cases of the Ottoman and Habsburg Empires, the opposite occurred. Ethnic nationalism, combined with religious differences, caused the empires to divide.

The Ottoman Empire

In the 1800s, the **Ottoman Empire** suffered overexpansion and a failure to modernize. As a result, it experienced palace coups, declining trade, weakening leadership, and rampant corruption. As the empire declined, long-standing ethnic and religious differences emerged which grew into rebellions and loss of territory.

Geography of the Balkans One region where the Ottomans lost power was in the **Balkans,** a mountainous region of southeastern Europe. Because the region is so mountainous, communication and transportation were always difficult. People remained separated and maintained distinct cultures more so than in less mountainous regions such as France or Germany.

Greece The Ottomans had ruled Greece since the crumbling of the Byzantine Empire in the 15th century. But the Greeks had kept a strong sense of national consciousness through the Greek language and the Greek Orthodox Church. As a sign of the growing nationalism in Europe, the Greeks began a war for independence in 1821. People known as philhellenes, lovers of Greek culture, throughout Europe donated money or even came to fight for the Greeks. The governments of Great Britain, France, and Russia added their support as a way to weaken the Ottomas. The European powers brokered a treaty in 1830, and Greek independence was settled in July 1832.

Read Closely: Point of View
Understanding all points of view will help you understand different people's motivations. If you were a Serbian citizen in 1800, how would you feel about the Ottoman Empire?

Serbia Serbians, though under Ottoman domination even longer than the Greeks, retained their cultural identity through their language and religion. Like the Greeks and the Russians, they were Orthodox Christians rather than Roman Catholics. In the early 1800s, Serbian uprisings against the Ottomans brought some autonomy, but not independence. However, with the aid of its Orthodox ally Russia, Serbia won independence in 1878.

Other Lands Wars and diplomatic maneuvering costs the Ottomans control over other ands throughout the late 1800s and the early 1900s. Most of the Balkans, the Mediterranean islands of Cyprus and Crete, and Egypt all became independent or under the control of another empire. By 1914, when World War I began, the Ottoman Empire was crumbling.

The Austro-Hungarian Empire

In 1848, citizens demanding greater participation in government, such as allowing more people to vote, rebelled in Paris and throughout Europe. In Vienna, the capital of Austria-Hungary, demands for political change combined with demands by ethnic groups for self-government. The Austrian ruler, Franz Joseph, tried to maintain absolute power. However, that became difficult as ethnic groups rebelled, often with the support of Austria's rivals such as France and Prussia.

- Hungarian nationalists led by Louis Kossuth disliked living under Austrian leadership. In 1867, they won local autonomy, and the empire was divided into a dual monarchy. However, Hungarians did not win full independence until after World War I.
- The Austro-Hungarian Empire including many groups of Slavs. Among the largest were the Czechs, Slovaks, Poles, and Croats.
- The king of Sardinia-Piedmont liberated northern Italy from Austrian control. The territory became part of the newly formed country of Italy.

Read Closely: Similarity
Understanding similarities will help you remember how different parts of history fit together. How is the fate of the Austro-Hungarian Empire similar to that of the Ottoman Empire?

World War I

The Ottoman Empire and Austria-Hungary joined with Germany in World War I. (The war is described in Chapter 5.) Their defeat, along with the spreading commitment to the idea that cultural groups had a right to determine their own government, brought an end to the two large multiethnic states.

Central and Southern Europe Austria and Hungary became separate, independent states. New states created included Czechoslovakia, Poland, and Yugoslavia (made up of several groups of Slavs).

Middle East The Ottoman Empire was reduced to just the independent state of Turkey. Other lands were stripped away and became either independent states or territories under the control of European powers. For example, Iraq came under the control of Great Britain, while France took over Syria and Lebanon.

Application

Read the excerpt and answer the questions that follow it.

Lajos (Louis) Kossuth, Speech in Washington, D.C., 1852

Yours is a happy country, gentlemen. You had more than fair play. You had active operative aid from Europe in your struggle for independence [from France], which, once achieved, you so wisely used as to become a prodigy of freedom, and welfare and a book of life to nations.

But we in Europe -- we, unhappily, have no such fair play. With us, against every palpitation of liberty all despots are united in a common league; and you may be sure that despots will never yield to the moral influence of your great example. They hate the very existence of this example. It is the sorrow of their thoughts, and the incubus [nightmare] of their dreams. To stop its moral influence abroad, and to check its spreading development at home, is what they wish, instead of yielding to its influence. . . .

Sir, I most fervently thank you for the acknowledgment that my country has proved worthy to be free. Yes, gentlemen, I feel proud at my nation's character, heroism, love of freedom and vitality, and I bow with reverential awe before the decree of Providence which placed my country in a position that, without its restoration to independence, there is no possibility for freedom and the independence of nations on the European continent. Even what now in France is about to pass proves the truth of this. Every disappointed hope with which Europe looked toward France is a degree more added to the importance of Hungary to the world. Upon our plains were fought the decisive battles for christendom; [sic] there will be fought the decisive battles for the independence of nations, for State rights, for international law, and for democratic liberty.

We will live free, or die like men; but should my people be doomed to die, it will be the first whose death will not be recorded as suicide, but as a martyrdom for the world, and future ages will mourn over the sad fate of the Magyar race, doomed to perish, not because we deserved it, but because in the nineteenth century there was nobody to protect the laws of nature and of nature's God.

Source: teachers.sduhsd.net/ltrupe/sources/nationalism/kossuth.htm.

1. Explain the historical context in which Kossuth is appealing for American help.

____

____

2. Interpret the reasoning that Kossuth uses to suggest the United States has a religious purpose in seeing Hungarians succeed.

____

____

3. Describe how Kossuth appeals to Americans to persuade them that they have a stake in the freedom of Hungary.

____

____

Chapter 2 Review

Multiple-Choice Questions

Directions (1–6): For each statement or question, choose the number of the word or expression that, of those given, best completes the statement or answers the question.

Base your answer to questions 1 and 2 on the passage below and your knowledge of social studies.

> Clause 9. The Sovereign is absolute; for there is no other authority but that which centers in his single Person that can act with a Vigor proportionate to the Extent of such a vast Dominion.
>
> Clause 10. The Extent of the Dominion requires an absolute Power to be vested in that Person who rules over it. It is expedient so to be that the quick Dispatch of Affairs, sent from distant Parts, might make ample Amends for the Delay occasioned by the great Distance of the Places.
>
> Clause 11. Every other Form of Government whatsoever would not only have been prejudicial to Russia, but would even have proved its entire Ruin. . . .
>
> Clause 13. What is the true End of Monarchy? Not to deprive People of their natural Liberty; but to correct their Actions, in order to attain the supreme Good.
>
> Clause 14. The Form of Government, therefore, which best attains this End, and at the same Time sets less Bounds than others to natural Liberty, is that which coincides with the Views and Purposes of rational Creatures, and answers the End, upon which we ought to fix a steadfast Eye in the Regulations of civil Polity.
>
> **Source:** Catherine the Great, Tsar of Russia, Instructions to the Legislative Commission, 1767

1. Which clause best supports the claim that Catherine was influenced by the ideas of the Enlightenment?
   (1) clause 9 stating that the sovereign is absolute and can "act with . . . Vigor"
   (2) clause 10 arguing that the "Extent of the Dominion requires an absolute Power"
   (3) clause 11 criticizing other forms of government that would have "proved its [Russia's] entire Ruin"
   (4) clause 14 mentioning the "natural Liberty" of "rational Creatures"

2. Based on this passage, which thinker and idea would Catherine the Great agree with?
   (1) Locke and his ideas about revolution
   (2) Rousseau and his ideas about the purpose of government
   (3) Wollstonecraft and her ideas about the slave trade
   (4) de Gouges and her ideas on the rights of women

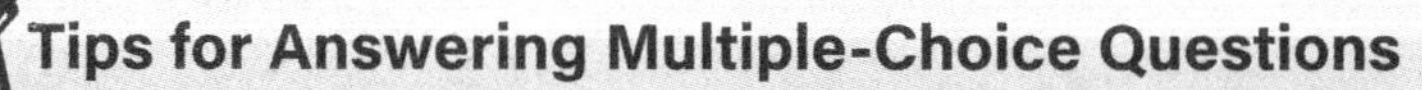

Tips for Answering Multiple-Choice Questions

If you are not sure which answer in a multiple-choice question is correct, try to identify and rule out the ones that you know are wrong. For example, in question 3, match each possible answer with the statement in the chart that demonstrates it is wrong. If you can find three matches, the remaining answer will be the correct one. For practice using this strategy, consider this question:

1. Which philosopher developed the idea of the noble savage?
   1. Locke
   2. Montesquieu
   3. Voltaire
   4. Rousseau

If you aren't sure that "Rousseau" is the correct answer, try to rule out other answers. The term "noble savage" describes the natural state of a person. The text did not discuss the ideas of Montesquieu and Voltaire on this topic, so they are not likely to be correct. You might recall Locke's idea of the *tabula rasa*. It is not consistent with the idea that a person is naturally noble or not noble. Therefore, the best choice is "Rousseau."

Base your answer to questions 3 and 4 on the table below and your knowledge of social studies.

John Locke on Government	
Topic	**Belief**
Human Nature	People are born with a mind that is a *tabula rasa*.
Equality	All people are naturally equal and independent.
Law	Natural laws govern human society, and they are more basic than laws written by legislatures.
Rights	People have no right to harm others or deprive them of their liberty or possessions.
Government	The legitimacy of a government is based on the consent of the people.

3. Based on the beliefs in the chart, which statement would John Locke support?
   (1) Rights are a reward given to people who behave morally.
   (2) The laws people write replace natural laws.
   (3) Individuals have a right to pursue life and liberty.
   (4) Political leaders derive their authority from God.

4. The statements in which row did Jean-Jacques Rousseau disagree most strongly with?
   (1) Human Nature
   (2) Equality
   (3) Law
   (4) Rights

Base your answer to questions 5 and 6 on the passages below and your knowledge of social studies.

Article 1. Men are born and remain free and equal in rights. Social distinctions may be founded only upon the general good.

Article 2. The aim of all political association is the preservation of the natural and imprescriptible [inalienable] rights of man. These rights are liberty, property, security, and resistance to oppression.

Source: French National Assembly, Declaration of the Rights of Man and of the Citizen, 1789

Article 1. Woman is born free and remains equal to man in rights. Social distinctions can only be founded on common utility.

Article 2. The purpose of any political association is the conservation of the natural and imprescriptible rights of Woman and Man: these rights are liberty, property, security, and especially resistance to oppression.

Source: Olympe de Gouges, Declaration of the Rights of Woman and the Female Citizen, 1791

5. Based on these passages, which action would most likely be supported by Olympe de Gouges?
   (1) executing the king so that a queen could reign
   (2) restricting access to education by gender
   (3) ending the enslavement of Africans
   (4) allowing women to serve in the legislature

6. Which statement is supported by both passages?
   (1) A government's authority comes from the people.
   (2) All people should have equal incomes.
   (3) Natural laws lead to the oppression of some people.
   (4) Men and women naturally have equal rights.

Tips for Answering Multiple-Choice Questions

One way to answer a question comparing two excerpts is to focus on one at a time. For example, in question 6

- identify which of the four possible answers are supported by the first excerpt
- identify which of the four possible answers are supported by the second excerpt
- choose the answer that is supported by both

Short-Answer Questions

CRQ Directions (7–9): Analyze the documents and answer the short-answer questions that follow each document in the space provided.

Base your answer to question 7 on Document 1 below and on your knowledge of social studies.

Document 1

Giuseppe (Joseph) Mazzini founded Young Italy to unify the nation under a representative government. He started several revolts that failed, and he was eventually exiled.

> This means [of infinitely multiplying your forces and powers of action] was provided for you by God, when he gave you a country; when, even as a wise overseer of labor distributes the various branches of employment according to the different capacities of the workmen, he divided humanity into distinct groups or nuclei upon the face of the earth, thus creating the germ of nationalities. Evil governments have disfigured the divine design. Nevertheless you may still trace it, distinctly marked out—at least as far as Europe is concerned—by the course of the great rivers, the direction of the higher mountains, and other geographical conditions. They have disfigured it by their conquests, their greed, and their jealousy even of the righteous power of others; disfigured it so far that, if we except England and France—there is not perhaps a single country whose present boundaries correspond to that design. . . .
>
> Then may each one of you, fortified by the power and affection of many millions, all speaking the same language, gifted with the same tendencies, and educated by the same historical tradition, hope even by your own single efforts to be able to benefit all humanity.
>
> Oh my brothers, love your country! Our country is our home, the house that God has given us, placing therein a numerous family that loves us, and whom we love; a family with whom we sympathize more readily and whom we understand more quickly than we do others; and which, from its being centered round a given spot, and from the homogeneous nature of its elements is adapted to a special branch of activity. . . .
>
> Country is not only a mere zone of territory. The true country is the idea to which it gives birth; it is the thought of love, the sense of communion [that] unites in one all the sons of that territory.
>
> **Source:** Joseph Mazzini, *The Duties of Man* (London: Chapman & Hall, 1862), pages 87–93.

7. Describe the geographic context, such as the status of boundaries, for Mazzini's ideas as expressed in this excerpt.

____

____

____

____

Base your answer to question 8 on Document 2 below and on your knowledge of social studies.

Document 2

Prussia and Austria fought the Seven Weeks' War over control of two small German states. After a quick victory, Bismarck reflected on the unification of Germans under one leader.

> We had to avoid wounding Austria too severely; we had to avoid leaving behind in her any unnecessary bitterness of feeling or desire for revenge; we ought rather to reserve the possibility of becoming friends again with our adversary of the moment, and in any case to regard the Austrian state as a piece on the European chessboard and the renewal of friendly relations with her as a move open to us. If Austria were severely injured, she would become the ally of France and of every other opponent of ours; she would even sacrifice her anti-Russian interests for the sake of revenge on Prussia. . . . German Austria we could neither wholly nor partly make use of. The acquisition of provinces like Austrian Silesia and portions of Bohemia could not strengthen the Prussian state; it would not lead to an amalgamation of German Austria with Prussia, and Vienna could not be governed from Berlin as a mere dependency. . . .
>
> Austria's conflict and rivalry with us was no more culpable [to be blamed] than ours with her; our task was the establishment or foundation of German national unity under the leadership of the King of Prussia.
>
> **Source:** Otto von Bismarck, *The Reflections and Reminiscences of Otto Prince von Bismarck*, Volume II. Translated by A. J. Butler (Leipzig, 1899), pages 229–231.

8. Based on this excerpt, identify Bismarck's point of view about unifying people who were culturally Germans.

____

____

____

____

____

____

Tips for Answering Short-Answer Questions

Exam questions often focus on the source of a document. Develop the habit of asking about the writer's bias, point of view, intended audience, and purpose. In particular, study the first and last sentence of a document for indications of what shaped the writer's thinking.

Base your answer to question 9 on both Documents 1 and 2 and on your knowledge of social studies.

Similarity—tells how something is alike or the same as something else.

Difference—tells how something is not alike or not the same as something else.

9. a) Identify a similarity or a difference in the nationalism expressed by Mazzini and Bismarck.

   b) Explain the similarity or difference you identified using evidence from both documents.

____

____

____

____

____

Speaking and Listening: Reflect on the Key Idea

Working with a partner or a small group, identify at least five ways that the Enlightenment changed how some people thought about religion, government, and society.

1. ____

____

2. ____

____

3. ____

____

4. ____

____

5. ____

____

CHAPTER 3

The Industrial Revolution

Chapter Overview

In Western Europe beginning in the mid-18th century, new technology in agriculture, manufacturing, and transportation resulted in what is now called the Industrial Revolution. These innovations spread throughout the world causing millions to move from farms to cities, and upended economic and social systems.

Origins One key factor leading to the Industrial Revolution was a set of new ideas and technologies used by farmers first in Great Britain. These innovations led to increased production and allowed farmers to work larger plots of land.

Similarly, new ideas about how to make a state wealthy, how to use coal and water power more effectively, and how to produce goods more efficiently changed life for everyone. One of the most important books in this revolution was *The Wealth of Nations* by Adam Smith (1776). It emphasized the importance of trade among countries. Other changes included new machines to improve production and steam engines that could power boats and trains.

Results These changes decreased the number of people needed to raise food and drew people into urban areas to work. They caused birthrates to fall yet death rates fell even faster, so total population rose rapidly. Countries industrialized differently. England ignited the Industrial Revolution in the mid-17th century and continued as an industrial leader for many years. In contrast, Japan didn't industrialize until the 1860s, but rapidly transformed into a global power.

Reactions The changes in industry prompted various social and political reforms. People demanded the right to vote, publicly funded schools, and the right to form labor unions so workers could protect themselves. Some ideas for change, such as ideas of German philosopher Karl Marx, included plans for transforming society to give workers ownership of the businesses they worked in. At times, changes in agricultural practices and ideas about trade combined for terrible results, such as the Irish potato famine.

An Enduring Issue: Innovation One enduring issue in this chapter is the importance of human inventiveness. Changes in technology revolutionized how people lived and thought.

New York Social Studies Framework: **Key Idea 10.3**

Innovations in agriculture, production, and transportation led to the Industrial Revolution, which originated in Western Europe and spread over time to Japan and other regions. This led to major population shifts and transformed economic and social systems.

Source: *New York State Grades 9–12 Social Studies Framework.*

1. Rewrite Key Idea 10.3 in your own words.

____

____

Identify Enduring Issues

One way to analyze an enduring issue is to consider it from a variety of points of view as expressed in different types of sources. For example, questions of war and peace are among the most common issues in world history. To understand this enduring issue, historians use many types of sources:

- letters of soldiers fighting in a war
- memoirs of political leaders trying to prevent war
- newspaper reports of anti-war protests
- statistics about the casualties and other costs of war
- speeches by individuals rallying a country to go to war

As the title of this chapter states, this chapter focuses on the Industrial Revolution, which is summarized in the Chapter Overview on the previous page. Select an example of a new technology that has been introduced or changed dramatically in the past 50 years. Write five examples of sources that might shed light on it.

Technology: ____________________

1. ____________________
2. ____________________
3. ____________________
4. ____________________
5. ____________________

Key Terms by Theme

Geography

China (p. 80)
Japan (p. 80)
United Kingdom (p. 89)

Social Structures

tenements (p. 77)
slums (p. 77)
blue collar (p. 78)
captains of industry (p. 78)
middle class (p. 78)
white collar (p. 78)
working class (p. 78)
cult of domesticity (p. 79)
samurai (p. 82)

Governance

daimyo (p. 82)

Civic Ideals

Meiji Restoration (p. 80)

Economics

Charles Townshend (p. 69)
commons (p. 69)
enclosure system (p. 69)
open-field system (p. 69)
crop rotation (p. 71)
Jethro Tull (p. 70)
Robert Bakewell (p. 70)
Jeremy Bentham (p. 85)
John Stuart Mill (p. 85)
Robert Owens (p. 85)
Louis Blanc (p. 85)

Lesson 1 *Origins of Industrialization*

Conceptual Understanding 10.3a Agricultural innovations and technologies enabled people to alter their environment, allowing them to increase and support farming on a large scale.

Conceptual Understanding 10.3b Factors including new economic theories and practices, new sources of energy, and technological innovations influenced the development of new communication and transportation systems and new methods of production. These developments had numerous effects.

Source: *New York State Grades 9–12 Social Studies Framework.*

In the late 1700s and early 1800s, English farm families experienced dramatic changes in how they lived. Many had supplemented their small incomes from selling crops or livestock by doing work for the textile industry. They could get a contract from a company to spin thread or weave cloth using simple tools in their homes. However, the development of new technology replaced much of this hand labor with machine labor. In the following excerpt, William Radcliffe describes this change.

Analyze a Primary Source

William Radcliffe, Industrialization in England, 1828

Read Closely: Setting
Note how writers provide the setting before describing a change.
Underline a phrase that Radcliffe uses to describe life before new machinery entered the region.

Read Closely: Details
To understand Radcliffe's general point, notice the specific details he uses to support it.

Read Closely: Continuity
One way writers emphasize a change is to contrast it with a more general continuity.
Circle the phrase that suggests one way in which the region did not change because of the introduction of machinery.

In the year 1770, the land in our township was occupied by between fifty to sixty farmers; rents, to the best of my recollection, did not exceed 10s. per statute acre, and out of these fifty or sixty farmers, there were only six or seven who raised their rents directly from the produce of their farms; all the rest got their rent partly in some branch of trade, such as spinning and weaving woolen, linen, or cotton. The cottagers were employed entirely in this manner, except for a few weeks in the harvest. . . .

From the year 1770 to 1788 a complete change had gradually been effected in the spinning of yarns, - that of wool had disappeared altogether, and that of linen was also nearly gone, - cotton, cotton, cotton, would become the almost universal material for employment, the hand wheels, with the exception of one establishment were all thrown into lumber-rooms, . . .

Although our family and some others in the neighborhood during the latter half of the time, earned from three-to four-fold wages to what the same families had heretofore done yet, upon the whole, the district was not much benefited by the change; for what was gained by some families who had the advantage of machinery, might, in a great measure, be said to be lost to the others.

Source: From William Radcliffe, *Origin of the New System of Manufacture, Commonly Called Power Loom Weaving* (London, 1828), pp. 9–10, 59–67; reprinted in J. F. C. Harrison, *Society and Politics in England, 1780–1960* (New York: Harper & Row, 1965), 58–61.

Changes in Agriculture and Population

In the early 1700s, Europe's population was beginning to grow. In response, landowners began experimenting to increase food production. They tried new methods of managing their land to get more out of it. Inventors designed new machines that increased the productivity of land. Together these changes both raised production and reduced the number of people needed to work the land. That meant that many laborers were free to—or were forced to—find other types of work.

The Enclosure System

One new approach to agriculture, the **enclosure system,** brought about some of the earliest and most drastic changes. It was first widely practiced in the Netherlands during the 1600s. When British farmers heard about the benefits of the system, they too adopted it.

Open-Field System For centuries, Europeans farmed under the **open-field system,** in which a landowner's land was divided into small strips and one farm family might be able to use several strips that were separated from each other, mostly to raise food to eat. Traditionally, they would cultivate two out of three strips each year. They would leave the third one fallow, or unused, so it could restore its fertility.

Read Closely: Central Cause
When you read about a cause-effect relationship, be aware that the text might describe multiple causes. Besides the introduction of new crops such as turnips and clover, what else caused increased agricultural production?

The Commons In addition, the landlords might have land that was not good for growing crops. It might be too rocky, or too damp, or too wooded. By tradition, landowners allowed local farmers to graze livestock in these areas. These jointly used lands were called **commons.**

Specializing Production The small strips of land in the open-field system were not efficient. They did not supply the surplus of agricultural goods necessary to meet the demands of a broader market. Landlords began to combine these small plots and enclose them with a fence or a wall. They then hired some of the people who used to grow food for themselves to be their laborers, growing food the landowner could sell for a profit.

Further, the growing demand for food caused landowners to also enclose the commons. They removed the rocks from the meadows, drained the swampy land, or cut down the forests, and hired workers to grow food crops. Small farmers could no longer use the large landowner's land to plant their own crops. As a result, many went from being farmers in their own right to laborers on the landowners' properties.

Read Closely: Plausible Claim
The text indicates that because of innovation in agriculture, farmers were able to raise cattle and sheep year-round. What impact could that change have made on the health of farm families?

Crop Rotation Farming changed from a way to provide food for farming families to a business raising crops to sell. As it did, landowners looked for new ways to increase their profits.

One way was to make each plot of land more productive. In the 1730s, **Charles Townshend,** an English nobleman, presented a new idea. He argued that none of the fields had to be kept fallow. They could be planted with turnips and clover. These plants return to the soil the nutrients that wheat and barley take from it. The turnips and clover could then be used for animal feed during the winter. Instead of killing many of their lambs and calves in the autumn, farmers could instead keep them to provide milk and wool year-round.

Landowners who used the enclosure system no longer grew a variety of crops to meet the needs of their workers. They could, therefore, respond more easily to changes in the market. They were able to plant all their fields with grain when prices for grain were high or use their fields as pastures when animal products brought better prices.

Agricultural Technology and Innovation

Inventions and new techniques in farming went hand-in-hand with changes in how the land was allocated. The chart below shows how these changes increased productivity.

Agricultural Improvements in the 18th Century			
Issue	**Traditional Method**	**Problem with Traditional Method**	**New Method**
Planting Seeds	Farmers scattered seeds by hand on the surface.	Many seeds were washed away or eaten by birds.	In 1701, **Jethro Tull,** an English farmer, invented the seed drill that planted seeds in rows below the surface.
Hoeing Soil	People hoed the land by hand.	Breaking up the soil was slow and difficult.	Jethro Tull developed a horse-drawn hoe.
Breeding Animals	People sometimes bred specific animals, but never systematically.	Male and female animals were kept together, so breeding was often random.	**Robert Bakewell,** in England, separated male and female animals and controlled which animals bred in order to get sheep with higher quality wool and cattle that put on weight more efficiently.

One example of the changing technology was the development of better methods for threshing grain, or separating the kernels of grain from the stems. For thousands of years, people had done this task with human labor. In many cultures around the world, people used some variation of a specially designed stick, called a flail, to hit the grain until the kernels fell off. It was slow, dull, and tiring work.

Around 1786, Andrew Meikle of Scotland developed a threshing machine that used animal power rather than human power. By walking around in a circle, a horse or other animal generated the power to move a set of gears and levers that could separate the kernels. Threshing machines made the task far faster and easier. Besides making farm life easier, it made each individual farmer more productive.

Source: Wikimedia Commons

The development of threshing machines was one of many innovations that decreased the need for labor on farms.

Effects on Small Farmers

The enclosure system and new machines were profitable for landowners. They made farming more efficient and provided more food for people in growing cities. However, the changes were a misfortune for many small farmers. They lost land they had traditionally cultivated and lost access to the commons. Some found work as laborers. Many felt their only choice was to leave the community where their family had lived for generations and move to a city to look for work. They, thus, were available to work in the factories that were being built.

Intellectual Changes

Innovations in technology and energy were essential to the Industrial Revolution. However, they did not, by themselves, cause this massive shift in every aspect of life. Several other factors helped cause the Industrial Revolution.

Run-Up to the Industrial Revolution

Before 1750, nearly all Europeans worked in agriculture. Some others were artisans, whose skills are still remembered in surnames such as Schmidt (German for "blacksmith"), Mullins (French for "miller"), or Cooper (English for "barrel maker"). They worked in small, family-owned shops. Some people, mostly women, worked in the household textile cottage industry. They spun thread, wove cotton cloth, or knitted woolens in their homes. What was happening within European societies, starting in Great Britain, the home of the Industrial Revolution, that made such a massive swing in economic practices and modes of work and life possible?

Read Closely: Meanings
One way to comprehend unfamiliar words is to make connections between them and ones you know that might share historical meanings. For example, how do you think Schmidt and Smith are related?

Population Growth Just before the Industrial Revolution, during the early 1700s, an agricultural revolution resulted in increased productivity. **Crop rotation** (rotating crops in and out of fields each year), inventions such as the seed drill, and scientific animal breeding helped greatly increase food production. Additionally, the introduction of the potato from South America contributed more calories to people's diets at a low cost.

The Impact of Potatoes on Nutrition in England

Crop	Yield per Acre (in bushels)	Calories per Acre (in millions)
Wheat	23	2.1
Barley	32	2.7
Oats	38	2.2
Potatoes	427	7.6

Source: Adapted from Nathan Nunn and Nancy Qian, "The Potato's Contribution to Population and Urbanization: Evidence from an Historical Experiment," August 2010. Later published in the *Quarterly Journal of Economics.* https://pdfs.semanticscholar.org/8c79/c624f388a9b774480f294f7734e6123e5abb.pdf

With more food available to more people, populations grew. And because of improved medical care, infant mortality rates declined and people lived longer. As these demographic changes developed, more people became available to work in factories and to provide a market for manufactured goods.

Urbanization However, the growing population would not remain in the countryside. Migration was sometimes the best of bad options. The enclosure of the commons made life unsustainable for many people who owned no land.

People who had survived as small farmers moved from rural to urban areas. In English cities, such as Manchester and Liverpool, they would become the new industrial workforce.

Britain's Advantages Britain had many geographical advantages in the process of industrialization. The first of these was water. Located on the Atlantic Ocean, the country was well placed to import raw materials and export finished goods. In addition, Britain had a natural network of rivers. Before the development of railroads and trucks, water was the least expensive way to transport supplies needed by factories and the products they produced.

Beneath Britain's surface lay immense coal deposits. Burning coal was vital to industrialization in multiple ways:

- It powered steam engines that were used to power factories, mills, and railroads. (The importance of the steam engine is discussed later.)
- It was used to separate iron from its ore. Iron production, and later steel production, allowed the building of larger bridges, taller buildings, and stronger and larger ships.
- It heated spaces more efficiently than did wood. This enabled people to work in larger factories and offices that would have been difficult otherwise.

An Enduring Issue: Technology
The improvements in agricultural and industrial technology in Great Britain revolutionized the way people worked. They are one example of the impact of technology on how people live.

As a colonial power, Britain had access to raw materials produced in its colonies such as cotton, sugar, and timber. These colonies would also serve as markets for manufactured goods. More important than these raw materials or manufactured goods was capital, money for investments. Buying machinery or opening a factory was very expensive. Largely because of the wealth accumulated from the trans-Atlantic slave trade and the products produced by enslaved workers, the British had a larger supply of capital than any other European country. They had money that private entrepreneurs could invest in new commercial ventures.

Finally, Great Britain industrialized quickly because it had a strong government that promoted economic growth:

- Britain had the world's most powerful navy. This navy could protect Britain's sea-going commercial ships and conquer and control trading ports throughout the world.
- The government added to the natural system of rivers by using money raised through taxes to build canals and harbors to facilitate trade.
- Britain's legal system protected private property. These protections gave entrepreneurs the confidence they needed to create and expand a business without fear that anyone would seize it from them.

Read Closely: Connections
To help you recall when important events happened, connect them with other events you already know. For example, in the year Adam Smith published his famous book, what event happened in the history of the United States?

Economic Theory

In the 17th and 18th centuries, economists began to criticize mercantilism. In the mercantile system, a country's government strictly regulated the economy through taxes and laws to increase exports and reduce imports.

Adam Smith In 1776, Adam Smith, a major economist of the Enlightenment, attacked mercantilism in a book entitled *An Inquiry into the Nature and Causes of the Wealth of Nations.* Instead of tightly regulating trade, Smith argued that a country's government should allow its businesspeople to compete freely. He believed that business is shaped by two natural laws: the law of supply and demand and the law of competition.

Supply and Demand Smith's theory stated basically that constant changes in supply and demand regulate prices. Demand for a product rises when it is very popular. If the supply is low, people might be willing to pay a high price for a popular item. Manufacturers who make the product decide that they can make large profits if they produce more of it. Once the supply of the product increases, however, the price for it drops. The manufacturers then compete for customers by lowering their prices even more or improving the product. Manufacturers who are unable to compete lose profits and might go out of business. When fewer manufacturers are making the product, the price for it again increases.

Competition and Laissez-faire Smith felt that markets regulate themselves through competition without extensive regulation. He believed competition motivated people to work more efficiently and make better products. If freely competitive private enterprise was encouraged, producers would have a chance to make more money. Consumers (buyers) would get better goods at the lower prices. This opposition to government regulation of business became known as *laissez-faire. (Laissez-faire* is a French phrase that means "leave it alone.")

While Smith opposed the extensive regulation of trade under mercantilism, he did think government should protect the public interest. For example, he noted that some businesses tried to limit competition in a market by creating a monopoly, or becoming the only manufacturer a particular product. When this happened, Smith supported government action to restore competition.

The doctrine of laissez-faire was popular with business owners during the Industrial Revolution. They did not want the government to interfere with the way they ran their businesses. They believed that the government should allow them to do whatever they choose to do to make and sell products.

Read Closely: Word Parts
To help you understand and learn unfamiliar words, note if parts of the word are used in words you already know. For example, *monopoly* shares its first four letters, with *monolog* (a speech by one character in a play) and *monolingual* (a person who speaks only one language). Based on these examples, what does *mono-* refer to?

Inventions and Innovations

The development of industry certainly had theoretical underpinnings, and it was helped by circumstances and fortuitous preconditions, but process innovation and technological advances drove the revolution.

The Textile Industry By the mid-18th century, new inventions had reduced the time needed to spin yarn and weave cloth. The spinning jenny, invented by James Hargreaves in 1764, allowed a weaver to spin more than one thread at a time. The water frame, patented by Richard Arkwright in 1769, used water power to drive the spinning machine. Then in 1784, Edmund Cartwright invented a more effective power loom. These developments increased demand for cotton.

Source: Getty Images

Making clothes is one of the most basic human tasks, but it was always time-consuming. As a result, textile manufacturing was among the first industries to benefit from new technology in the 18th century.

The United States supplied most of the cotton for Britain's weaving industry. After the development of the cotton gin by Eli Whitney in 1793, cotton became the leading export of the southern United States. The gin made it possible to separate the seeds from cotton fibers much faster than the process could be done by hand.

Read Closely: Change
Readers often miss the significance of an innovation because it has become so common today that understanding life before it is difficult. How widely is mass production based on production of identical, interchangeable parts used today?

Interchangeable Parts Whitney is also responsible for another key development in making machines easier to use. In 1798, he created a system of interchangeable parts for manufacturing firearms for the U.S. military. In Whitney's system, when one component of a gun broke, it could be easily replaced with a new, identical part. Entrepreneurs adapted this method of making firearms to the manufacture of other products.

Mass Production The system of interchangeable parts was a pivotal contribution to industrial technology. Instead of relying on skilled workers to craft every component of a product, Whitney's system allowed relatively unskilled workers to specialize in a specific task that was just one part of the overall manufacturing process. This led directly to a division of labor among workers. Because the workers repeated a few simple tasks over and over again, they became very fast. By using the mass production system, a factory could turn out great quantities of an item in a very short time. The items were inexpensive to produce and could be sold at a low price.

Steam Engine The new machinery and methods of work benefited from a new power source, one much more mobile than rivers and streams. The version of the steam engine made by James Watt in 1765 provided an inexpensive way to harness coal power to create steam, which in turn generated energy for machinery in textile factories. A steam-powered locomotive came almost fifty years later and produced power for railway trains.

Just as important was the development of the steamship in the late 18th century. Steam-powered ships were able to travel quickly upstream on rivers, instead of having to sail up, or be pulled up, by people and animals along the shore. Steamships revolutionized transportation on lakes and oceans as well because ship captains were no longer dependent on wind for power. The need to travel long distances across oceans led to the creation of coaling stations at critical points, such as in Cape Colony in South Africa and on various islands in the Pacific Ocean.

The Issues of Industrializaion Many of the issues that emerged with the origins of industrialization endure today. Population has continued to shift from rural to urban areas. People still debate the role of government in promoting economic growth. New technology remains a source of constant change.

Economic Change in Europe

Pre-industrial Europe	Post-industrial Europe
Serfdom: Peasants are tied to land where they are born and owe their labor to landed nobility.	Capitalism: Working class labors in factories being paid for their time on the job.
Mercantilism: Governments control the economy to encourage exports and discourage imports.	Capitalism: Governments allow business people to compete more freely with one another.
Agriculture: People work on farms, growing food to feed themselves and the landowners.	Industry: People work in factories for wages, which they spend on food and other necessities.
Artisanal production: A highly skilled artisan creates every part of the goods he or she produces and sells.	Mass production: A semi-skilled worker repeats the same task over and over, creating or assembling only one part of a mass produced good.

Application

Read the excerpt and answer the questions that follow it.

Adam Smith, The Division of Labor, 1776

> The greatest improvement in the productive powers of labor, and the greater part of the skill, dexterity, and judgment with which it is anywhere directed, or applied, seem to have been the effects of the division of labor....
>
> To take an example, therefore, the trade of the pin-maker; a workman not educated to this business, nor acquainted with the use of the machinery employed in it, could scarce, perhaps, with his utmost industry, make one pin in a day, and certainly could not make twenty. But in the way in which this business is now carried on, not only the whole work is a peculiar trade, but it is divided into a number of branches, of which the greater part are likewise peculiar trades.
>
> One man draws out the wire, another straightens it, a third cuts it, a fourth points it, a fifth grinds it at the top for receiving the head; to make the head requires two or three distinct operations; to put it on is a peculiar business, to whiten the pins is another; it is even a trade by itself to put them into the paper; and the important business of making a pin is, in this manner, divided into about eighteen distinct operations, which, in some factories, are all performed by distinct hands, though in others the same man will sometimes perform two or three of them.
>
> I have seen a small manufactory of this kind where ten men only were employed . . . [who] could make among them upwards of forty-eight thousand pins in a day. Each person, therefore, making a tenth part of forty-eight thousand pins, might be considered as making four thousand eight hundred pins in a day.
>
> **Source:** Adam Smith, *An Inquiry into the Nature and Causes of the Wealth of Nations,* 1776

1. Describe the context in which Smith is writing about the pin industry.

____

____

2. Explain why might Smith have chosen the production of pins, rather than a more complex item such as a clock, to demonstrate his point.

____

____

3. Detail the benefit for consumers in the system described by Smith.

____

____

4. Identify the change, according to Smith, in how people thought about work that allowed a pin company to make more pins than it formerly did.

____

____

Lesson 2 *Industrialization and Society*

Conceptual Understanding 10.3c Shifts in population from rural to urban areas led to social changes in class structure, family structure, and the daily lives of people.

Source: *New York State Grades 9–12 Social Studies Framework.*

In 1832, the British government appointed a committee to look into working conditions in factories. Leading the investigation was Michael Sadler.

Analyze a Primary Source

Peter Smart, Interviewed by the Sadler Committee, 1832

You say you were locked up night and day?
—Yes.

Do the children ever attempt to run away?
—Very often.

Were they pursued and brought back again?
—Yes, the overseer pursued them and brought them back.

Did you ever attempt to run away?
—Yes, I ran away twice.

And you were brought back?
—Yes, and I was sent up to the master's loft and thrashed with a whip for running away.

What were the hours of labor in that mill?
—My master told me that I had to produce a certain quantity of yarn; the hours were at that time fourteen; I said that I was not able to produce the quantity of yarn that was required; I told him if he took the timepiece out of the mill I would produce that quantity, and after that time I found no difficulty in producing the quantity.

How long have you worked per day in order to produce the quantity your master required?
—I have wrought nineteen hours.

Did you find that the children were unable to pursue their labor properly to that extent?
—Yes, they have been brought to that condition, that I have gone and fetched up the doctor to them, to see what was the matter with them, and to know whether they were able to rise or not able to rise; they were not at all able to rise; we have had great difficulty in getting them up.

When that was the case, how long have they been in bed, generally speaking?
—Perhaps not above four or five hours in their beds.

Source: Parliamentary Papers, 1831–1832, vol. XV. pp. 44, 95–97, 115, 195, 197, 339, 341–342, reprinted in Jonathan F. Scott and Alexander Baltzly, eds., *Readings in European History Since 1814* (New York: Appleton-Century-Crofts, Inc., 1930).

Read Closely: Impact
Consider the audience for any piece of writing. In this document, the audience could be either the general public or the members of Parliament.

Read Closely: Order
Note the order that the questions are asked. By asking the questions in a particular order, the interviewer ends with the most dramatic information. *Underline two questions that are asked in an order to make the answers seem more dramatic.*

Read Closely: Bias
Watch for how the text appeals to sympathies of the reader. *Circle a passage where the answer given would elicit sympathy for the working children.*

Social Changes from Industrialization

As industrialization spread from Great Britain throughout Europe, it changed far more than just how people made products and how they worked. It caused several pronounced social changes. For example, industrialization quickened the existing trend of people moving from rural to urban areas. By the beginning of the 1900s, British society was more urban than rural. The new workplace and the growth of business created an entirely new class structure. Women and children at every rung of society saw their roles in the family change dramatically.

Effects on Families

Prior to industrialization, family members worked near one another. Whether women spun fabric in their own homes or men worked a landlord's fields, parents and children usually spent their days together. Industrialization disrupted this pattern. However, industrial machinery was large and expensive. It required people to leave their homes and work in factories. Parents and children were separated more than ever before.

Work by the Clock In a factory, work schedules were nothing like they were on a farm or in a cottage industry. Traditionally, farmers and cottage workers set their own hours. They decided when to start, when to stop, and when to take breaks. Working in a factory shocked them. The shrill sounds of the whistle controlled their work lives.

In addition, since machines never got tired, employers expected workers to work very long days. People commonly spent fourteen hours a day, six days a week in a factory. Exhaustion was common. As a result, on-the-job injuries and death were also common.

Child Labor The low wages of factory workers forced them to send their children to work in the factories, also. In the early decades of industrialization, children as young as five worked in textile mills. Because of their small size and nimble fingers, children could climb into equipment and make repairs that adults could not. They were also able to fit into tight spaces in mines more easily than most adults.

Read Closely: Cause and Effect
Recognize how a text presents causation. For example, in the paragraph on child labor, the word "because" indicates a cause-effect relationship between ideas. What about the size of children caused factory and mine owners to hire them?

Miners Coal miners had difficult lives. Though their labor fueled the growth and prosperity of the Industrial Revolution, many died from their work. Some died suddenly from a single catastrophe. For example, a mine could collapse or flood, or underground gases could cause an explosion or a fire. Many more died early from long-term causes. For example, miners suffered from lung disease caused by inhaling coal dust. Others were simply worn out by the exhausting physical labor they did, such as hammering the coal out of the earth and carting it out of the mine.

Effects on Urban Areas

Industrialization increased urbanization. For the first half of the 19th century, urban areas grew rapidly and with little planning and few government services. This left a damaging ecological footprint and created inhumane living conditions, particularly for poor residents:

- Working families crowded into shoddily constructed apartment buildings called **tenements**. These buildings were often owned by factory owners themselves.
- Neighborhoods filled with low-income families, poor housing, and environmental problems were called **slums**.

- Industrial waste products combined with untreated human waste and animal waste polluted the water and the air. Cities did not have underground sewage systems, so waste was removed through open sewers. These unsanitary conditions were breeding grounds for diseases such as cholera, dysentery, and tuberculosis.

Effects on Class Structure

Before industrialization, the class structure in Europe was quite stable. Nearly everyone was a farmer. Wealth was measured in land. Life changed very little from one generation to the next. As industrialization spread, three new classes of society emerged in Britain.

The Working Class One of these new classes was the **working class,** which included people who labored in factories and coal mines. Since the supply of workers fleeing rural areas in search of work was high, the members of the working class had little ability to negotiate for good wages. In the 20th century, people who relied primarily on their manual skills became known as **blue-collar** workers from the blue cotton work shirts that many wore.

Further, members of the working class had little chance to enjoy their work. Factories were very efficient at producing goods quickly and cheaply. However, the use of machines, division of labor, and interchangeable parts made work dull. Workers never got the satisfaction, as artisans did, to develop their skills or to create a complete product. Factory managers treated workers just as they did machines: replaceable tools used to make goods.

The Middle Class Another new class produced by industrialization was called the **middle class**. It included the people with the education and the skills to manage a factory. They purchased raw materials, kept track of the finances, and marketed the products. The middle class included the growing number of merchants and small business owners who bought and sold goods for a living, as well as lawyers, accountants, and other professionals who provided services in an industrial economy. In the 20th century, people who worked primarily with their mental skills became known as **white-collar** workers because of the custom of wearing white shirts in offices.

Read Closely: Relationships
One way to understand a cluster of new concepts is to think of them as a group of related ideas. How were the rises of the working class, the middle class, and the wealthy elite related to each other?

The Wealthy Elite A third class emerged that was more powerful than the other two new classes. This was the small group of wealthy industrialists, bankers, and owners of large corporations known as the **captains of industry**. As they became more powerful, they often battled against the traditional leaders of society and government, the landed aristocracy. The new class measured its wealth not in land, but in stocks and other forms of money.

Effects on Women's Lives

The Industrial Revolution affected women in different ways, depending on their class position. Because their families needed the money, working-class women worked in coal mines (until the practice of hiring women for coal mining was declared illegal in Britain in the 1840s) and were the primary laborers in textile factories. Factory owners preferred to hire women because they could pay them half of what they paid men.

Housewives Middle-class women were spared factory work, yet in many ways, they lived more limited lives than working-class women. Middle-class men had to leave the house and work at an office to provide for their families. If a wife stayed at home, it was an indication that her husband was capable of being the family's sole provider. So, being a housewife became a kind of status symbol.

Idealized Roles By the late 1800s, advertising and consumer culture contributed to an idealized image of the female homemaker, a **cult of domesticity**. Advertising encouraged these middle-class housewives to buy products that would supposedly make the home a husband's refuge from a harsh modern world. Pamphlets instructed middle-class women on how to care for the home, raise children, and behave in polite society, urging them to be pious, submissive, pure, and domestic. For working-class women, the cult of domesticity was even more taxing as they had to manage the household, care for the children, and work full time.

Effects on Mass Culture

A culture of consumerism as well as of leisure developed among the working and middle classes of society in Great Britain. Consumption needed to keep up with production, so companies began to advertise heavily, particularly to the middle class who had some disposable income, or money that can be spent on nonessential goods.

Leisure activities such as biking and boating became popular in the late 1800s. Companies encouraged their workers to participate in athletics, because they believed that sports rewarded virtues such as self-discipline and playing by the rules. The sales of athletic equipment also generated business for those who made everything from soccer balls to sports stadiums.

Perhaps because workers spent most of their waking hours in a bleak industrial environment, material goods and leisure entertainment became important escapes. In particular, first in Great Britain and later throughout Europe and beyond, soccer (known in Europe as football) became immensely popular. It developed out of earlier games based on kicking a ball toward a goal.

Read Closely: Continuity
To understand the significance of a historical development, always consider how it grew out of what came before it. What did soccer grow out of?

Landmarks in the Development of Popular Culture

Date	Development	Country or Region
1843	Princes Park near Liverpool opened. It provided open space for the enjoyment of residents in a densely industrial urban area.	Great Britain
1863	The Football Association was formed, becoming the first organization to set rules for a game known in the United States as soccer.	Great Britain
1867	New rules for boxing published by the Marquess of Queensbury made boxing a more popular entertainment.	Great Britain
1882	The Berlin Philharmonic Orchestra was founded, one of several musical organizations started throughout Europe in the late 1800s. Prior to the 1800s, musicians had been hired by kings or other nobles to perform at their courts.	Germany
1885	A new style of bicycle was introduced that was safer and easier to ride. Because of these changes, bicycling became more popular.	Great Britain
1891	The game of basketball was invented by James Naismith, a Canadian working at a YMCA in Springfield, Massachusetts.	United States

Meiji Japan

> ***An Enduring Issue: Diffusion***
> Japan resisted the influence of foreign ideas before the Meiji Restoration but eagerly embraced some ideas afterward. The adoption or rejection of elements of other cultures is an ongoing issue in most cultures.

Japan entered the industrial era under vastly different circumstances from those of Great Britain or any Western country. Japan had been nearly isolated from almost all outside interactions and influences beginning in the early 17th century. This isolation lasted until the mid-19th century.

From Isolation to Industrialization

Japan did not end its isolation by choice. Great Britain, the United States, and other Western countries were eager to set up ports in Japan where they could refuel their coal-powered ships and trade with the Japanese. Westerners pressured Japan diplomatically to open up.

While Japan resisted the diplomatic efforts, it was fearful. It had seen what happened to its larger and more powerful neighbor **China** when it resisted Western ideas about trade. In 1839, when China tried to stop the British from selling opium in China, the British went to war. China lost badly.

So when the United States sent warships into Tokyo Bay to force Japan to accept foreign trade, Japan knew it faced a hard choice. The cost of resistance would be a war the nation would probably lose.

Meiji Restoration

To protect their independence and traditional culture, some Japanese leaders decided they had to adopt some Western ideas, particularly ones that would strengthen their military. In 1868, the conflict over how to respond to Westerners touched off the **Meiji Restoration.** The power of the *shogun*, a military dictator who ruled in place of the emperor, aided by local lords, had been brought to an end. Returning to power was the young Emperor Mutsuhito, who adopted Meiji - which means "enlightened rule" - as a description of his rule. But his rule depended directly on the powerful officials and advisers who had placed him at the center of government. The Meiji Restoration period, which lasted until 1912, saw a drastic overhaul of Japanese society, economics, and politics.

Source: Shutterstock

Emperor Komei (left) ruled Japan from 1846 to 1867. He was the last emperor to always dress in traditional fashion. In contrast, his son and successor, Emperor Meiji (right), reflected Western influences in his clothing.

Reforms in Meiji Japan The emperor and his allies, many of whom were young and committed to modernizing the country, instituted a number of reforms to bring Japan in line with the practices and ideals of Western powers. In the coming years, Japan went through as rapid and intense industrialization as any country ever has. After the Meiji Restoration, Japan made many changes:

- It formally abolished feudalism (1868) in the "Charter Oath," a statement of policy for the new Japanese government.
- It established equality before the law and abolished cruel and unusual punishments.
- It established a constitutional monarchy based on the Prussian model, in which the emperor exercised political power and oversaw foreign policy, and the Diet (the legislature) focused on domestic policy.
- It remodeled the military, creating an army based on the Prussian army, building a new navy, and instituting conscription (mandatory military service).
- It started a postal service.
- It created a new educational system modeled after Western systems.
- It promoted industrialization and financed it with funding from both the Japanese government and foreign investors.
- It started a railroad network with the help of British engineers that rapidly expanded throughout the country.
- It instituted religious freedom.

The education and economic reforms worked well. The new schools quickly improved literacy rates, and Japan became wealthier. However, the political changes were less successful. Japan began moving slowly toward becoming more democratic. However, unlike Great Britain and France, but more like Germany and Italy, landlords and military officers remained quite powerful. This difference would become very important in later years.

Read Closely: Significance
Note when a text suggests how history will unfold. For example, during the process of industrialization, the histories of Japan, Germany, and Italy diverged from the histories of Great Britain and France. How was this divergence reflected in the alliances formed during World War II (see Chapter 5 for help)?

Industrialization and Economic Modernization The Meiji emperors wanted citizens who were educated and competent but also loyal and obedient. Industrialization, much of it paid for by careful government financing, created new jobs. The government provided massive subsidies for training new workers in the key industries of tea, silk, weaponry, shipbuilding, and rice wine (sake) production.

In addition, the government set up technical schools and instituted universal education. The central government modernized the transportation and communication systems, including new railroads and roads. A high agricultural tax financed much of the government investment that created industries and jobs. These increased taxes also provided revenue for the bureaucracy centered in Tokyo.

While the relationship between industry and centralized government was key to modernization in Japan, private investment from overseas was also important. Once new industries flourished, they were sometimes sold to powerful Japanese business organizations that were similar to Western business conglomerates. The prospect of attracting investors encouraged innovation in technology. For example, a carpenter founded a company in 1906 called Toyoda Loom Works, which made an automatic loom. The company prospered, modified its name, and grew into today's Toyota Motor Company.

The Decline of the Samurai Japanese **samurai** were fighting men who supported the feudal system of the regional lords, or ***daimyo,*** and received their livelihood from it. They emerged in the 12th century and were highly respected. Their swords symbolized their importance.

However, the two centuries of isolation had been fairly peaceful. As a result, the samurai had begun losing status and had begun to take other positions in society. Then, after the Meiji Restoration, they fell victim to rapid modernization. In 1871, the government made a final lump-sum payment to the samurai and legally dissolved their position. They were no longer fighting men and could no longer legally carry their swords.

Read Closely: Symbols
When reading a history text, note small details that have great symbolic significance. By 1871, swords were not important weapons, and people did not need to carry them daily. Why was the ban on samurai carrying swords so important in Japan?

Several groups of samurai rebelled. They tried to hold onto and restore their former position and way of life. In 1877, the defeat of a samurai uprising by Japan's newly modernized and mechanized army marked the end of the traditional role of the samurai and *daimyo* in Japanese society.

The Rise of a New Elite While the samurai and *daimyo* were losing power, a new class of leaders was emerging. It consisted of wealthy industrial leaders, educated professionals, military leaders, and government. Unlike earlier Japanese society, where prestige reflected one's birth, this new class consisted of people whose prestige reflected what they had done. Unlike Great Britain, where leaders often maintained large country estates, in Japan, this new elite was very urban, without ties to the land.

For the most part, Japan's society and economy were still peasant-based. Most lower-class people lived in small villages or the countryside and were relatively poorly educated and poor. During this period as well, an urban middle class failed, for the most part, to develop. There existed a large gap in wealth between the upper and lower classes with relatively few people in between.

Improvements in Japanese Life Life in Japan changed dramatically with modernization. The development of better public health measures to dispose of sewage, provide clean water, and fight the spread of disease, combined with advances in medicine, enabled people to live longer lives. In this change, Japan was part of a global trend. Life expectancy increased in countries throughout the world in the 20th century.

Life Expectancy, 1800, 1900, and 2000

Country	1800	1900	2000
Argentina	33	37	74
China	32	32	72
Germany	38	44	78
Great Britain	39	46	78
India	25	18	61
Japan	36	37	81
Russia	30	31	65
Saudi Arabia	32	32	76
United States	39	49	77

Application

Read the excerpt and answer the questions that follow it.

Yamamoto Tsunetomo, Decline in Masculine Culture in Japan, c. 1700

In the practice of medicine there is a differentiation of treatment . . . [between] men and women. There is also a difference in pulse. In the last fifty years, however, men's pulse has become the same as women's. . . . Thus I knew that men's spirit had weakened and that they had become the same as women, and the end of the world had come. . . . When looking at the men of today with this in mind, those who could be thought to have a woman's pulse are many indeed, and those who seem like real men few. . . .

All of man's work is a bloody business. That fact, today, is considered foolish, affairs are finished clearly with words alone, and jobs that require effort are avoided. I would like young men to have some understanding of this. . . .

The brave men of old times were for the most part rowdies. As they were of the disposition to be out running amok, their vitality was strong and they were brave. When I had doubts this and asked, Tsunetomo said, "It is understandable that since their vitality was strong they were generally ought and went about running amok. These days rowdiness is nonexistent because man's vitality has weakened. Vitality has fallen behind, but man's character has improved. Valor is yet a different thing. Although men have become gentle these days because of the lack of vitality, this does not mean that they are inferior in being crazy to die. This has nothing to do with vitality.

Source: *Hagakure: The Book of the Samuri* by Yamamoto Tsunetomo. Based on comments made 1709 to 1716.

1. Explain the main observation in this excerpt.

____

____

2. Describe the context in 18th-century Japan that might explain the change observed in the excerpt.

____

____

3. Explain how Tsunetomo's point of view affected his opinions as expressed in the excerpt.

____

____

4. Quote a phrase or sentence that indicates the audience for this excerpt.

____

____

Lesson 3 *Industrialization and Politics*

Conceptual Understanding
10.3d Social and political reform, as well as new ideologies, developed in response to industrial growth.

Source: *New York State Grades 9–12 Social Studies Framework.*

The dramatic changes from the Industrial Revolution changed who had power in society. These were then reflected in the political system. They also promoted a renewed debate about ethical behavior. One of the leaders in this debate was a British philosopher, John Stuart Mill.

Analyze a Primary Source

John Stuart Mill, *Utilitarianism,* 1871

Read Closely: Definitions
One way to recognize the importance of a definition is to consider counter examples. In the case of Mill's definition of utility, try to think of an example of something that most people would consider right but that does not promote happiness.

Read Closely: Significance
Note when a writer uses a key phrase that reflects his or her goal. Mill is trying to establish a "moral standard," the guidelines for ethical behavior.
Underline the phrase that explains Mill's Greatest Happiness Principle.

Read Closely: Divisions
Writers sometimes clarify what they mean by drawing distinctions between aspects of a larger concept. Here, he begins to distinguish between two features of pleasure: quantity and quality.

Read Closely: Generalization
Note how Mill broadens his task to include more than how humans treat each other.
Circle the phrase that states these beliefs.

The creed which accepts as the foundation of morals, Utility, or the Greatest Happiness Principle, holds that actions are right in proportion as they tend to promote happiness, wrong as they tend to produce the reverse of happiness.

By happiness is intended pleasure, and the absence of pain; by unhappiness, pain, and the privation [denial] of pleasure. To give a clear view of the moral standard set up by the theory, much more requires to be said; in particular, what things it includes in the ideas of pain and pleasure; and to what extent this is left an open question. But these supplementary explanations do not affect the theory of life on which this theory of morality is grounded—namely, that pleasure, and freedom from pain, are the only things desirable as ends. . . .

According to the Greatest Happiness Principle, the ultimate end, for the sake of which all other things are desirable (whether we are considering our own good or that of other people), is an existence exempt as far as possible from pain, and as rich as possible in enjoyments, both in point of quantity and quality. . . .

This, being, according to the utilitarian opinion, the end of human action, is necessarily also the standard of morality; which may accordingly be defined, the rules and precepts for human conduct, . . . [which, if observed, would lead to the Greatest Happiness], to the greatest extent possible, secured to all mankind; and not to them only, but, so far as the nature of things admits, to the whole sentient [alive] creation.

Source: From Chapter 2 of John Stuart Mill's *Utilitarianism* (London: Longmans, Green, Ryder, and Dyer, 1871). https://www.uua.org/re/tapestry/adults/ethics/workshop3/191792.shtml.

The Political Impact of Industrialization

The Industrial Revolution created jobs for thousands of people and increased the wealth of the middle and upper classes. However, it also caused many problems. Most serious was the extreme poverty suffered by factory workers and rural workers. The plight of the poor caused people to question old ideas about societies, economic systems, and governments. As a result, many reforms, ranging from minor to radical, were proposed and implemented during the era.

Utilitarianism

Some thinkers wanted to base reforms on a simple principle: an action is right and should be promoted if its result is more happiness for more people, and it is wrong if the opposite is the result. This was the basic belief of a group of economists and philosophers, most notably **Jeremy Bentham** and **John Stuart Mill**, known as **utilitarians**.

Finding that *laissez-faire* capitalism was often inhumane to workers, the utilitarians advocated for reform to try to achieve "the greatest good for the greatest number of people." Mill, in particular, was a champion of three social reforms:

- laws allowing workers to form labor unions so they could bargain for higher wages and safer working conditions
- laws limiting the labor that children could perform
- laws ensuring safe working conditions in factories

Read Closely: Change
One way to understand the importance of a development is to think about how it differed from what was before. For example, Mill's utilitarianism was unusual for its time because it was not based on biblical teachings. How was utilitarianism more compatible with democracy than with feudalism?

The Socialist Movement

Socialists believed that setting up a new form of government and economic system was the best solution for the problems caused by the Industrial Revolution. They wanted the people as a whole, rather than a few wealthy individuals, to own factories, mines, and farms. Socialists attacked the practice of producing goods for profit. Instead, they wanted the basic goods everyone needed to be produced at prices everyone could afford. Most importantly, socialists demanded that governments serve the needs of all the people and not just the wealthy landowners and industrialists.

Utopianism One wealthy business owner, **Robert Owen** (1771–1858), shared the goals of socialists. To show how society could be reorganized, Owen bought a cotton mill in Scotland and used it as an example to show how to provide safe, healthy working conditions for his employees. Further, he turned the nearby town of New Lanark into a model community with good schools and a high standard of living.

Owen and other 19th-century socialists who shared his beliefs were **utopians**, reformers who believed that they could create ideal communities. They tried to establish places where residents contributed to and shared in economic success equally. Owen succeeded in New Lanark. But other utopian communities he set up in Britain and the United States failed. Most people could not cooperate and work together for the common good to the degree required to make the communities successful.

Louis Blanc The French utopian socialist **Louis Blanc** began his movement as a newspaper owner. In his writings, he attacked the French government for giving the industrialists, or capitalists, too much freedom. Blanc believed that the government should set up workshops to provide all workers with employment. Eventually, the workers would take over the workshops and run them. Blanc also

Read Closely: Trends
Historians group developments together to show trends during a period. To understand these developments, keep in mind the similarities that make them a trend, but also the differences that make them distinctive. How were Owen and Blanc similar and different?

had the idea that workers should produce according to their ability and be paid according to their needs. Some national workshops were set up in France in 1848, but they failed to become widespread.

The Communist Movement

Other reformers criticized Owens and Blanc for not basing their ideas on how people actually lived. For example, **Karl Marx** (1818–1883), a German philosopher and economist who lived much of his life in London, argued for what he called "scientific socialism." His solutions to problems of industrialization were more radical than those proposed by most other socialists and came to be called **communism**. In 1848, Marx and his longtime collaborator **Friedrich Engels** (1820–1895) summarized their ideas in a pamphlet titled *The Communist Manifesto*.

Class Struggle Marx was struck by the contrast between the growing wealth of society—the rapidly growing output of goods—with the growing misery of workers who made the goods—their low wages and dangerous working conditions. He explained this contrast by his analysis of how capitalism worked. Investors put up the money, or capital, needed to bring workers, machines, and raw materials together to produce goods. In return, they received some of the income of the company. As a result, workers never received in wages the full value of the products they created. In addition, the constant pressure of competition from other companies required owners to drive wages as low as possible.

Based on his analysis, Marx thought that capitalism placed the **proletariat**, the class of people who worked for wages, into a constant conflict with the **bourgeoisie**, the class of people who prospered by investing money. He called this conflict the "class struggle."

Revolution For Marx, the only way to end the class struggle was revolution. He urged workers of every country to unite and seize ownership of the means of production, or the sources of wealth. He envisioned a world in which everything would be shared and businesses would be cooperative instead of competitive. Over time, the state would no longer be necessary. People would be truly free.

Limited Acceptance The theories developed by Marx and Engels appealed to many. They were especially attractive to those who saw no other solution to problems such as poverty and unemployment.

However, the worldwide revolution Marx predicted never occurred. Instead, conditions for workers organized into unions gradually won higher wages and better working conditions. By the beginning of the 20th century, the standard of living for most people in the Western world had begun to rise higher than ever before.

Communist Governments During the 20th century, two of the world's largest countries, Russia and China, went through revolutions that resulted in Communist governments. In Russia, widespread poverty and lack of freedom were long-standing problems under the tsarist government. Then, when Russia was drawn into World War I in 1914, the suffering got worse. Russia was so poor it could not afford to provide guns for all the soldiers it sent into battle. Disruptions caused by the war caused widespread hunger and disease. Early in 1917, several political factions participated in a revolution to overthrow the tsar. By the end of the year, one faction, the Communists led by Vladimir Lenin, had seized power. Russia remained ruled by Communists until 1991, when the system collapsed.

In China, civil war broke out in 1927. The opposing sides set aside their conflict to fight against Japan in World War II, but then resumed fighting. In 1949, the Communists declared victory. Today, China remains officially a Communist country, but it has adopted many elements of capitalism.

Neither Russia nor China followed the path to communism the way Marx had predicted. He thought that only a country that had become wealthy through extensive industrialization would be ready for communism. In neither country did industrialists control the government. Similarly, none of the other three countries led by Communist today, Vietnam, North Korea, and Cuba, had fully industrialized before Communists took power

The Labor Union Movement

While utopians and other thinkers tried to design the perfect society, workers followed the example of the utilitarians: they sought more immediate and practical solutions to their problems. The eventual success of their attempts was one of the reasons that communism did not replace capitalism throughout Europe.

Source: Shutterstock

Mass meetings of laborers, such as this one in mid-19th century England, were part of the effort to organize workers into unions.

Organizing People who worked in the same occupations or industries joined together in organizations called **unions** to improve their wages and working and living conditions. As a group, they could put more pressure on employers to raise wages or improve workplace safety than they could as individuals.

Tactics Union members elected representatives to present their requests or demands to employers. This process is called collective bargaining. If an employer did not grant their requests or demands, the workers might strike, to stop working until they reached an agreement with the employer. Sometimes unions organized a boycott of an employer's products. They refused to buy the products and urged others not to buy them until the employer compromised.

To stop a strike, an employer might hire strikebreakers to replace the striking workers. Police or military troops might be called in to end a strike. Some employers tried to weaken union causes by blacklisting outspoken members or leaders. This list, which was sent to other employers, branded selected workers as undesirable employees. Blacklisting meant that the selected workers could not get jobs in their chosen line of work. British workers could not legally organize unions until 1824. Efforts to form a national union in the late 1830s had only short periods of success. Until 1871, the government and the factory owners forcefully discouraged attempts to form unions. However, by the early 20th century, unions became more acceptable and membership increased. Unions improved workers' lives by demanding and winning on several issues:

- laws setting a minimum wage
- limits on the number of hours worked in a day or week
- higher pay for overtime work
- establishment of a five-day work week

Read Closely: Point of View
Be aware of how a historical change can be seen by different groups of people. Unions improved the lives of workers in many ways. Why would some people have opposed changes such as overtime pay?

Unions in France did not become strong until the late 1880s. The German labor movement gained power in the 1890s. The Industrial Revolution did not take hold in Russia until the very end of the 19th century. As a result, labor unions did not become important there until shortly before the revolution of 1917.

Political Reforms

In Great Britain, reformers pressured Parliament to pass laws that gave suffrage, or the right to vote, to all males who owned a certain amount of property. As a result, middle-class men gained the right to vote and the right to hold public office. This victory encouraged people to demand suffrage for all men with or without property and the right to vote by secret ballot. By 1885, Parliament had passed laws that met these demands. Working-class men now also had the right to vote. However, women did not win equal suffrage until 1928, after decades of protest and pressure.

Read Closely: Causes
Note how reasons change over time. For example, today, people often praise education for giving people economic opportunity. Why did the British support expansion of their school system in 1880?

Education of Voters As the right to vote was extended to poor, uneducated people, reformist leaders realized how important it was that the new voters be able to make responsible political decisions. Consequently, reformers urged the passage of the Elementary Education Act of 1880, which made it possible for all children in Great Britain to get an elementary school education. Parliament also passed laws giving Catholics and non-Anglican Protestants the right to engage in political activity.

Labor Issues In the early 19th century, religious and political groups started concerning themselves with the abuses of factory workers. One reformer, **Michael Sadler,** set up a Select Committee on Child Labor in Parliament. The reports made by this committee resulted in an 1833 law limiting the working day of children aged 9 to 12 to eight hours and those aged 13 to 17 to twelve hours. Mills and factories were so dependent on child labor that when the children left for the day, they closed. Therefore, the bill limiting children's workdays effectively reduced the number of hours that adults had to work as well.

Source: Getty Images

In Ireland during the famine, people were desperate for food.

Ireland's Great Famine

In the 1840s, Ireland was part of the **United Kingdom**. A few wealthy Protestant Irish families owned the country's great estates. The poor Catholic Irish worked on the estates for very low wages. Following the practices of the agricultural revolution, the wealthy landowners used their land to grow cash crops—agricultural products they could sell for profits, usually in England. They gave their tenant farmers small plots on which to grow food crops for themselves.

Irish peasants found that potatoes were the best crop to grow. They were easy to plant, took up little room, and thrived in Ireland's damp climate and dense soil. Best of all, potatoes are extremely nourishing. Because it had so many advantages, small Irish farmers planted no other major food crop.

However, between 1845 and 1851, a fungus from America destroyed the yearly potato crops. The Irish were so dependent on the potato that without it, a massive, deadly famine gripped Ireland.

Read Closely: Risks of Progress
Identify how elements of progress often come with costs. Growing potatoes caused Ireland's population to grow and become healthier. What was the cost of relying heavily on potatoes as a food source?

> ***An Enduring Issue: Scarcity***
> The Irish Potato Famine is an extreme example of a scarcity problem. People starved to death for lack of food and were not helped by British policies. Scarcity of resources exists in every society.

The Failure of Support The British government was not prepared to handle this disaster. When the famine first started, charitable organizations opened soup kitchens in Ireland. But when British banks experienced a financial crisis, the government stopped the charitable aid. British leaders then turned the problem over to the Irish Poor Law system. Under this law, the government was authorized only to set up workhouses where poor people could live and work. Many, though starving, were put to work building stone fences simply so they would not be getting aid without working for it. There were no facilities for sick and dying people who were too weak to work.

The Failure of Ideology The British were not only incompetent in handling the situation, they were also unbending. Though tenants had no food, wealthy estate owners could still demand that the tenants pay their rents. When the starving tenants were unable to come up with the money or to do their farm work, the landlords evicted them. British troops often forced the tenants to leave their homes.

The famine and the treatment of the Irish by the British sparked a mass exodus from the island. Between 1845 and 1851, as many as two million people emigrated, with a million of those going to the United States. Another 500,000 to 750,000 people starved to death or died from diseases caused by malnutrition.

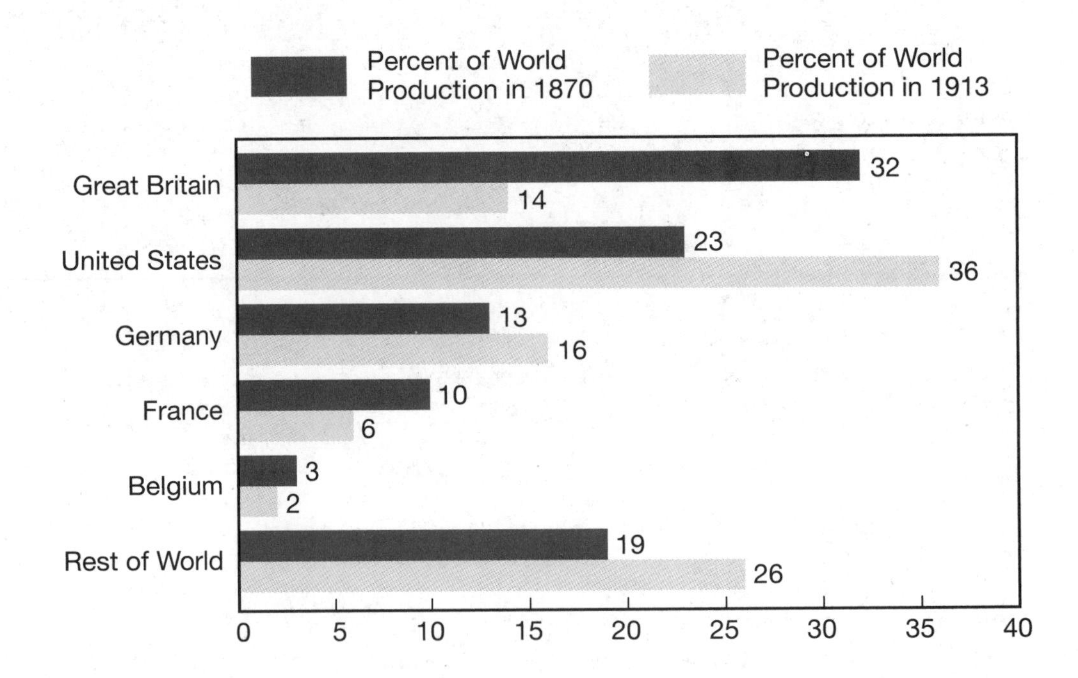

Application

Reporter for the ***Cork Reporter*** [Southwest Ireland], January 5, 1847

Read the excerpt and answer the questions that follow it.

"It is my painful duty to inform you of six inquests [legal inquiries into the cause of a person's death]. . . . The jury unanimously agreed without a moment's hesitation, that the following persons came to their deaths by starvation, vis:

"Catherine Sheehan, a child, two years old, who died on the 26th of December last, and had lived for several days previous to her death on seaweed. . . .

"Michael Sullivan died at Skahana, on or about the 4th of December, from the effects of eating too hearty a meal, which he had received through charity, after being previously exhausted from overlong fasting.

"Richard Finn was conveyed into this town on the 14th of December, in a car, for the purpose of taking him to the workhouse, when in the street, the Very Rev. Thomas Barry, parish priest, was obliged to hear confession before the public, and before he had time to complete his sacred duties the poor man expired.

"John Driscoll was working on one of the public works on the 29th of December; on his return home he fell exhausted for want of food, and was found dead. . . . His wife proved that he had eaten nothing for two days previous to his death, except a small quantity of boiled wheat, and that he frequently had a similar fast.

"Jeremiah Carthy entered the shop of Mr. Robert Vickery, of this town, when he fell senseless, and died in three hours after at the workhouse. . . .

"Michael Linehan was found dead on the lands of Ibane on the 18th of December last. He was on his way home from Bantry after purchasing some food for his mother and brother (which were all his family) who were then lying in fever. . . .

"It is our opinion that if the Government of the country shall persevere in its determination of refusing to use the means available to it for the purpose of lowering the price of food, so as to place it within the reach of the laboring poor, the result will be a sacrifice of human life from starvation to a frightful extent, and endangerment of property and of the public peace."

Source: *The Cork Reporter*. "Findings of Inquests Conducted Today on Six Famine Victims, Including Two-Year-Old Catherine Sheehan," January 5, 1847. Reprinted in *The Times*, January 11, 1847. Dublin.

1. Describe the geographic context in which these inquests were conducted.

____

____

2. Detail the motives of the investigators to report the death of Catherine Sheehan first.

____

____

3. Explain what the investigators imply should result from the death of the six people.

____

____

Chapter 3 *Review*

Multiple-Choice Questions

Directions (1–6): For each statement or question, choose the number of the word or expression that, of those given, best completes the statement or answers the question.

Base your answers to questions 1 and 2 on the table below and your knowledge of social studies.

Changes in English Agriculture, 1550 to 1859

Decade	Productivity (1860=100)	Percentage of Men Working in Agriculture	Agricultural Output (millions of British pounds)	Productivity (1860-69)
1550-1559	43	58	7	46
1600-1609	64	59	21	64
1650-1659	67	57	34	67
1700-1709	74	55	32	73
1750-1759	79	53	40	79
1800-1809	72	37	78	71
1850-1859	99	24	103	99

Source: Gregory Clark, "The Agricultural Revolution and the Industrial Revolution: England, 1500-1912," June 2002. faculty.econ.ucdavis.edu/faculty/gclark/papers/prod2002.pdf

1. Which claim about the cause of the Industrial Revolution is best supported by this chart?
   (1) Increases in agricultural productivity provided the foundation for the Industrial Revolution.
   (2) The start of the Industrial Revolution caused agricultural productivity to decrease because people left rural areas to take jobs in factories.
   (3) Decreases in agricultural productivity caused people to find ways to make goods more efficiently
   (4) Changes in agricultural productivity were unrelated to changes in production of manufactured goods.

2. Which change in England in the 1700s best explains the changes in the perecentage of men working in agriculture as shown in this chart?
   (1) an increase in factory employment
   (2) an increase in gender equality
   (3) an increase in the length of the workday
   (4) an increases in imports as mercantilist ideas lost popularity

Base your answers to questions 3 and 4 on the passages below and your knowledge of social studies.

Tokugawa Nariaki to the Japanese Government, August 14, 1853

It is widely stated that [apart from trade] the foreigners have no other evil designs and that if only the *bakufu* [government] will permit trade there will be no further difficulty. However, it is their practice first to seek a foothold by means of trade and then to go on to propagate Christianity and make other unreasonable demands. Thus we would be repeating the blunders of others, seen remotely in the Christianity incidents of the Kanei period (1624–1644) and before [in Japan] and more recently in the Opium War in China. That is the fifth reason why we must never choose the policy of peace.

Source: *Japan: A Documentary History: Volume 2: The Late Tokugawa Period to the Present*, ed. David J. Lu.

Ii Naosuke to the Japanese Government, October 1, 1853

There is a saying that when one is besieged in a castle, to raise the drawbridge is to imprison oneself and make it impossible to hold out indefinitely; and again, that when opposing forces face each other across a river, victory is obtained by those who cross the river and attack. It seems clear throughout history that he who takes action is in a position to advance, while he who remains inactive must retreat. . . . We must revive the licensed trading vessels that existed before the Kanei period (1624–1644) . . . We must construct new steamships, especially powerful warships, and these we will load with goods not needed in Japan. For a time, we will have to employ Dutchmen as masters and mariners, but we will put on board with them Japanese of ability and integrity who must study the use of large guns, the handling of ships, and the rules of navigation. Openly they will be called merchant vessels, but they will in fact have the secret purpose of training a navy. . . . We will eventually complete the organization of a navy.

Source: *Japan: A Documentary History: Volume 2: The Late Tokugawa Period to the Present*, ed. David J. Lu.

3. Which statement best describes a similarity in the advice between Tokugawa Nariaki and Ii Naosuke?

   (1) Both wanted to prevent increased Western influence in Japan.

   (2) Both encouraged greater trade as a route toward Japanese prosperity.

   (3) Both believed Japan could win a war with Westerners if it began quickly.

   (4) Both thought peace should be Japan's primary concern.

4. How were the ideas of Tokugawa Nariaki and Ii Naosuke reflected in the Meiji Restoration?

   (1) After the Meiji Restoration, Japan followed the ideas of Ii Naosuke more than Tokugawa Nariaki.

   (2) The conflict between Tokugawa Nariaki and Ii Naosuke caused the Meiji Restoration.

   (3) Tokugawa Nariaki probably supported the Meiji Restoration more than did Ii Naosuke.

   (4) Tokugawa Nariaki and Ii Naosuke went on to become leaders in the Meiji Restoration.

Base your answers to questions 5 and 6 on the passage below and your knowledge of social studies.

Petition from the Yorkshire Cloth Workers, 1786

The scribbling-machines [machines that separate strands of wool before the wool is spun into cloth] have thrown thousands of your petitioners out of employ, whereby they are brought into great distress, and are not able to [support] their families, and deprived them of the opportunity of bringing up their children to labor: We are therefore to request that prejudice and self-interest may be laid aside, and that you may pay that attention to the following facts, which the nature of the case requires.

The number of scribbling-machines extending about seventeen miles south-west of Leeds, exceeds all belief, being no less than *one hundred and seventy!* And as each machine will do as much work in twelve hours, as ten men can in that time do by hand (speaking within bounds) and they working night and day, one machine will do as much work in one day as would otherwise employ twenty men.

Twelve men are though out of employ for every single machine used in scribbling; and as it may be supposed the number of machines in all the other quarters [regions] together [are] nearly equal those in the south-west, full four thousand men are left to shift for a living how they can. . . . Allowing one boy to be bound apprentice from each family out of work, eight thousand hands are deprived of the opportunity of getting a livelihood.

We therefore hope that the feeling of humanity will lead those who have it in their power to prevent the use of those machines.

Source: *Leeds Intelligencer*, June 13, 1786. Quoted in J. F. C. Harrison, *Society and Politics in England, 1780–1960.* Harper and Row, 1965.

5. What is the most useful information about the context in which this petition was written?

   (1) The use of machinery in factories was spreading.
   (2) Population growth was increasing demand for clothing.
   (3) Workers were moving from rural to urban areas.
   (4) The roles for men and women were changing.

6. What is the point of view of the petitioners?

   (1) They were concerned about losing their jobs.
   (2) They wanted the company to make a profit.
   (3) They wanted consumers to have the best clothes, which are hand-made.
   (4) They were focused on expanding markets into new countries.

Short-Answer Questions

CRQ Directions (7-9): Analyze the documents and answer the short-answer questions that follow each document in the space provided.

Base your answer to question 7 on Document 1 below and on your knowledge of social studies.

Document 1

In response to problems many in the lowest classes experienced during the Industrial Revolution, Friedrich Engels wrote "A Communist Confession of Faith" in June 1847.

> The proletariat came into being as a result of the introduction of the machines which have been invented since the middle of the last century and the most important of which are: the steam-engine, the spinning machine and the power loom. These machines, which were very expensive and could therefore only be purchased by rich people, supplanted the workers of the time, because by the use of machinery it was possible to produce commodities more quickly and cheaply than could the workers with their imperfect spinning wheels and hand-looms.
>
> The machines thus delivered industry entirely into the hands of the big capitalists and rendered the workers' scanty property which consisted mainly of their tools, looms, etc., quite worthless, so that the capitalist was left with everything, the worker with nothing. In this way the factory system was introduced. Once the capitalists saw how advantageous this was for them, they sought to extend it to more and more branches of labor. . . .
>
> We have gradually arrived at the position where almost *all* branches of labor are run on a factory basis. This has increasingly brought about the ruin of the previously existing middle class, especially of the small master craftsmen, completely transformed the previous position of the workers, and two new classes which are gradually swallowing up all other classes have come into being, namely:
>
> I. The class of the big capitalists who in all advanced countries are in almost exclusive possession of the means of subsistence and those means (machines, factories, workshops, etc.) by which these means of subsistence are produced. This is the *bourgeois* class, or the *bourgeoisie.*
>
> II. The class of the completely propertyless, who are compelled to sell their labor to the first class, the bourgeois, simply to obtain from them in return their means of subsistence. Since the parties to this trading in labor are not *equal*, but the bourgeois have the advantage, the propertyless must submit to the bad conditions laid down by the bourgeois. This class, dependent on the bourgeois, is called the class of the *proletarians* or the *proletariat.*
>
> **Source:** https://www.marxists.org/archive/marx/works/download/pdf/Manifesto.pdf

7. Describe the time period that provided the context in which Engels wrote the excerpt.

____

____

____

____

Base your answer to question 8 on Document 2 below and on your knowledge of social studies

Document 2

German economist Friedrich List wrote *The National System of Political Economy* in 1841 after serving as American consul in Germany and assisting in the development of railways in Germany.

> The more that man and the community perfect themselves, the more are they enabled to make use of the natural powers which are within their reach for the accomplishment of their objects, and the more does the sphere of what is within their reach extends itself.
>
> The hunter does not employ the thousandth part, the shepherd not the hundredth part, of those natural advantages which surround him. The sea, foreign climates and countries, yield him either none, or at least only an inconsiderable amount of enjoyment, assistance, or stimulants to exertion.
>
> In the case of a people in a primitive agricultural condition, a large portion of the existing natural resources lies yet unutilized, and man still continues limited to his nearest surroundings. . . .
>
> Through the establishment of manufacturing power in an agricultural state, roads are made, railways constructed, canals excavated, rivers rendered navigable, and lines of steamers established. By these not merely is the surplus produce of the agricultural land converted into machinery for yielding income, not merely are the powers of labor of those who are employed by it brought into activity, not only is the agricultural population enabled to obtain from the natural resources which it possesses an infinitely greater return than before, but all minerals, all metals, which heretofore were lying idle in the earth are now rendered useful and valuable.
>
> **Source:** Friedrich List, *The National System of Political Economy,* 1841

8. Using Document 2, identify List's purpose in writing the excerpt.

Base your answer to question 9 on both Documents 1 and 2 and on your knowledge of social studies.

Similarity—tells how something is alike or the same as something else.
Difference—tells how something is not alike or not the same as something else.

9. a) Identify a similarity or a difference in the ideas about industrialization held by Engels and List.
   b) Explain the similarity or difference you identified using evidence from both documents.

Speaking and Listening: Reflect on the Key Idea

Working with a partner or a small group, fill in the chart below describing ways that the Industrial Revolution changed how some people thought about their world. Note that the first letter of each category in the chart together spell out SPEECH-G. Remembering this is a useful way to recall the categories of information to review any historical topic.

Reviewing the Industrial Revolution

Category	Information
Social	
Political	
Economic	
Environmental	
Cultural	
Historical	
Geographical	

CHAPTER 4

Imperialism

Chapter Overview

Throughout the 19th century and into the 20th, Western nations and Japan aggressively expanded their influence throughout Asia and Africa. Advances in technology and increases in trade transformed international interactions. Instead of being primarily limited regional contacts along the coast, they became connections throughout these regions.

Economic and Military Interests Imperialist nations such as Great Britain and France sought to dominate other countries economically, politically, and militarily. Competing industrialized states desired raw materials from Africa and Asia as well as access to markets to sell manufactured goods. Economic competition sometimes escalated to large-scale military conflicts.

Cultural Clashes Imperial rivalries often reshaped borders drastically, with little regard for traditional cultures and commerce. In some cases, people of various cultural groups were thrown together in the same political state. In others, people of one cultural group were divided by state boundaries. Christian missionaries, indigenous peoples, women, merchants, and government officials often viewed these cultural clashes quite differently.

Resistance Many people resisted colonial rule. In Africa, major resistance movements included the Ethiopians (who were never colonized) in eastern Africa, the Zulu in South Africa and the Sudanese in the region south of Egypt. In Asia, the governments of China and Japan each reacted against Western attempts to control their countries.

An Enduring Issue: Power One enduring issue in this chapter is the power of countries such as Great Britain and France to establish colonies and the power of people in colonies to resist these efforts. European countries, the United States, and Japan exerted their power through economic influence, military assaults, and cultural ideas. Responses varied. For example, Zulus fought militarily, while the Chinese tried to adopt new European technology.

New York Social Studies Framework: **Key Idea 10.4**

Western European interactions with Africa and Asia shifted from limited regional contacts along the coast to greater influence and connections throughout these regions. Competing industrialized states sought to control and transport raw materials and create new markets across the world.

Source: *New York State Grades 9–12 Social Studies Framework.*

1. Rewrite Key Idea 10.4 in your own words.

____

____

Identify Enduring Issues

While enduring issues are ones faced by many people in various places and time periods, they are more important in some places and time periods than others. Compare Chapter 2, "Enlightenment, Revolution, and Nationalism," with Chapter 3, "The Industrial Revolution." Chapter 2 focused more on issues of political rights and revolution, while Chapter 3 focused more on issues of how people work and their relationships to each other.

Re-read the Chapter Overview on the previous page, and scan the headings used throughout the chapter. As you do, list two enduring issues that each lesson in this chapter will address.

Lesson	Enduring Issues
1. The Growth of European and Japanese Power	1. ____________ ____________ 2. ____________ ____________
2. Responses to Colonial Rule	1. ____________ ____________ 2. ____________ ____________
3. Conflicts Among Imperial Powers	1. ____________ ____________ 2. ____________ ____________

Key Terms by Theme

Identity

Boers (p. 103)
Zulu (p. 103)

Geography

Indochina (p. 106)

Social Structures

sepoys (p. 101)

Governance

imperialism (p. 101)
Seven Years' War (p. 101)
Indian Rebellion of 1857 (p. 102)
Cecil Rhodes (p. 103)
Congo Free State (p. 103)
King Leopold II (p. 103)
Opium War (p. 104)
spheres of influence (p. 105)
Taiping Rebellion (p. 105)
Russo-Japanese War (p. 106)
Anglo-Zulu War (p. 109)
Cetshwayo (p. 109)
Menelik II (p. 109)
Shaka (p. 109)
Battle of Adowa (p. 110)
Empress Cixi (p. 111)
Boxer Rebellion (p. 112)
Berlin Conference (1884–1885) (p. 115)

Civics

Dadabhai Naoroji (p. 102)
Indian National Congress (INC) (p. 102)
Self-Strengthening Movement (p. 111)
Righteous and Harmonious Order of Fists (p. 112)

Exchange

British East India Company (p. 101)

Lesson 1 *European and Japanese Power*

Conceptual Understanding 10.4a Note that Fabri avoids the question of whether imperialism is justified morally. Rather, he compares the rights of Germany and other countries.

Source: *New York State Grades 9–12 Social Studies Framework.*

Portugal, Spain, France, and Great Britain led the European states in seizing colonies around the world. Germany was slow to join the competition. Divided in many small states until unification in 1871, Germany was too fragmented to claim colonies in the Americas or south Asia. To some Germans, establishing colonies in Africa and east Asia was essential to national pride and prosperity.

Analyze a Primary Source

Friedrich Fabri, "Does Germany Need Colonies?", 1879

Read Closely: Direct Questioning
One technique writers use to draw readers into their argument is to make a statement phrased as a question. Fabri's opening statement is phrased in this manner.

Read Closely: Problem and Solution
Fabri uses attempts to appeal to readers by organizing his writing as a problem and a solution. Readers who recognize the problem might also agree with his solution. *Underline the solution that Fabri suggests to gain reader support.*

Read Closely: Comparison
Fabri compares his Germany of 1879 to Germany of the past, comparisons that his readers would be familiar with.

Read Closely: Call to Action
Fabri appeals to the emotions of readers by urging them to make their country great. *Circle a phrase in which Fabri makes this appeal.*

Should not the German nation, so seaworthy, so industrially and commercially minded, more than other peoples geared to agricultural colonization, and possessing a rich and available supply of labor, all these to a greater extent than other modern culture-peoples, should not this nation successfully pave a new path on the road of imperialism? We are convinced beyond doubt that the colonial question has become a matter of life-or-death for the development of Germany. Colonies will have a salutary [positive] effect on our economic situation as well as on our entire national progress.

Here is a solution for many of the problems that face us. In this new Reich [new imperial Germany] of ours there is so much bitterness, so much unfruitful, sour, and poisoned political wrangling, that the opening of a new, promising road of national effort will act as a kind of liberating influence. Our national spirit will be renewed, a gratifying thing, a great asset. A people that has been led to a high level of power can maintain its historical position only as long as it understands and proves itself to be the bearer of the culture-mission. At the same time, this is the only way to stability and to the growth of national welfare, the necessary foundation for a lasting expansion of power.

At one time Germany contributed only intellectual and literary activity to the tasks of our century. That era is now over. As a people we have become politically minded and powerful. But if political power becomes the primal [most important] goal of a nation, it will lead to harshness, even to barbarism. We must be ready to serve for the ideal, moral, and economic culture-tasks of our time. The French national-economist, Leroy Beaulieu, closed his work on colonization with these words: "That nation is the greatest in the world which colonizes most; if she does not achieve that rank today, she will make it tomorrow."

Source: Friedrich Fabri, *"Does Germany Need Colonies?"*, 1879

Industrialization and National Power

The Industrial Revolution built several countries in Europe and Japan into economic powers in the last half of the 19th century. These countries ventured outward in search of raw materials, markets, and global power.

Empire Building in the 19th Century

During the Age of Discovery in the 16th and 17th centuries, Spain, Portugal, Great Britain, the Netherlands, and France colonized parts of Africa, Asia, and the Americas. As Europeans moved into these new regions, they brought their goods and ideas with them. During the "new **imperialism**" of the late 1800s, European expansion reached its peak. Industrialization, technology, and military might gave European countries enormous power and influence in the world.

Great Britain Leads In the early 1800s, Great Britain had more colonies than any other Western nation. It controlled Canada, British Honduras (now Belize) in Central America, British Guiana (now Guyana) in South America, several islands in the Caribbean, much of the eastern half of Africa, part of India, Australia, and New Zealand. By 1900, it also controlled much of Southeast Asia, Hong Kong, and islands in the Mediterranean and the Pacific. At the peak of Britain's colonial power, people said that "the sun never sets on the British Empire."

Read Closely: Explanation Look for reasons that explain a pattern described in a text. For example, what information explains why Britain had more colonies than did other Western nations?

Other Nations Follow Britain By the late 1800s, three other European countries also had sizeable empires:

- France controlled several islands in the Caribbean, French Guiana in South America, much of northern and western Africa, and Indochina (today, Vietnam, Laos, and Cambodia).
- Germany entered the race for colonies after 1870 but took control of sections of eastern and southwestern Africa and several islands in the Pacific.
- Italy acquired areas in northeastern Africa in the late 19th century.

Belgium, the Netherlands, Portugal, and Spain each had a few colonies scattered throughout the world. The United States acquired territories in the late 1800s and early 1900s in the Caribbean and South Pacific. From the 1890s to the 1940s, Japan engaged in imperialism in east Asia.

Read Closely: Central Cause While events have many causes, identify what the text claims are the main ones. What were the most important causes that led European countries to acquire colonies?

The British in India

During the 1700s, the Mogul Empire in India became weaker and weaker. At the same time, the British and the French East India trading companies gained strength. They competed for control of India.

The British East India Company The major aim of the **British East India Company** was to profit from selling Indian cotton, cloth, silk, and sugar to other countries. Victory over France in the **Seven Years' War** (1756–1763) left Britain the major power in India. The portions of India not directly governed by Britain were ruled by Indian princes. These local leaders eventually signed treaties that placed their states under British protection.

With some restrictions placed on it by the British government, the East India Company ruled India until 1857. The company built telegraph, railroad, and irrigation systems there. In addition, it set up a postal service and a number of schools. The company also organized a large army of Indian soldiers, called **sepoys**, to defend company interests and India's borders. British officers commanded the sepoys, and units of the British Army provided additional support. Missionaries arrived to spread Christianity in India, where most people were Hindus or Muslims.

Reaction of Indians Although some Indians benefited from changes brought about by British rule, many resented it. The East India Company brought new technology and industrialization, but most of the benefits went to British colonists. Indian factory workers and servants received very low wages. Farmers received very little for their produce. Indians could not hold high-level positions in the East India Company. Schools taught English and Western ideas and paid little attention to the long history and advanced culture of India. Many Indians suspected that the British wanted to undermine India's traditional religions. In addition, many British treated the Indian people as inferiors.

Indian Rebellion of 1857 The resentment turned violent in what became known as the Indian Rebellion of 1857, or the Sepoy Rebellion. The spark for the rebellion occurred when soldiers were issued new rifles. The ammunition for these rifles were greased cartridges, with ends that had to be bitten off to be used. Rumors spread that the grease was either from beef or pork. Hindu soldiers had religious objections to consuming beef products. Muslim soldiers had religious objections to consuming pork products.

Read Closely: Change
To understand the significance of an event, identify what change it caused. While this change might have far-reaching effects, it is usually most noticeable in a particular region. How was life in India different after the Sepoy Rebellion?

A number of soldiers were jailed for refusing to use the ammunition. In response, thousands of sepoys rebelled against British authority. The sepoys released the prisoners, killed the British officers, and headed for the city of Delhi to set up a new government. Civilians and princes joined the revolt. However, regular army forces from Britain arrived in 1858 and crushed the uprising. Fighting lasted into 1859. By the time it ended, deaths from fighting and the famines and diseases made worse by the conflict might have exceeded 100,000. Both sides had committed atrocities that bred longstanding suspicion and anger between the British and the Indians.

After the sepoy mutiny, the British government took over direct control of India from the East India Company. It appointed a viceroy (governor) to head the Indian government. Local civil and police officers were trained in Britain, and the Indian civil service was staffed with young British men. Few Indians qualified for jobs with the civil service as a result of the strict rules set up by the British. Then in 1876, Queen Victoria became empress of India.

The Indian National Congress In 1885, a group of Indians organized to push for reforms in how the British ruled India. The organization, called the **Indian National Congress (INC)**, consisted mostly of middle class and British-educated Indians. They began with moderate goals, such as informing the British public about the Indian point of view of policies that affected Indian people. The INC included Indians of many religions, which was important because religion often divided the people and was used by the British to keep opposition weak. But one of the INC's founding members, **Dadabhai Naoroji**, made plain the need for unity in the face of British imperialism:

Read Closely: Purpose
Writers often include quotations or anecdotes to support a claim. For example, what claim is supported by the quotation from Dadabhai Naorjori?

"Let us always remember that we are all children of our mother country. Indeed, I have never worked in any other spirit than that I am an Indian, and owe duty to my country and all my countrymen. Whether I am a Hindu, a Mohammedan [Muslim], a Parsi, a Christian, or any other creed, I am above all an Indian. Our country is India; our nationality is Indian."

The Indian National Congress later became the Congress Party, a leading force in India's drive for independence in the 20th century.

South Africa

Britain's richest African colonies were in the south. It had acquired South Africa from the Dutch in the early 1800s during the Napoleonic Wars. The Dutch farmers, called **Boers,** resented British rule. They moved north in the hope of escaping the British.

When trying to settle the new territory, however, the Boers met with resistance from an African people called the **Zulu**, whose land they had invaded. Eventually, the Boers, using modern weapons and backed up by British troops, defeated the Zulu, who had only spears and shields. (See Lesson 2 for more on the Zulu.) The Boers set up the independent republics of the Transvaal and the Orange Free State. Both are today part of the Republic of South Africa.

In 1867, diamonds were discovered near the Boer territory. The area became the richest source of diamonds in the world. Then, gold was discovered in a nearby area in 1886. A leading developer of the diamond and gold industries in South Africa was **Cecil Rhodes**, an Englishman. At the insistence of Rhodes and other mine owners, laws were passed to force the black African population off the land and into towns or mining compounds where their only source of income would be to work in the mines. This type of action—annexation of land and domination of black Africans—was repeated throughout the history of South Africa as more whites settled in the area.

Read Closely: Point of View
People always see and report on events from a point of view, whether it is strongly biased or very fair-minded. What does the use of forced labor tell you about the point of view of the British toward African natives?

Congo Free State

British-American explorer Henry Morton Stanley's expeditions in the Congo River basin in the mid-1870s increased the interest of Europeans in this region. **King Leopold II** of Belgium set out to open trade along the river into Africa's interior. Stanley helped establish trading posts all along the river. He negotiated trade deals with hundreds of different groups in the interior. Leopold used these agreements to claim the right to rule over the whole area. He established the **Congo Free State**.

The Congo, unlike other areas that belonged to European states, was virtually Leopold's own personal colony. Leopold's agents forced the Congolese to work for him in brutal conditions, harvesting ivory and rubber. Laborers often received no payment for their backbreaking work. His agents severed the hands of Congolese workers in order to terrorize others into submission. Workers who could not meet their quotas were beaten or killed, while others were worked to death. To insure that they did not run away, their spouses were sometimes held captive. Overall, three million to eight million people perished under King Leopold's reign of terror in the Congo. The king's profits from the Congo totaled some $1 billion.

First-hand accounts by Belgian officials working in the Congo documented the brutal treatment people suffered. For example, a British diplomat in the Congo in 1899 reported that a Belgian officer had described to him how people were treated:"This officer['s] . . . method . . . was to arrive in canoes at a village, the inhabitants of which invariably bolted on their arrival; the soldiers then landed, and commenced looting, taking all the chickens, grain, etc., out of the houses; after this they attacked the natives until able to seize their women; these women were kept as hostages until the chief of the district brought in the required number of kilograms of rubber. The rubber having been brought, the women were sold back to their owners for a couple of goats apiece, and so he continued from village to village until the requisite amount of rubber had been collected."

In 1908 Belgium itself took over control of the Congo as a regular colony. Conditions improved, although the Congo remained a colony.

Read Closely: Course of Action
One way to engage with a history text is to consider the best course of action available to people in the text. How could the Congolese have resisted Belgian oppression?

Spheres of Influence in China

By the 19th century, China had been a world leader in developing art and technology for over 1,000 years. However, it had been slow to industrialize:

- China's rulers felt that Europeans had nothing to teach them, so they paid little attention to new European technology, such as improved weapons.
- China's taxes were so low that the government could not afford to pay for better roads and canals and to support new industries the way Europe and the United States could.

> **Read Closely: Patterns**
> As you read, identify patterns such as how success can lead to problems. For example, China's centuries of success created a problem in recognizing European development. How did China's success at keeping taxes low lead to problems?

Europeans saw great opportunities in China. They could hire inexpensive labor, sell goods to China's millions of consumers, and use abundant natural resources such as iron and coal. China was too weak to resist European power effectively. .

SPHERES OF COLONIAL INFLUENCE IN ASIA

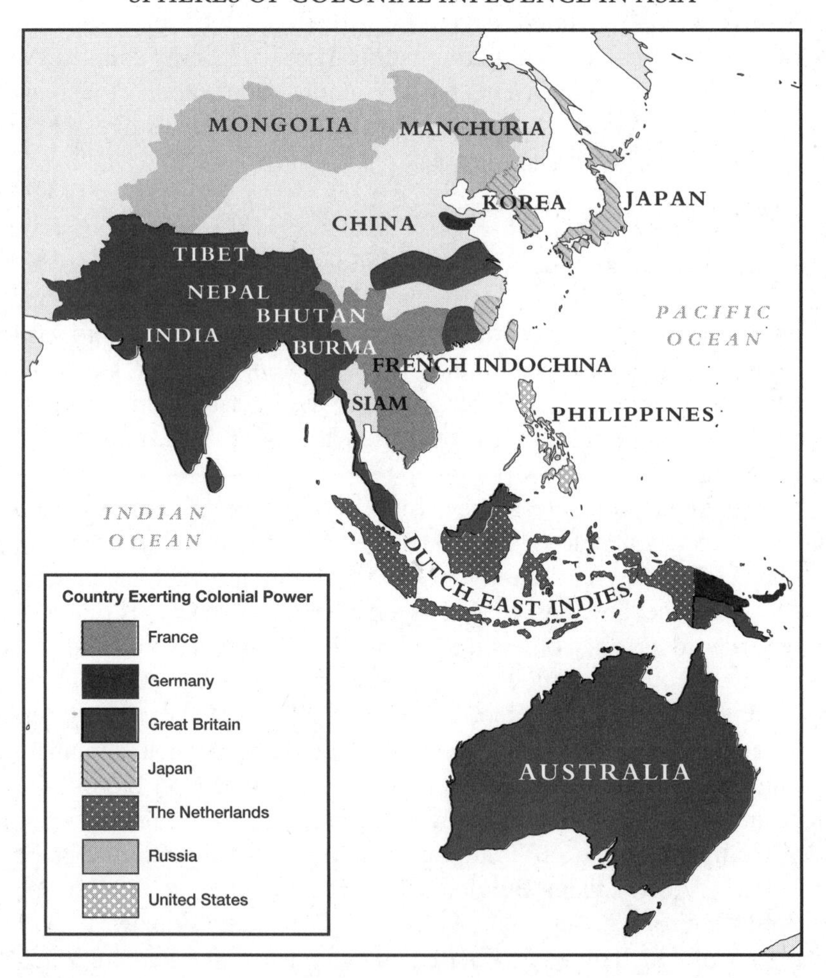

The Opium War China's rulers, the Qing Dynasty, tried to limit foreign influence in their country. In particular, they objected to the British selling opium. The flow of money out of China to pay for the opium severely damaged the country's economy. Far worse, many Chinese were becoming addicted to opium. In 1839, Chinese officials destroyed many tons of the drug and imprisoned the British opium merchants. The British responded by defending the principle of free trade, and they sent a fleet of warships to invade China. Without a modern navy and weapons, the Chinese could not defend themselves against British military power. The British forced the Chinese government to sign the Treaty of Nanjing in 1842.

As a result of the treaty, the British and other foreigners gained new privileges in China. It allowed foreigners to trade in six Chinese ports, rather than just one, and Britain gained complete control of the island of Hong Kong. (China did not regain control of Hong Kong until 1997.) These ports and their surrounding areas were known as the countries' **spheres of influence**. In addition, foreign traders accused of crimes in China gained the right to be tried in courts of and under the laws of their own country, not China.

Weakening of China's Government The Qing Dynasty lost popular support because of its failure to protect the Chinese people from foreign invasion and drug addiction. It never recovered. In the 1850s and 1860s, China suffered a handful of large-scale uprisings.

The largest of these uprisings was the **Taiping Rebellion**. It began in 1850. To end it, China's rulers asked for Western help. After 14 years of fighting, the Taiping were defeated. However, it resulted in 20 million deaths, making it one of the worst wars in human history.

During the rebellion, the French and British attacked China in an attempt to coerce even further trade concessions. Again easily defeated by Western forces, the Chinese were forced to sign the Treaty of Tientsin in 1858. This treaty gave Europeans more power within China:

- It opened 11 more Chinese ports to Western traders.
- It made it legal once again for traders to import opium into China.
- It allowed foreign traders and Christian missionaries to move into the Chinese interior.

Read Closely: Differences Recognizing distinctions is one way to understand the different options available in history. China and India were both large Asian countries. How did Western countries use different methods to exert their influence on China and India?

The second half of the 19th century saw a continued erosion of Chinese power in east Asia. Western colonial powers chipped away at territories formerly controlled by China. Japan and France were major players in that process.

Source: Shutterstock

In 1951, China issued a stamp to honor the 100th anniversary of the date the Taiping declared their rebellion against the Qing Dynasty. Two of China's most important 20th century leaders, Sun Yat-sen and Mao Zhedong, grew up hearing stories about how the Taiping rebelled against an oppressive government.

Japanese Imperialism

Japan's push for modernization prompted it to also become imperialist. Having a centralized government with an active emperor increased feelings of nationalism throughout Japan. Population growth and economic needs also contributed to Japan's desire to expand. The success of new industries relied upon raw materials and expanded markets. Two wars promoted Japan's expansion:

- The **Sino-Japanese War** between China and Japan ended in a Japanese victory in 1895. China gave up control of the island of Formosa (Taiwan) to Japan, and Japan became influential in Korea.
- The **Russo-Japanese War** between Russia and Japan ended in a Japanese victory in 1905. In the Treaty of Portsmouth (New Hampshire), Japan gained control of territory in southern Manchuria, a region bordering China and Russia. It also made Korea into a colony.

An Enduring Issue: Industrialization
Japan's defeat of China and Russia in wars showed the power of its industrialization. No society has gone untouched by the impact of industrialization.

Japan's victory over Russia shocked the world. It was the first victory by an Asian country over Europeans in modern times. It inspired nationalists from Turkey to India to China, and it worried European colonial powers.

French Indochina

In addition to its colonies in north and west Africa, the French government had a major imperial presence in southeast Asia. This region, known as **Indochina**, includes the modern-day countries of Cambodia, Laos, and Vietnam.

The Importance of Missionaries French missionaries had been present in Indochina starting in the 17th century. The large number of Catholic missionaries and local converts played a direct role in the progress of French colonialism. During the second half of the 19th century, uprisings and other attacks that targeted missionaries and local converts increasingly brought a protective military response from French forces. The increase in attacks against Catholics coincided with increasing French economic interests in Southeast Asia.

Read Closely: Motivations
In reading about rebellions and revolutions, note the combination of ideas and goals that motivate people. What are three reasons that motivated Indochinese nationalists to oppose French control?

Soon, the French government could use the security concerns as a reason to justify establishing a permanent foothold in Indochina. In the estimation of one French newspaper owner, missionaries "who seem to work only for God have been the most marvelous instrument of civilization, incomparable workers for French power overseas." By the 1890s, France had taken control of Indochina.

Economic and Political Consequences With the establishment of French power in the region, rubber plantations soon dotted the landscape of Cambodia and Vietnam. French influence in Indochina continued even after World War II ended in 1945, when a nationalist movement finally forced the French out.

French Involvement in Southeast Asia

Date	Action
1615	Jesuits establish an outpost in Hanoi.
1800s	Vietnamese begin using a new writing system developed by missionaries.
1858	France sends 3,000 troops to Vietnam to protect French citizens there.
1887	France formally organizes its rule of Indochina.
1946	The Viet Minh launch a war of independence against the French.
1954	The Viet Minh defeat the French at Dien Bien Phu.

Application

Read the excerpt and answer the questions that follow it.

J. A. Hobson, *Imperialism: A Study*, 1902

> As for the territories acquired under the new Imperialism, except in one instance, no serious attempt to regard them as satisfactory business assets is possible. Egypt alone yields a trade of some magnitude; of the other possessions, three only—Lagos, Niger Coast Protectorate, and North Borneo—are proved to do a trade with Great Britain exceeding one million pounds in value… Apart from its quantity, the quality of the new tropical export trade is of the lowest, consisting for the most part…of the cheapest textile goods of Lancashire, the cheapest metal goods of Birmingham and Sheffield, and large quantities of gun-powder, spirits, and tobacco.
>
> Such evidence leads to the following conclusions bearing upon the economics of the new Imperialism. First, the external trade of Great Britain bears a small and diminishing proportion to its internal industry and trade. Secondly, of the external trade, that with British possessions bears a diminishing proportion to that with foreign countries. Thirdly, of the trade with British possessions, the tropical trade, and in particular the trade with the new tropical possessions, is the smallest, least progressive, and most fluctuating in quantity, while it is lowest in the character of the goods which it embraces.
>
> **Source:** Hobson, J.A. *Imperialism: A Study*, 1902.

1. Quote one phrase that explains Hobson's point of view of the relationship between imperialism and economics.

____

____

____

2. Compare and contrast the aspects of imperialism as outlined by Hobson.

____

____

____

3. Explain Hobson's three conclusions about imperialism.

____

____

____

4. Identify one leader from this time and explain why he or she would disagree with Hobson about imperialism.

____

____

____

Lesson 2 *Responses to Colonial Rule*

Conceptual Understanding
10.4b Those who faced being colonized engaged in varying forms of resistance and adaptation to colonial rule with varying degrees of success.

Source: *New York State Grades 9–12 Social Studies Framework.*

Throughout the world, people fought back having European and Japanese imperialists attempting to take over their lands and cultures. The excerpt below focuses on one example in Africa.

Analyze a Primary Source

Ndansi Kumalo, chief of the Ndebele people in southern Africa, 1890s

Read Closely: Examples
Writers often use details to make their writing more persuasive. However, Kumalo uses a vague description and lets readers infer his meaning. *Underline a vague passage used by the author.*

Read Closely: Quotations
The use of a direct quotation—even if it is something that was not said exactly that way by anyone—creates an image of a group of people committed to acting as one.

Read Closely: Comparison
Kumalo uses a comparison to highlight the Ndebele people's very limited options to respond to the Europeans. *Circle a phrase used in this comparison.*

They [the British] came and were overbearing, and we were ordered to carry their clothes and bundles. They interfered with our wives and our daughters and molested them. In fact, the treatment was intolerable. We thought it best to fight and die rather than bear it.

How the rebellion started I do not know; there was no organization; it was like a fire that suddenly flames up. We had been flogged by native police and then they rubbed salt water in the wounds. There was much bitterness because so many of our cattle were branded and taken away from us; we had no property, nothing we could call our own. We said, "It is not good living under such conditions; death would be better—let us fight."

Our King gone, we had submitted to the white people and they ill-treated us until we became desperate and tried to make an end of it all. We knew that we had very little chance because their weapons were so much superior to ours. But we meant to fight to the last, feeling that even if we could not beat them we might at least kill a few of them and so have some sort of revenge.

Source: Ndansi Kumalo, Margery Perham, eds. *Ten Africans* (London: Faber and Faber, 1936). Reprinted in Denis Gainty, Walter D. Ward, eds. *Sources of World Societies, Volume 2: Since 1450*, 209–211.

Resistance to Colonization

Imperialism had tremendous effects on people who were its subjects and, often, its victims. Colonized peoples were forced to adapt to the conditions imposed upon them by powerful outsiders. In response, many people resisted their colonizers, but with varying degrees of success.

The Zulu and the British

Before the 19th century, the Zulu people were a modestly sized group of no more than 3,000 people. They lived in the northeastern region of what is today the Republic of South Africa. A ruler named **Shaka** took control of the Zulu in 1816 and proceeded to expand their territory and absorb new populations. By 1820, Shaka could send 100,000 trained warriors into a battle. The Zulu were a major power in southern Africa.

Power of the Zulu Empire The growth of the Zulu Empire brought them into conflict with two groups of Europeans in the region. One consisted of the Dutch settlers known as the Boers. The other was the British. As the British expanded inward from the coast, the Boers retreated, hoping to maintain their independence. As they moved, they came into conflict with the Zulu, causing several clashes.

Read Closely: Problem
Words such as "conflict" and "clash" indicate a problem exists between two groups of people. What problem led to the clashes between the British and the Zulu?

The Anglo-Zulu War The larger battle occurred as the Zulu resisted British expansion in the region. In early 1879, the British invaded Zulu land, starting the Anglo-Zulu War. The Zulu leader, **Cetshwayo**, had assembled an army of roughly 50,000.

The first battle of the invasion ended in a stunning victory for the Zulu. At Isandlwana, 20,000 Zulu warriors routed a British detachment of 2,000, killing more than 1,200 British and African auxiliary troops. However, by August of 1879, the British had defeated the Zulu and captured Cetshwayo.

During the war, the British had traded some Zulu territory to the Boers in return for military help. The British annexed the majority of what remained in 1887.

Ethiopia

At the outset of the 19th century, the ancient kingdom of Ethiopia was independent, but it was in disarray. The central government had lost its grip on the kingdom, and power moved instead into the hands of regional rulers. By mid-century, Ethiopia again had a strong emperor, so it was prepared to defend itself against European imperialism. In 1889, when Italian troops invaded Ethiopia, the Ethiopian leader **Menelik II** resisted. He kept most of the country free, but he did sign a treaty that granted Italy control over the coastal region of Eritrea.

Source: Shutterstock

Menelik II of Ethiopia lived from 1844 to 1913.

Read Closely: Exceptions
History is a story of patterns and exceptions. To understand an event in its context, identify both ways it was part of a trend and ways it was unusual. In a time when Europeans defeated African forces regularly, why was Menelik able to resist European domination?

However, the Italians claimed that the treaty gave them a protectorate over all of Ethiopia effectively making it a colony. Menelik gathered his forces and waited for the Italians to attempt to subdue Ethiopia. The attempt came at the **Battle of Adowa**, also known as Adwa or Adua. An attachment of 14,500 Italian troops was met by nearly 100,000 Ethiopian fighters who defeated the Italians in short order. Some six months later the Treaty of Addis Ababa (Ethiopia's present-day capital) was signed, in which Italy renounced its claims to the kingdom.

The Significance of Adowa With its victory at Adowa, Ethiopia maintained its independence. In 1935, the Italians again attacked Ethiopia, this time successfully, and occupied Ethiopia for five years. Other than this period, Ethiopia remained free. It and the tiny country of Liberia in West Africa were the only parts of the continent to successfully resist colonization.

In addition, the Battle at Adowa took on a larger significance. It became one of the most influential battles fought in Africa in the modern era. The success of the Ethiopians provided an inspiration to later Africans in their battles to throw off European colonization.

AFRICA IN 1914

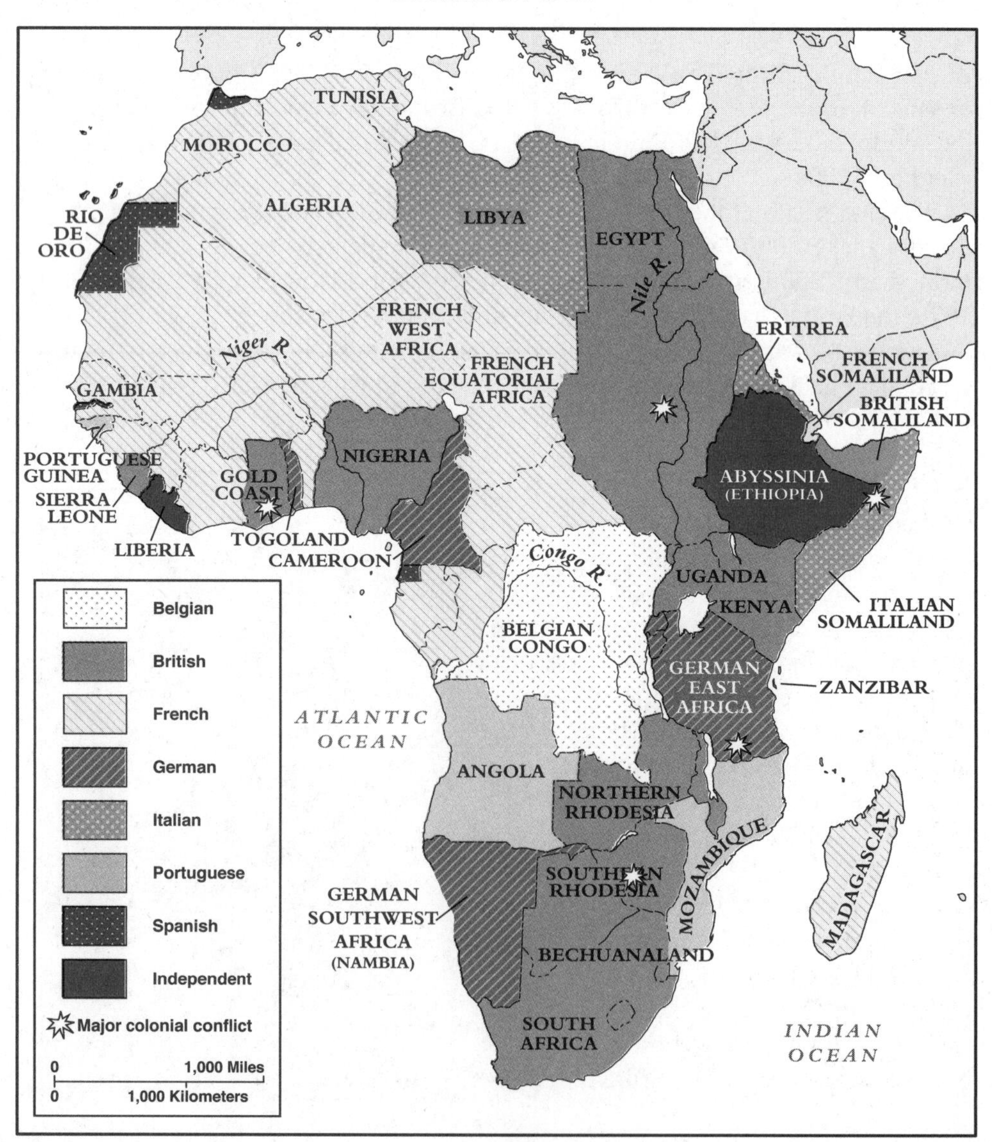

Reform and Resistance in China

By the late 1800s, the Qing Dynasty was widely unpopular in China. It had always faced resentment because the Qing were not Chinese—they were Manchus, from a region northeast of China. Worse, the dynasty had failed to protect the country from foreign assaults, such as the flow of opium into the country by British traders. Finally, the Taiping Rebellion and other uprisings had devastated the country. Between 1850 and 1873, China's population decreased 15 percent.

Reform Efforts The Qing attempted to address the internal and external problems facing the country through a major reform movement known as the **Self-Strengthening Movement**. The movement included several intiatives:

- improving China's military technology and readiness
- training Chinese artisans in the manufacture of items for shipyards and arsenals
- strengthening the customs service to collect taxes on imports and exports
- repaying China's foreign debts
- participating more in international trade
- creating a diplomatic corps to deal with other countries more effectively

To help in these reforms, particularly of the customs service, China hired French and British advisors. For the Chinese, their existence as an independent nation depended upon economic solvency. Reform in the name of modernization seemed inevitable. The government's strategy in the reform efforts was to graft modern methods and technologies onto Chinese tradition rather than to create major change in cultural or political ideas.

Read Closely: Effects
To fully appreciate the significance of a historical decision, be alert to any contradictory effects it has. For example, when the Qing Dynasty hired foreign economic advisors, it helped the economy. How did it also undermine the economy?

Cixi's Conservatism Demand for reform increased after China's defeat in the Sino-Japanese War. People formed clubs to call for change. One club, led by a civil servant named Kang Youwei, gained momentum and convinced the emperor to support a set of sweeping reforms known as the "Hundred Days of Reform." The reforms attempted to transform all aspects of Chinese society, including the abolition of the outdated civil servant exam, the elimination of corruption, and the establishment of Western-style industrial, commercial, and medical systems.

However, the emperor did not really run the government. The power was exercised by his aunt and adoptive mother, **Empress Cixi**, whose title was Empress Dowager. Cixi was more conservative than he was. She was more fearful that Japanese and European influence would undermine Chinese traditions and sovereignty. To slow the pace of reform, Cixi had the emperor confined to a house on the palace grounds. To prevent the spread of foreign ideas, she blocked the extension of railroad lines and telegraph networks into the Chinese interior.

The Chinese Civil Service Cixi was suspicious of but not completely opposed to reform. For example, she recognized the problems with the country's civil service system. It was designed according to Confucian ideals of respect for rank and hierarchy as well as values of civic participation and action. By the 19th century, though, the wealthy were manipulating civil servants to secure favors. Revenue dropped off for the government as a result of bribes going into the pockets of corrupt public officials. Moreover, unqualified persons were purchasing civil service posts. In some cases, young men took the exam for others.

An Enduring Issue: Empire
China's response to European empire building highlighted the difficulty many societies faced. From Ghana in western Africa to Japan in eastern Asia, countries had to decide what to accept and what to reject of European influence.

The Boxer Rebellion Cixi's fear of outside influence was shared by a group of Chinese who called themselves the **Righteous and Harmonious Order of Fists**, or as Westerners called them, "the Boxers." It was a secret society in northern China based on training and rituals that they believed made them invulnerable. The Boxers opposed the presence of all foreigners in the country. From 1899 to 1901, the central government in league with the society waged a violent anti-foreigner campaign known as the **Boxer Rebellion**. The campaign targeted Christian missionaries and converts. .

However, provincial governors in southern China opposed the central government's actions and protected foreigners and Christians. In 1900, a military force of Japanese, British, Americans, and soldiers from other countries defeated the Boxers. The successful foreign powers forced Cixi to admit she had erred and the Chinese government to pay an enormous indemnity. Further, existing foreign powers in China retained their spheres of influence.

After the failures in the war against Japan and in the Boxer Rebellion, Cixi recognized that the conservative response to foreign ideas was failing China. The country was not able to defend itself or confront the problems it faced in the modern world. Cixi became more supportive of reform, looking to Meiji Japan as a model for how to adapt foreign ideas and still maintain cultural traditions. In one of her most dramatic moves, she abolished the civil service exam in 1905. This ended a system going back 2,500 years.

Source: Library of Congress

The largest number of foreigners who fought the Boxers were from Japan. Here, the forces from several countries are attacking a Boxer-held fort.

Application

Read the excerpt and answer the questions that follow it.

"The Ferment in China," *The Nation*, June 21, 1900

The rationale of the troubles in China is beginning to appear in a clearer light as events move on. That a formidable reaction is shaking the Empire has been obvious enough, but it has not been plainly seen that it has a domestic side as well as an international aspect. The truth is, however, that the movement of which the "Boxers" have taken the murderous lead, is directed against not only foreign interlopers, but native reformers as well.

These are normally the two phases of the agitation. The revolt is one against modern ideas and methods, whether imposed from without or advocates from within. Missionaries are murdered and foreigners hunted on exactly the same principle that led to the execution of six native reformers at Pekin [Beijing], and sent [constitutional monarchist] Kang-Yu and other educated Chinamen, hospitable to the new enlightenment, fleeing from the land for safety.

Source: "The Ferment in China," *The Nation*, June 21, 1900.

1. Quote one phrase that describes whether or not the author is sympathetic to the Boxer resistance.

___

___

___

2. Explain what the author means by the "two phases of the agitation."

___

___

___

3. Describe how the author compares the Boxer resistance to the executions in Pekin.

___

___

___

4. Explain how the author feels about individuals such as Kang-Yu.

___

___

___

Lesson 3 Conflicts Among Imperial Powers

Conceptual Understanding
10.4c International conflicts developed as imperial powers competed for control. Claims over land often resulted in borders being shifted on political maps, often with little regard for traditional cultures and commerce (e.g., the Berlin Conference).

Source: *New York State Grades 9–12 Social Studies Framework.*

Europeans had been at war with each other for centuries before the competition for colonies began. The race to seize control of lands in Africa and Asia was just one more cause of conflict. For example, English and French armies had been fighting each other on and off since the Hundred Years' War, which began in the 14th century. In the 18th and 19th century, they faced off in North America, South Asia, and West Africa. The following source describes the struggle between the English and the French for power in West Africa.

Analyze a Primary Source

Harold Frederic, *The New York Times*, October 17, 1897

Although as was said last week, people of the highest authority are confident that the Anglo-French dispute in the matter of the West African boundaries will be amicably settled, the discussion of the various phases of the subject occupies so much journalistic attention, both in London and Paris, and is engendering so much heat, that it is impossible not to treat it as a matter of importance.

The French hardly take the trouble to deny that they are bound by treaty not to do what they have been doing on the Niger. They rest satisfiedly on the statement that their adoption of a new policy alters everything, and that, having occupied a great deal of territory in which they had no business whatever, they are now compelled to defend it tooth and nail. There is, of course, the unusual cackle as well about England also breaking treaties and grabbing territories she had promised to respect.

Even if this retort were as true as the most ignorant boulevardier [fashionable man] supposes it to be, it still remains a fact that what England takes is held in trust for the whole world, with free trade in open markets; whereas every colonial acquisition of nations like France and Germany means so much waste country, expensively fenced off from contact with humanity in general.

Source: Harold Frederic, *The New York Times*, October 17, 1897.

Read Closely: Descriptions
Frederic uses expressive language to describe the relationship between Britain and France.
Circle a description used by the author to show how these nations feel about each other.

Read Closely: Word Choices
Writers use phrases such as "of course" to suggest to readers that all reasonable people agree on an issue. The word "grabbing" also paints a clear picture of the methods England used to claim new land.

Read Closely: Points of View
The first half of the commentary criticizes England, but this final paragraph defends it. Showing other points of view helps strengthen the ultimate argument.
Circle a phrase that states Frederic's view that England's actions were good for the world.

Conflicts Among Imperial Powers

As European countries increased their desire for overseas colonies, they came into conflict with each other. The imperial powers tried to reduce these conflicts through agreements regarding who could colonize where. However, the agreements were not as powerful as their desire for colonies.

Read Closely: Similarity Recognizing similarities in historical events is one way to see how they fit into a broader context. What is one similarity between European imperialism in Africa and Asia?

The Scramble for Africa

European countries' push for colonial holdings surged after 1875. As Belgium, Germany, Italy, Portugal, and Spain industrialized, they wanted to join Great Britain and France in claiming overseas lands. They, too, wanted sources of raw material and cheap labor, along with markets in which to sell their goods. The result was a "scramble for Africa" that caused an effort to create some diplomatic rules to govern colonization.

Imperialism Expands The spread of industrialization not only created a desire by more countries for colonies, but it also made imperialism easier. The advances in technology that helped these newer industrial powers challenge Britain and France economically also helped them, potentially, challenge the established powers militarily. Advances in naval technology—armored ships with high-powered guns—posed a particular challenge to Great Britain's dominance of the seas. All this was occurring while Britain and France continued to vie for dominance in north and west Africa.

The colonies of France and Great Britain in Africa were almost exclusively along the coast of the continent. The one exception was Britain's Cape Colony on the southern tip of the continent, which extended farther inland. Portugal, too, held onto colonial outposts on the west coast of Africa, in what are now Angola and Guinea-Bissau, and on the east coast in what is now Mozambique. But explorers, missionaries, and traders were busy making inroads into the continent.

Read Closely: Geography Many readers understand history best when they visualize in their minds where events occurred. Why did most European colonization take place primarily along the coasts?

The Berlin Conference The stage was set for colonization of the interior just as Germany made its big colonial move, annexing territory in three regions on the west coast (Togo, Cameroon, and Namibia today) as well as a substantial area in east Africa. King Leopold was also attempting to control the Congo. European diplomats realized that without some sort of guidelines in place, their countries could soon be in conflicts that might escalate.

In 1884–1885, the European countries, Turkey, and the United States held the **Berlin Conference** to set rules for dividing Africa. No Africans were present. The attendees decided to recognize a country's right to a colony if that country first made a formal announcement of its claim and then occupied the claimed territory. Before this decision, a country could gain legal right to a colony by establishing that it had historical claim to it. For example, a country might assert ownership of an area by providing evidence that, in the past, the area had been inhabited and governed by the country's citizens.

The new procedure was adopted to add clarity to the colonization process. It succeeded in making clear that any European country that wanted territory in Africa should grab it before any other country did. Competition for African holdings among the Western powers intensified almost instantly. They all rushed to send troops, officials, and settlers to the lands they felt they had a right to own or influence.

An Enduring Issue: Colonization
The Berlin Conference demonstrated the idea of imperialism held by many Europeans in the late 19th century. This idea would lead to wars and conflict for many decades.

The Berlin Conference clarified how European countries could compete for land in Africa. They could exert imperial control in three ways:

- establish colonies that they owned and governed directly
- mark an area as a sphere of influence, in which they had sole investment or trading rights
- turn a weak country into a protectorate, in which the African region's ruler was kept on, but the imperial power set policy for that ruler to follow

Post-Conference Competition Britain and France vied for territory in east Africa around present-day Sudan. Each country had militarily subdued all of the peoples who lived in the regions they claimed. The two countries almost went to war over what is today Sudan, but the conflict was averted again through an agreement that gave each some of the territory it wanted. Italy took control of Eritrea on the northern border of Ethiopia in 1890 and Somaliland on Ethiopia's southern border in 1896. (It had much less success in Ethiopia proper, as described in Lesson 2.) Portugal extended its holdings on both coasts, and even Spain claimed a protectorate in Río de Oro in northwest Africa.

The Europeans seizing land in Africa did not consider traditional or cultural borders. They simply drew boundaries between new colonial entities for political expediency and geographical convenience. As a result, some African cultural groups were divided between new countries. Others were forced to live together with traditional enemies. In the eyes of many of the colonizers, an African was an African. These randomly drawn borders caused major tensions among Africans, and many of these problems remain to the present day.

Read Closely: Plausible Claim
To understand the importance of past events, note how current events are based on them. For example, give an example of tensions that still exist in Africa as a result of European imperialism.

Source: Getty Images

At the beginning of the 20th century, various black African groups made up about two-thirds of South African society. However, the whites who descended from British and Dutch settlers held most positions of power.

Application

Read the excerpt and answer the questions that follow it.

Hans Delbruck, editorial in a German newspaper, *Die Post*, January 14, 1912

In Africa we see possibilities worth cultivating, but not in British Africa. I am thinking of what seems to me the inevitable, eventual collapse of Portuguese power in Africa, and a division of the Republic's possessions there between England and Germany. There would have been such a division long ago, I doubt not, but there again British repugnance to the idea of German expansion has intervened to our disadvantage.

France has North Africa; Britain dominates South Africa; Germany must get Central Africa. We must strike now while the iron is hot. Britain should be given an immediate opportunity to prove their words that they do not oppose Germany's expansion. Perhaps it may eventually be possible to induce England to cede Rhodesia, and France the remainder of the mutilated Congo. If we in the meantime secure the Portuguese possessions, a mighty German Empire in Central Africa would then be assured.

Source: Hans Delbruck, *Die Post*, January 14, 1912.

1. Identify the four countries disputing territory on the African continent.

____

____

____

2. Cite a passage that supports the author's view regarding Germany's feelings toward the actions of England.

____

____

____

3. Explain what opportunity the writer believes England should be given immediately.

____

____

____

4. Identify the writer's bias that would explain why he thinks Germany must secure land in Central Africa.

____

____

____

Chapter 4 *Review*

Multiple-Choice Questions

Directions (1–6): For each statement or question, choose the number of the word or expression that, of those given, best completes the statement or answers the question.

Base your answers to questions 1 and 2 on the passage below and your knowledge of social studies.

> "The village, or town, is well-built; the houses are very lofty; and the inhabitants are employed, according to the season, in the manufacture of cotton and the cultivation of rice. The principal pagoda, situated on the threshold of the rice fields, near a grove of graceful coryphe palms, is richly ornamented in the interior, and among other curiosities, contains an ancient carved *portecierges* of wood.
>
> At the time of Garnier's visit, some Birman traders had displayed the contents of their packs on the steps of the temple, and were selling to the natives their bright-colored cotton stuffs and English hardware. A road having been made westward from Houten, Muong Mai is only a hundred leagues from Moulmein, which lies in the nearly same latitude, and is, as the reader knows, an English colony, and a busy commercial port, at the mouth of the Saluen [River].
>
> From this point spread over the interior of Laos the [people . . .] whose knowledge of the wares most readily purchased by European merchants, and the high price at which they sell to the natives their English goods, enable them to accumulate considerable wealth.
>
> **Source:** *The French in Indo-China, With a Narrative of Garnier's Explorations in Cochin China, Annam, and Tonquin* (London: T. Nelson and Sons, 1884), 70–73.

1. Which statement best describes the geographical context in which this passage is set?

   (1) It was a region dominated by French imperialists.

   (2) It was a region of conflict between English and French interests.

   (3) It was a region controlled by China until Europeans arrived.

   (4) It was a region where Europeans had little success in establishing colonies.

2. Which general claim about European imperialism is best supported by the information in the passage?

   (1) The influence of Europeans benefited some native groups more than others.

   (2) One impact of the arrival of Europeans was that all native people identified with each other.

   (3) Europeans found that few native people wanted the goods they had to sell.

   (4) Trade in goods was primarily Europeans buying raw materials from natives.

Base your answer to questions 3 and 4 on the passage below and your knowledge of social studies.

> When I was thoroughly convinced that neither the reformation nor the regeneration of China was to come from the Taipings, I at once turned my thoughts to the idea of making a big fortune as my first duty, and as the first element in the successful carrying out of other plans for the future.
>
> One day, while sauntering about in the tea garden inside the city of Shanghai, I came across a few tea-merchants regaling themselves with that beverage in a booth by themselves, evidently having a very social time. . . . It was stated that an immense quantity of green tea could be found there [a region controlled by the Taiping], all packed and boxed ready for shipment, and that the rebels were in possession of the goods, and that whoever had the hardihood and courage to risk his life to gain possession of it would become a millionaire. . . . [The region was] a country where highway robbery, lawlessness and murder were of daily occurrence. But with the glamor of a big fortune confronting me, all privations, dangers and risks of life seemed small and faded into airy nothing. . . .
>
> On the way up the Wuhu River, we passed three cities mostly deserted by their inhabitants, but occupied by rebels. Paddy fields on both sides of the river were mostly left uncultivated and deserted, overrun with rank weeds and tall grass. As we ascended towards Taiping, the whole region presented a heart-rending and depressing scene of wild waste and devastation. Whole villages were depopulated and left in a dilapidated condition. Out of a population of 500,000 only a few dozen people were seen wandering about in a listless, hopeless condition, very much emaciated [made thin from lack of food] and looking like walking skeletons.
>
> **Source:** Joseph Wing Yung, *My Life in China and America* (New York: Henry Holt, 1909), 123–127.

3. What is the point of view of the writer toward the Taiping?
   (1) They were not going to solve the problems that China faced through a rebellion.
   (2) They had great resources, such as tea, they could use to finance the rebellion.
   (3) They were a good example of the influence of Christianity in China.
   (4) They were made stronger because people blamed the government for the danger of starvation.

4. Which individual would most agree with the information in this passage?
   (1) A leader of the Qing government who opposed the Taiping Rebellion
   (2) An English soldier who went to China to fight to suppress the Taiping Rebellion
   (3) A European Christian who supported the Taiping Rebellion for religious reasons
   (4) A Chinese soldier who was fighting with the Taiping rebels for nationalist reasons

Base your answers to questions 5 and 6 on the passage below and your knowledge of social studies

> In the *Daily Telegraph* of November 2, 1877, the following words of mine were published. They will, at least, prove my own consistency of belief.
>
> "I feel convinced that the question of this mighty waterway [the Congo River] will become a political one in time. As yet, however, no European Power seems to have put forth the right of control. Portugal claims it because she discovered its mouth; but the great Powers—England, America, and France—refuse to recognize her right. If it were not that I fear to damp any interest you may have in Africa, or in this magnificent stream, by the length of my letters, I could show you very strong reasons why it would be a political deed to settle this momentous question immediately. I could prove to you that the Power possessing the Congo, despite the cataracts [waterfalls], would absorb to itself the trade of the whole of the enormous basin behind. This river is and will be the grand highway of commerce to West Central Africa.
>
> Gambetta, the great French statesman, in July, 1878, also uttered a prediction which has been since verified.
>
> "You have thrown the light of knowledge of what you have well-described as the Dark Continent. Not only, if have you opened up a new Continent to our view, but you have given an impulse to scientific and philanthropic enterprise which will have a material effect on the progress of the world. It is not only in the action of private individuals that this is seen. What you have done has influenced Governments—proverbially so difficult to be moved—and the impulse you have imparted to them will, I am convinced, go on growing year after year."
>
> **Source:** Henry Morton Stanley, *The Congo and the Founding of the Free State*, (New York: Harper and Brothers, 1885), v–vii.

5. Which statement about imperialism in Africa is reflected in this passage?
   (1) Disputes over imperialism will cause conflicts among European powers.
   (2) Most Africans will negotiate agreements that allow them to keep control over their land.
   (3) Water transportation will quickly become less important than roads in Africa.
   (4) The Congo River will remain free of European control.

6. How are the statements by Stanley and Gambetta related?
   (1) Both believed that European imperialism would benefit Africa.
   (2) Both had more confidence in private individuals than in governments.
   (3) They disagreed on whether Africa would provide wealth and opportunity to Europeans.
   (4) They disagreed on which foreign countries had rights to claim parts of Africa.

Short-Answer Questions

CRQ Directions (7-9): Analyze the documents and answer the short-answer questions that follow each document in the space provided.

Base your answer to question 7 on Document 1 below and on your knowledge of social studies.

Document 1

The Boxer movement in the province had grown apace, and had spread to our own immediate neighborhood. Corps were being rapidly organized in every city; and in towns and villages recruiting was brisk. . . .

It was now clear to us all that we were face to face with a crisis the nature and extent of which it was impossible fully to gauge, but whose gravity was sufficiently apparent. We could not be sure that the recent action of the officials in showing themselves our friends and protectors was something of a guarantee of security. Moreover, we knew that in general a heavy discount must be allowed on all street rumor; and so we hoped and encouraged one another to believe that things were not as black as they looked. . . .

It was clear that matters were heading to a definite issue, and we began to ask ourselves seriously: Ought we not at least to be ready for flight in case of sudden emergency! The climax, however, was reached when positive news was brought in later that the edict which it was rumored the Empress Dowager had issued for our destruction might be seen posted up outside the yamen [Chinese government headquarters]; and that our death was not the topic of the hour. Not only so, but the actual day had been fixed for our execution—the tenth day of the sixth month.

Source: Archibald E. Glover, *A Thousand Miles of Miracle in China*. (London: Hodder and Stoughton Publishers, 1907), 86–88. First written in 1904.

7. Specify the context in which this excerpt was written.

___

___

___

___

___

Tips for Answering Short-Answer Questions

One way to think about the context of a source is to position it in time. Picture the event as the middle entry on a timeline.

- What events occurred right before it?
- What events occurred right after it?

A second way to think about the context of a soure is to position it in space. Picture the event on a map.

- What events occurred in nearby places?
- What events occurred in places around the world?

Base your answer to question 8 on Document 2 below and on your knowledge of social studies

Document 2

This excerpt is from Sir Garnet Wolseley, a British general. He is speaking shortly after the British-Zulu Conflict, where Britain defeated the Zulus capturing their leader, Cetshwayo.

> This monument must hereafter be looked upon by all who see it, not only as a record of the gallant deeds of those who erected it, but also as a lasting denial of the statements one so frequently hears made, that Christianity interferes or disagrees with the martial spirit of a native race, or that it deteriorates them as soldiers. In the future those who would assert that the native converted under Christianity is thereby injured socially or physically, either as a citizen or as a soldier, must come to Edendale and see this monument, and see the prosperous condition this village has attained.
>
> I have heard it said that Cetewayo [Cetshwayo] frequently asserted that a Zulu made a Christian was a Zulu spoiled, and that the day he became a Christian he was useless as a soldier. I have only to appeal to the history of the late war to prove how untrue this statement in regard to the native races is. I would appeal to all those gallant officers who had the good fortune to be associated with these Edendale men to come forward and say how well those men fought. . . . The men of Edendale proved themselves to be worthy of standing shoulder to shoulder with the best soldiers of the British army.
>
> **Source:** Quoted in Annie Margaret Wilkinson, *A Lady's Life and Travels in Zululand and the Transvaal During Cetewayo's Reign* (London: J. T. Hayes, 1882), 260–262.

8. Using the excerpt, identify Wolseley's purpose in making the statement.

____

____

____

____

____

Base your answer to question 9 on both Documents 1 and 2 and on your knowledge of social studies.

Similarity—tells how something is alike or the same as something else.
Difference—tells how something is not alike or not the same as something else.

9. Identify and explain the most important differences between the beliefs expressed in Documents 1 and 2. Use evidence from both Documents 1 and 2 in your response.

Speaking and Listening: Reflect on the Key Idea

Working with a partner or a small group, create a chart or diagram summarizing the conflicts among European countries and between Europeans and Africans regarding colonization.

Period 2 *Enduring Issue Extended Essay*

Directions

An enduring issue is an issue that exists across time. It is one that many societies have attempted to address with varying degrees of success. Read the following documents and take notes in the margin identifying at least two themes in each one. Then use these notes and the Planning Page to prepare to write the essay. Finally, on a separate sheet of paper or on a computer, write your extended essay.

In your essay:

Identify the issue based on a historically accurate interpretation of **three** documents.

Define the issue using evidence from three documents.

Argue that this is a significant issue that has endured by showing:

- How the issue has affected people or been affected by people.
- How the issue has continued to be an issue or changed over time.

Include outside information from your knowledge of social studies and evidence from the documents.

Keep in mind these terms:

Identify—means to put a name or to name

Define—means to explain features of a thing or concept so that it can be understood

Argue—means to provide a series of statements that provide evidence and reasons to support a conclusion.

Topics to consider for your essay: (See page xvii.)

- Conflict
- Coperation
- Power
- Inequality
- Innovation
- Interconnectedness
- Ideas and Beliefs
- Environmental Issues
- Scarcity

Document 1

Shaikh Hasan al-Kafrawi, Professor of Islamic Law in Cairo, Muslims and Non-Muslims, 1772.

The decision given by [earlier Islamic scholars] may be worded as follows: "It is forbidden to the tolerated peoples living on Muslim territory to clothe themselves in the same manner as the chiefs, the scholars, and the nobles. They should not be allowed to clothe themselves in costly fabrics which have been cut in the modes which are forbidden to them, in order that they may not offend the sensibilities of poor Muslims and in order that their faith in their religion should not be shaken by this [who might doubt their faith after seeing prosperous Jews and Christians].

"They should not be permitted to employ mounts like the Muslims. They must use neither saddles, nor iron-stirrups, in order to be distinguished from the true believers. They must under no circumstance ride horses because of the noble character of this animal. The Most-High [Allah] has said: 'And through powerful squadrons [of horses] through which you will strike terror into your own and God's enemies.'

"They should not be permitted to take Muslims into their service because God has glorified the people of Islam. He has given them His aid and has given them a guarantee by these words: 'Surely God will never give preeminence to unbelievers over the true believers.'"

Source: Jacob Marcus, *The Jew in the Medieval World: A Sourcebook, 315–1791* (New York: JPS, 1938). pages 15–19. Reprinted online at www.bu.edu/mzank/Jerusalem/tx/fatwa.htm.

Document 2

Religious Composition of the Ottoman Empire.

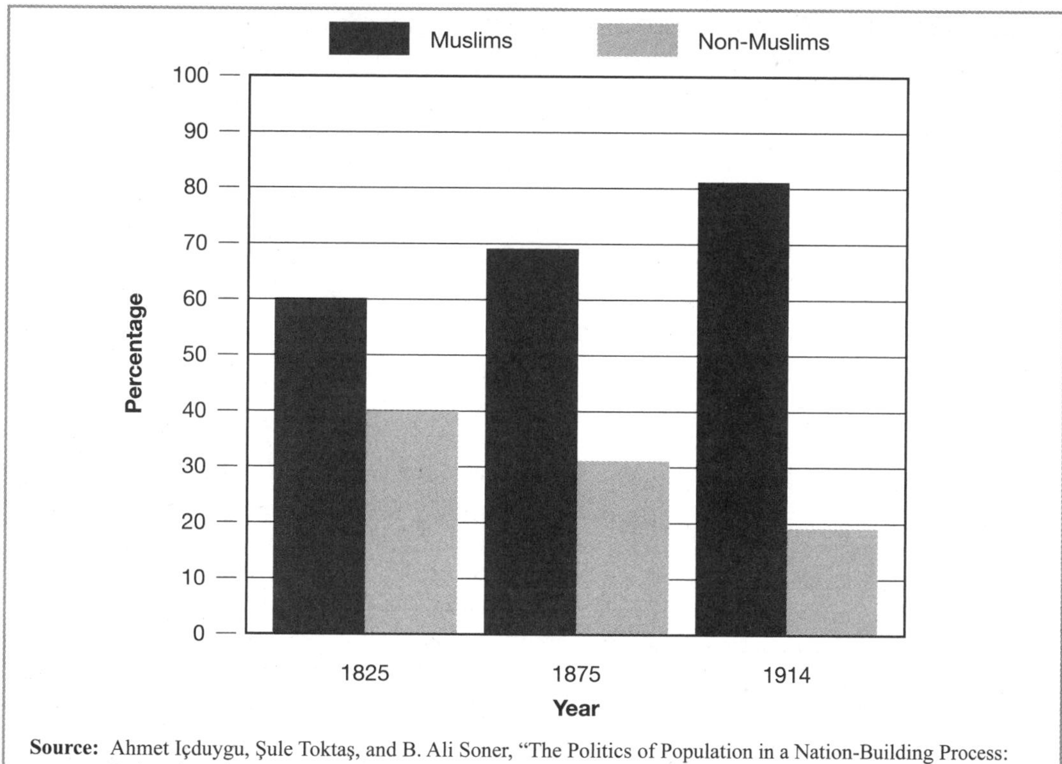

Source: Ahmet Içduygu, Şule Toktaş, and B. Ali Soner, "The Politics of Population in a Nation-Building Process: Emigration of Non-Muslims from Turkey," *Ethnic and Racial Studies,* Vol. 31, Number 2, February 1, 2008, pages 358–389.

Document 3

The excerpt is a letter from French writer and Enlightenment philosopher, Voltaire, describing English society in 1733.

This [England] is the country of sects. An Englishman, as a free man, goes to Heaven by whatever road he pleases. . . .

Go into the Exchange [where merchants bought and sold goods] in London, that place more venerable [honored] than many a court, and you will see representatives of all the nations assembled there for the profit of mankind. There the Jew, the Mahometan [Muslim], and the Christian deal with one another as if they were of the same religion, and reserve the name of infidel for those who go bankrupt. There the Presbyterian trusts the Anabaptist, and the Church of England man accepts the promise of the Quaker. . . .

If there were only one religion in England, there would be danger of tyranny; if there were two, they would cut each other's throats; but there are thirty, and they live happily together in peace.

Source: Voltaire, *Philosophical Letters: Letters Concerning the English Nation*. Translated by Ernest Dilworth. Mineola, New York: Dover Publications, 2003. Republication of a book published by Bobbs-Merrill Company, 1961. Pages 22–26.

Document 4

Japan in the early 19th century was resisting Western influences. Aizawa Seishisai, Japanese scholar and politician wrote ***New Theses*** in 1825.

The bakufu [government of Japan] once made it plain to Russia that Japanese law requires us to destroy on sight any barbarian ship approaching our coasts. But now the English regularly appear and anchor off our shores, and we do not lift a finger to drive them away. When they have the gall to land, we go out of our way to provide for their needs and send them merrily along. Will the barbarians have any respect for our laws after they hear about this? The English come and go as they please, draw maps and sketch our terrain, disrupt our inter-island transport system, and win over our commoners with their occult religion and the lure of profit. If smuggling increases and we fail to stop commoners from aiding and abetting the barbarians, who knows what future conspiracies may hatch?

But our temporizing, gloss-it-over officials reply, "The foreigners are just fishermen and merchants doing nothing out of the ordinary; there is no cause for alarm." What simpletons! The barbarians live ten thousand miles across the sea; when they set off on foreign conquests, "they must procure supplies and provisions from the enemy." That is why they trade and fish. Their men-of-war are self-sufficient away from home. If their only motive for harpooning whales was to obtain whale meat, they could do so in their own waters. Why should they risk long, difficult voyages just to harpoon whales in eastern seas?

Their ships can be outfitted for trading, or fishing, *or fighting*. Can anyone guarantee that their merchant vessels and fishing boats of today will not turn into warships tomorrow?

Source: Bob Tadashi Wakabayashi, *Anti-Foreignism and Western Learning in Early-Modern Japan*, (Council on East Asian Studies, Harvard University, 1986), pages 208-209, 213. Reprinted online by Asia for Educators, http://afe.easia.columbia.edu/ps/japan/aizawa_seishisai_shinron.pdf.

Document 5

Cecil Rhodes was an Englishman who lead the way in developing diamond and gold industries in Africa during the colonization of the continent. The excerpt is from "Confession of Faith," 1877.

> I have felt that at the present day we are actually limiting our children and perhaps bringing into the world half the human beings we might owing to the lack of country for them to inhabit that if we had retained America there would at this moment be millions more of English living. I contend that we are the finest race in the world and that the more of the world we inhabit the better it is for the human race. . . .
>
> Why should we not form a secret society with but one object the furtherance of the British Empire and the bringing of the whole uncivilized world under British rule for the recovery of the United States for the making the Anglo-Saxon race but one Empire. What a dream, but yet it is probable, it is possible. . . . Think of those countless 000's of Englishmen that during the last 100 years would have crossed the Atlantic and settled and populated the United States. Would they have not made without any prejudice a finer country of it than the low class Irish and German emigrants?
>
> **Source:** http://pages.uoregon.edu/kimball/Rhodes-Confession.htm.

Preparing to Write an Extended Essay

MY ENDURING ISSUE IS: ____

You may use the Enduring Issues Planning Page organizer to prepare to write your essay. Writing on this Planning Page will NOT count toward your final score.

You may also choose to prepare to write the Enduring Issues Essay by creating an outline or graphic organizer on your own sheet of paper.

ENDURING ISSUES PLANNING PAGE

Essay Requirements	Yes	Circle documents that apply	One or two possible ideas for outside info
Is this an issue supported by at least three documents? Which documents support this issue?		1 2 3 4 5	
Which documents can be used to develop the definition for this issue?		1 2 3 4 5	
Has this issue significantly affected people or been affected by people?		1 2 3 4 5	
Has this issue endured across time or changed over time? In which document or documents do you see this?		1 2 3 4 5	

Period 3

Crisis and Achievement in the 20th Century, 1914–Present

Chapter 5

World War I, the Great Depression, and World War II

Chapter 6

The Cold War

Chapter 7

Rebellions Against Imperialism

Map Notes

A

The creation of the United Nations, based in New York City, reflected that countries of the world recognized that that they were becoming more interconnected.

B

During the 20th century, many countries in South America made the transition from dictatorship to democracy.

C

The world included the first 2 urban areas with more than 10 million people: New York and London. Today, at least 20 urban areas are that large.

D

The assassination of a political leader in Sarajevo in 1914 ignited the conflict now called World War I. New technology made it one of the bloodiest wars ever.

E

Russia and China began the 20th century as the world's last large imperial dynasties. By 1950, they were the first two large countries with Communist governments.

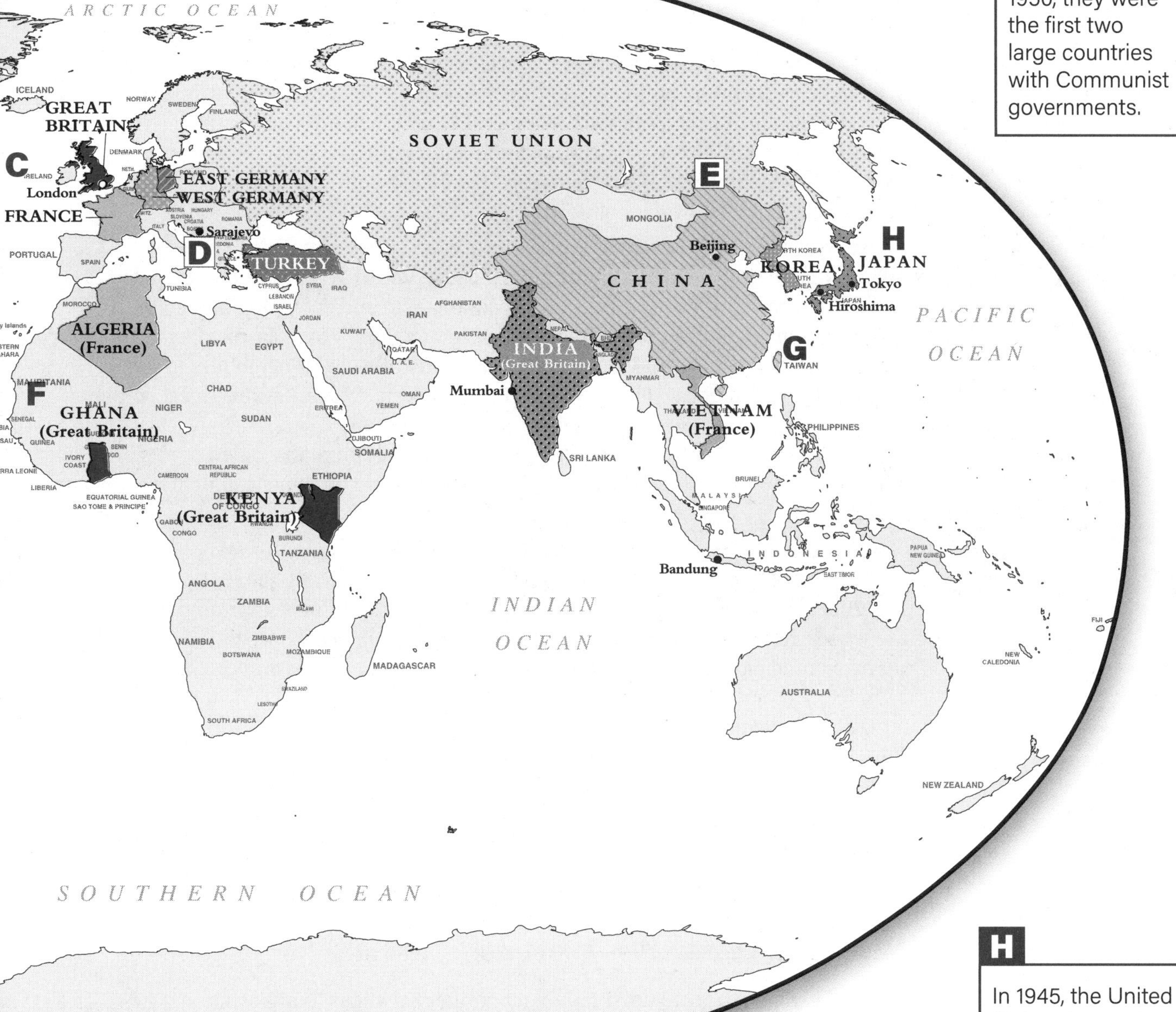

F

Ghana declared its independence from Great Britain in 1957. During the following two decades, nearly every part of Africa won independence.

G

An ideological battle between the United States and the Soviet Union known as the Cold War fed into military conflicts in Korea, Vietnam, and elsewhere.

H

In 1945, the United States dropped atomic bombs on Japan. At least eight countries now have atomic weapons, but no country has used them since.

CHAPTER 5

World War I, the Great Depression, and World War II

Chapter Overview

World War I and World War II led to the deaths of tens of millions of people and caused huge shifts in the political relationships among countries. The wars were sparked by the spirit of international competition and fueled by nationalism, imperialism, and militarism. Industrialization and high-tech weapons powered these massive conflicts. The long-term results of these conflicts included forming organizations to prevent future conflicts.

Two World Wars World War I and World War II were connected. The problems resulting from World War I helped cause World War II. The time between the wars was a period of growing nationalism and economic hardship. As a result, some countries turned to totalitarian dictators. For example, Germany suffered terribly from World War I and lost key territories to its neighbors in the treaties that ended the war. This provided the context in which Adolph Hitler came to power promising to restore Germany to greatness.

In the Soviet Union, another totalitarian dictator, Joseph Stalin, ruled. However, he and Hitler had sharply opposing ideologies and they became fierce enemies.

Responses to Mass Murder Several examples of the murder or starvation of hundreds of thousands, or millions, of people occurred during the first half of the 20th century. The Armenians, Ukrainians, Jews, and Poles were among those who suffered the most from these events. Preventing such atrocities from happening again was one reason that the countries of the world organized the United Nations after the end of World War II. People hoped that a strong international organization could preserve peace and step in before conflicts resulted in massacres.

An Enduring Issue: Cooperation The complicated results of countries working together is an enduring issue in this chapter. Alliances helped cause World War I, defeat totalitarian countries in World War II, create organizations to promote peace, and hold people responsible for committing atrocities.

New York Social Studies Framework: **Key Idea 10.5**

World War I and World War II led to geopolitical changes, human and environmental devastation, and attempts to bring stability and peace.

Source: *New York State Grades 9–12 Social Studies Framework*

1. Rewrite Key Idea 10.5 in your own words..

____

____

Identify Enduring Issues

Comparing two sources often highlights enduring issues that appear in both. One way to organize information is by type of theme. As you study this chapter, look for similarities and differences in the causes of World War I and World War II, and complete the chart below.

Comparing Causes of Two World Wars			
Type of Cause	**World War I**	**World War II**	**Similarities and Differences**
Economic and Technological			
Political and Diplomatic			
Military			
Ethnic and Religious			
Other			

Key Terms by Theme

Identity

nationalism (p. 134)
anti-Semitism (p. 157)
scientific racism (p. 157)

Geography

Stalingrad (p. 138)
Hiroshima (p. 139)
Israel (p. 140)
Palestine (p. 140)
Ukraine (p. 155)
USSR (p. 155)

Governance

alliances (p. 133)
Archduke Franz Ferdinand (p. 133)
Gavrilo Princip (p. 133)
militarism (p. 133)
World War I (p. 133)
World War II (p. 133)
self-determination (p. 134)
trench warfare (p. 135)
isolationism (p. 136)
Treaty of Versailles (p. 136)
appeasement (p. 137)
blitzkrieg (p. 137)
fascism (p. 137)
nonaggression pact (p. 137)
D-Day (p. 139)
Marshall Plan (p. 139)
Cold War (p. 140)
Holocaust (p. 140)
NATO (p. 140)
Warsaw Pact (p. 140)
Fourteen Points (p. 149)
League of Nations (p. 150)
Bolsheviks (p. 155)
United Nations (p. 152)
Joseph Stalin (p. 155)
Vladimir I. Lenin (p. 155)
Nazi (p. 156)
Jiang Jieshi (p. 158)
Great Depression (p. 160)
Armenians (p. 163)
Mustafa Kemal (p. 163)
Holodomor (p. 165)

Technology

atomic bomb (p. 139)
barbed wire (p. 143)
chemical weapons (p. 143)
machine gun (p. 143)
submarines (p. 143)
airplane (p. 144)
tank (p. 144)
computer (p. 146)
nuclear weapon (p. 146)
radar (p. 146)

Lesson 1 Causes of World Wars

Conceptual Understanding 10.5a International competition, fueled by nationalism, imperialism, and militarism, along with shifts in the balance of power and alliances, led to world wars.

Source: *New York State Grades 9–12 Social Studies Framework.*

World War I (1914 to 1918) was a global conflict. In Europe, much of the fighting occurred in trench warfare. While trench warfare was not an innovation, new weapons made it more deadly than ever. Below is one soldier's recollection of the fighting.

Analyze a Primary Source

Arthur Guy Empey, American soldier in the British Army during World War I

All along our trench, rifles and machine guns spoke; our shrapnel was bursting over their heads. They went down in heaps, but new ones took the place of the fallen. Nothing could stop that mad rush. The Germans reached our barbed wire, which had previously been demolished by their shells, then it was bomb against bomb, and the devil for all.

Suddenly, my head seemed to burst from a loud crack [noise] in my ear. Then my head began to swim, my throat got dry, and a heavy pressure on the lungs warned me that my helmet was leaking. The trench started to wind like a snake, and sandbags appeared to be floating in the air. The noise was horrible; I sank onto the fire step, needles seemed to be pricking my flesh, then blackness. They told me that I had been out for three hours; they thought I was dead.

The attack had been repulsed [stopped] after a hard fight. Twice the Germans had gained a foothold in our trench, but had been driven out by counter-attacks. The trench was filled with their dead and ours. Through a periscope, I counted eighteen dead Germans in our wire; they were a ghastly sight in their horrible-looking respirators.

I examined my first smoke helmet; a bullet had gone through it on the left side, just grazing my ear. The gas had penetrated through the hole made in the cloth. Out of our crew of six, we lost two killed and two wounded. That night we buried all of the dead, excepting those in No Man's Land. In death there is not much distinction; friend and foe are treated alike.

Source: Arthur Guy Empey, *Over the Top,* 1917.

Read Closely: Comparisons
One way to make a comparison vivid is to use personification, providing human traits to an animal or object.
Circle a word that treats machine guns as if they had human abilities.

Read Closely: Implication
Part of reading is to understand what is implied without being said directly. The author doesn't directly say he was shot in the first three paragraphs, but he does give clues.
Underline the passages that suggest he was shot and injured in battle.

Read Closely: Specific Details
Note how the use of details adds legitimacy to a story. By including the number of enemy soldiers killed and the fact that the Germans wore different respirators, the writer makes the story more concrete and believable.

Read Closely: Characters
Identify how writers make individuals sympathetic characters, ones that readers will like or admire. For example, by explaining that all the dead are buried—even the enemies—the author shows a human side to war that helps readers see soldiers as complex humans.

Events Leading to Global Conflict

European imperialism resulted in conflicts among the colonial powers. This competition was one of many factors that resulted in the Great War, a conflict now called **World War I.** But the end of this war left unresolved issues and lingering resentments. These led to **World War II,** which dwarfed the "Great War."

Immediate Causes of World War I

The specific incident that ignited World War I occurred on June 28, 1914. That day, a Serbian nationalist, **Gavrilo Princip,** assassinated the Austro-Hungarian **Archduke Franz Ferdinand** and his wife, Sophie, in Sarajevo, Bosnia-Herzegovina. Austria-Hungary had annexed the Balkan province of Bosnia and Herzegovina in 1908, effectively taking it from the Ottoman Empire. But Serbia badly wanted the Austro-Hungarians out of the Balkans altogether. Princip was a member of the Black Hand, a secret organization committed to uniting Serbians throughout the Balkans with Serbia proper. From the Austro-Hungarian perspective, the Black Hand was a terrorist group, but it was one with close connections to the Serbian military.

Read Closely: Contrasts
The word "but" can often signify a contrast in two competing points. How does "but" link the relationship between the Austro-Hungarians and the Serbians?

Immediately following the assassinations, the Austro-Hungarian Empire sent an ultimatum to the Serbian government: end all anti-Austrian agitation in the Balkans and allow Austrian officials to investigate the assassinations in Belgrade. The Serbian government rejected the ultimatum. Next, the Austro-Hungarian Empire asked its powerful ally, Germany, to help punish Serbia. Since Serbia was ethnically Slavic, it asked the most powerful Slavic country, Russia, for help. Russia's and Germany's involvement changed a small, regional conflict into a large, global war.

Long-term Causes of World War I

Princip's actions led, in less than two months, to the start of World War I. However, tensions among the powers of Europe had been simmering for decades. These tensions had several causes.

Militarism Defined as "aggressive military preparedness," **militarism** celebrates war and the armed forces. European powers had long been competing for dominance, and one way to prove their strength was to invest in the military. Great Britain and Germany, in particular, poured money into building up their armies and navies. They recruited young men to join their armed forces and bought more ships, guns, and other military hardware. Each nation's militaristic attitude influenced its public to view war as a festive competition rather than a deadly and gravely serious matter.

Read Closely: Details
Writers often start a paragraph with a general idea and then support it with specific details. When the first sentence of a paragraph seems general, look for details in the following sentences. How does the paragraph on militarism show this pattern?

Alliances In their quest for power, European nations also formed secret **alliances**, groups whose members secretly agree to protect one another when attacked. When one member of an alliance was attacked in any way, the other members of the alliance were expected to stand up for that particular member. For example, Germany and Russia were ready to jump into the conflict between Austria-Hungary and Serbia.

Further, countries that had joined these alliances were often sworn enemies of the members of other alliances. When the war started, most of Europe joined one side or the other:

- The Triple Entente started with Britain, France, and Russia, but it later added China, Japan, and the United States. They were sometimes called the Allies during World War I.

- The Triple Alliance included Germany, Austria-Hungary, and Italy before the war. However, when the war began, Italy remained neutral and then in 1915, joined the Allies. The Ottoman Empire joined the Triple Alliance. They were sometimes called the Central Powers.

Read Closely: Analysis
One way to grasp complicated events is to analyze them—break them into smaller or more specific parts that are easier to understand. How did nationalism support militarism in Great Britain and Germany?

Imperialism The alliance system developed because Western European countries were bitter rivals for global power. Each wanted overseas colonies. In the later 19th century, they scrambled for additional lands in Africa, South and Southeast Asia, the Pacific, and the Americas.

Nationalism The assassination of Archduke Ferdinand in June, 1914 reflected the growth of **nationalism**, a pride in one's identity as a member of state that shared cultural traits. Multinational empires such as the Ottoman Empire and the Austro-Hungarian Empire tried to defeat nationalist movements for independence among their ethnically diverse subject peoples.

For example, Serbs had endured centuries of domination by the Ottoman Empire to the south. They were loath to merely exchange that for what they saw as interference from the Austro-Hungarian Empire to the north. Likewise, Arabs in southwest Asia had grown tired of the limitations imposed on them by the Ottoman Turks.

These groups sought **self-determination**—the idea that people of the same ethnicity, language, culture, and political ideas should be united and should have the right to form an independent nation-state. Militant nationalists among Serbs and Arabs fought on the side of the Allies, thus extending the boundaries of the Great War.

Source: The Newberry Library

In 1914, the countries of Europe blamed each other for killing "The Peace of Europe."

The Course of the Great War

During the four years of World War I, it pulled in most large nations of the world. Most battles occurred in Europe, but others took place in Africa, the Middle East, Asia, and on both the Atlantic and Pacific oceans.

The Western Front The bloodiest fighting of the war occurred in France. German armies struck through Belgium and invaded France. Their attempt to capture Paris was stopped at the Marne River in September 1914. From then through 1917, the British and French engaged the Germans in **trench warfare** on a scale that had never before been known. Each side dug ditches from which they fought and in which they lived. Since each side had a strong defensive position, neither side could advance. The markedly improved killing technology, such as machine guns and poison gas, made battles very deadly. The result was a bloody stalemate. (See Lesson 2 for more on technology in the world wars.)

The Eastern Front The Central Powers won major victories in Eastern Europe in 1914. They defeated and occupied Serbia in 1915 and stopped a British attempt to capture the Dardanelles, a narrow, strategically important waterway that connects the Aegean Sea and the Black Sea.

More crucially, they fended off Russian attacks. Anger and discontent among Russians, which were already high before the war, spilled over into revolution. Russians overthrew the czarist regime in 1917. The Communists took power later in the year, promising peace. By early 1918, Russia had signed a separate peace treaty with the Central Powers. Germany became free to fight entirely on the Western Front.

U.S. Entry into the War The United States remained officially neutral when the war began in 1914. Most Americans preferred to let the Europeans settle their own differences. However, the country loaned money and supplies to the Allies, which drew responses from Germany. German submarines sank American ships traveling to Europe. Some were carrying war materials to the Allies, but they resulted in many civilian deaths. These attacks angered Americans, and the United States joined the Allies in 1917.

The U.S. entry provided new supplies and fresh troops to the Allies. The Germany people, seeing that the war was turning against them, rose up against their government. Kaiser Wilhelm, the German leader, resigned and fled. Germany became a republic, and its new leaders asked for peace. The armistice, or agreement to stop the fighting, of November 11, 1918, ended World War I.

Some, such as U.S. President Woodrow Wilson, said that the treaty ending the war would be "peace without victory," a settlement that punished neither side. However, the terms of the actual Treaty of Versailles punished Germany harshly. It had to admit guilt for the war, pay huge monetary reparations, and surrender large parts of its territory.

Read Closely: Effects
Identifying the links between causes and effects of historical events helps highlight the significance of these events. How do the events caused by the Treaty of Versailles show the treaty's significance?

Effects of the Great War

The importance of World War I is sometimes overshadowed by World War II, which was much larger. However, World War I had crucial short- and long-term effects.

Short-term Effects One short-term effect of the war was the creation of the League of Nations. The League of Nations grew out of the belief of U.S. President Woodrow Wilson and others that an international organization of countries might prevent future wars. However, the League was ineffective. Several European countries joined but were not committed to it, and the United States never joined. It ended in 1945.

The unwillingness of the United States to join the League reflected another short-term effect of the war. The United States adopted **isolationism**, a policy of staying out of events in Europe. The United States did not want to get pulled into another deadly European war. The United States followed isolationism until December, 1941 when Japan attacked Pearl Harbor, Hawaii. This involved the United States in World War II.

European societies and landscapes were affected, too, but in a much more profound way. Casualty figures from the war's main European actors were devastating.

Casualties in World War I

Country	Total Forces	Killed/Died	Wounded
Austria-Hungary	7,800,000	1,200,000	3,620,000
British Empire	8,905,000	908,000	2,100,000
France	8,410,000	1,360,000	4,270,000
Germany	11,000,000	1,775,000	4,220,000
Italy	5,615,000	650,000	947,000
Russia	12,000,000	1,700,000	4,950,000
Turkey	2,850,000	325,000	400,000

Source: Adapted from *Encyclopedia Britannica*, https://www.britannica.com/event/World-War-I/Killed-wounded-and-missing

Before the war, Europe had been making technological and economic progress. People were hopeful about the future. However, the slaughter of a generation of men left Europeans bitter and disenchanted.

Long-Term Effects The impact of the Great War was felt strongly over the next few decades:

- Empires collapsed. The Russian, German, and Austro-Hungarian empires all ceased to exist. They were replaced by smaller states.
- New nation-states formed. From these defeated empires, new or reformed countries based on ethnic nationalism sprung from the postwar belief in self-determination, including Finland, Latvia, Lithuania, Estonia, Czechoslovakia, Poland, Hungary, Austria, and Yugoslavia.
- Communism took hold. Although the ideas of Communism had been around for several decades, it became the ruling ideology in a large country (Russia) for the first time in 1917. This subject is covered in more detail in Lesson 4.
- Technology made warfare more deadly. The intensive application of technology to the battlefield made warfare more deadly than in the past. This subject is covered in more detail in Lesson 2.

Causes of World War II

The causes of World War I—militarism, alliances, imperialism, and nationalism—did not disappear with the end of the war. They set the context for three basic causes of World War II.

The Treaty of Versailles The Treaty of Versailles ended the war but poisonously embittered those on the losing side, especially the Germans.

They were required to admit guilt for the war and make massive payments, called reparations, to the Allies for the cost of the war. Germany lost territories to its neighbors and overseas colonies to its rivals.

Italy and Japan, though on the victorious side, felt mistreated by their allies the British and the French. They each wanted more territory as a reward for their participation.

The Rise of Fascism First Italy (under Benito Mussolini, 1922) and then Germany (under Adolf Hitler, 1934) fell under authoritarian governments. They each developed a version of **fascism**, a political doctrine that rejected democracy, praised violence, and emphasized extreme nationalism. Mussolini and Hitler skillfully used propaganda to portray themselves as strong leaders who were the only ones capable of returning their nations to their past glories and could stand up to socialism and communism. Hitler blamed Germany's problems on the country's Jews, thereby encouraging the spread of anti-Semitism. Under pressure from Hitler, Mussolini eventually adopted anti-Semitic policies as well.

Appeasement Hitler wanted Germany to expand to the south and east to become a larger, more powerful country. He argued that Germany had a right to these lands, in part because many German-speaking people lived in some of those areas. In addition, Hitler believed that Germans were biologically superior to the Slavic people living on those lands, so Germany could take them. In 1938, Hitler demanded control over the Sudetenland, a portion of Czechoslovakia where many Germans lived. He vowed to invade if the Czechs did not give up the region peacefully.

Britain and France refused to support the Czechs against the much more powerful Germany. Some leaders accepted Hitler as a strong leader who would prevent the spread of Communism. Others simply recalled the terrible bloodshed of World War I and were determine not to risk another war. Facing no significant opposition, Hitler claimed the Sudetenland. The following year, he seized the rest of Czechoslovakia.

War Breaks Out

After Germany's aggression against Czechoslovakia, Britain and France feared that Hitler would expand until he was stopped. His allies, Italy and Japan, seemed equally aggressive. (Together, the three were known as the Axis Powers.) War was on the way.

Invasion of Poland In August 1939, Germany and the Soviet Union signed a **nonaggression pact**, an agreement not to attack each other. Since the two were fierce ideological foes, the pact surprised people. However, each received a clear benefit. The Soviet leader, Joseph Stalin, gained time to build up his military forces. Hitler insured that he would not have to fight a war on both the east and west fronts, for the present.

On September 1, 1939, German forces poured into Poland using **blitzkrieg**, or "lightning war," tactics based on speed and mobility. Britain, which had signed a mutual assistance treaty with Poland, demanded the attack be called off. Hitler refused. On September 3, Britain and France declared war on Germany. World War II had begun, just 25 years after the start of what was supposed to be the "Great War."

An Enduring Issue: Conflict
After feeling that World War I was a mistake, many Europeans and Americans avoided a war to stop fascism. Countries repeatedly confront the issue of when to engage in conflict.

Germany's blitzkrieg was effective. Using tanks, planes, and artillery, Germany crushed Poland in less than one month.

Moves North and West By June 1940, German forces had overrun Denmark and Norway, Belgium and Holland, and France. Britain stood alone. Germany prepared to invade. The German Air Force began a massive bombing campaign against Britain, which the British Air Force fought off. By June 1941, Britain seemed safe from invasion.

Source: Shutterstock

The "Stand to the Death" memorial honors the Soviets who stopped Hitler's invasion of the Soviet Union at Stalingrad in 1942 and 1943.

The Tide Turns in Europe

Hitler and his allies firmly controlled most of mainland Europe. However, their power soon began to fail.

Invading the Soviet Union In June 1941, Hitler broke the nonaggression pact with Stalin and invaded the Soviet Union. German forces advanced almost to Moscow, but a Soviet counterattack and the harsh winter halted the German offensive.The United States enters the war during the early morning hours of December 7, 1941, when Japanese planes bombed the U.S. naval base at Pearl Harbor in Hawaii. Much of the U.S. Pacific fleet was destroyed or severely damaged. As a result, the United States could not prevent the Japanese from taking over East Asia and key islands in the Pacific. In less than a week, the United States was formally at war with Japan, Germany, and Italy.

Read Closely: Similarities
Identifying similarities in events often suggests underlying factors that caused both. For example, recognizing how World War I and World War II were alike can make understanding the cause of each war easier. What is one important similarity between World War I and World War II?

The Allies Strike Back In 1942, the Allied Powers, as Britain, Russia, the United States,and its allies were known, began to achieve some victories, giving hope to the peoples of occupied Europe. Their first came in North Africa.

The turning point of the conflict in Europe came at **Stalingrad**, a city in the southwestern Soviet Union. Between August 1942 and February 1943, the Russians fended off German attacks, starvation, and bitter cold. However, they held on. The Germans surrendered. Total casualties in this one fight were tremendous, nearly twice the number in the entire American Civil War.

Allied forces invaded Sicily in July 1943. Later that month, Mussolini was forced out of office and imprisoned. He was later shot by anti-Fascists. A new Italian government signed an armistice with the Allies in September.

The greatest seaborne invasion of modern times, Operation Overlord, was launched on June 6, 1944 (D-Day). Allied troops crossed the English Channel and landed in Normandy, France. From there, they steadily advanced, pushing German forces out of France, Belgium, and Holland.

In March 1945, the Allies moved into Germany. As the Russians entered Berlin, Hitler committed suicide. On May 7, the new German leaders surrendered. The next day, the end of the war in Europe, V-E Day (Victory in Europe), was officially declared.

Read Closely: Indirect Results
As you read about historical events, note the direct, immediate, and local consequences of an action and the indirect consequences that occur over many years and a wider region. The bombing of Hiroshima directly killed more than 80,000 people. What was the indirect consequence on international relations over the next two decades?

The Tide Turns in Asia

The pattern in Europe was mirrored in the Pacific. Japan quickly conquered much of East and Southeast Asia and many Pacific Islands. However, by mid-1942, the Japanese were bogged down in China and the United States had won key battles at the Coral Sea, and Midway. For the following three years, U.S. forces drew ever closer to invading Japan. By the summer of 1945, some leaders within the Japanese government had begun to explore options for ending the fighting.

By mid-1945, the United States had developed a powerful new type of weapon: nuclear bombs. The advisers to U.S. President Harry Truman disagreed on whether to deploy these weapons. Truman decided to use them rather than risk the casualties from an invasion of Japan. On August 6, 1945, the United States dropped an atomic bomb on **Hiroshima.** On August 9, a second bomb was dropped, this time on Nagasaki. (For more on nuclear weapons, see Lesson 2) Japan officially surrendered on September 2, 1945, V-J Day (Victory in Japan).

Short-term Effects of World War II

The immediate impact of World War II was devastating. Six years of intense fighting, the use of powerful new weapons, and the willingness of leaders to continue fighting long after defeat was certain resulted in suffering and death.

Population Loss Estimates for the total number of people who died as a result of the war run as high as 80,000,000. The number of deaths includes soldiers and civilians, including those who were targets of the Nazi persecution of Jews (about 5,700,000) and targeted ethnic, political, and other groups. (For more about Axis atrocities committed during World War II, see Lesson 5.) The Soviet Union was particularly hard hit, with military and civilian deaths numbering as many as 20,000,000.

Read Closely: Shifts
The word "although" indicates a shift in direction, such as contradiction or even a surprise, is coming. What is the shift in the description of the Marshall Plan?

Physical Devastation In countries that saw significant ground fighting and aerial bombardment, the damage to buildings was substantial. Large numbers of houses were significantly damaged or destroyed—anywhere from 20 percent in Holland and Belgium, to 30 percent in Great Britain, and up to 40 percent in the cities of Germany. Poland reported 30 percent of all of its buildings destroyed. Numerous cities throughout Japan were destroyed by firebombing, and both Hiroshima and Nagasaki were leveled by atomic bombs.

Marshall Plan The European Recovery Program, also known as the Marshall Plan after the man who proposed it, U.S. Secretary of State, George C. Marshall, helped rebuild Europe. Between April 1948 and December 1951, the United States disbursed about $13 billion in aid to restore Europe's agriculture, industries, and trade. Although the offer was extended to all of the countries of Europe, the nations of Eastern Europe soon left the program. These were countries that fell under the sway of the Soviet Union after the war.

Long-term Effects of World War II

The defining historic event of the 20th century, World War II had many long-term effects. Probably every aspect of life was influenced by the war. Some effects were very general and others very specific.

International Connections One of the war's broadest impacts was to make people around the world aware of how interconnected they were. The impact of war on trade, the mobility of ships and planes, and the danger of deadly fallout from nuclear weapons meant that every part of the world was threatened by a war. In response, countries formed several international organizations, such as the United Nations, to deal with problems on a global level.

Cold War Almost immediately after the end of the war, the United States and the Soviet Union became adversaries. This sometimes aggressive, adversarial relationship—more or less an ongoing, global competition for political and military dominance—was known as the Cold War. It was called "cold" due to its lack of direct warfare between the two sides. (For more on the Cold War, see Chapter 6.)

Partition of Europe Part of the Cold War was the partition of Europe. The states of Eastern Europe that came under Soviet control as the war wound down remained under its direct control until the early 1990s. These nations of the "Eastern Bloc" joined in a Soviet-dominated military treaty called the **Warsaw Pact**. They faced off against the countries of Western Europe. Most of the western countries came together in an alliance with the United States and a few other countries known as the **North Atlantic Treaty Organization**, or **NATO**. Separating the two regions of Europe was the "Iron Curtain," a term to describe the line running from from the Baltic Sea in the north to the Adriatic Sea in the south. The Warsaw Pact went away in the early 1990s with the end of the Soviet Union. NATO still exists today.

Read Closely: Alternatives
When reading history, recognize that people who made decisions did so without knowing the consequences of their decisions. If the leaders who decided to use the atomic bomb had known about the arms race that followed World War II, do you think they would have made the same decision?

Nuclear Threat The atomic weapons caused huge losses of life and physical devastation in Japan Asia, and they threatened the people of Earth from that time forward. As technology advanced, weapons grew ever stronger, and delivery systems grew more robust and accurate.

Within several years of the end of World War II, both the Soviet Union and the United States could deliver several hundred nuclear-armed missiles anywhere in the world at a moment's notice. The threat of total destruction of all human life on the planet shaped war and diplomacy, as well as books, movies, and other forms of popular culture. (For more on the impact of technologies of the world wars, see Lesson 2.)

Israel and Palestine The break-up of Ottoman territory after World War I led to a British "mandate" over the area of **Palestine.** Encouraged by the British, Zionists began to immigrate to this area with hopes of establishing a state where Jews could live safely. This migration brought conflict with the established population of Arab Muslims living there.

After World War II, large numbers of Jews, many of whom were **Holocaust** survivors, fled Europe for Palestine. By 1948, the UN had taken over administrering the territory. It divided Palestine into Jewish and Arab sections. The Jewish section declared itself to be a new country: **Israel.** This led to an immediate war between Israel and the Palestinians. Israel won this war, but the conflict in the region resulted in ongoing tension and violence in the Middle East. (For more on the Israeli-Palestinian conflict, see Chapter 7, Lesson 3.)

Application

Read the excerpts and answer the questions that follow them.

Bruce Bliven Jr., A German Bombing Run, December 25, 1944

When the bombs went off and I realized that I hadn't been hit, I found I couldn't draw a full breath. My chest felt contracted and tight. . . . Another bomber roared overhead, quite low, and I saw the first of a string of flares splash into flame; it was dead ahead of me and it looked close enough to touch. I flopped back on the bottom of the trench and began to shake. The whine started again and I thought, "They are going to get me this time, they are systematically bombing the CP in a pattern of strips and this time I am right in the middle of the strip." I tried to sink my head into my shoulders, turtle fashion, and I closed my eyes. The whine crept down the scale and I shook, not like shivering from cold but slower and bigger. Some of my weight was on my arms and they shook in particular, but the source of the shaking was nowhere and all over; I remember feeling my knees bumping the ground.

Source: Bruce Bliven Jr., "A Soldier's Vivid, Candid Diary of What it was Like to Fight in World War ll," *War Letters Lost and Found* (Smithsonian, National Postal Museum)

George Evans, a British Soldier During World War II

In July 1942 the garrison was overwhelmed, we were taken prisoner and transported to Benghazi. The prison camp there was grim, and I contracted dysentery. On November 16, 1942, we were transported to Italy and were taken to a concentration camp at Porto St. Georgio on the Adriatic coast.

This was somewhat of an improvement as we were given Red Cross parcels containing food, which augmented our meager rations. I suffered frostbite, which resulted in my toes becoming septic, my left big toe being the worst and requiring surgery. I recovered and in May 1943 volunteered for a working camp in Northern Italy. We were transported to the region of Vercelli to work in the rice fields that were situated in the Po Valley. Here living conditions were much improved, for apart from receiving better rations, the people we worked for also gave us food.

We surveyed the situation and decided, when darkness fell, to escape rather than stay in the camp. When all was quiet that night we removed the barbed wire from the gate and our working party, numbering around twelve, went to the farm where we had been working. It was here in a barn we spent our first night of freedom.

Source: George Evans, "A British PoW becomes a Partisan, 1943-1945," bbc.co.uk.

1. Explain how each excerpt helps you understand the experiences of soldiers during World War II.

____

____

2. Compare the context for the experiences of each writer.

____

____

Lesson 2 *Technology in World Wars*

Conceptual Understanding 10.5b Technological developments increased the extent of damage and casualties in both World War I and World War II.

Source: *New York State Grades 9–12 Social Studies Framework.*

World War I was the first conflict in which countries used airplanes as weapons of war. While armies used planes to drop bombs and shoot at opposing troops, they were most valuable for gathering information on the enemy. Between the start and end of the war, countries began to learn how to use air power effectively, as the document below describes.

Analyze a Primary Source

Brigadier General Charles Lee, Chief of the British Aviation Mission, August 18, 1918

Read Closely: Historical Reference
Consider whether historical examples used by writers to support a claim are persuasive. *Circle the example that Lee uses to demonstrate his claim that people have made progress in aviation.*

At first, the standard of proficiency necessary in pilots before they went overseas is what we now consider very low. In fact, in those days, as soon as a man could take off and land and fly around the airdrome without crashing—and had a certain amount of elementary knowledge of the engine and machine—he was given his pilot's certificate.

Read Closely: Use of Data
The author supports his claim by using specific details about flying. To evaluate the strength of this support, a reader would need to know if the facts are accurate.

In those days Bleriot machines were considered fast. Pilots were considered skillful and fearless to fly them. Their speed, however, was only about 60 miles an hour, and their ceiling was about 5,000 to 6,000 feet. Nowadays flying takes place at altitudes from 20,000 feet and upward, and as low as necessary, and machines are capable of a speed of 145 miles per hour, and we have now developed a machine which will go a great deal faster.

Read Closely: Bias
Active readers look for words and phrases that indicate one-sided or biased viewpoints. *Underline a statement that shows the author's bias.*

There have been ups and downs in serial supremacy according to the development of machines. There were times when the Germans had better machines than ours, and we had to fight hard to keep our supremacy which at one time was sorely menaced. Now, however, things are different. We have the machines and we have the men. Our supremacy has been unquestioned for a long time. That is definite.

Read Closely: Rhetorical Question
Note how the writer asks a question to lead readers to a particular conclusion.

How can we destroy and bring to book the powers in Germany which started this war? Undoubtedly we can do it by bringing war into the heart of Germany, but we have got a good long way to go before we can do that on land. What is open to us is the air.

Source: Charles Lee, *Air Service Journal,* volume 3 (August 18, 1918) 263.

Innovations in Warfare

Both World War I and World War II involved many countries and millions of potential combatants. There were bound to be substantial numbers of casualties. But in each war, the introduction of new technologies and new weapons that were improvements on or new uses of existing technologies added greatly to each war's human and environmental devastation.

World War I

During the first few months of World War I, hundreds of thousands of young men enthusiastically enlisted in the military, dreaming of heroism. Wartime assemblies sounded more like high school pep rallies in which speakers naively predicted swift and easy victories in battles against supposedly inferior enemies. At the time, few people actually understood how brutal 20th-century warfare could be. Only over the years of fighting would the horrific effects of new advances in war technology become apparent.

Read Closely: Change
Notice how often the phrase "at the time" indicates a situation that was about to change or has changed. How does that apply to the pre-World War I mentality?

Chemical Weapons The use of **chemical weapons** by both sides remains one of the Great War's more chilling aspects. The first large-scale use of a lethal chemical agent occurred in April 1915. German troops released a massive cloud of chlorine gas that overwhelmed the opposing, and unprepared, French and Algerian troops. Soon, both sides were using poison gas, including phosgene and mustard gas. In response, soldiers were equipped with gas masks, which were effective when used in a timely fashion. In all, about 90,000 were killed by chemical weapons during World War I, and another million were injured, with many veterans suffering permanent damage to their lungs.

Machine Guns Developed in the late 1800s, the **machine gun** completely changed warfare by massively increasing the number of rounds a soldier could fire in a minute. Early machine guns, such as the Gatling gun, were hand-cranked, heavy, and jammed often. But by the time of the Great War, automatic, relatively lightweight, and reliable machine guns were able to fire up to 600 rounds per minute. As soldiers went "over the top" of their trenches and advanced through "no-man's-land" to try to take enemy positions, these machine guns were able to mow the attackers down at an alarming rate.

Submarines Like the machine gun, the submarine developed in the second half of the 19th century. Although Great Britain had a small number of them, it was Germany's more advanced U-boats that became effective weapons and hinted at their crucial role in the navies of the future. German U-boats of the time could carry up to a dozen torpedoes, and they could stay underwater for up to two hours. U-boats terrorized Allied shipping, and their unrestricted use on neutral shipping played a role in bringing the United States into the war. To combat **submarines**, arms makers developed another new technology—the depth charge. These underwater bombs were launched over the side of a surface vessel and were set to explode at a predetermined depth.

Barbed Wire Although it was originally invented as a way to corral livestock, barbed wire quickly showed its usefulness in military applications. As trench warfare settled in, particularly on the western front, both sides used lines and bundles of **barbed wire** to protect their trenches from frontal infantry assaults. But barbed wire was also strategically placed to funnel enemy attackers into kill zones where machine gunners and artillery fire awaited.

Tanks The **tank** developed as a way to securely traverse no-man's-land and break through barbed wire entanglements and other barricades. Early tanks often got stuck in mud and broke down, and they were difficult to steer. More reliable and useful models appeared as the war progressed, but tanks did not play a major role in World War I. However, they became major weapons some 20 years later in World War II.

Airplanes When World War I began, the first successful controlled flight had occurred only 11 years previously. **Airplane** technology developed quickly during the war. Though planes began as instruments of reconnaissance, they quickly became weaponized. Once the technology was developed that synchronized machine gun fire with the rotation of the propeller, allowing pilots to aim accurately, duels between pilots became common, and pilots could strafe soldiers on the ground. By the end of the war, larger "bombers" could carry as much as 2,000 pounds of bombs and could be fitted with up to four machine guns. Other new technologies associated with the development of aerial warfare during World War I include anti-aircraft guns and the first aircraft carrier, the British Navy's *Argus*, completed two months before war's end.

Read Closely: Technology
When reading, look for themes that cover multiple time periods. For example, throughout human history, war has often driven technological progress. How did World War I improvements lead to modern transportation?

Mobile X-ray Machines Most of the war's new technologies brought death and destruction. However, one advance helped save lives. The x-ray machine had been developed in the 1890s. By creating images of the inside of a patient's body, it helped doctors diagnose problems and surgeons work efficiently. But when World War I began, x-ray machines were not mobile and could be found only in city hospitals.

In France, Marie Curie, who had already won Nobel Prizes in physics and chemistry, developed mobile x-ray machines. Special vehicles were built that each carried an x-ray machine, a darkroom to develop the image, and an electrical generator to power the x-ray. To fund the production of her new invention, Curie obtained money from a charity called The United Women of France, as well as from many wealthy Parisian women.

Then, with the help of her daughter Irène, Curie trained a group of women as x-ray technicians and accompanied them to bring the first 20 "radiological cars" to the battlefields of the raging war. Curie's mobile x-ray cars helped doctors treat the wounded at numerous battles, including the crucial Allied victory at the Battle of the Marne in 1914. In addition to her mobile x-ray machines, Curie supervised the building of 200 x-ray rooms in battlefield hospitals. More than one million wounded soldiers benefitted from x-ray exams during World War I.

World War II

In the 20 years between the two world wars, all of the above technologies, except poison gas (which was not used in World War II) and barbed wire, became more deadly:

- Machine guns became more portable (lighter weight), and others were produced that fired larger rounds.
- Submarines could carry more torpedoes and stay under water much longer.
- Tanks could maneuver better, go faster, withstand fire better, and deliver deadlier fire.
- Airplanes could fly much faster and farther and carry more and deadlier bombs.
- Vastly improved aircraft carriers could transport attack aircraft anywhere in the world by sea.

Source: Shutterstock

In World War I, planes such as the Sopworth Pup, were still very new technology.

Source: Bill VanderMolen

By World War II, planes such as the B-29 Superfortress, were larger, faster, and more deadly.

These all contributed to World War II being a broader and deadlier conflict. But many new technologies evolved from the turmoil and urgency of this deadly conflict.

Nuclear Weapons In 1939, a number of prominent scientists in the United States, some of them émigrés from the oppressive dictatorships of Germany and Italy, approached the U.S. government about the possibility of a weapon based on an uncontrolled nuclear fission chain reaction. After the U.S. entry into World War II, work on the project intensified under the code name "Manhattan Project." The project employed hundreds of scientists who tackled the many theoretical and practical obstacles to making an atomic weapon at sites all over the country. But the final steps and construction of a weapon took place at the project's laboratory at Los Alamos, New Mexico.

Read Closely: Transitions Transitions that show the passing of time help you keep information connected. "In 1939" and "After the U.S. entry into World War II" are transitions. Where else do you see transitions in these paragraphs?

The United States dropped atomic bombs on the Japanese cities of Hiroshima and Nagasaki in August 1945. Of the two, Hiroshima, a city of 340,000 people, was harder hit, with 80,000 people killed instantly and more than 100,000 dead within six months. The city's center was completely flattened, and about 70 percent of its buildings were seriously damaged or destroyed.

By 1949, the Soviet Union—an ally of the United States turned enemy—had successfully tested its own atomic bomb. In 1952, the United States successfully tested a nuclear fusion device—a thermonuclear, or hydrogen, bomb. This device had the power of 10,000,000 tons of TNT, whereas the Hiroshima bomb's force was only around that of 20,000 tons. The Soviets had their own thermonuclear device by the following year, and the nuclear arms race that loomed over civilization was under way.

Rockletry Although the Chinese started using simple rockets in the 13th century, rockets as effective weapons were not used until World War II. Both sides developed effective, short-range rocket weapons that burned solid fuel. But the true technological innovation came in the form of the German V-2 rocket. It used liquid, rather than solid, fuel which allowed for more efficient and greater thrust. Its range was 200 miles and it was equipped with more than 1,500 pounds of explosives. Over 1,000 V-2s were fired at London alone in the final nine months of the war, and more than 2,700 people were killed across Britain.

The true impact of these rockets, however, came later. At war's end, captured V-2 rockets (and the surrender of their main inventor, Wernher von Braun, to U.S. forces) helped both the United States and the Soviet Union further develop their own rocket programs. Eventually, this led to intercontinental ballistic missiles (upon which **nuclear weapons** could be delivered) and to the space programs that put satellites in orbit around the earth and men on the moon.

Read Closely: Side-Effects
While reading, pay attention to side-effects. The main effect of military technology is in violent conflicts. However, how did radar initially make things more peaceful?

Radar Radar is an acronym of the term *radio detection and ranging.* **Radar** is a way of detecting distant objects by analysis of radio waves reflected from an object's surface. Using radar, the position, velocity, size, and direction of things such as aircraft, ships, and even weather events can be determined.

Like many other technologies, radar did not fully develop until military necessity spurred research in the run-up to World War II. A British radar system was in place by 1938; it played an important role in helping the Royal Air Force (RAF) deploy its limited resources effectively during the Battle of Britain, in which the RAF beat back the German air onslaught and, most likely, a German invasion. During the war, further research by the British and then Americans led to the development of more effective microwave radar. One of its most effective uses was as a targeting mechanism for antiaircraft guns.

After the war, radar technology improved greatly and found a number of civilian applications, most importantly in civilian air traffic control and weather forecasting.

Computers During World War II, the world's first programmable, electronic, digital **computer,** the Electronic Numeral Integrator and Computer (ENIAC) was developed at the University of Pennsylvania. The university undertook to produce the ENIAC under contract from the U.S. Army, with the computer's specific function to compute artillery range tables. The ENIAC was enormous—an 8' × 80' × 2' monstrosity of cables, flashing lights, and vacuum tubes that occupied a 50' × 30' basement room at the university. This device is effectively the beginning of the computer age, a revolution that has fundamentally changed how modern people work and live.

An Enduring Issue: Technology
Before the modern era, technology changed slowly. Since the 1750s, how to respond to new technology has been an ongoing concern.

Code-Breaking Another computer advance, led by British mathematician Alan Turing, became central to the Allied victory. Turing led a team trying to break the German coding system called Enigma. Enigma used an encryption machine that resembled a typewriter. It scrambled letters in a message, which could then be decoded only by a receiver with the same complex settings.

French and Polish analysts had obtained an Enigma before the war and had been working on breaking its code. Building on their work, Turing's team created a bank of machines able to figure out Enigma's settings and decode German messages. These machines were ancestors of today's computers.

By early 1942, Turing's team was decoding about 39,000 German messages a month. Later, this total would double. The messages, according to U.S. General Dwight D. Eisenhower, "saved thousands of British and American lives and . . . contributed to the speed with which the enemy was . . . forced to surrender."

Application

Read the excerpt and answer the questions that follow it.

Frederick W. Barker, President of the Aeronautical Society of America, June 22, 1917

> The Aeronautical Society of America has no wish to put itself forward in appearing to advise or even in making suggestions to the Government, which, through the Signal Corps and the Aircraft Production Board, is devoting earnest thought and action to the task of creating an air fleet. But the society has a distinct duty to perform in submitting to the Government whatever information it may possess or be able to acquire that may be of service. And the conviction has been growing upon us that all is not right in the aviation field.
>
> By that we do not intend a personal criticism of [Aircraft Production Board Chair Howard Coffin] or of his associates on the board. But the fact remains that after a month's existence the board yesterday in Washington made partial announcement of plans which, to give their sentiment the mildest characterization, have roused in aeronautical engineers the most extreme apprehension.
>
> This announcement told of the board's intention to enlist the services of automobile motor builders…to manufacture small steel parts, and of other similarly detached industries, in the general scheme for effecting rapid quantity production of airplane parts.
>
> **Source:** Frederick W. Barker, President of the Aeronautical Society of America, June 22, 1917.

1. Identify one pair of statements in the author's account that may contradict each other.

____

____

____

2. Explain what duty the author believes he has.

____

____

____

3. Quote one phrase that demonstrates how the author builds suspense.

____

____

____

4. Explain why the author might be bothered by the revelation in the final paragraph.

____

____

____

Lesson 3 *Efforts to Prevent New Wars*

Conceptual Understanding
10.5c The devastation of the world wars and use of total war led people to explore ways to prevent future world wars.

Source: *New York State Grades 9–12 Social Studies Framework.*

After the horrendous results of World War I, some world leaders wanted an organization that might be able to protect peace. They hoped the League of Nations could accomplish that. One of its defenders was an English politician, Anthony Eden.

Analyze a Primary Source

Anthony Eden, Former Foreign Secretary of Great Britain. January 27, 1938

This is the 100th meeting of the League of Nations. This fact is in itself sufficient to show that the League has given its proofs; it has a record of achievements [that] should not be forgotten by those who are more apt to contemplate its failures. Diplomatic successes have little news value, while diplomatic failures have resounding consequences [that] continue for long to be heard and felt.

For the moment we must realize that, in present circumstances, the League is not in a position to achieve all that was hoped of it. It was designed to hold all the nations of the world together in resistance to war and injustice. It was born of the universal desire to avoid a recurrence of the horrors through which the world had just passed. It was an idea hailed by all nations as responding to an urgent and spontaneous impulse.

Believing as we do that that impulse survives, we can hope that it will ultimately prevail and that differences will be narrowed to those of method. For the present, if and for so long as other great nations withhold their collaboration, the field of action by the League is to that extent, in practice, inevitably restricted.

Let us hold fast to our principles, if we believe in them, and devote our whole energies to proving their worth. Let us not be drawn into any sterile and embittering controversy with those who do not think and work with us at this moment. Let us rather hope that an appeasement may be achieved that will unite all nations in the desire once again to find the way of peace through cooperation.

Source: Anthony Eden, Former Foreign Secretary of Great Britain. January 27, 1938

Read Closely: Tone
From the first sentences, a reader might note the defensive tone used by the writer. The author accepts that the League of Nations had failures.
Underline a phrase that suggests he intends to focus on the positive attributes instead.

Read Closely: Parallelism
Parallel structure is a pattern in the writing style that emphasizes similar levels of importance. Using repetition creates a clear rhythm in a passage and suggests that several ideas are related.
Circle the words at the beginnings of three sentences that create parallel structure.

Read Closely: Responsibility
The writer implies that if the League of Nations fails, it will not be the fault of nations that choose to work together. Rather, it will be the fault of the nations that refuse to collaborate. However, he does not say this bluntly. Some readers will appreciate his restraint, while others might prefer more clarity.

Read Closely: Call to Action
Readers of historical documents should be aware of how the meanings of words change over time. In 1938, "appeasement" was not viewed as negatively as it is today.

Post-war Attempts at Peace

In its direct aftermath, the shocking loss of life and destruction wrought by World War I led it to be referred to as "the war to end all wars." Although we now know all too well that this was not the case, at the time, there was an earnest desire to see to it that nothing of this sort should occur again. In fact, after both World War I and World War II, numerous and differing approaches were taken in an attempt to head off any similar future conflicts.

World War I

The large-scale suffering of World War I caught almost everyone—civilians, soldiers, and governments—by surprise. To many, the longer it went on, the more irrational it seemed. The armistice that brought an end to the fighting provided relief, but the settling of accounts and the shaping of the future still lay ahead. Leaders from the victorious countries approached the negotiations for a treaty to end the war differently, and the consequences for these differing approaches were tremendous.

Read Closely: Similarities
To understand an event in its context, consider similar events you know about in history. Based on what you know about the treatment of defeated countries in other wars, what were some of the options for ending World War I?

Wilson's Fourteen Points In fall of 1917, U.S. President Woodrow Wilson had assembled a team of academics and political experts called "The Inquiry" to help him gather and analyze data concerning the history, economy, geography, and ethnology of Europe and other regions involved in World War I. Wilson wanted to prepare himself for what must eventually come—negotiations to remake the world at war's end.

Wilson had announced in January 1917, before the United States entered the war, that he hoped the war would end in "peace without victory." In light of later events, his hopes made him seem able to predict the future: "Victory would mean peace forced upon a loser, a victor's terms imposed upon the vanquished. It would be accepted in humiliation, under duress, at an intolerable sacrifice, and would leave a sting, a resentment, a bitter memory upon which terms of peace would rest, not permanently, but only as upon quicksand."

The work of The Inquiry, as well as the ideas and analysis of Wilson himself (who had a Ph.D. in history and political science), led to what is known as the **Fourteen Points.** Wilson delivered the points as part of an address to Congress on January 8, 1918. Five of the points proposed long-term changes to promote a peaceful future:

- **No more secret treaties** Agreements between states should be agreed upon through open negotiations and openly revealed to all other states.
- **Freedom of the seas** Absolute freedom of navigation should be maintained in international waters, whether in peacetime or in time of war.
- **Free trade** Economic barriers should be removed and fair trade established among all nations.
- **Arms reduction** Nations should reduce their weapons stocks to "the lowest point consistent with domestic safety."
- **Fair adjustment of colonial claims** All colonial issues created by the war should take into account the voice of the people equally with the governments involved.

Most of the rest of the points deal with specific issues involving countries affected by the war:

- allowing Russia to have a government of its own choosing and giving it respect and assistance
- restoring the sovereignty of Belgium
- restoring all French territories—including Alsace and Lorraine, long points of conflict between France and Germany
- readjusting Italy's frontiers along clear lines of nationality
- affording the right of national self-determination to the ethnic nationalities of Austria-Hungary and the Ottoman Empire
- restoring the autonomy of Romania, Serbia, and Montenegro
- creating an independent Polish nation

The final point would eventually lead to the creation of the **League of Nations:** "A general association of nations must be formed under specific covenants for the purpose of affording mutual guarantees of political independence and territorial integrity to great and small states alike." (See below for more on the League of Nations.)

Wilson hoped that the Fourteen Points would be the basis of any future armistice or treaty to end the war, but in this, he was to be largely disappointed.

Read Closely: Context
A word such as "eventually" indicates that a people felt a process took a long time. The definition of "long" depends on the context. Based on the context, explain whether it took days, months, or years for the Allies to insist that they alone should set the terms for the armistice.

Armistice and the Treaty of Versailles In October 1918, the German military finally admitted to itself and the German people that victory was impossible. The country was exhausted. The German chancellor sent a note to President Wilson requesting an armistice and an end to the war based on the Fourteen Points. However, other leaders of the Allies did not share his views. Eventually, the Allies insisted that the armistice's terms must be determined by them alone; as a result, the terms were harsh. But Germany's military situation and general war weariness were such that its civilian leaders felt they had no choice but to sign.

Negotiations for the treaty to officially end the war took place between the leaders of the victorious "Big Four" of France, England, the United States, and Italy. No one from the defeated Central Powers took part; the final Treaty of Versailles was presented to them, and they were compelled to sign. In spite of Wilson's hope for an honorable and reasonable "peace without victory," his European allies, particularly the leaders of Britain and France, wanted to punish Germany. They also thought they could prevent any future wars by making Germany smaller and weaker—essentially removing its capacity for any future aggression.

The final treaty (1919) included a clause wherein Germany admitted it was the aggressor and caused the war—the "war guilt clause." As such, Germany would have to pay the Allied nations for damages. The figure for damages and reparations was set at $33 billion. Germany itself was reduced by 10 percent, it lost all of its overseas colonies, its military was capped at 100,000 men, and the manufacture of heavy weapons was forbidden.

Many Germans harbored deep bitterness in regard to the Treaty of Versailles. In many ways, its terms did not reflect Wilson's Fourteen Points. Germany's economy, territorial integrity, and sovereignty were compromised, and its people felt humiliated. Many, especially in the military, blamed the civilian leaders for accepting it, claiming it was a "stab in the back." This delusion helped the military leadership put the blame elsewhere for their disastrous policies, which had led Germany to the hopeless situation it found itself in at war's end. In simple terms, the Allies' harsh terms, which they hoped would preclude any future European war, had the exact opposite effect.

The League of Nations

U.S. President Woodrow Wilson was extremely disappointed by the final Treaty of Versailles. But he was encouraged that his idea for an international peace organization, the League of Nations, had made it into the treaty.

THE LEAGUE OF NATIONS, 1920

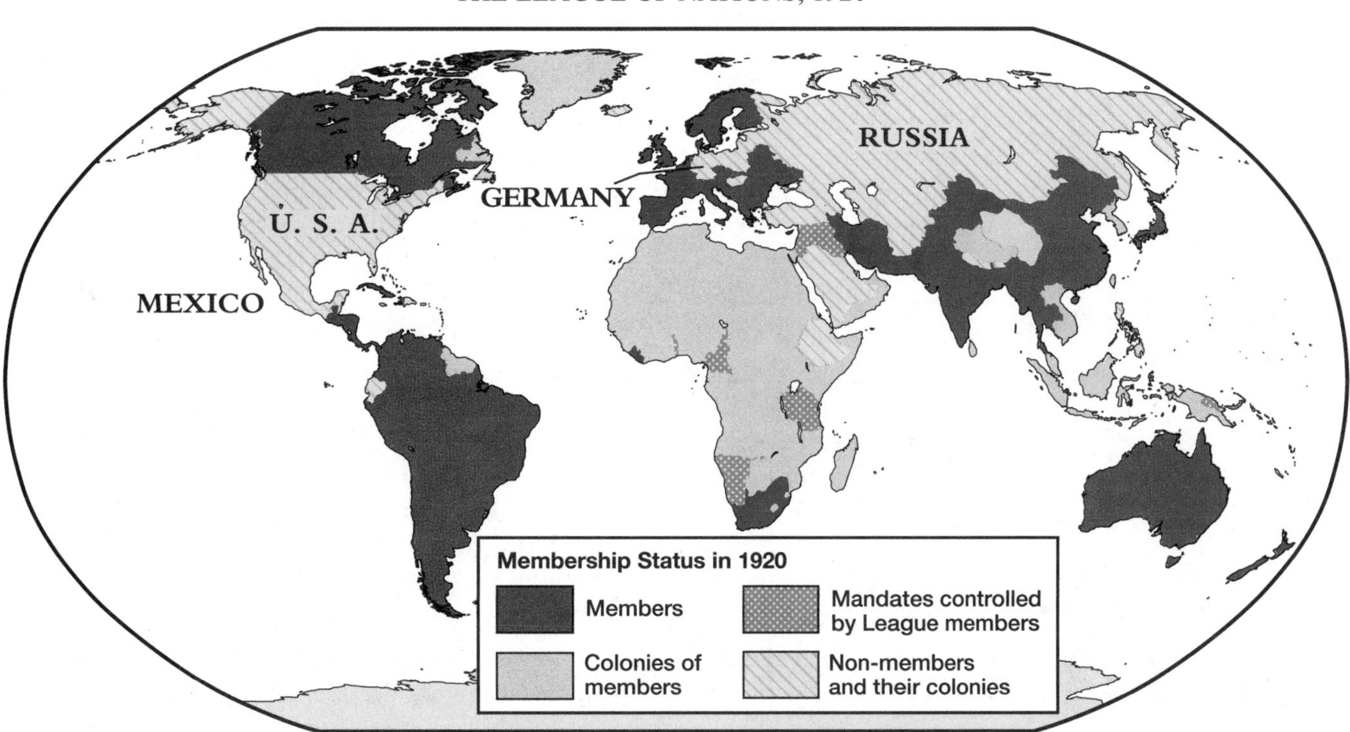

The new League of Nations marked a recognition that all countries in the world were part of a single, global system:

- It established initial members (all Allies and any nations that were neutral in the war and wanted to join).
- It decided that the Big Four and Japan would be on the permanent council.
- It agreed that the headquarters would be in Geneva, Switzerland.
- It mandated arms reductions for all nations.
- It set up a system for collective security, based on the idea that aggression against one member is a matter for all members to confront.

> ***An Enduring Issue: Cooperation***
> The creation of the League of Nations was one of the most ambitious attempts at international cooperation before the 1940s. How and when to cooperate has always been an important issue for states.

Members pledged to solve all disputes between them by peaceful means. Those actors who undertook aggression against other nations were subject to economic sanctions that could be followed by joint military action.

However, the possibility for the League to fulfill its potential to promote world peace and justice was undermined from its beginning. The Republican-dominated U.S. Senate, claiming membership in the League of Nations would compromise U.S. sovereignty, voted not to ratify the Treaty of Versailles. (The U.S. Constitution states that the Senate must ratify all treaties by a two-thirds margin.)

Read Closely: Details
Recognize how even simple details can appear different depending on the context. Explain why someone could argue that World War I ended in 1918 or 1919 or 1921.

The United States agreed a separate peace treaty with Germany and Austria-Hungary in 1921, but it never joined the League of Nations.

While the League reflected the growing interconnectedness of the world, it failed to stop aggression. Japan invaded Manchuria in northern China in 1931, Bolivia and Paraguay fought a war that lasted from 1932 to 1935, Italy invaded Ethiopia in 1935, annexing it in 1936, Italy and Germany directly assisted the "Nationalists" in their rebellion against the rightful Republican government of Spain, Germany annexed Austria in 1938, and so on. And then, of course, World War II began. If anything, the success of the League can be measured in terms of setting an example and a framework for what does and does not work for a future, similar organization—one that would follow World War II.

The United Nations

The successor organization to the League of Nations, the **United Nations** (UN), began as the group of nations allied against the Axis Powers in World War II. Although negotiations were ongoing concerning the organization among Great Britain, the Soviet Union, and the United States throughout the war, an agreement was mostly reached at their meeting at Yalta in February 1945. In San Francisco in June 1945, the UN Charter was adopted.

The General Assembly The United Nations General Assembly is where all the member nations have equal representation and where a number of the general duties of the organization are fulfilled. One of these duties is choosing nonpermanent members of the Security Council, one of the important arms of the organization when it comes to preserving international peace. It has five permanent members: China, France, Russia (until 1991, the Soviet Union), the United Kingdom, and the United States. The number of nonpermanent members began at six. As overall membership in the UN grew, this increased to 10.

The Security Council It is within the Security Council that serious issues that could lead to war have been addressed. But the fact that each permanent member has the power to veto any resolution of the council rendered the Security Council quite ineffective during the Cold War. The generally opposing opinions and aims of the Soviet Union and the United States mostly saw to that.

Read Closely: Examples
When you read a sentence or paragraph or paragraph that begins "For example," keep in mind the larger point the writer is making. In the example about the Soviet Union and Hungary, what is the larger point?

For example, in 1956 when the Soviet Union invaded Hungary, it vetoed a Security Council resolution that opposed the aggression. In 1983, the United States vetoed a resolution that called on it to end its invasion of the Caribbean island nation of Grenada. Other vetoes were used by permanent members to aid countries they supported and/or who had taken their side in the Cold War.

Since the end of the Cold War, the Security Council veto has been used much less frequently, but it has been used most frequently by the United States. Most of these uses have been in favor of Israel, halting motions concerned with war or human rights issues.

Peacekeeping The Security Council also operates peacekeeping missions. Peacekeepers are military or policing units drawn from around the world and sent to areas of conflict. Many have helped prevent violence, but others have been notable failures. In the former Yugoslavia in 1995, the number of UN peacekeepers was too low to guard civilian "safe areas." Further, they failed to treat local Bosnian-Serb paramilitary as the primary aggressor. The result was that Bosnian-Serb fighters seized and masacred more than 7,000 Bosniak Muslim men and boys at Srebrenica. To this day, the UN uses the lessons learned from this disaster to try to improve its peacekeeping missions.

Application

Use the photo to answer the questions that follow it.

United Nations Peacekeepers

Source: Monusco Photos

1. Identify the purpose of troops such as those portrayed in the photo.

____

____

2. Explain whether the photo indicates the troops are prepared for their work.

____

____

3. Evaluate the success that United Nations troops, as seen in the photo, have had in their missions.

____

____

Lesson 4 *Ideology Between the World Wars*

Conceptual Understanding
10.5d Nationalism and ideology played a significant role in shaping the period between the world wars.

Source: *New York State Grades 9–12 Social Studies Framework.*

The 1930s were one of the worst economic periods in Europe, the United States, and much of the world since the start of the Industrial Revolution. Photographers captured the protests and poverty of the era.

Analyze a Primary Source

Read Closely: Sympathetic Characters
The most emotionally charged images from the Great Depression include children. *Circle parts of the photos that might create sympathy from a viewer.*

Read Closely: Context
For readers to appreciate photos from the Great Depression, they need to understand the difficulties faced by migrant farmworkers. They lived in tents, trailers, and other temporary housing, and they relied on farmwork such as picking vegetables or fruits for survival. One poor growing season could devastate a family.

Read Closely: Class Separation
One child is holding a sign that mentions Rarig. He was an engineer who owned a company and continued to make money during the Great Depression. The children in the photo are those of unemployed workers. Class distinctions grew wider during the Great Depression as the poor became more poorer.

Read Closely: Use of Questioning
By framing their concerns as questions, the children force all who see their signs to consider their role in the possible answer.

Source: Getty Images

The 1920s and 1930s

Revolution in Russia

At first, World War I seemed to unify Russia. Russians of all social classes and political leanings drew together to defend their country. But this unity was short-lived. Defeats in battle, the loss of millions of men at the front, and food shortages made the Russian people desperate. They demanded an end to Russia's participation in the war. When the Russian leader, Czar Nicholas II, ignored these demands, his people rebelled.

Read Closely: Alternatives
When you see the word "seemed," you should assume that something is not as it appears. How does that apply to post-World War I Russia?

Revolution and the Bolsheviks In March 1917, the Russian Revolution began. Czar Nicholas II was driven from his throne, and a provisional government of moderate leaders took charge. Soon, however, their pledges of democracy and reform were not enough: they, like the czar, refused to take Russia out of the war. The hunger, misery, and massive military casualties continued. Finally, in November 1917, a second revolution, led by **Vladimir I. Lenin**, occurred. He promised the Russian people what they wanted—peace, bread, and land.

Lenin's party, the **Bolsheviks** (later called the Communists), took over the government. One of the new government's first acts was to stop fighting in World War I. Russia agreed to the Treaty of Brest-Litovsk with the Central Powers. This action cost the Russians dearly, as they resulted in the loss of the **Ukraine** and other territories that were home to one-third of Russia's population and agriculture and one-half of its industry.

Lenin's Political and Economic Policy Under Lenin's regime, workers and peasants could elect representatives to a lawmaking body, but this congress was controlled by Lenin and the Communist Party. Atheism (the belief that God does not exist) became official government policy, as did the elimination of class distinctions. (Russians were encouraged to address each other as "comrade.") The Communist Party was the only political party allowed to exist. In order to prevent criticism of Communism, the government censored newspapers and other forms of communication.

The effort to rapidly change Russia's traditional economy into a Communist one was difficult. Lenin did not change his ideals, but he did agree to slow down the transition. In 1921, Lenin instituted the New Economic Policy (NEP). The NEP made some compromises with Communist doctrine. For example, peasants were allowed to sell surplus grain for profit, and some small manufacturers were allowed to resume control over their businesses. Under the NEP, the Russian economy improved. In 1922, Russia changed its name to the **Union of Soviet Socialist Republics** (USSR), the **Soviet Union**.

Read Closely: Leaders
Pay attention to major changes in leadership. New rulers often signify a significant change in the way people think or behave. New rulers can also impose new military or social policies that have wide-ranging implications. How is this true with Vladimir Lenin and Joseph Stalin?

Joseph Stalin's Totalitarian State

By the time of his death in 1924, Lenin had already set the USSR on a path toward an authoritarian government. The next leader, **Joseph Stalin**, remained in control until he died in 1953. Stalin abolished the NEP and replaced it with a highly centralized command economy.

A Command Economy A command economy is one in which the state makes all basic economic decisions. For example, the state determines what and how much is to be produced, and it sets prices for everything that the economy produces. Stalin believed that Communism would result in more equality and prosperity for Soviet citizens. In addition, he wanted the Soviet Union to avoid being destroyed economically by the more industrialized nations. He put forth two Five-Year Plans for socializing and industrializing the USSR:

- *First Five-Year Plan* In 1929 plan called for the total industrial output to increase by 250 percent in just over five years. Soviet laborers were compelled to work long hours for very low wages in factories and mines and on construction sites. After only three years, Stalin declared the plan a success. In reality, the economy had not grown as fast as Stalin hoped it would.
- *Second Five-Year Plan* Taking effect in 1933, this plan encouraged heavy industry, such as steel production. By 1938, the Soviet Union was among the major industrial powers of the world, a dramatic improvement from where it had been when the Communists seized power just two decades earlier. The only two countries that outranked it in industrial production were Germany and the United States.

Read Closely: Cause and Effect
Words such as "as a result" and "consequently" signal the effect of an action or policy. What was the cause of the famine between 1932 and 1933?

Stalin also ordered collectivization of farms, in which peasants' land was taken from them and incorporated into large government-owned farms. Many peasants resisted collectivization, sabotaging farm produce, and among those who went to work on collective farms, many worked half-heartedly.

Consequently, grain production did not increase, causing a famine. Between 1932 and 1933, millions died of starvation and diseases related to malnutrition. In the end, however, the government succeeded in collectivizing agriculture because it had stripped the peasants of their political power.

Stalinist Repression Stalin kept an iron grip on the country by means of terror. His secret police tracked down dissidents, and people were encouraged to inform on coworkers, friends, and even family members. Stalin also instituted periodic purges, accusing officials throughout the government of disloyalty and even treason. To be accused at any level was as good as a conviction, and the condemned were either killed, imprisoned, or exiled to labor camps (gulags) in Siberia. The worst of these persecutions occurred in the mid-1930s; in the great purges of the era, millions were arrested, imprisoned, and killed.

Read Closely: Comparison
As you move from reading about the USSR to Germany, consider how conditions in each nation may help explain the rise of authoritarianism.

The Rise of Nazism in Germany

Germany's defeat in 1918 brought an end to the kaiser's monarchical rule. But modern Germans had never known anything but authoritarian rule. How would they respond to pluralistic governance in a time of crisis?

The Weimar Republic The democratically elected **Weimar Republic** governed after the war. Under the terms of the Treaty of Versailles, the new German government not only had to pay billions in war reparations, it was also not allowed to have an army. The numbers of unemployed workers swelled due to the weak German economy. Such an environment fostered anger and alienation. Many Germans perceived their democratic government as utterly incapable of solving the country's problems, so they looked to right-wing political parties that promised strong action.

Authoritarianism Returns The National Socialist German Workers' Party, or the **Nazis**, came to power legally after the party did well in the 1932 parliamentary elections. In early 1933, the aging and infirm president of Germany, Paul von Hindenburg, invited Adolf Hitler to form a government as chancellor, which he did. Hindenburg died in 1934, giving Hitler the opening he needed to declare himself president.

Through intimidation and manipulation, the Nazi Party instilled fear and panic in the German people, making them believe that they were in a state of emergency. For example, the Nazis secretly set fire to the Reichstag, the German parliament building, and then blamed it on Communists and socialists. Hitler used this as a pretext to crack down on these groups, who opposed him. Using the need for domestic security as justification, Hitler later outlawed all other political parties and all forms of resistance to his rule.

Like the emperors of earlier times, Hitler expected his subjects to follow his direction without question. Various factors enabled Hitler to persuade many Germans to accept his leadership:

- **The Economy** Hitler's regime reduced unemployment through public works and rearmament programs. Aside from providing jobs, these programs made powerful German industrialists wealthy, which helped to garner their support.
- **Propaganda** A powerful orator, Hitler held audiences at huge rallies spellbound as he ranted against the enemies of Germany—primarily Jews and Communists whom he blamed for the country's ills. The Nazis took complete control of all forms of media through which they constantly trumpeted their worldview. People listened to it because it fit their bias about why Germany had lost World War I.
- **National Pride** The Nazi party's propaganda was designed to wipe away the shame Germans felt after World War I. It told Germans they were superior to all other peoples—a "master race." If this was so, it only made sense that all other races existed to serve them.
- **Youth and Education** The Nazis strictly controlled the curriculum of all schools. Young people were compelled to join groups such as the Hitler Youth, which further indoctrinated them in Nazi ideology. Parents who objected were threatened with the loss of their children.

Read Closely: Analysis
To understand complex topics, historians break them into separate topics, or factors. What factors help explain why so many Germans accepted Hitler's leadership?

Nazi Anti-Semitism and Terror

Hitler promoted **scientific racism**—a pseudo-scientific movement that claimed that certain races were genetically superior to others. He also advanced an extreme form of **anti-Semitism**, or hostility toward Jews. He filled his speeches with accusations against German Jews, who Hitler claimed were responsible for the nation's domestic problems. Nazi propaganda emphasized the need for a "pure" German nation of "Aryans," purged of "outsiders"—not only Jews, but Slavs, Communists, Romani, and gay men and women. He declared that these groups must be removed from German society.

To this end, the Nuremberg Laws of 1935 stripped Jews of their German citizenship and finalized their social and professional isolation. Hitler's propaganda and the Nuremberg Laws successfully created an atmosphere of hostility, hatred, and distrust in Germany. In November 1938, *Kristallnacht*, the "Night of the Broken Glass," saw supposedly spontaneous anti-Jewish riots. But, in fact, the attacks were entirely orchestrated by the Nazis.

Read Closely: Us vs. Them
Authoritarian regimes typically target certain groups as the source of national problems, unifying many by dividing them from others. Who were among the "others" in Nazi Germany?

The riots resulted in the deaths of more than 90 German Jews and the destruction of nearly every synagogue in Germany. About 7,000 Jewish shops were also wrecked, and some 30,000 Jews were dragged from their homes and sent to concentration camps. These horrifying crimes turned out to be only the beginning of Adolf Hitler's deadly campaign against Jews and other Nazi scapegoats in Germany and beyond.

Conflicting Beliefs of Communists and Fascists

Issue	Communists	Fascists
Capitalism	Opposed: argued that it exploited workers	Opposed: argued that worker-management conflicts undermined national unity
Internationalism	Supported: believed in international worker solidarity and opposed colonialism	Opposed: emphasized strong nationalism and defended colonialism
Peace	Supported: hoped people would live in peace after a revolution	Opposed: argued that war was noble and was important for developing strong men
Equality	Supported: emphasized political and economic equality for all people	Opposed: believed that inequalities based on gender and ethnicity were natural

Militarism and Nationalism in Japan

Read Closely: Comparisons
Comparing countries operating at the same time can help you understand the time period more clearly. How were Japan and Germany similar at the beginning of the 20th century?

After its military and commercial successes in the early 1900s, many in Japan (and beyond) began to see the country as the natural, dominant power in East Asia. It was on the winning side in World War I and received some of Germany's Asian colonial holdings—Tsingtao on the Chinese coast facing Korea and Pacific islands in Micronesia—as a result. Japanese nationalists wanted to increase the nation's power and influence, but Japan has few natural resources. To run its industries, it wanted raw materials from other countries. In the 1920s and 1930s, the industrial and military leaders of Japan developed a long-range plan to acquire the resources the country needed. The plan called for conquering East Asia. Control of China was the most important aim of Japan's plan.

Attacking China Then, in September 1931, the Japanese seized Manchuria, a region of northeast China. Renamed Manchukuo, it declared its independence from China in 1932. However, Japan actually controlled the government. Japan had direct access to the rich natural resources of their new colony.

Next, in 1937, Japan opened a full-scale attack on China. Japanese forces quickly overran much of the northern part of the country. They captured the capital, Nanking (now Nanjing), committing horrible atrocities on the citizens of that city. But General **Jiang Jieshi,** head of the Chinese government, refused to surrender. He moved the Nationalist government into western China and set up a new capital. The Japanese then realized that the war in China would be a long one. It lasted from 1937 to 1945, until Japan was defeated in World War II.

Reaction of the West The League of Nations condemned Japan's aggression in China. The United States, the Soviet Union, and other nations also protested Japan's actions and gave aid to China. Because no one was willing to use military force against Japan, the Japanese continued their conquests in China. In 1940, they moved into northern Indochina (now Vietnam). In mid-1941, as the Japanese pushed farther south in Indochina, the United States instituted an oil embargo against Japan. Relations between the two countries worsened. The United States demanded that Japan fully withdraw from both China and Indochina on November 26. That day, a Japanese fleet set sail into the Pacific. On December 7, it would launch a surprise attack on the U.S. Naval Base at Pearl Harbor, Hawaii.

Read Closely: Chronology
List three transitions in the section "Militarism and Nationalism in Japan," that help organize the text abou the worsening relations between Japan and the West.

Roots of the Great Depression

During the 1930s, the largest economic collapse of modern times hit the industrialized countries. It reshaped politics and economics for the entire world.

Instability The Great Depression was unusually severe, but smaller depressions were frequent before the 1930s. Modern, industrial capitalism had never been stable. Prices, wages, and prosperity continually went up and down. Several reasons contributed to this constant variation.

- Inventions kept changing the market. For example, the development of the automobile created millions of new jobs in manufacturing and sales. It also put many people who made and sold buggies and carts out of business.
- Manufacturers hoped to increase profits by increasing production and sales. When they produced more than they could sell, they would slash production, which meant firing workers. Without income, the unemployed then had to cut back on their purchases.
- Workers had little bargaining power with employers to win higher wages. As a result, wages were low. The people of the country had too little money to purchase everything they could produce. Again, businesses would build up their inventories, and then either layoff workers or go out of business.

Read Closely: Cause and Effect
Identify an example of the cycle of causes and effects that made industrial capitalism unstable.

Problems in the United States In the United States, a booming stock market throughout the 1920s disguised many important economic problems. Vital industries, such as agriculture, were in trouble. Farmers were receiving such low prices for their crops that many could not pay the mortgages on their farms. Banks that relied on mortgage payments for their income failed.

Another weakness was the growing trend to buy goods on credit. When people failed to make timely payments, stores suffered.

Then, in October 1929, prices on the New York stock market started to fall a little. Many investors had bought stocks "on margin." This meant that they borrowed money to buy stocks. When stock prices fell, investors feared they would not be able to repay their loans. They were eager to sell before prices declined any more. Fear increased that prices would continue to fall. Within days, many people wanted to sell stocks and very few wanted to buy. Stock prices spiraled downward. Within weeks, people with large fortunes, or just small savings for their retirement, were wiped out financially.

Worldwide Depression

The depression in the United States affected economies all over the world. American investors who had lent money to businesses in Europe began to demand payment. This drew capital from countries that had not yet recovered from the expenses of World War I. Manufacturers everywhere tried frantically to sell their products in order to raise money to repay loans. Few people were able to buy these goods, and world prices collapsed. With the loss of markets, production fell and thus so too did employment.

Loss of Jobs and Hope Millions of people all over the world lost their jobs in the **Great Depression.** For example, in 1932, unemployment in Great Britain was about 17 percent of the workforce. In 1933 in the United States, it was almost 25 percent. Germany was the hardest hit of all. In causing unemployment, the Great Depression caused many social problems as well. Unable to earn money, people felt worthless as well as hopeless. Angry and fearful, the German people began to seek answers from Fascist leaders who gave them convenient scapegoats and aggressive solutions.

An Enduring Issue: The Environment
The agricultural crisis of the 1930s was severe in part because farming practices contributed to soil erosion. This is one of many examples of the impact of humans on the environment.

Read Closely: Solutions
When a passage does not fully address the solution to a major problem, you should note whether it is discussed later. What major event ultimately ended the Great Depression in the United States?

Reaction in the United States Different governments tried different ways to end the depression. President Franklin Roosevelt of the United States introduced a program called the New Deal. One part of it was putting people back to work through government-funded public works projects—the construction of highways, bridges, and public buildings. By giving jobs to desperate people, the New Deal undercut the appeal of more radical solutions in the United States.

European Solutions British leaders did not make major changes in their government's economic policies. They balanced the country's budget and provided subsistence welfare for the unemployed. After 1932, the economy began to recover by itself.

French leaders were never able to solve the social and political problems cause by the depression. Conflicts broke out among various political factions. Fascist organizations rioted and spread propaganda. Socialists, Radicals, and Communists joined together in the Popular Front Party. Léon Blum, the leader of the Popular Front, was elected to office in 1936. When his party tried to pass programs similar to the ones Roosevelt had successfully passed in the United States, conservatives and Fascists threatened a revolution. Blum resigned in June 1937. Divided and impoverished at this time, France also had to face the renewed threat of German aggression.

Application

Use the photo of Joseph Stalin to answer the questions that follow.

Source: Getty Images

1. Describe the mid-20th century context in which this photo of Joseph Stalin was taken.

2. Explain if this image of Stalin is consistent with how he is remembered as ruler of the Soviet Union.

Lesson 5 *Atrocities from 1914 to 1945*

Conceptual Understanding
10.5e Human atrocities and mass murders occurred in this time period.

Source: *New York State Grades 9–12 Social Studies Framework.*

The deaths of hundreds of thousands of Armenians living in Turkey during World War I was one of many terrible atrocities that occurred between the start of World War I and the end of World War II. Since then, they have continued, despite international efforts to prevent them.

Analyze a Primary Source

Shogher Tonoyan, "The Turkish Attack on the Armenian village of Vardenis, 1915"

They came to our village and robbed everything. They took away our sheep, oxen and properties. Those who were good-looking were taken away.

My aunt's young son, who was staying with me, was also taken away, together with all the males in the town. They gathered the young and the elderly in the stables of the Avzut Village, set fire and burned them alive. Those cattle sheds were as large as those of our collective farms. They shut people in the stables, they piled up stacks of hay round them, poured kerosene and set them on fire. Sixty members of our great family were burned in those stables. I do not wish my enemy to see the days I have seen! Only I and my brother were saved.

From the beginning, they took away the young pretty brides and girls to Turkify them, and also they pulled away the male infants from their mothers' arms to make them policemen in the future. The stable was filled with smoke and fire; people started to cough and to choke. Mothers forgot about their children.

It was a real Sodom and Gomorrah. People ran, on fire, to and fro, struck against the walls, trod upon the infants and children who had fallen on the ground. I wish I and my little brother had been burned down in that stable and had not seen how sixty souls were burned alive.

Source: Shogher Tonoyan, Armenian village of Vardenis, 1915

Read Closely: Details
Specific details can be used to show suffering and destruction. *Underline three examples of specific details that the writer lists to show the destruction caused by the Ottomans.*

Read Closely: Emotive Language
The author's descriptive details about the fires, as well as her statements that she wished she would have died instead of been a witness, elicit a strong emotional response.

Read Closely: Inferences
Based on the author's information about both the young pretty girls and the male infants and young men, readers can figure out why the author and her brother were spared death.

Read Closely: References
Readers might sometimes need to look up references used by writers.
Circle a reference to an outside source that the writer assumes the readers will understand.

Ethnic and Religious Violence

During the tumultuous three decades covered in this chapter, several governments committed acts of mass murder against ethnic or religious minorities. The Holocaust is the best-known of these, but it followed events against the Armenians and Ukrainians. Since the end of World War II, many people have vowed never to let large-scale atrocities occur again, but the world community has not found a way to prevent them.

Atrocity Against the Armenians

For centuries, the Ottoman Empire was a sprawling empire. It was centered in Turkey, but it spread through northern Africa, southeastern Europe, and southwestern Asia. The population of the empire was very diverse religously and ethnically. For much of its history, the Ottomans had some laws that discriminated against people based on religion. However, the empire rarely persecuted people for their faith. During the religious wars in Europe, both Protestants and Catholics fled to the Ottoman Empire for its relatively tolerant practices.

In the region northeast of Turkey most people belonged to the ethnic group of **Armenians.** As Christians, the Armenians did not enjoy equality with the Muslim Turks, but the two groups generally lived in harmony.

However, in the late 19th and early 20th centuries, conflict increased. Fearful of the growing nationalism of the Young Turk movement and distrustful of Christian minorities, the Ottoman sultan ordered persecutions. Hundreds of thousands of Armenians were killed between 1894 and 1897.

The victory of the Young Turks in 1908 ended the oppressive rule of the sultans in Turkey. Many Armenians had supported the Young Turks in the hope that political reform and modernization would improve their lives. However, the new government was strongly nationalist. It regarded the Armenians as an obstacle to Turkish unity and expansion.

Read Closely: Chronology When reading, look for passages that can keep you oriented in time. Noting the date, year, or even century, can help you fit events you are reading about with ones you have already learned. This will help you get context for what you read. When did the conflict between the Turks and Armenians increase?

Deaths During World War I The outbreak of World War I unleashed even greater suffering for the Armenians. The Turks who led the Ottoman government feared that the Armenians were not loyal. This fear lead to several policies that resulted in the deaths of Armenians:

- Hundreds of leaders of the Armenian community were summoned to Istanbul, the Turkish capital, and murdered or deported.
- Far more Armenians were drafted into the Turkish Army. Many were forced to do hard labor, and died from the work.
- Many Armenian women, children, and the elderly died while being forcibly marched from their homes into the deserts of Syria and Iraq.

When World War I began, more than 2 million Armenians lived in the Ottoman Empire. By the end of the war, more than 1 million had died. Others, with the help of Turks, Arabs, or foreign missionaries, had fled to someplace outside of Turkish-controlled territory.

World War I ended in 1918. However, in 1923, Turkey became a republic under the presidency of **Mustafa Kemal,** and another wave of persecutions took place. By 2016, only between 10,000 and 30,000 Armenians lived under Turkish rule.

Disagreement over Genocide Much of the world considers the Turkish treatment of the Armenians as genocide. The Turkish government rejects that description, arguing that the Turks never wished to kill all Armenians. It says that the loss of life among the Armenians was the result of famine, disease, and the turmoil of war.

Source: Shutterstock

Around the world, people of Armenian heritage hold events to keep alive the memory of what happened to their ancestors during World War I.

The Ukrainian Holodomor

Soviet leader Joseph Stalin instituted his first Five-Year Plan in 1928. This sweeping economic and social plan greatly accelerated the country's industrial production. It also sought to move peasants from their private plots of land onto collective, factory-like farms run by the government. Peasants everywhere resisted this move to some extent, but maybe nowhere like in Ukraine, the Soviet republic to the west of Russia.

Read Closely: Order
To help you understand cause and effect, pay attention to words that call attention to the order of events. These can include "it began," "later," "eventually," or "finally," although there are many others. What is an example of a word with this function in the paragraph that begins "Stalin's plan."

A History of Conflict Ukraine had long been known as the "breadbasket of Europe" for its prodigious production, chiefly of wheat. The region had a long history of struggle against Russian domination, and its farmers were successful and fiercely independent.

Stalin's plan to collectivize the farms of Ukraine at any cost had disastrous consequences. It began with a campaign against "kulaks," or rich farmers, who were targeted with high taxes and grain confiscations to begin with. Later, many were deported to far-off regions in the freezing east with no compensation and few resources. As collectivization continued and intensified, the Ukraine's peasants fought back by destroying produce and farm equipment and starting small-scale revolts. Stalin responded with brutality and more deportations. He intended to crush the independent spirit of Ukrainian nationalism.

Famine These conflicts set the stage for the massive famine of 1932–1933. The yield from the harvest of 1932 was less than expected, but it was large enough to feed the region's people. However, the government confiscated the majority of it to send to cities or to export. The money gained was used to fuel burgeoning Soviet industries. In addition, special government squads charged with collecting farm produce went as far as searching individual homes and removing any food they could find. Ukrainians would receive no assistance from the Soviet authorities.

By the spring and summer of 1933, the famine had reached devastating proportions, with mass starvation hitting people in Ukrainian cities and in the countryside. By one estimate, as many as 30,000 people a day were dying of starvation or malnutrition-related diseases by June 1933. When the famine finally broke after the harvest of 1933, its toll was clear: between 4 million and 5 million dead and large parts of the Ukraine depopulated.

Source: Thinkstock

Memorials in Ukraine recall the famine of 1933.

A Opportunity for Stalin Stalin took this opportunity to settle ethnic Russians and people from other Soviet regions in Ukraine. This resettlement was another step in the process of trying to break Ukrainian resistance to Soviet control. This atrocity against the Ukrainians is known as the **Holodomor**.

The Holocaust

The early World War II victories of the German Army allowed Hitler to establish a "New Order" in Europe. He planned to colonize Eastern Europe with Germans. Hitler believed that members of the German "master race" deserved to be given farms, factories, and businesses. The original owners—Czechs, Poles, Russians, and others whom the Nazis considered inferior—were to work as slave laborers to produce food and goods for Germany.

Millions of Europeans of all nationalities and cultural groups met such a fate. Most were transported to factories inside the dreaded concentration camps. Besides Jews and Slavs (Russians, Czechs, Poles, and so on), Hitler wanted to eliminate the Romani people (then known as Gypsies), gay and lesbian individuals, Communists, and people with disabilities.

Attacks on Jews in Germany Hitler had especially marked the Jews of Europe for destruction. As you have read, the Nuremburg Laws of 1935 took away the citizenship of German Jews. On *Kristallnacht*, or the "Night of the Broken Glass," (November 9–10, 1938), Nazis killed and beat Jewish people throughout Germany and Austria. Their homes, shops, and places of worship were smashed and looted, and tens of thousands were dragged off to concentration camps.

Jews Attempt to Save Themselves Many Jews then fled to other parts of Europe to escape the misery of life in the Third Reich. Some also went to Britain

An Enduring Issue: Migration
Jewish intellectuals who fled Germany under Hitler contributed greatly to the culture of the United States and other countries. Migrations caused by terrible events can have wide-ranging impact.

> **Read Closely: Imagination**
> When you are reading, try to put yourself in the mindset of important figures or peoples. If you were a refugee fleeing Germany under the Nazis, how would you decide where to go?

and North and South America. Many more would have left but could not find anywhere to go. Most countries, including the United States, limited the number of Jews they would take in. Families did try to send children to safe places, with varying degrees of success.

As the Nazis overran Europe, the Jews who had moved to other European countries once again found themselves at Hitler's mercy. The Nazis referred to the continuing presence of Jewish people in Europe as "the Jewish problem." In 1942, Nazi leaders officially decided to murder all of the Jews of Europe. At the Wannsee Conference in January of that year, they worked out their plans for carrying out this "final solution."

Death Camps In every country they conquered, the Nazis rounded up Jews and sent them to death camps. In Poland and the Soviet Union in particular, special killing squads rounded up and murdered more than a million people in mass shootings of Jews, Communist officials, religious leaders, and anyone else who opposed the Nazi presence. People resisted, most notably the Jews in Warsaw, but the Nazi power was too great. One of the largest and most infamous death camps was Auschwitz in Poland. In this place alone, some 3 million Jews were murdered. In all, the Nazis killed at least 6 million Jews and an equal number of Poles, Russians, Romani, homosexuals, disabled people, and others.

Three Atrocities in the 20th Century

	Ottoman Empire, particularly Armenia	The Ukraine region in the Soviet Union	Lands controlled by the Nazis, particularly Poland
Perpetrators	Government of the Young Turks	Joseph Stalin's Soviet regime	Adolf Hitler's Nazi regime
Reasons	Distrust of an ethnic minority that was mostly Christian during World War I	Collectivization of farms and desire to dominate Ukraine	Hitler's racism, anti-Semitism, and desire to expand German lands
Methods	Deportations, hard labor, forced marches, murders	Artificially produced famine and resulting mass starvation	Mobile killing squads, death camps
Death Tolls	More than 1 million	4 to 5 million	Around 12 million, half of whom were Jews

Application

Read the excerpt and answer the questions that follow it.

Galina Gubenko, "The Ukrainian famine, 1933"

At that time I lived in the village of Yaressky of the Poltava region. More than half of the village population perished as a result of the famine. It was terrifying to walk through the village: swollen people moaning and dying. The bodies of the dead were buried together, because there was no one to dig the graves.

There were no dogs and no cats. People died at work; it was of no concern whether your body was swollen, whether you could work, whether you have eaten, whether you could—you had to go and work. Otherwise, you are the enemy of the people.

Many people never lived to see the crops of 1933 and those crops were considerable. A more severe famine and other sufferings were awaiting ahead. Rye was starting to become ripe. Those who were still able made their way to the fields. This road, however, was covered with dead bodies. Some could not reach the fields, some ate grain and died right away. The patrol was hunting them down, collecting everything, beating the people, coming into their homes, seizing everything. What they could not take, they burned.

Source: Galina Gubenko, Poltava region of Ukraine, 1933

1. Quote one passage where emotional language is used, and explain the type of response it might generate.

____

____

2. Quote one passage that describes the suffering of villagers.

____

____

3. Explain the importance of agriculture to the author's community.

____

____

4. Explain how this description qualifies what happened in Ukraine as a genocide.

____

____

Chapter 5 *Review*

Multiple-Choice Questions

Directions (1–6): For each statement or question, choose the number of the word or expression that, of those given, best completes the statement or answers the question.

Base your answers to questions 1 and 2 on the passage below and your knowledge of social studies.

> And what do [the League of Nations countries] unite for? They enter into a solemn promise to one another that they will never use their power against one another for aggression; that they never will impair the territorial integrity of a neighbor; that they never will interfere with the political independence of a neighbor; that they will abide by the principle that great populations are entitled to determine their own destiny and that they will not interfere with that destiny; and that no matter what differences arise amongst them they will never resort to war without first having done one or other of two things - either submitted the matter of controversy to arbitration, in which case they agree to abide by the result without question, or submitted it to the consideration of the council of the League of Nations, laying before that council all the documents, all the facts, agreeing that the council can publish the documents and the facts to the whole world, agreeing that there shall be six months allowed for the mature consideration of those facts by the council, and agreeing that at the expiration of the six months, even if they are not then ready to accept the advice of the council with regard to the settlement of the dispute, they will still not go to war for another three months.
>
> **Source:** www.firstworldwar.com Woodrow Wilson's Address in Favor of the League of Nations, September 25, 1919

1. Which principle is best demonstrated in Wilson's speech?

   (1) the importance of national self-determination
   (2) the concept of a balance of power
   (3) the policy of realpolitik
   (4) the goal of supporting democracy

2. World War II provides evidence to support which conclusion about the League of Nations?

   (1) The League successfully promoted cooperation among nations.
   (2) The League demonstrated that sanctions against countries never work.
   (3) The League was damaged by the decision of the United States to join.
   (4) The League was too weak to enforce its provisions.

Base your answers to questions 3 and 4 on the cartoon below and on your knowledge of social studies.

Source: CartoonStock.com

3. The cartoonist criticized the United Nations because it:
   (1) acted too slowly to solve problems.
   (2) spent more time debating issues than for solving disagreements.
   (3) allowed dictators too much power.
   (4) suffered from the problem of tyranny of the majority.

4. One goal of both the League of Nations and the United Nations was to:
   (1) establish peaceful cooperation between nations.
   (2) create democratic societies to replace dictatorships.
   (3) abolish trade barriers between nations.
   (4) destroy Communism.

Tips for Answering Multiple-Choice Questions

In a question that includes "both," the best answer must address both parts of the question. Often, incorrect responses will address only one. Reading all possible answers before selecting one as correct will prevent you from choosing a response that is only half-correct.

Base your answers to questions 5 and 6 on the passage below and your knowledge of social studies.

Adolf Hitler on Genocide, August 22, 1939

> Accordingly, I have placed my death-head formations in readiness – for the present only in the East - with orders to send to death mercilessly and without compassion, men and women of Polish derivation. Only then shall we gain the living space which we need. Who, after all, speaks today of the annihilation of the Armenians.
>
> **Source:** Danny S. Parker, *Hitler's Warrior: The Life and Wars of SS Colonel Jochen Peiper* (Philadelphia: Da Capo Press, 2014), 35.

5. Adolf Hitler made the statement above because he wanted to:

   (1) show similarities between the Poles and the Armenians.

   (2) express sympathy for the genocide of the Armenians.

   (3) explain why he was confident in attacking Poland.

   (4) demonstrate support for German nationalism.

6. Which event best represents the continuation of the process described in the quotation from Adolf Hitler?

   (1) the establishment of Auschwitz

   (2) the aerial bombing of Berlin

   (3) the dropping of the atomic bomb on Hiroshima

   (4) the attack on Pearl Harbor

Tips for Answering Multiple-Choice Questions

Historical questions often have many reasonable answers. For example, one event usually has many causes, many effects, many ways it is like other events, and many generalizations that it supports. However, a question should have one "best" answer. As a result, reading all the possible choices before picking one is important.

Short-Answer Questions

CRQ Directions (7-9): Analyze the documents and answer the short-answer questions that follow each document in the space provided.

Base your answer to question 7 on Document 1 below and on your knowledge of social studies.

Document 1

British Soldier T. Harold Watts, June 18th, 1915, describes the conditions that soldiers are forced to endure during the first year of World War I.

> We live in a trench and it is a mercy it doesn't rain or we'd be washed away. The fighting lately has been terrible. Our shells knock the enemy all ways and the sight in the trenches is awful. We wear our respirators because of the awful smell of the dead. I'll never get the sight out of my eyes; it will be an everlasting nightmare. If I am spared to come home, I'll be able to tell you all about it, but I cannot possibly write as words fail me. I can't describe things.
>
> **Source:** http://www.nationalarchives.gov.uk/education/resources/letters-first-world-war-1915/dardanelles-everlasting-nightmare/

7. Explain how the context of life in 1915 affected the reaction of soldiers to the war.

____

____

____

____

____

____

Tips for Answering Multiple-Choice Questions

In a question that includes "both," the best answer must address both parts of the question. Often, incorrect responses will address only one. Reading all possible answers before selecting one as correct will prevent you from choosing a response that is only half-correct.

Base your answer to question 8 on Document 2 below and on your knowledge of social studies

Document 2

An account of being the subject of a German bombing run by American journalist Bruce Bliven Jr., December 25, 1944

> When the bombs went off and I realized that I hadn't been hit, I found I couldn't draw a full breath. My chest felt contracted and tight. I was cold and vaguely dissatisfied with my slit-trench.
>
> Another bomber roared overhead, quite low, and I saw the first of a string of flares splash into flame; it was dead ahead of me and it looked close enough to touch. I flopped back on the bottom of the trench and began to shake. The whine started again and I thought, "They are going to get me this time, they are systematically bombing the CP in a pattern of strips and this time I am right in the middle of the strip." I tried to sink my head into my shoulders, turtle fashion, and I closed my eyes. The whine crept down the scale and I shook, not like shivering from cold but slower and bigger. Some of my weight was on my arms and they shook in particular, but the source of the shaking was nowhere and all over; I remember feeling my knees bumping the ground.
>
> **Source:** Bruce Bliven Jr., "A Soldier's Vivid, Candid Diary of What it was Like to Fight in World War II," *War Letters Lost and Found* (Smithsonian, National Postal Museum)

8. Based on this excerpt, describe the audience Bliven was writing for.

____

____

____

____

____

Base your answer to question 9 on both Documents 1 and 2 and on your knowledge of social studies.

Similarity—tells how something is alike or the same as something else.

Difference—tells how something is not alike or not the same as something else.

9. a) Identify a similarity or a difference in the ideas about war expressed by Watts and Bliven.
   b) Explain the similarity or difference you identified using evidence from both documents.

Speaking and Listening: Reflect on the Key Idea

Working with a partner or a small group, make a list of ways that World War I and World War II caused changes in politics, including in country boundaries.

CHAPTER 6

The Cold War

Chapter Overview

The United States and the Soviet Union fought together against fascism in World War II. However, even before that war ended, they were also foes. The ideological conflict between them, known as the Cold War, shaped every aspect of life, from warfare to education to novels in the second half of the 20th century.

The Beginnings of the Cold War As World War II ended, the United States wanted to create capitalist countries that would ally with it. The Soviets wanted countries to adopt its communist ideology and ally with them. Most of Western Europe joined the United States in a military alliance called the North Atlantic Treaty Organization. Countries in Eastern Europe joined with the Soviets to form their own alliance, the **Warsaw Pact**.

Confrontations in the Cold War The Cold War shaped events in many countries. A Cuban revolution established an alliance with the Soviets, Vietnam experienced a civil war that resulted in a Communist regime, and Afghanistan struggled with both superpowers to maintain autonomy. Some countries, such as Egypt and India, avoided taking sides in the Cold War.

By the late 1960s, both the United States and the Soviet Union wanted relief from the high costs of military programs and the fear of nuclear war. Tensions relaxed briefly, a period known as détente. The two countries did sign some significant arms control treaties, but by 1980, tensions were rising again.

The End of the Cold War In the 1980s, Soviet leaders tried to save the communist government by reforming the country's weak economy and repressive political system. Aiding the reform movements was the willingness of the United States to again sign arms control measures. The results were dramatic and unexpected. The Soviet Union lost control of Eastern Europe and broke apart. The Cold War ended. The U.S.-Soviet rivalry no longer dominated world affairs.

An Enduring Issue: Conflict One enduring issue in this chapter is the long-running rivalry between the United States and the Soviet Union. The causes, impact, and results of this conflict confronted Americans, Soviets, and people around the world.

New York Social Studies Framework: **Key Idea 10.6**

The second half of the 20th century was shaped by the Cold War, a legacy of World War II. The United States and the Soviet Union emerged as global superpowers engaged in ideological, political, economic, and military competition.

Source: *New York State Grades 9–12 Social Studies Framework.*

1. Rewrite Key Idea 10.6 in your own words.

____

____

Identify Enduring Issues

To prepare to write the enduring issues essay, practice identifying issues that reappear throughout history. In the chart below, the left column lists some enduring issues. The middle column lists examples of those issues from Chapters 1 and 2. Fill in the third column with examples from Chapters 3, 4, and 5, as well as this chapter as you study it. Use the bottom row to add an additional issue.

Enduring Issues	Examples from Chapters 1 and 2	Examples from Chapters 3, 4, 5, and 6
Efforts by countries to build alliances or to avoid conflicts with other countries	Japan under the Tokugawa Shogunate	1.
The importance of new technology in a country's power	The Industrial Revolution	2.
The role of outside powers in shaping internal affairs of other countries	Revolutions in the Americas in the 1700s and 1800s	3.
Ideas about how to organize an economy	Adam Smith and the Wealth of Nations	4.
5.	6.	7.

Key Terms by Theme

Geography

Iron Curtain (p. 178)
Berlin Airlift (p. 179)
Berlin Blockade (p. 179)

Governance

Big Three (p. 177)
Potsdam Conference (p. 177)
Tehran Conference (p. 177)
Yalta Conference (p. 177)
Cold War (p. 178)
Marshall Plan (p. 179)
satellite countries (p. 179)
Truman Doctrine (p. 179)
NATO (p. 180)
Warsaw Pact (p. 180)
arms race (p. 183)
containment (p. 185)
nonaligned movement (p. 185)
Bay of Pigs (p. 186)
domino theory (p. 186)
Fidel Castro (p. 186)
Vietnam (p. 186)
Afghanistan (p. 187)
Tet Offensive (p. 187)
Mikhail Gorbachev (p. 191)

Civic Ideals

détente (p. 188)
glasnost (p. 191)
Solidarity (p. 193)

Economics

perestroika (p. 191)

Technology

intercontinental ballistic missiles (p. 183)
military-industrial complex (p. 184)

Lesson 1 The American-Soviet Conflict

Conceptual Understanding
10.6a The Cold War originated from tensions near the end of World War II as plans for peace were made and implemented. The Cold War was characterized by competition for power and ideological differences between the United States and the Soviet Union.

Source: *New York State Grades 9–12 Social Studies Framework.*

As the Allies began to see that World War II would be ending, their leaders began to meet to plan for the post-war world. Without the clear shared goal of defeating Germany and Japan, conflicting interests among Allies led to sharp disagreements. In particular, the United States and Soviet Union clashed repeatedly. Some of these clashes appeared at a meeting of Allied leaders at Potsdam, Germany.

Analyze a Primary Source

Statement of Allied Leaders at Potsdam, July 1945

Throughout the Conference, besides the daily meetings of the heads of governments and the Foreign Secretaries, separate meetings of the three Foreign Secretaries, and their advisers have also been held daily.

These meetings have proved of the utmost value and the Conference agreed that permanent machinery should be set up for regular consultation between the three Foreign Secretaries. They will, therefore, meet as often as may be necessary, probably about every three or four months. These meetings will be held in rotation in the three capitals, the first meeting being held in London, after the United Nations Conference on World Organization.

Our meeting here in the Crimea has reaffirmed our common determination to maintain and strengthen in the peace to come that unity of purpose and of action which has made victory possible and certain for the United Nations in this war. We believe that this is a sacred obligation which our Governments owe to our peoples and to all the peoples of the world.

Only with the continuing and growing cooperation and understanding among our three countries and among all the peace-loving Nations can the highest aspiration of humanity be realized—a secure and lasting peace which will, in the words of the Atlantic Charter, "afford assurance that all the men in all the lands may live out their lives in freedom from fear and want."

Victory in this war and establishment of the proposed international organization will provide the greatest opportunity in all history to create in the years to come the essential conditions of such a peace.

Source: Winston S. Churchill, Prime Minister of Great Britain; Franklin D. Roosevelt, President of the United States of America; and Marshal J. V. Stalin, Chairman of the Council of Peoples' Commissars of the Union of Soviet Socialist Republics. Potsdam Conference. July 1945.

Read Closely: Language
One way to understand the formal language of diplomatic documents is to reword it, phrase by phrase.
Underline the sentence that could be reworded as "Our gathering has proven our intention to create a peaceful existence after our World War II victory."

Read Closely: Key Point
This excerpt appears near the end of a lengthy document. This is a good place for authors to state their main point: a secure and lasting peace.

Read Closely: Allusion
The words in quotation marks refer to a famous speech by Roosevelt in which he identified four basic freedoms: freedom of speech, freedom of worship, freedom from want, and freedom from fear.

Read Closely: Context
When this document was written, tensions were increasing between the Soviet Union and Western countries. *Circle the phrase that suggests they wanted to look forward with hope.*

Allies Become Opponents

As World War II ended, Allies disagreed on the shape of the post-war world. These differences resulted in decades of conflict.

The Big Three

The most powerful Allied nations in World War II—Great Britain, the United States, and the Soviet Union—were known as the **Big Three**. Beginning in 1943, they met in a series of conferences to discuss strategy for winning the war and for shaping the world after the war ended.

Tehran The first of these meetings took place in Tehran, Iran's capital. During the **Tehran Conference** in November 1943, the Allies were generally in agreement. The Soviet Union would focus on freeing Eastern Europe from German control, while Britain and the United States would concentrate on Western Europe. Britain and the United States agreed to a Soviet demand to shift some Polish territory to the Soviet Union, to be made up by Poland gaining territory elsewhere, mostly from Germany.

An Enduring Issue: Cooperation
To defeat the Nazis, the United States produced immense quantities of guns, tanks, and planes, while the Soviets contributed many millions of lives. Their cooperation is one example of the influence of cooperation among states.

Yalta The second meeting took place in February 1945 at Yalta, on the Crimean Peninsula in Ukraine. At the **Yalta Conference**, the Soviet leader Joseph Stalin revealed his distrust of his allies. He recalled that the British had rejected an anti-Nazi alliance in the 1930s and had refused to help Russia by invading France early in the war. He felt that the other Allies failed to respect the level of Russian sacrifices in the war. Together, Great Britain and the United States lost fewer than 1 million lives, while Russia lost more than 20 million.

Stalin wanted influence over the countries of Eastern Europe so that the region would serve as a buffer between the USSR and Western Europe. U.S. President Franklin Roosevelt wanted these countries to rule themselves through free, democratic elections. In the end, Stalin agreed, accepting the "earliest possible establishment through free elections of governments responsive to the will of the people."

Roosevelt also wanted Soviet support in the war against Japan. Stalin asked for numerous concessions in return for his commitment to fight Japan:

- possession of Japanese territory in the southern Sakhalin and Kuril Islands
- control of two Chinese ports
- an ownership interest in a Manchurian railroad

Read Closely: Predictions
When you are reading, look for patterns in events that help you predict what will happen next. In the case of the first two "Big Three" conferences, Stalin's relationship with Great Britain and the United States became increasingly strained. If the pattern continues, what will happen at the third conference?

Roosevelt hoped that agreeing to Stalin's demands would lead to self-determination for Eastern Europe, the ability of the people of this region to choose their own government. The conference ended with only vague assurances of this.

One important agreement was that the world needed a new international organization to solve future disputes peacefully. This organization became known as the United Nations.

Potsdam In July and August 1945 at the **Potsdam Conference**, which took place in a suburb of Berlin, the Big Three met for the final time. Harry Truman, who had become U.S. president after Roosevelt died in April 1945, represented the United States. Churchill started the conference but lost his position as prime minister midway through and was replaced by Clement Attlee. The leaders agreed to occupy Germany by dividing it into four occupation zones administered by France, Great Britain, the Soviet Union, and the United States. Austria and the cities of Berlin and Vienna were also similarly divided.

> **Read Closely: Shifts**
> Paying attention to words that indicate a change is coming, such as "however," will help you see how events are shifting. What do you think the significance is of this paragraph beginning with "however"?

However, the agreement reached at Yalta concerning the status of the Eastern European countries occupied by Soviet forces did not stand up. When pressed by Truman on the subject of free elections in Poland, Romania, Hungary, and Bulgaria, Stalin adamantly refused. The two countries lacked trust in one another and began the aggressive rhetoric that would develop into the **Cold War**.

Developments Through 1949

The Big Three conferences produced plans for how the peace should be administrated in Europe. However, events on the ground between 1945 and 1949 challenged these plans.

Soviet Occupation of Eastern Europe In a speech delivered in Fulton, Missouri, in March 1946, Winston Churchill famously assessed the worsening situation of the countries of Eastern Europe. He declared that "an iron curtain has descended across the continent" of Europe. The metaphor of the **Iron Curtain** described the split between Eastern and Western Europe. The Soviets were determined to make the governments of Eastern Europe as much like the Soviet government as they could. Therefore the Soviets directed East Germany, Poland, Hungary, Romania, and Bulgaria to develop five-year economic plans focused on developing industry and collective agriculture at the expense of consumer products. In addition, they outlawed all political parties other than the Communists.

Source: Shutterstock

This patrol tower on the border of the Czech Republic is a reminder of the Iron Curtain that separated Europe in the Cold War.

These actions allowed the USSR to exploit the Eastern European countries to benefit the Soviet Union, rather than helping them to grow and prosper. These **satellite countries**—small states that are militarily, politically, and economically dominated by a larger, more powerful state—were forced to import only Soviet goods and to export only to the Soviet Union. Moreover, the governments of these countries were just as totalitarian as the government of the USSR.

> **Read Closely: Bias**
> Understanding a person's bias for their actions is crucial to understanding history. What do you think Winston Churchill's bias was when he described the split in Europe as an Iron Curtain?

The Marshall Plan After World War II, the United States was deeply concerned about rebuilding Europe. At a time when the U.S. government budget was about $30 billion per year, the United States spent about $12 billion in the years following the war to provide relief and to rebuild infrastructure.

However, many U.S. leaders thought that was not enough. Fearing that economic instability could lead to communist revolutions, the U.S. launched a larger plan to rebuild Europe into a prosperous and stable region. The **Marshall Plan**, enacted in June 1947, offered $13 billion more in aid to all countries of Europe, including Germany. This money would be used to modernize industrial and agricultural operations, stabilize finances, and promote free trade. However, the Soviet Union and its satellites refused to participate in the plan.

The Marshall Plan was a success. In the countries that participated, economic output in the countries was 35 percent higher in 1951 than it had been in 1938.

The Truman Doctrine Although Americans and Soviets disapproved of each other's actions, neither wanted a direct military confrontation. Americans wanted their soldiers, who had fought so long overseas, to come back home. Because the Soviet Union did not yet have an atomic bomb, many Americans felt that Soviet expansion was not a serious threat to their own freedom and safety.

However, the conflict between the Soviet Union and the United States worsened. Tensions increased in three regions:

- In Greece, efforts by Soviet-backed communist guerrillas who wanted to overthrow the Greek government led to a civil war.
- In Turkey, the Soviet Union was pressuring the country to give up land to give up control of the Dardanelles, the passageway between the Mediterranean Sea and the Black Sea, to the Soviets.
- In Iran, the Soviets were demanding territory.

> **Read Closely: Issues**
> You can more clearly understand the context for events if you pay attention to major themes while you are reading. Powerful leaders often set up plans or strategies they want carried out in the coming years. What issues do the Truman Doctrine and the Marshall Plan share?

In March 1947, President Truman responded to the USSR's actions with military and economic aid to Greece, Iran, and Turkey. The idea behind this aid came to be called the **Truman Doctrine**. The doctrine stated that the United States would "support free peoples" who resist being taken over by outside forces. Greece, Iran, and Turkey did not become Communist.

Berlin Blockade In 1948, the Soviets again tested the will of the Western Allies to contain the spread of communism. The city of Berlin was located within the Soviet-controlled region of East Germany. However, the city was so important that control of it was divided among the Soviets, the United States, Great Britain, and France. The Soviet sector was called East Berlin, and the other three were known as West Berlin.

In 1948, the Soviets tried to take over the entire city of Berlin. They shut down all highways and railroad lines into West Berlin. The city was blockaded. It could not receive supplies by land. Rather than try to break the blockade by sending in troops and possibly starting a war, the United States and its allies decided to build new airstrips and airlift supplies to Berlin.

Although the blockade caused West Berliners much suffering, the **Berlin Airlift** kept them from starving. Planes landed at a rate of one a minute. They brought in more than 7,000 tons of food, fuel, machinery, and other goods every day. After 11 months, the Soviets ended the blockade and once again opened up land routes across East Germany and into West Berlin. The Berlin Airlift demonstrated Allied determination to oppose Soviet moves. It had been a dazzling technological achievement—one that ended up costing a staggering $224 million and one that Soviet experts had told their leaders could not be done.

Source: Library of Congress

In 1948 and 1949, a massive airlift of food and other supplies to the two million civilians in Berlin eventually broke the Soviet blockade.

Read Closely: Benchmarks
As you read, note benchmarks that set long-term patterns. Alliances and agreements are often examples of this. Which alliances set the course of the Cold War for decades?

NATO In April 1949, ten countries of Western Europe, Canada, and the United States formed a new military alliance, the **North Atlantic Treaty Organization (NATO).** Membership would more than double. Members agreed to the principle of collective defense. It meant that an attack against one member was an attack against all of them. This phrase warned the Soviets that if they attacked a NATO member, they would be at war with the United States. However, the first use of collective defense came after the September 11, 2001, terrorist attacks on the United States. European countries sent troops to fight alongside the United States military in the war in Afghanistan.

The Warsaw Pact and Berlin Wall In response to NATO, the Soviet Union and its satellites, known as the Eastern Bloc, formed their own alliance, the **Warsaw Pact**, in 1955. In 1961, the Communists further divided Europe by building a wall separating east and west Berlin. The Berlin Wall symbolized the global divide. The two superpowers and their allies faced off for influence in the rest of the world for three more decades, until 1991.

Application

Read the excerpt and answer the questions that follow it.

Soviet View of NATO, 1949

The statements contained in the North Atlantic treaty that it is designated for defense and that it recognizes the principles of the United Nations organization serve aims which have nothing in common, either with the tasks of self-defense of the parties to the treaty or with real recognition of the aims and principles of the United Nations organization.

Of the great powers, only the Soviet Union is excluded from among the parties to this treaty, which can be explained only by the fact that this treaty is directed against the Soviet Union. The fact that the North Atlantic treaty is directed against the U.S.S.R. as well as against the countries of peoples' democracy was definitely pointed out also by the official representatives of the United States of America, Great Britain and France.

The North Atlantic pact is designed to daunt [scare] the states which do not agree to obey the dictate [orders] of the Anglo-American grouping of powers that lay claim to world domination, though the untenability [impossibility] of such claims was once again affirmed by the second World War which ended in the debacle [defeat] of Fascist Germany, which also had laid claim to world domination.

Conclusion: The North Atlantic treaty runs counter to agreements between the Soviet Union, the United States of America and Great Britain concluded at the Yalta and Potsdam conferences as well as at other conferences of representatives of these powers held both during and after the second World War under which the United States of America and Great Britain, like the Soviet Union, assumed the obligation to cooperate in consolidation of general peace and international security and to the consolidation of the United Nations organization.

Source: *Soviet Monitor*, April 1949.

1. Quote one passage that identifies the point of view of the writer.

____

____

2. Explain the author's purpose in comparing the United Nations to Nazi Germany.

____

____

3. Identify two possible audiences for this piece. Explain the type of response the author would hope to receive from each of them.

____

____

4. Summarize the author's conclusion in your own words.

____

____

Lesson 2 *Confrontation and Coexistence*

Conceptual Understanding
10.6b The Cold War was a period of confrontations and attempts at peaceful coexistence.

Source: *New York State Grades 9–12 Social Studies Framework.*

Many countries believed it was in their self-interest not to be too closely aligned with either the United States or the Soviet Union. By keeping their distance, these nonaligned countries could appeal to each of the leading combatants in the Cold War for diplomatic and economic aid. One meeting of nonaligned countries occurred in Belgrade. In 1961, Belgrade was part of Yugoslavia. Today, it is the capital of Serbia.

Analyze a Primary Source

M.S. Handler, Changing Views of Communists on Nonalignment, *New York Times*. August 28, 1961

Read Closely: News Story
Journalists structure stories in the shape of a reverse pyramid: the most important information comes in the first sentence, and increasingly less significant information follows in each subsequent paragraph.

Read Closely: Audience
When reading historical documents, you might need outside help to understand topics that were very familiar to the original audience. *Underline a reference used by Handler without explanation, but that might not be familiar to readers today.*

Read Closely: Sources
To protect a source, journalists sometimes use phrases such as "it is said" or "reports suggest" without saying who said or reported something. *Circle an example where the writer does not make clear who is doing the action.*

The Soviet Union, Communist China and East European Communist regimes have begun to display interest in the coming Belgrade conference of heads of uncommitted nations. The conference, which begins Friday in the Yugoslav capital, has been ignored until now by the Communist press.

The unannounced arrival in Belgrade of a contingent of seven Chinese Communist correspondents was the first indication of Communist interest in what the representatives of the twenty-four uncommitted governments at the meeting will have to say on the Berlin crisis, reorganization of the United Nations Secretariat, colonialism and disarmament.

The conference's press secretariat received word also that the Soviet Union was planning to send four of its leading correspondents to cover the meeting. It was indicated today that the Hungarians, the Poles and probably other East European regimes would also send newsmen.

Moscow and Peiping are believed to be perturbed at seeing their ideological rival, President Tito of Yugoslavia, succeed in bringing together leaders of nonaligned countries. The participants will include Prime Minister Jawaharlal Nehru of India, President Sukarno of Indonesia, President Kwame Nkrumah of Ghana and other leaders noted for their stand of nonalignment with either the Communist or the Western bloc.

Source: M.S. Handler "Reds Shift View on Belgrade Talk," *New York Times*. August 28, 1961.

Superpower Rivalry

In the Cold War, the United States and the Soviet Union both feared the results of a direct confrontation between them. It could quickly escalate to a full-scale nuclear war that could destroy all civilization. However, the two superpowers often fought indirectly. They supported opposing sides in conflicts around the world in which millions of people died. The United States and the Soviet Union coexisted, but at a very high cost.

Read Closely: Summary
Writers often summarize a section or paragraph in the final line to emphasize a point or wrap up a series of facts. In "The Arms Race", what point does the final sentence make?

Nuclear Arms and Proliferation

The development of nuclear weapons had serious effects on global politics. They gave tremendous power to the United States and the Soviet Union.

The Arms Race The Soviet Union tested its own atomic bomb in August 1949. This marked the beginning of the nuclear **arms race** between the USSR and the United States. Each country developed much more powerful and deadly thermonuclear weapons (also called hydrogen bombs) by 1952. By the end of 1959, each had also developed **intercontinental ballistic missiles**—rockets that could precisely deliver nuclear warheads to any part of the other's territory. Over time, both superpowers developed systems to launch missiles from submarines or from planes (so-called cruise missiles). There seemed to be no limit to the lethal ingenuity employed by the scientists and military personnel on both sides.

Source: CartoonStock.com

Nuclear weapons threatened to kill more people more quickly than any weapons ever had.

The Military-Industrial Complex Even by 1961, one serious consequence of this continuing, escalating arms race was the development of what the U.S. President (and former five-star general) Dwight Eisenhower called the "military-industrial complex." In a capitalist country such as the United States, the arms race fostered close ties between private companies that manufactured weapons and their counterparts in the military and government. Eisenhower and many who followed him saw that this relationship could be a serious threat both to world peace and to democracy itself. In his farewell speech after eight years as U.S. president, he said:

"In the councils of government, we must guard against the acquisition of unwarranted influence, whether sought or unsought, by the **military-industrial complex**. The potential for the disastrous rise of misplaced power exists, and will persist. . . . Until the latest of our world conflicts, the United States had no armaments industry. American makers of ploughshares could, with time and as required, make swords as well. But we can no longer risk emergency improvisation of national defense; we have been compelled to create a permanent armaments industry of vast proportions."

Eisenhower feared that the enormous profit motive of war to these private industries could drive foreign policy decision-making. He also worried that peaceful, everyday needs—schools, hospitals, roads, and so on—would suffer as government poured money into the military-industrial complex.

Nuclear Proliferation Other countries also wanted to develop nuclear weapons, either for defense against nuclear-armed foes or simply to remain relevant powers on the world stage. Below is a list of countries that developed or obtained nuclear weapons:

- United Kingdom (atomic bomb, 1952; thermonuclear device, 1957)
- France (atomic bomb, 1960; thermonuclear device, 1968)
- China (atomic bomb, 1964; thermonuclear device, 1967)
- India (atomic bomb, 1974)
- Pakistan (atomic bomb, 1998)
- Israel (atomic bomb, 1967—never tested and officially denied)
- South Africa (atomic bomb, 1985; dismantled, 1990)
- North Korea (atomic bomb, early 1990s)

Read Closely: Problems
In history, people often take actions in response to problems. Try to identify problems as you read and then evaluate how people responded to them. How was the nuclear arms race a response to problems people perceived?

Recognizing the unprecedented risks of nuclear destruction, countries formed international organizations and treaties to maintain peace. Two were particularly important:

- The International Atomic Energy Agency (IAEA) was founded in 1957 as an independent United Nations agency. By 2018, it had 169 members. The IAEA was established to encourage the peaceful use of atomic energy and discourage the building of nuclear weapons.
- The Nuclear Non-Proliferation Treaty (NNT or NPT) was designed to halt the spread of nuclear weapons. By 1968, more than 175 nations had signed it. The signers of the treaty agreed to allow inspections of their nuclear power facilities by the International Atomic Energy Agency. As of 2018, 190 states had joined the NNT.

New Military Alliances

The tense, adversarial nature of the Cold War drove the development of several regional military alliances. In 1955, to counter NATO, the Soviet Union created the Warsaw Pact with the following members: Albania, Bulgaria, Czechoslovakia, East Germany, Hungary, Poland, Romania, and the Soviet Union. Warsaw Pact nations combined their armed forces and based their military leaders in Moscow, the capital of the USSR. These nations were known as the Communist, or Eastern, Bloc.

Additional treaty organizations were formed in an attempt to halt the spread of communism in other regions. In 1954, Australia, France, Great Britain, New Zealand, Pakistan, the Philippines, Thailand, and the United States formed the Southeast Asia Treaty Organization (SEATO).

The Central Treaty Organization (CENTO) was an anti-Soviet treaty organization formed by Great Britain, Iran, Iraq, Pakistan, and Turkey in 1955 to prevent the spread of communism in the Middle East. The United States was not a full member, but it joined CENTO's military committee. (CENTO disbanded in 1979.) During the Cold War era, the United States formed alliances with more than 40 nations.

The Nonaligned Movement

Most countries were not aligned with either the Soviet Union or the United States. They might have good relations with one power or the other or with both. Many developing countries played the superpowers against one another in a bid to receive foreign aid from both. Important nonaligned countries in the Cold War period included Gamal Abdel Nasser's Egypt, Kwame Nkrumah's Ghana, Jawaharlal Nehru's India, and Sukarno's Indonesia. These leaders set up the **nonaligned movement** in the 1950s. Most member nations were developing countries of Asia and Africa that wished to avoid becoming involved in the Cold War. They saw world peace and cooperation as in their own nations' best interests.

Despite attempts to remain neutral, nonaligned nations found themselves used as pawns in the Cold War. For example, when war broke out between the nonaligned nations of Somalia and Ethiopia (1977–1978), the Soviet Union supplied aid to Ethiopia, prompting the United States to supply aid to Somalia.

The superpowers also meddled in the internal affairs of nonaligned nations. Alarmed by the land reforms instituted by Jacobo Árbenz, the Communist leader of Guatemala, the United Fruit Company lobbied friends in the U.S. government to have him removed. In 1954, the Eisenhower administration ordered the CIA to execute a coup d'état to replace the Árbenz government with one aligned with U.S. interests.

Read Closely: Motivation
Looking for a nation's motivations for their actions can be a helpful tool in understanding history. Countries in the nonaligned movement attempted to stay out of the Cold War. Why do you think they wished to do this?

Communist Expansion and Containment

The United States and the Soviet Union competed with each other for influence around the world. The United States, realizing that overthrowing Communist governments would lead to nonstop war, adopted a policy of **containment**, to check the spread of communism into any country where it did not already exist in the wake of World War II.

Cuba's Revolution In the 1950s, Cuba was ruled by a corrupt dictator, Fulgencio Batista. Most of the country's wealth was controlled by a tiny elite and by foreign investors. Many investors were from the United States. Anger at the corruption, concentration of wealth, and foreign influence caused many Cubans to support overthrowing the government. Beginning in 1956, a guerrilla movement headed by **Fidel Castro** steadily gained ground against the dictator's forces. The Batista regime collapsed on January 1, 1959. Fearing what Castro might do, many Cubans fled the country.

> ***An Enduring Issue: Migration***
> After Castro seized power, many Cubans fled to the United States for safety. They became a powerful political group, particularly in Florida. This migration was one of many cases where upheaval in one country had an impact on politics elsewhere.

The "Fidelistas" began to reshape Cuban society. They promised to help the working class through educational and economic reform. Cuba's new government was similar to those of communist nations. For example, only the Communist Party was allowed, and it was led by one person, Castro. He soon began to nationalize, or put under government control, foreign-owned industries, including vast sugar cane plantations owned by Americans.

In protest against nationalization, the United States broke off trade with Cuba and cut diplomatic ties. Castro, in turn, accepted Soviet aid and aligned Cuban foreign policy with that of the Soviet Union. The Cuban-Soviet alliance strengthened in 1961. In that year, a group of Cuban exiles, with American support, invaded the country at the **Bay of Pigs**. They hoped to overthrow Castro, but failed.

The Cuban Missle Crisis In 1962, the United States discovered that Soviet ships were sailing toward Cuba. They carried nuclear missiles that the Soviets planned to install in Cuba. This was a direct threat to U.S. security. Some American leaders advocated bombing the Soviet ships immediately. Others argued for a diplomatic solution. For almost two weeks, the world was close to nuclear war. However, diplomacy worked. Soviet leader Nikita Khrushchev recalled the ships. In return, the United States pledged not to invade Cuba and to remove missiles based in Turkey that were very close to Soviet territory.

Vietnam and France In Southeast Asia, France had controlled **Vietnam** since the mid-19th century. Following World War II, under the leadership of Ho Chi Minh, the Vietnamese rebelled against French rule. Like leaders in China and Cuba, Ho created a powerful movement by combining the nationalist idea of self-determination with the internationalist idea of communism.

France responded by attempting to reestablish its colonial rule. This sparked a Vietnamese war of independence that finally succeeded in 1954 with the defeat of French forces at Dien Bien Phu. The peace treaty split the country into North and South Vietnam. The split was supposed to be temporary, with elections planned for 1956 that would unite the country. However, many in South Vietnam, along with the United States, opposed the Communists and feared that Ho would win the election. No election was held.

War Continues in Vietnam The division of Vietnam resulted in ongoing fighting. Ho wanted to reunite the country under his control. Supporting him were guerilla fighters in South Vietnam known as the Viet Cong. U.S. officials feared that if Communists won in Vietnam they would also seize power in vulnerable neighboring countries. This belief was known as the **domino theory**. As a result, the United States began sending advisers and then combat troops to help South Vietnam. By the late 1960s, the United States had 500,000 troops in Vietnam. The United States also launched an intense bombing of North Vietnam and neighboring Cambodia, through which the "Ho Chi Minh Trail" snaked to bring supplies to the Viet Cong.

Source: Wikimedia Commons.

American soldiers fought in Vietnam longer than in any other conflict to that time.

A turning point in the war came in 1968. The North Vietnamese and Viet Cong troops launched a series of attacks known as the **Tet Offensive**. As a military action, the Tet Offensive failed. However, the strength of the attacks demonstrated that South Vietnam was failing to win the war. Even massive aid from the United States was not enough to save it.

As opposition to the war increased in the United States, President Richard Nixon began to withdraw troops in 1971. The last U.S. troops left in 1975. North Vietnam soon gained control of South Vietnam. The united country was called the Socialist Republic of Vietnam.

The Vietnam War resulted in the deaths of between one and two million people, including about 58,000 Americans. In the turmoil caused by the war, Communists gained control of Laos and Cambodia. However, they did not continue to spread as the domino theory had predicted. Thailand, the Philippines, Singapore, and Malaysia often had authoritarian governments, but all remained noncommunist nations with free-market economies.

Afghanistan

Beginning in 1978, **Afghanistan** started a long period of turmoil. Internal conflicts were deepened by the involvement of outside forces:

- In 1978, Marxists overthrew the corrupt but moderate Afghan government.
- In 1979, the Soviet Union supported the Marxist government but feared the rise of Islamic fundamentalism. It invaded and formed a new government.
- From 1979 to 1989, Muslims from many countries, known as mujahideen, or "those who wage holy war," went to Afghanistan to fight the Soviets. They received funds and arms from the United States and other countries.
- In 1989, after 10 years of warfare and maybe a million or more Afghani deaths, the Soviets withdrew their troops. Factional fighting continued.
- In 2001, some Afghans provided support for the terrorists who attacked the United States on September 11, 2001. In response, the United States and its NATO allies invaded Afghanistan. This war officially ended in 2014, but U.S. troops remained in the country and violence continued.

Read Closely: Similarities
Even with countries in bitter conflict, often basic beliefs can still share some values. By recognizing these similar ideas, you can better understand the context for the conflict. In what ways were the United States and the Soviet Union similar in the Cold War?

Détente

By the late 1960s, both the Soviet Union and the United States wanted to slow down the nuclear arms race and the constant tension that surrounded it. This movement toward improved relations was known as **détente**.

Motives for Détente to Reduce Tension The Soviet Union and the United States each had their own reasons for wanting to reduce tension with the other. The Soviet Union was concerned about the breakdown of their relationship with China. During the 1950s, they had often been allies on the world stage as the only two large Communist-led countries. But disagreements over how to implement communism led to other conflicts. In 1969, they had a seven-month standoff over a border dispute. The dispute turned violent at times, resulting in military clashes. Around 120 people died in these clashes. As the two countries grew farther apart, each hoped that closer ties with the United States would strengthen them diplomatically.

Similarly, as the United States watched the growing split between the Soviets and the Chinese, it wanted each as an ally. The United States was fighting a difficult war in Vietnam. It hoped that the Soviets might have influence with North Vietnam that could help the United States negotiate a way out of it.

In addition to diplomatic help, both countries were looking for economic relief. Each country was spending large sums of money out of fear of the other. Reduced tensions might allow for them to reduce military expenses.

Agreements to Reduce Tension The United States and the Soviet Union took several steps to relax their relationship:

- In 1972, after negotiations known as the Strategic Arms Limitation Talks (SALT I), the two countries adopted the Anti-Ballistic Missile Treaty (ABM). It reduced the number of missiles for each country.
- During the 1970s, the Soviet Union began buying grain from the United States. This benefited both U.S. farmers and Soviet consumers.
- In 1975, the Soviet Union and the United States were among the 35 countries that signed the Helsinki Accords, by which they all accepted the political boundaries set at the end of World War II. While this brought some stability to Europe, it also recognized Soviet control of Eastern Europe and the Baltic states of Latvia, Lithuania, and Estonia.

Tensions Increase Again In 1979, the Soviets and the Americans nearly agreed to another arms control treaty, known as SALT II. However, when the USSR invaded Afghanistan, U.S. President Jimmy Carter removed the treaty from Senate consideration. In addition, Carter pulled the United States out of the 1980 Olympics, which were being held in Moscow that year. The Soviet invasion of Afghanistan and the American response to it effectively ended the détente era.

Nuclear Weapons Stockpiles, 1945 to 2015

Country	1945	1955	1965	1975	1985	1995	2005	2015
United States	6	3,057	31,982	27,826	24,237	12,144	10,295	7,100
Soviet Union	0	200	6,129	19,055	39,197	27,000	17,000	7,700

Source: Hans M. Kristensen and Robert S. Norris, "Global Nuclear Stockpiles, 1945–2006," *Bulletin of the Atomic Scientists,* July 1, 2006. Data from the Arms Control Association, armscontrol.org.

Application

Read the excerpts and answer the questions that follow them.

Nikita Khrushchev, Comments Upon Arrival in France, May 15, 1960

Though all the peoples desire the strengthening of peace and a détente in international relations, it is common knowledge that, particularly of late, influential quarters who are seeking to revive the cold war and hinder the invigoration of the international atmosphere have noticeably intensified their activities in certain countries. Let us hope that their efforts will yield no success, and that the discussion of such questions and universal and complete disarmament, elimination of the vestiges of World War II and the conclusion of a German peace treaty and East-West relations will yield useful results for the cause of universal peace.

Source: Nikita Khrushchev, speech in France, May 15, 1960.

Adlai Stevenson, Comments in Chicago, June 2, 1960

Great progress toward a nuclear test ban and a break in the arms deadlock was made since last fall. That progress must not be lost. The United States, which has been the source of most of the revolutionary concepts of human and political freedom, should be the tireless, fearless leader of the cause of freedom from war in this revolutionary century. To seize that role and pursue it with passion should be our national policy. I think the time has come to put this important business on a permanent and professional basis. I think we need a special agency under the Secretary of State charged with the great, complex and neglected task of peace and disarmament which will be a symbol of our determination to lead the world away from madness.

Source: Adlai Stevenson, speech in Chicago, June 2, 1960.

1. Identify one way in which the two countries view détente similarly.

____

____

2. Identify one way in which the two countries view détente differently.

____

____

3. Explain the level of trust the author of the first excerpt has in the rest of the world.

____

____

4. Describe the role, according to the author of the second excerpt, that the United States should take in the establishment of world peace.

____

____

Lesson 3 *The End of the Cold War*

Conceptual Understanding
10.6c The end of the Cold War and the collapse of the communist bloc in Europe had a global impact.

Source: *New York State Grades 9–12 Social Studies Framework.*

The Berlin Wall was the clearest physical symbol of the division of Europe into regions aligned with either the United States or the Soviet Union. So, when the East German government allowed the Berlin Wall to be knocked down, it was a sign that the Cold War was ending.

Analyze a Primary Source

The Destruction of the Berlin Wall, 1989

Source: Getty Images

Read Closely: Differences
When analyzing a photo, note differences. In this photo, on the East German side, only uniformed soldiers can be seen. On the West German side, both soldiers and civilians are shown. This suggests that the West Germans were more relaxed about the wall than were the East Germans.

Read Closely: Details
To analyze an image, pay attention to details. One of the West Germans has a camera. *Circle details that might show the historical importance of this moment.*

Read Closely: Questions
Like any other source, a photo cannot communicate everything. Note the graffiti on the West German side of the wall. This suggests that West Germans could safely get close to the wall. A photo from the other side would indicate whether East Germans could do that as well.

The U.S.-Soviet Thaw

After more than 40 years of tension between the Soviet Union and the United States, the Cold War ended in the late 1980s. However, the end of the rivalry created new uncertainty worldwide.

Gorbachev and the Era of Reform

In 1985, **Mikhail Gorbachev** became the leader of the Soviet Union. Recognizing that the country faced serious problems, he attempted reforms to strengthen the Communist government. By signing a nuclear arms control agreement with the United States, he was able to weaken the power of conservatives within the Soviet Union. This allowed him to push for changes in the two broad categories described in the following chart.

Gorbachev's Reform Programs

	Perestroika	Glasnost
English translation	Restructuring	Openness
Reform goal	To make the economy more efficient	To increase individual freedom
Policies	• Allow citizens to start their own businesses more easily • Reduce central planning and management of businesses • Reduce government support for industries	• Grant more freedom of speech and the press to Soviet citizens • Become more tolerant of criticism of government officials • Change election laws to make multiparty, multicandidate elections more common

Because of these reforms, relations with the West improved. In 1987 and 1991, the Soviet Union and the United States signed major nuclear arms reduction treaties. Gorbachev ordered Soviet forces out of Afghanistan in 1989. Also, to end the economic drain on the country, he stopped supporting Marxist governments and movements around the world.

Read Closely: Comparisons One way to understand ideas new to you is to compare them to ideas you already know well. How do the concepts of *perestroika* and *glasnost* relate to the United States Constitution?

Opposition and Devolution Some Communists opposed Gorbachev. They believed that his reforms undermined the Soviet system, even though he was clear this was not his goal. In August 1991, these Communists led an unsuccessful coup attempt against Gorbachev. To reduce the power of the Communists, Gorbachev resigned from the party. The Soviet Parliament suspended all party activities. The Communist Party no longer controlled the government, the economy, or the military.

Gorbachev continued his reforms. In spite of his efforts to keep the Soviet Union together, it broke apart. Russia, Ukraine, and the 13 other satellites declared their independence. At the end of 1991, Gorbachev resigned as president. Most of the former Soviet republics then formed the Commonwealth of Independent States (CIS). The Soviet Union no longer existed. Russia was the dominant state in the CIS. This succession of events in 1991 ended the Cold War.

After the fall of the Soviet Union, the leaders of the newly independent republics struggled to develop new political systems and to solve severe economic problems. Eager to promote democracy and free-market economies in these new nations, the United States and other Western nations provided financial aid and advisers.

COUNTRIES FORMED FROM THE SOVIET UNION

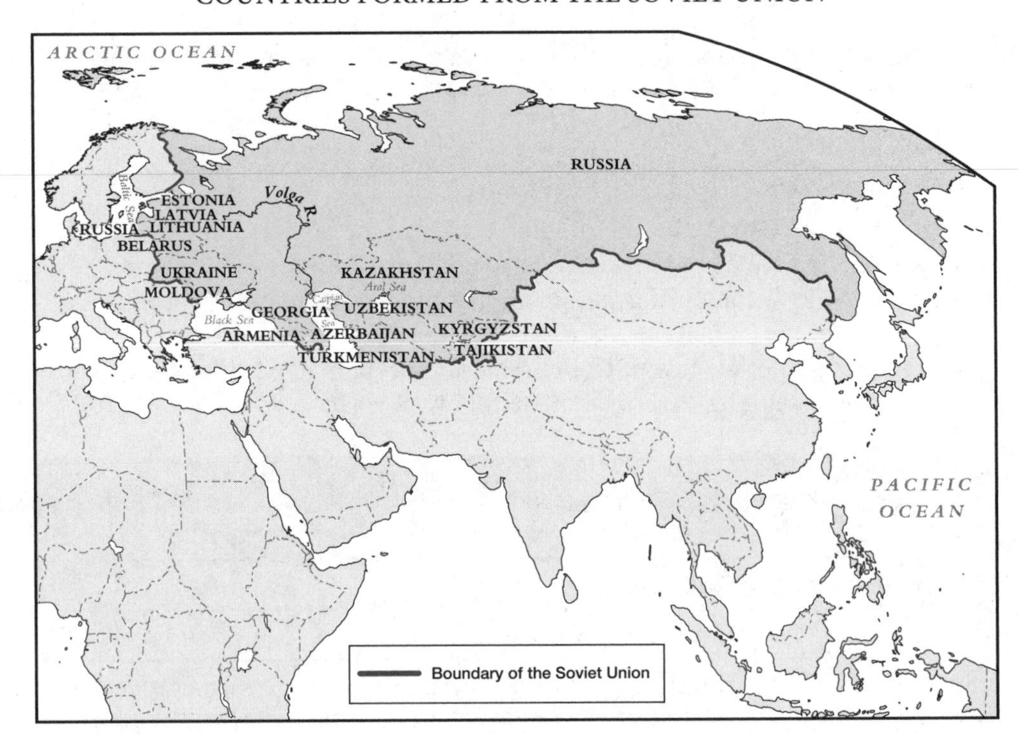

An Enduring Issue: Nationalism
The breakup of the Soviet Union released a wave of nationalism in parts of Europe and Asia. For over two centuries, nationalism has shaped politics around the world.

Yeltsin Continues Boris Yeltsin was elected president of the Republic of Russia in 1990. He had been a leader in the Communist Party and had supported Gorbachev's reforms. In Russia, Communists and strongly nationalist conservatives opposed Yeltsin's attempts to establish democracy and a free-market economy. In October 1993, these "hard-liners" attempted to remove Yeltsin from office. They failed.

New national elections were held in December 1993. Yeltsin won, and a new constitution was approved. However, a large number of seats in the State Duma (the new lower house of parliament) went to ultranationalists and others opposed to Yeltsin's reforms. Clashes between the president and parliament continued.

Economic problems made solving the political crisis difficult. Prices spiraled upward at a dizzying pace. Economic officials tried to ease people's hardship. They slowed down privatization (the process of selling state-run businesses to private investors), printed more paper money, and tried to increase production. Some reformers feared that Russia might turn back to its old methods of rigid central control. Although in poor health, Yeltsin won another presidential election in 1998. He continued his efforts to adopt some elements of capitalism and to maintain good relations with the West.

Read Closely: Relationships
Understanding the relationship between citizens and rulers will help you appreciate why people in the past made decisions as they did. How do you think a middle-class Russian citizen would feel about Boris Yeltsin?

The Fall of Communism in Eastern Europe

Until 1989, the Soviet Union closely supervised the governments of its Eastern European satellites. It intervened to stop any challenge to the Communist government. Soviet troops put down prodemocracy movements in Hungary in 1956 and in Czechoslovakia in 1968.

The Soviets also cracked down on protests and strikes by Polish workers, students, and intellectuals in 1956, 1968, 1970, and 1976. Poland, more than any other satellite, was culturally united by religion. Most Poles had a strong attachment to the Roman Catholic Church.

Solidarity In 1980, Lech Walesa, an electrician in the shipyards of the city of Gdansk, Poland, became head of **Solidarity**, a trade union organization. Solidarity demanded trade unions free of communist control and a reexamination of Poland's alliance with the Soviet Union. After making some early concessions, the Polish authorities, encouraged by the Soviets, outlawed Solidarity in 1981. They arrested Walesa and thousands of others and imposed military rule on the country. These harsh actions drew strong criticism from the United States and other Western countries. Walesa was released in 1982, and martial law was lifted in 1983.

Rising prices and shortages of consumer goods led to protests in Poland. The Communist Party yielded to the people's demands for free elections in 1989, which the Solidarity movement won. It formed the first noncommunist government in a former Soviet satellite country. In 1990, Lech Walesa was elected president of his country.

Source: Shutterstock.

In Gdansk, Poland, the union workers who challenged the Polish Communist government remain honored.

Read Closely: Symbols
Recognizing which historical figures became important symbols for their period is one way to understand the general changes in that period. How was Lech Walesa a symbol for the fate of communism?

Soviet Reaction and Its Fallout Mikhail Gorbachev changed the way the Soviet Union dealt with its satellites. He abandoned the "Brezhnev Doctrine," named for an earlier Soviet leader, which asserted the right of the Soviet Union to interfere in the affairs of its satellites to protect communism. Thus, when the people of Eastern Europe protested against their communist governments in 1989, the Soviet Union did little in response.

In addition to Poland, other Eastern European countries recognized that Soviet-led communism was failing. It could not provide goods, services, and freedom equal to what was enjoyed in the West. In Hungary, Czechoslovakia, Albania, and Bulgaria, demands for free elections led to the peaceful end of communist rule between 1989 and 1991. In Romania, when the communist leaders did not agree to free elections, they were overthrown. The president, the brutal dictator Nicolae Ceausescu, was executed.

Read Closely: Summaries
Identify those sentences that summarize the details of a section. They reinforce the main point. Which line summarizes "Soviet Reaction and Its Fallout"?

In East Germany, too, the people demanded greater personal freedoms and economic opportunity. In 1989, they forced the East German government to open the Berlin Wall and allow unrestricted travel across its borders. In 1990, free elections in East Germany led to the fall from power of the Communist Party. In October 1990, East and West Germany were united. The unified Germany has become a leading economic and political power in Europe.

NATO and Eastern Europe

After the Cold War, many countries once part of the Soviet empire wanted to avoid Russian domination again. Therefore, they sought membership in NATO. If they joined NATO, troops from the United States, Canada, and West Europe would be required to defend them from attack by Russia.

Existing NATO members were cautious about adding new countries. They did not want to offend Russia—nor get drawn into a war. They urged the East Europeans to be patient and to start by first joining a "Partnership for Peace." Gradually, Russian leaders accepted the idea of NATO membership for Eastern European countries. In 1997, Yeltsin signed an agreement preparing the way for these countries to become full NATO members. Between 1999 and 2004, ten countries in Eastern Europe joined NATO.

Effects on Cuba

Soviet aid to Cuba continued until the Soviet Union dissolved in 1991. Without Soviet aid, the Cuban economy declined sharply. A drop in trade with Eastern Europe and shortages of fuel made Cuba's problems even worse.

In 1993 and 1994, Cuban President Fidel Castro and the Communist Party leadership introduced limited free-market reforms similar to those in China. People were allowed to form small private businesses, legally possess foreign currency, and establish their own agricultural cooperatives. However, the reforms caused little immediate improvement in Cuba's economy.

In 1994, the Cuban government allowed more than 30,000 people to leave. This rid the country of many citizens most displeased with the Castro government. Most went to the United States. Later, the United States agreed to admit 20,000 Cubans yearly, with Cuba's cooperation.

The Fall of Communism

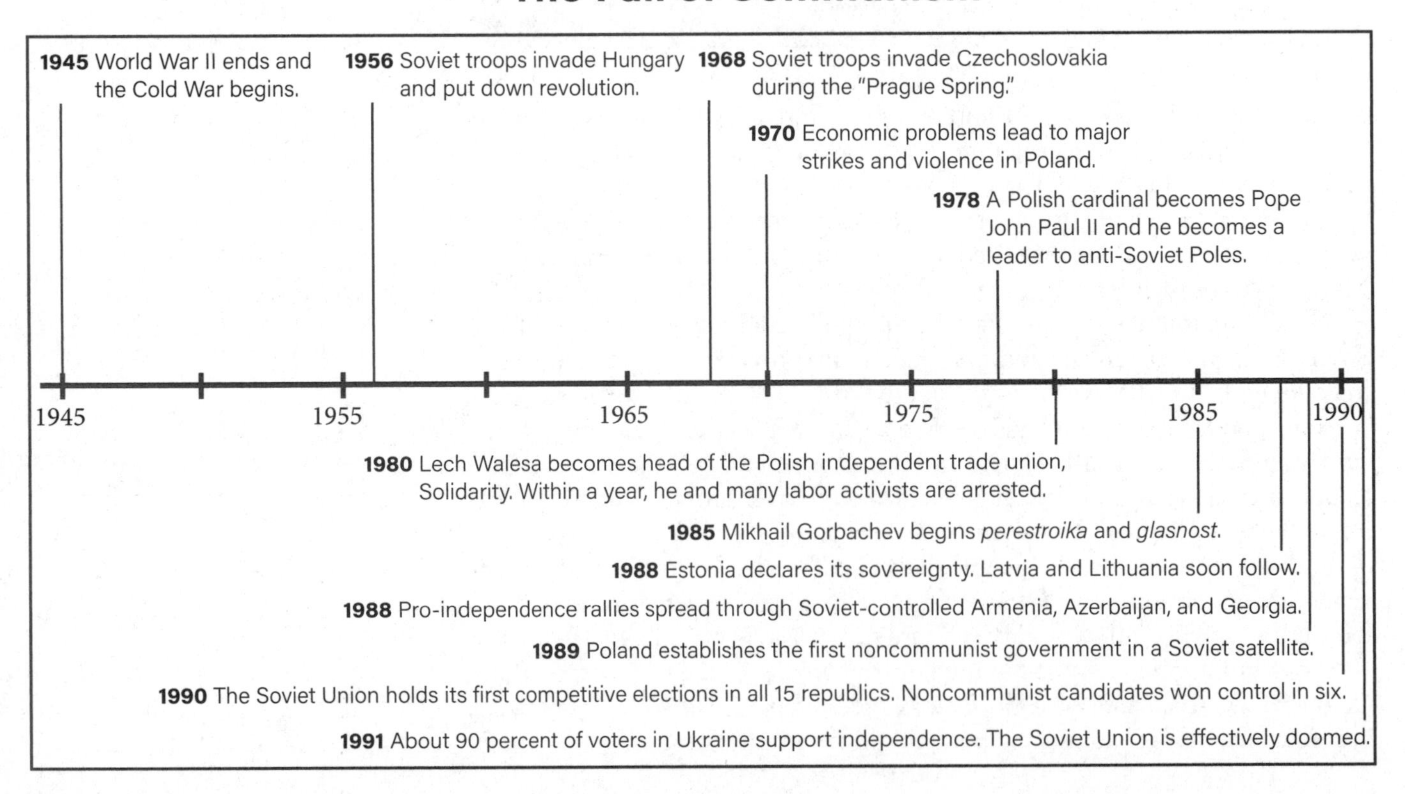

Application

Read the excerpt and answer the questions that follow it.

Elena Yurievna S., Memories of Soviet Life

Is it really already time to tell the story of socialism? To whom? Everyone around is still a witness. It was 1989. By then, I was the third secretary of the district Party committee. I was recruited to work in the Party from the school where I'd taught Russian language and literature. When they first offered me the job, I was intimidated. What a huge responsibility! But I didn't hesitate for a moment. I had a real burst of desire to serve the Party. Did I believe in the Party? I did. And I still do. Did I believe in communism? I believed in the possibility of life being governed fairly. I still believe in that.

The last years of the Soviet Union. What do I remember? The ever-present shame. I was ashamed that people had taken to calling the Kremlin a comfortable retirement home. I was ashamed of the empty store shelves. We were meeting and even surpassing production quotas, but somehow the stores were completely empty. Where was our milk? Our meat? I still don't understand where it all went. Stores would run out of milk within an hour of opening. After noon, the sales clerks just stood there behind clean, empty display cases. The only things on the shelves were three-liter jars of birch juice and packages of salt.

Perestroika. There was a moment when people wanted to turn to us again. They were joining the party. Everyone had great expectations. Back then, everyone was naïve, on the left and on the right—the communists and anti-Soviets alike. Everyone was a romantic. And everyone understood that we couldn't go on the way we were. Caught in a web of lies.

Source: Elena Yurievna S., third secretary of the district Party committee. Excerpted from *Secondhand Time* by Svetlana Alexievich, 2016.

1. Explain the author's role in the Communist Party in 1989.

____

____

2. Identify one quote that shows how difficult life was for everyday people under communism.

____

____

3. Contrast the author's assumption of communism to the reality she witnessed.

____

____

4. Explain when and how the author reluctantly realized that the communist model was not working.

____

____

Chapter 6 *Review*

Multiple-Choice Questions

Directions (1–6): For each statement or question, choose the number of the word or expression that, of those given, best completes the statement or answers the question.

Base your answers to questions 1 and 2 on the passage below and your knowledge of social studies

> [Unity] binds the 14 nations of the Atlantic Alliance together. I stress the word unity because that is what matters more than anything else: that is the real answer to the threat of aggression, that is what potential enemies fear more than anything else; that is what they want to destroy more than anything else. We must be on guard against the sometimes persuasive whispers and insinuations of propagandists who seek to magnify our differences and try to drive a wedge in our unity. Nations cannot afford to stand alone to be picked off one by one. We have the eloquent evidence of countries that formerly were free, independent, and important members of the Western European community, who now have fallen under the domination and imperialistic exploitation of the Soviet.
>
> Clearly we must arm up to the limit in order to be as strong as possible as rapidly as possible, but not at the expense of national bankruptcy. We cannot afford, through excessive haste to avert the hot war, to lose the cold one. Our alliance, it cannot be too often repeated, is purely defensive. Not a ship, not a plane, not a gun will ever be used except in self-defense. And no one knows better than the Soviet General Staff that the forces we plan are of a magnitude which can never be put to offensive or aggressive purposes.
>
> **Source:** nato.int/docu/speech/1952/s19521018.html. Press Statement by Lord Ismay, Vice Chairman of the North Atlantic Council and Secretary General of NATO, October 18, 1952

1. Which country best fits the description by Lord Ismay in the last sentence of the first paragraph?
   (1) France
   (2) East Germany
   (3) Greece
   (4) Korea

2. What development was the most direct response to the point of view expressed by Lord Ismay and others between 1945 and 1960?
   (1) outbreak of the Korean War
   (2) formation of Warsaw Pact
   (3) failure of the Hungarian Revolution
   (4) success of the Communist Party in China

Base your answers to questions 3 and 4 on the passages below and on your knowledge of social studies

Nikita Khrushchev's letters to President Kennedy, October 27, 1962

> I propose: We, for our part, will declare that our ships, bound for Cuba, will not carry any kind of armaments. You would declare that the United States will not invade Cuba with its forces and will not support any sort of forces which might intend to carry out an invasion of Cuba. Then the necessity for the presence of our military specialists in Cuba would disappear.
>
> **Source:** http://microsites.jfklibrary.org/cmc/oct27/doc4.html.

Nikita Khrushchev's letters to President Kennedy, October 27, 1962

> I think it would be possible to end the controversy quickly and normalize the situation, and then the people could breathe more easily, considering that statesmen charged with responsibility are of sober mind and have an awareness of their responsibility combined with the ability to solve complex questions and not bring things to a military catastrophe.
>
> I therefore make this proposal: We are willing to remove from Cuba the means which you regard as offensive. We are willing to carry this out and to make this pledge in the United Nations. Your representatives will make a declaration to the effect that the United States, for its part, considering the uneasiness and anxiety of the Soviet State, will remove its analogous [similar] means from Turkey. Let us reach agreement as to the period of time needed by you and by us to bring this about. And, after that, persons entrusted by the United Nations Security Council could inspect on the spot the fulfillment of the pledges made.
>
> **Source:** http://microsites.jfklibrary.org/cmc/oct27/doc4.html.

3. Compared to the first letter, in the second letter Khrushchev emphasized
   (1) the dangers of a nuclear conflict if no solution could be found
   (2) the importance to Russia of Cuban independence
   (3) the two countries probably could not find a realistic solution
   (4) the Soviets possessed nuclear superiority over the United States

4. What conclusion can you draw from President Kennedy's decision to answer the first rather than the second letter?
   (1) He did not want U.S. forces to invade Cuba.
   (2) He believed he could claim victory without giving up anything.
   (3) He thought giving up missiles in Turkey was too high a price to pay for resolving the crisis.
   (4) He wanted a peaceful resolution that had little effect on U.S. military power overseas.

Base your answers to questions 5 and 6 on the photos below and your knowledge of social studies.

Source: Getty Images These images show the Berlin Wall in 1961 (left) and 1989 (right).

5. Which statement best explains the official reason that the East German government justified the action shown in the photo on the left?
   (1) It would create jobs needed by people in East Berlin.
   (2) It would keep capitalist aggressors out of East Germany.
   (3) It would fulfill one of the orders issued by the Soviet Union.
   (4) It would improve trade between Communist and capitalist countries

6. The contrast between the two photos suggests that
   (1) the Berlin Wall successfully protected Communism
   (2) Germans demonstrated a strong nationalist feeling
   (3) capitalism triumphed over Communism
   (4) East Germany later absorbed West Germany.

Tips for Answering Multiple-Choice Questions

When reading primary sources, it is sometimes necessary to use context clues within the text to understand the meaning. Many primary sources were not written in the style of common speech today. Therefore, readers sometimes need to figure out the meaning of confusing text by using words and phrases around unfamiliar words. If a word is not identifiable, try to plug in words that you know that might fit within this main idea. Using context clues and synonyms will help you understand the author's intent in the primary source.

Short-Answer Questions

CRQ Directions (7-9): Analyze the documents and answer the short-answer questions that follow each document in the space provided.

Base your answer to question 7 on Document 1 below and on your knowledge of social studies.

Document 1

This excerpt is from the "Iron Curtain" speech given by Winston Churchill in Fulton, Missouri, March 5, 1946.

> A shadow has fallen upon the scenes so lately lighted by the Allied victory. Nobody knows what Soviet Russia and its Communist international organization intends to do in the immediate future, or what are its limits, to their expansive and proselytizing tendencies. I have a strong admiration for the valiant Russian people and my wartime comrade, Marshall Stalin. . . . It is my duty, however . . . for me to state the facts as I see them to you. . . . From Stettin in the Baltic to Trieste in the Adriatic, an Iron Curtain has descended across the Continent. Behind that line lie all the capitals of the ancient states of Central and Eastern Europe, Warsaw, Berlin, Prague, Vienna, Budapest, Belgrade, Bucharest and Sofia, all these famous cities and the population around them lie in what I must call the Soviet sphere and all are subject in one form or another, to what I must call the Soviet sphere, not only to Soviet influence, but to a very high degree . . . of control from Moscow.
>
> If the Western democracies stand together in strict adherence to the principles of the United Nations Charter . . . no one is likely to molest them. If, however, they become divided or falter in their duty . . . then indeed catastrophe may overwhelm us all.
>
> **Source:** http://www.historyplace.com/speeches/ironcurtain.htm.

7. Explain the geographic context of this speech by Churchill.

____

____

____

____

____

Tips for Answering Short-Answer Questions

To understand the geographic context of a document, consider two types of questions:

- Why was the document created where it was? For example, in Churchill's Iron Curtain speech, consider whether it was significant that Churchill was speaking in the United States, in the state of Missouri, on a college campus.
- How did geography shape the content of the document? For example, consider the political geography of Europe at the time of Churchill's speech.

Base your answer to question 8 on Document 2 below and on your knowledge of social studies.

Document 2

This quotation from Joseph Stalin appeared in a state-run Soviet newspaper on March 14, 1946.

> In substance, Mr. Churchill now stands in the position of a firebrand of war. And Mr. Churchill is not alone here. He has friends not only in England but also in the United States of America.
>
> In this respect, one is reminded of Hitler and his friends. Hitler began to set war loose by announcing his racial theory, declaring that only people speaking the German language represent a fully valuable nation. Mr. Churchill began to set war loose, also by a racial theory, maintaining that only nations speaking the English language are fully valuable nations, called upon to decide the destinies of the entire world. . . . It may be that some quarters are trying to push into oblivion the sacrifices of the Soviet people which insured the liberation of Europe from the Hitlerite yoke. But the Soviet Union cannot forget them. One can ask therefore, what can be surprising in the fact that the Soviet Union, in a desire to ensure its security for the future, tries to achieve that these countries should have governments whose relations to the Soviet Union are loyal? How can one, without having lost one's reason, qualify these peaceful aspirations of the Soviet Union as "expansionist tendencies" of our Government?
>
> **Source:** Joseph Stalin, "Answer to *Pravada* Correspondent," *New York Times,* March 14, 1946.

8. Using this excerpt, identify Stalin's audience for these comments.

Base your answer to question 9 on both Documents 1 and 2 and on your knowledge of social studies.

Cause—refers to something that contributes to the occurrence of an event, the rise of an idea, or the bringing about of a development.

Effect—refers to what happens as a consequence (result, impact, outcome) of an event, an idea, or a development.

9. Identify and explain a cause-and-effect relationship associated with the historical developments in Documents 1 and 2. Use evidence from both Documents 1 and 2 in your response.

Speaking and Listening: Reflect on the Key Idea

Working with a small group, design a poster that displays the main theme and events of the Cold War.

CHAPTER 7

Rebellions Against Imperialism

Chapter Overview

During the 20th century, colonies began to regain their independence. The two world wars weakened European nations making it difficult for them to control colonies. Decolonization movements, as in India, succeeded through nonviolent resistance, while others succeeded through armed struggle, as in Algeria and Vietnam.

Nationalism Anticolonial movements built on the idea of nationalism. While nationalism united people enough to throw out colonial rulers, it was often too weak to overcome cultural differences within an independent country. For example, India won its independence from the British after World War II, but it remained a country of hundreds of languages and cultural groups.

Middle East The Middle East faced great turmoil because of a combination of religious and political conflicts. The rivalry between followers of different branches of Islam led to rivalries, including a large-scale war between Iran and Iraq. The creation of a Jewish-majority country in the Middle East after World War II was an ongoing cause of tension and sometimes war.

China Nationalistic pride was growing in China as the old imperial government showed weakness in the face of Western power. A 1911 rebellion overthrew the Qing Dynasty and created a Chinese republic with elected leaders.

However, the new central government was too weak to keep order. Ruthless regional leaders, a civil war, and an invasion by Japan during World War II resulted in the deaths of millions of people. In 1947, the Communists defeated their rivals and seized control of the government. Years later, dramatic changes in China's version of communism resulted in rapid economic growth. China emerged in the 21st century as one of the most influential countries in the world.

An Enduring Issue: Inequality One enduring issue in this chapter is the unequal relationship between the imperialist countries and the territories they dominated. Countries such as Great Britain, France, the United States, and Japan used their economic, political, and military power to dominate regions of Asia and Africa. In response, these regions followed various strategies to be able to govern themselves.

New York Social Studies Framework: **Key Idea 10.7**

Nationalist and decolonization movements employed a variety of methods, including nonviolent resistance and armed struggle. Tensions and conflicts often continued after independence as new challenges arose.

Source: *New York State Grades 9–12 Social Studies Framework.*

1. Rewrite Key Idea 10.7 in your own words.

____

____

Identify Enduring Issues

A first step in identifying enduring issues among multiple documents is to note all issues that one document expresses. Consider one of the most famous lines ever spoken, the words of astronaut Neil Armstrong on July 20, 1969, when he became the first human to step on the moon: "That's one small step for [a] man, one giant leap for mankind." This line addresses several enduring issues:

- the interaction between humans and nature
- the rivalry between powerful countries for leadership
- the impact of science and technology on human thoughts and behavior
- the desire by people to explore and innovate

Below is a quotation attributed to Mohandas Gandhi. Identify at least three issues that you think it addresses. As you read this chapter, you might add more.

> I believe that the civilization India evolved is not to be beaten in the world. Nothing can equal the seeds sown by our ancestors, Rome went, Greece shared the same fate; the might of the Pharaohs was broken; Japan has become Westernized; of China nothing can be said; but India is still, somehow or other, sound at the foundation.

1. ______________________________
2. ______________________________
3. ______________________________
4. ______________________________
5. ______________________________

Key Terms and Names

Identity

Pan-Africanism (p. 211)
Zionism (p. 217)
Balfour Declaration (p. 217)
Long March (p. 224)

Geography

Amritsar (p. 205)
Gold Coast (p. 211)
Ghana (p. 211)
Algeria (p. 212)
Kenya (p. 212)
Angola (p. 213)

Social Structures

Mohandas K. Gandhi (p. 205)
Dreyfus Affair (p. 217)

Governance

Muhammad Ali Jinnah (p. 205)
Jawaharlal Nehru (p. 205)
Ho Chi Minh (p. 207)
Dien Bien Phu (p. 207)
Kwame Nkrumah (p. 211)
Mau Mau (p. 212)
Theodor Herzl (p. 217)
mandate system (p. 218)
Camp David Accords (p. 220)
Sun Yat-sen (Sun Yixian) (p. 223)
Chinese Communist Party (CCP) (p. 223)
Mao Zedong (p. 223)
Chiang Kai-shek (Jiang Jieshi) (p. 224)
Great Leap Forward (p. 225)
Cultural Revolution (p. 225)
Deng Xiaoping (p. 226)

Civics

Salt March (p. 205)
Tiananmen Square (p. 226)

Lesson 1 *Independence Movements in India and Indochina*

Conceptual Understanding
10.7a Independence movements in India and Indochina developed in response to European control.

Source: *New York State Grades 9–12 Social Studies Framework.*

Under the leadership of Mohandas Gandhi, the people of India organized to demand self-government or independence from Great Britain. Gandhi was committed to using nonviolent pressure through a campaign of civil disobedience, deliberate efforts to break a law to highlight the injustice of the law.

Analyze a Primary Source

Letter from Mohandas Gandhi to Lord Irwin, Great Britain's top official in India, March 1930

Read Closely: Point of View
Readers should note how Gandhi focuses on what he believes by using words such as "faith," "intentionally," "hold," and "intend." Then readers should decide whether Gandhi's actions reflect his beliefs.

Read Closely: Ideas
Gandhi tries to present his ideas in the context of his general beliefs about people. This excerpt provides insight into Gandhi's view of human nature.
Underline phrases that show how Gandhi felt about British individuals.

Read Closely: Details
Writers often ask a question as a way of leading into details they want to provide to support a generalization.
Circle a question Gandhi asks and then answers.

Before embarking on Civil Disobedience . . . I would again approach you and find a way out.

My personal faith is absolutely clear. I cannot intentionally hurt anything that lives, much less fellow human beings, even though they may do the greatest wrong to me and mine. Whilst, therefore, I hold the British rule to be a curse, I do not intend harm to a single Englishman or to any legitimate interest he may have in India.

I must not be misunderstood. Though I hold the British rule in India to be a curse, I do not, therefore, consider Englishmen in general to be worse than any other people on earth. I have the privilege of claiming many Englishmen as dearest friends. Indeed much that I have learnt of the evil of British rule is due to the writings of frank and courageous Englishmen who have not hesitated to tell the unpalatable [unappealing] truth about that rule.

And why do I regard the British rule as a curse?

It has impoverished the dumb millions by a system of progressive exploitation and by a ruinously expensive military and civil administration which the country can never afford.

Source: http://www.bl.uk/reshelp/findhelpregion/asia/india/indianindependence/indiannat/source3/index.html

Asian Opposition to Imperialism

When the 20th century began, large parts of Asia had been under Western imperial control for centuries. But a wave of nationalism and decolonization was rising, particularly after World War II.

Reading Closely: Prior Knowledge
Draw upon information you already read to help you understand new content. What do you know about other independence movements that suggest problems Asian independence movements will face?

Decolonization of India

In India, a group of nationalists, mostly middle-class Hindu professionals, formed the Indian National Congress in 1885. Indian Muslims formed a comparable nationalist group, the Muslim League, in 1906. The goal of these groups was to change, diminish, and eventually eliminate the British domination of their country.

Indian troops fought for the British in World War I. When they returned to India, many demanded more respect from British authorities. Protests against British rule became more widespread after the war. Authorities often contained the protests without resorting to violence. But in April 1919, British soldiers opened fire on a peaceful gathering of about 10,000 Indian men, women, and children in the city of **Amritsar**. About 400 were killed and another 1,200 were wounded.

Gandhi The Amritsar massacre stirred up demands for greater self-rule. In the 1920s and 1930s, **Mohandas K. Gandhi**, an Indian lawyer who had studied in London and been an activist for the rights of Indians in South Africa, became a leader in the Indian National Congress. Gandhi persuaded many Indians to practice passive (nonviolent) resistance to British rule. For example, many Indians refused to buy or use British goods, serve in the armed forces, pay taxes, or obey some British laws. Anyone who protested British rule faced arrest. Great numbers of Indians went to jail.

One symbol of British authority was its control of and tax on the sale of salt. To protest British rule, then, Gandhi led a long protest in 1930 known as the **Salt March**. Walking to the ocean, the marchers filled containers with seawater, set them in the sun, and let the water evaporate till only salt remained. By making their own salt, they were breaking the law. More importantly, they threatened British control. About 60,000 Indians were arrested for their salt protest.

Gandhi's followers showed their respect for him by calling him Mahatma, "the great one." His resistance activities often caused the British authorities to jail him. He also used the tactic of fasting to get his way. He would go without food for weeks until his demands were met.

Jinnah In 1934, **Muhammad Ali Jinnah** became president of the Muslim League. The organization had been founded to protect Muslim interests in the region. Jinnah cooperated with the Indian National Congress at times. At other times, he worked with the British to get protection for Muslims from the Hindu majority. During the 1940s, Jinnah called for a separate Muslim state.

Nehru One of the strong Hindu nationalist leaders was **Jawaharlal Nehru**. His father had worked closely with Gandhi in the wake of the Amritsar massacre, and father and son were arrested for their political activities in 1921. Jawaharlal Nehru was to be imprisoned for his activism another eight times over the following 20-plus years. Between 1929 and 1954, Nehru was elected president of the Indian National Congress on six occasions.

Independence The British proposed power-sharing agreements with the Indians, but the leaders held out for full independence. With the outbreak of World War II in 1939, any talk about self-rule or independence was set aside.

When World War II ended, Indian efforts to end colonial rule resumed. However, the leaders disagreed on how to move forward. Gandhi believed strongly in uniting people of all faiths into one single country. Jinnah feared Hindu domination of Muslims, so he demanded a separate Islamic country. Lord Mountbatten, the British colonial leader, proposed partitioning the colony into two countries. Pakistan would be almost entirely Islamic. India would be mostly Hindu, but with a large Muslim minority. The Mountbatten plan was adopted.

However, many regions included both Hindus and Muslims, so a simple separation was impossible. People began fleeing their homes. Hindus tried to get to India and Muslims sought safety in Pakistan. The result was chaos and violence. About 15 million people relocated and over 1 million died.

Source: Getty Images

The partition between India and Pakistan resulted in more deaths than the American Civil War and left the two countries bitter foes.

Reading Closely: Stakeholders
Stakeholders in society always have possible gains and risk possible losses in a major transition in leadership. Which major stakeholders in India in the early 20th century might have benefited from decolonialization?

Nehru became the first prime minister of India under the new constitution adopted in 1948. Jinnah headed the government in Pakistan. Gandhi was assassinated in 1948 by a Hindu extremist, who objected to his call for fair treatment of Muslims. This event caused worldwide outrage and plunged India into mourning.

Vietnam and Ho Chi Minh

Like India, Vietnam had experienced European colonialism for many years. Both desired self-rule. But while India followed nonviolent resistance, Vietnam suffered through decades of war.

The leader of the Vietnamese anticolonial movement was **Ho Chi Minh**. The impoverished child of a teacher, Ho Chi Minh received a good education and in 1911 at the age of 21, he went to sea to work on a French ship. From 1917 to 1923, he lived in France, where he studied the Enlightenment thinkers including Thomas Jefferson. Ho joined the cause for Vietnamese independence. He soon combined his Vietnamese nationalism with a belief in communism. While studying in Moscow, Ho developed his belief in the importance of Vietnam's peasantry in any future revolutionary movement.

Reading Closely: Preparation To understand a person's actions, look for forces that shaped their lives. Events that occur early in someone's life can set them up for accomplishments in the future. What about Ho Chi Minh's early life prepared him to lead the Vietnamese people later?

The turmoil of World War II gave Ho a chance to return to Vietnam and fight for independence. During the war, the Japanese liberated Vietnam from France but seized the country for themselves. Ho and his followers started a guerrilla war against Japan. When the Japanese surrendered to the United States, Ho declared Vietnam independent.

However, the French attempted to regain control of their colony. They occupied several major cities. Ho's Viet Minh forces opposed the French, just as they had the Japanese. The Viet Minh won a decisive victory over the French at **Dien Bien Phu** in May 1954.

Peace negotiations established a temporarily divided Vietnam. Ho Chi Minh's Viet Minh ruled the north and a U.S.-backed government led the south. Elections were to establish a unified country in 1956, but the American and South Vietnamese leaders thought Ho might win, so they prevented the elections. The fight between the North and the South continued in Vietnam, with the United States providing up to 600,000 troops to support the South. The North eventually won, and Vietnam was unified under a Communist government in 1976.

Reading Closely: Exceptions Look for cases when events don't follow typical patterns. For example, most rebellions fail. What is distinctive about Ho Chi Minh and his Viet Minh soldiers that helped them defeat their former rulers?

Source: Shutterstock

The Vietnamese won their independence from the French with a victory at Dien Bien Phu in 1954.

The Special Case of Siam (Thailand)

In the 19th century, the British colonized India and the French colonized Indochina (Vietnam, Laos, and Cambodia). Located between India and Indochina was the kingdom of Siam, known since 1939 as Thailand. Siam kept its freedom while most of Asia was falling under Western imperialist influence.

> ***An Enduring Issue: Diffusion***
> The cultures of India and Indochina have each influenced Siam (Thailand). They demonstrate how cultures spread and interact.

Effective Diplomacy One reason Siam remained independent was that its leaders were skilled diplomats. While they made small concessions over trade and territory to Britain and France, they also used the European powers against each other. As a result, Siam remained a buffer zone between them.

A Strong Military Faced with the threat of 19th-century Western imperialism, Siam built a strong military. The government invested in training its officers well and obtaining the latest weapons. As a result, potential invaders recognized that conquest would be costly. In addition, the military became a stabilizing force for independence and nationalism.

Modernization Economic modernization also helped Siam prevent Western domination. The monarchs accepted reforms that built a modern, centralized, and efficient government. This government built canals, expanded electrification, and encouraged trade. Increased trade brought Westerners to Siam, but as partners not conquerers. They helped establish hospitals, schools, and printing plants.

As did countries around the world, Siam suffered in the global economic depression in the 1930s. The stress lead to a rebellion in 1932. This coup forced the king to agree to a constitutional government.

Geography Thailand's location had helped it remain independent in the 19th century. Similarly, its location promoted the country's independence during the Cold War of the 1950s and 1960s. The establishment of communism in China in 1949 made Western powers worry about the spread of that ideology throughout Asia. They saw an independent Thailand as a barrier against this. The United States provided massive amounts of financial aid to strengthen Thailand in order to discourage the appeal of communism.

Source: Getty Images.

Buddhism has long been one of the forces uniting the people of Thailand.

Application

Read the excerpt and answer the questions that follow it.

Ho Chi Minh, letter to the French minister of colonies in the newspaper *La Paria*, August 1, 1922

> We know very well that your affection for the natives; of the colonies in general, and the Annamese [Vietnamese] in particular is great.
>
> Under your proconsulate [leadership] the Annamese people have known true prosperity and real happiness, the happiness of seeing their country dotted all over with an increasing number of spirit and opium shops which, together with firing squads, prisons, "democracy" and all the improved apparatus of modern civilization, are combining to make the Annamese the most advanced of the Asians and the happiest of mortals.
>
> These acts of benevolence [kindness] save us the trouble of recalling all the others, such as enforced recruitment and loans, bloody repressions, the dethronement and exile of kings, profanation of sacred places, etc.
>
> **Source:** https://www.marxists.org/reference/archive/ho-chi-minh/works/1922/08/01b.htm

1. Explain who is the audience for Ho's letter, and explain how you can determine this.

____

____

____

2. Identify the evidence that Ho provides to support his view of the minister's "affection" for the Annamese.

____

____

____

3. Specify the goal of Ho Chi Minh in writing this open letter.

____

____

____

4. Describe the tone of Ho's letter.

____

____

____

Lesson 2 *Independence Movements in Africa*

Following World War II, people throughout Africa organized to free themselves from colonial rule. Along with this, many leaders advocated for unity among Africans as a way to promote independence, peace, and prosperity. Jomo Kenyatta was a leader in both the Kenyan independence movement and the African unity movement.

Conceptual Understanding
10.7b African independence movements gained strength as European states struggled economically after World War II. European efforts to limit African nationalist movements were often unsuccessful.

Source: *New York State Grades 9–12 Social Studies Framework.*

Analyze a Primary Source

Jomo Kenyatta, speech at the Kenya African Union meeting at Nyeri, July 26, 1952

I want you to know the purpose of the K.A.U. [the Kenya African Union]. It is the biggest purpose the African has. It involves every African in Kenya and it is their mouthpiece [messenger] which asks for freedom. K.A.U. is you and you are the K.A.U.

If we unite now, each and every one of us, and each tribe to another, we will cause the implementation [achievement] in this country of that which the European calls democracy. True democracy has no colour [color] distinction [difference]. It does not choose between black and white.

We are here in this tremendous gathering under the K.A.U. flag to find which road leads us from darkness into democracy. In order to find it we Africans must first achieve the right to elect our own representatives. That is surely the first principle of democracy. We are the only race in Kenya which does not elect its own representatives in the Legislature and we are going to set about to rectify [fix] this situation. We feel we are dominated by a handful of others who refuse to be just. God said this is our land . . . .

We want our cattle to get fat on our land so that our children grow up in prosperity [wealth]; we do not want that fat removed to feed others . . . . We want to prosper as a nation, and as a nation we demand equality, that is equal pay for equal work. Whether it is a chief, headman, or laborer he needs in these days increased salary. He needs a salary that compares with a salary of a European who does equal work. We will never get our freedom unless we succeed in this issue. We do not want equal pay for equal work tomorrow—we want it right now.

If we work together as one, we must succeed. . . .

Source: https://sourcebooks.fordham.edu/mod/1952kenyatta-kau1.html

Read Closely: Context
Based on the context from which it is read, Kenyatta makes a statement that could be intepreted as his disagreement with democracy. Or the same statement could be interpreted as he doesn't think readers will know the meaning of democracy.
Circle a statement that could be interpreted two opposing ways.

Read Closely: Authority
Kenyatta could support his claim that Kenyans have a right to elect their leaders by appealing to facts, logic, informed opinion, or other forms of authority. The authority he appeals to is God.

Read Closely: Emphasis
Writers sometimes summarize and highlight an important point in a short sentence or phrase after a dash or colon.
Circle an example where Kenyatta uses this technique.

African Opposition to Imperialism

At the end of World War II in 1945, demands by Africans for an end to European colonization grew strong. Many Africans had fought on behalf of Britian or France, and they were ready to fight for their country. African newspapers and radio stations advocated for nationalism and independence. Communist leaders, including many educated in the Soviet Union or other Communist countries, promoted independence and state-run economies. However, unlike other Communist regimes, African ones usually retained elements of capitalism.

Ghana

The first British colony in West Africa to win independence was the **Gold Coast**. This colony combined with the former British Togoland to form **Ghana.** Ghana gained independence in 1957 through negotiations led by the United Nations.

Nkrumah Ghana's first president, **Kwame Nkrumah**, took office in the newly established republic in 1960. He was responsible for numerous public works and development projects, such as hydroelectric plants. He was also accused of running the country into debt and allowing widespread corruption, an economic pattern that would often be seen in subsequent African dictatorships. In 1964, he claimed dictatorial powers when the voters agreed to a one-party state with Nkrumah as party leader.

Reading Closely: Context
As you read, pay attention to the location where events take place. Often, the events in one country will affect those in neighboring countries. How did changes in Ghana affect nearby African countries?

Pan-Africanism Nkrumah was a vocal supporter of **Pan-Africanism**, a term he used to mean a celebration of cultural bonds that united people throughout the continent and a rejection of European colonialism. (The term had a different meaning in the 19th century. Some British and American abolitionists believed that whites and blacks could never live together successfully. They proposed to send freed slaves to Africa. They called their ideas Pan-Africanism. The country of Liberia was founded on this vision.)

In keeping with his Pan-Africanist vision, Nkrumah founded the Organization of African Unity (OAU) in 1963. However, three years later, the Nkrumah government was overthrown in a military coup, during which many foreigners were expelled from the country. Not until 2000 would Ghana witness a peaceful transfer of civilian power from one elected president to another.

Source: Shutterstock

For the OAU summit held in Accra, Ghana, in 1965, a gold medallion was created to honor Ghana's leader, Kwame Nkrumah.

Algeria

In North Africa, the French colony of **Algeria** also struggled for independence. Like Ghana, Algeria gained its independence in the years after World War II, fell under the control of a strong leader, and developed into a single-party state. However, Algeria endured far more violence in the process of gaining its independence.

The Algerian War for Independence Algerians' battle for independence from France began in 1954, although many Algerians had been campaigning for independence since World War II. The war was a complicated affair with many groups involved. Since so many French people lived in Algeria as settlers, the French government considered Algeria a part of France and was adamant that it could not become a separate country. But the French in Algeria were a minority.

The Algerian movement for independence was led by the National Liberation Front (NLF), which used effective guerrilla techniques against half a million French forces sent to keep hold of Algeria. While French military casualties were relatively low, hundreds of thousands of Algerians died in the war.

Reading Closely: Stakeholders
Historical conflicts occur between people who have opposing interests in the outcome of an event. Examining positions of stakeholders can help you understand an event from multiple perspectives. Who were the stakeholders in the Algerian conflict?

The Algerian conflict caused sharp divisions in France. The French Communist Party, which was quite powerful at the time, favored Algerian independence. Violence broke out in urban areas throughout France. In 1958, French president Charles de Gaulle, with a new mandate for expanded presidential power under the constitution of the new Fifth Republic, planned the steps through which Algeria would gain independence. He then went straight to the people of France and Algeria to gain approval of his plan in a referendum, thereby bypassing the French National Assembly.

Struggles with New Independence In Algeria, independence caused many thousands of pro-French residents to flee the country. Many of these were middle-class professionals, and their absence caused economic problems. In addition, the large influx of these refugees arriving in France created housing and employment problems as well as an increase in anti-immigration sentiment.

The new Algerian Republic faced problems. Its first leader was overthrown in a coup led by his former ally in 1965. The country was a single-party state for many years, with little tolerance for dissent. Meanwhile, the government led a drive for modernization of industry and collectivization of agriculture.

Algerian Civil War In 1991, violence again surfaced in Algeria, this time in reaction to one-party rule. The Islamic Salvation Front won the first round in an election that was then canceled. A bloody civil war followed (1991–2002), during which the NLF continued its control. President Abdelaziz Bouteflika was chosen by the army in 1999. In his second term, he attempted to be more inclusive of political opponents, although suicide bombings continued. In 2011, the military state of emergency, in place since 1992, was lifted in response to protests in the wake of major uprisings in nearby states, including Tunisia, Egypt, and Libya.

Reading Closely: Motivation
Examining the motivations of specific individuals provides understanding into historical events. What were President Abdelaziz Bouteflika's motivations for his actions?

Kenya

East Africa was a culturally diverse region. It was home to many long-standing African cultures. In addition, so many merchants from the Middle East traded and settled in the region that the Bantu language of Swahili shows a heavy influence of Arabic. In addition, many laborers from India settled in the region. For example, in **Kenya**, the British brought 35,000 workers from India between 1886 and 1901 to help build the Mombasa-Kisumu Railway. After completion of the railway, these workers settled on unoccupied lands in Kenya. Over the years, their descendants became merchants and professionals, forming part of Kenya's middle class. Their prosperity made them targets for violence by other Kenyans.

Mau Mau Rebellion Before independence, many Kenyans resisted European control. A group called the **Mau Mau** carried out terror campaigns in 1952 in protest against economic conditions as well as British colonialism. Kenya's government, with British support, attempted to put down the Mau Mau rebellion. However, the fighting escalated into a civil war, and the Mau Mau gained support throughout Kenya. The British ultimately gave up the area, granting independence in 1963. The first elected president was Jomo Kenyatta, who ruled from 1964 to 1978. A long-time advocate for independence, Kenyatta had served a prison term for supporting the Mau Mau.

Ethnic Conflict Attempts to unify the people living in Kenya were difficult. The differences among the various African groups, combined with the many people of Indian heritage, made creating a single national identity slow.

Ethnic Diversity in Kenya

Ethnic Group	Percentage of the Total Population
Kikuyu	22%
Luhya	14%
Luo	13%
Kalenjin	12%,
Kamba	11%
Kisii	6%
Meru	6%
other African	15%
non-African	1%

Source: *World Factbook,* United States Central Intelligence Agency.

Reading Closely: Comparisons
To understand situations in other countries, compare them to ones you are already familiar with. Both Kenya and the United States include people of many ethnic groups. How are ethnic relations in the two countries similar and different?

Independent Kenya had only one political party, the Kenya African National Union (KANU). Following the death of Kenyatta in 1978, Vice President Daniel arap Moi ruled for 24 years while Kenyan stability disintegrated in the face of increasing corruption. Finally, the International Monetary Fund (IMF) threatened to withdraw loans if the corruption continued. In the 2000s, the government pledged to crack down on bribery and kickbacks.

Violence between Kenya's ethnic groups was common, especially during elections. The 2007 presidential elections resulted in more than 1,000 deaths. In addition, it displaced more than 600,000 people. The formation of a coalition government brought some peace. However, attacks on Asians, particularly Indians, continued.

Angola The Portuguese colony of **Angola** in southwest Africa won its independence in 1975. Like the Algerians and the Vietnamese, the Angolans had to fight to end their colonial status. The armed struggle for independence lasted 14 years.

However, Angola faced greater ethnic conflict than did Algeria or Vietnam. The borders of Angola, like the borders of many newly independent African countries, had been set by European colonial powers with little regard for the makeup of the ethnic groups thrown together under one government. The country was more like a multiethnic empire than a nation-state.

> ***An Enduring Issue: Trade***
> Various factions in Angola fought for control of valuable resources. This was one place where trade led not to greater wealth and prosperity but to conflict.

While the various groups had all fought for independence, they fought each other after winning in 1975. Each wanted to control the country's lucrative diamond mines. Civil war broke out. Each group was supported by a different country:

- The Mbundu people were backed by the U.S.S.R. and Cuba.
- The Ovimbundu people were backed by South Africa.
- The Bakongo people were backed by the United States.

In 2002, after 27 years of fighting, the rivals agreed on a cease-fire. However, this did not end the country's problems. Angola remained beset by poverty, corruption, and human rights abuses.

AFRICAN INDEPENDENCE

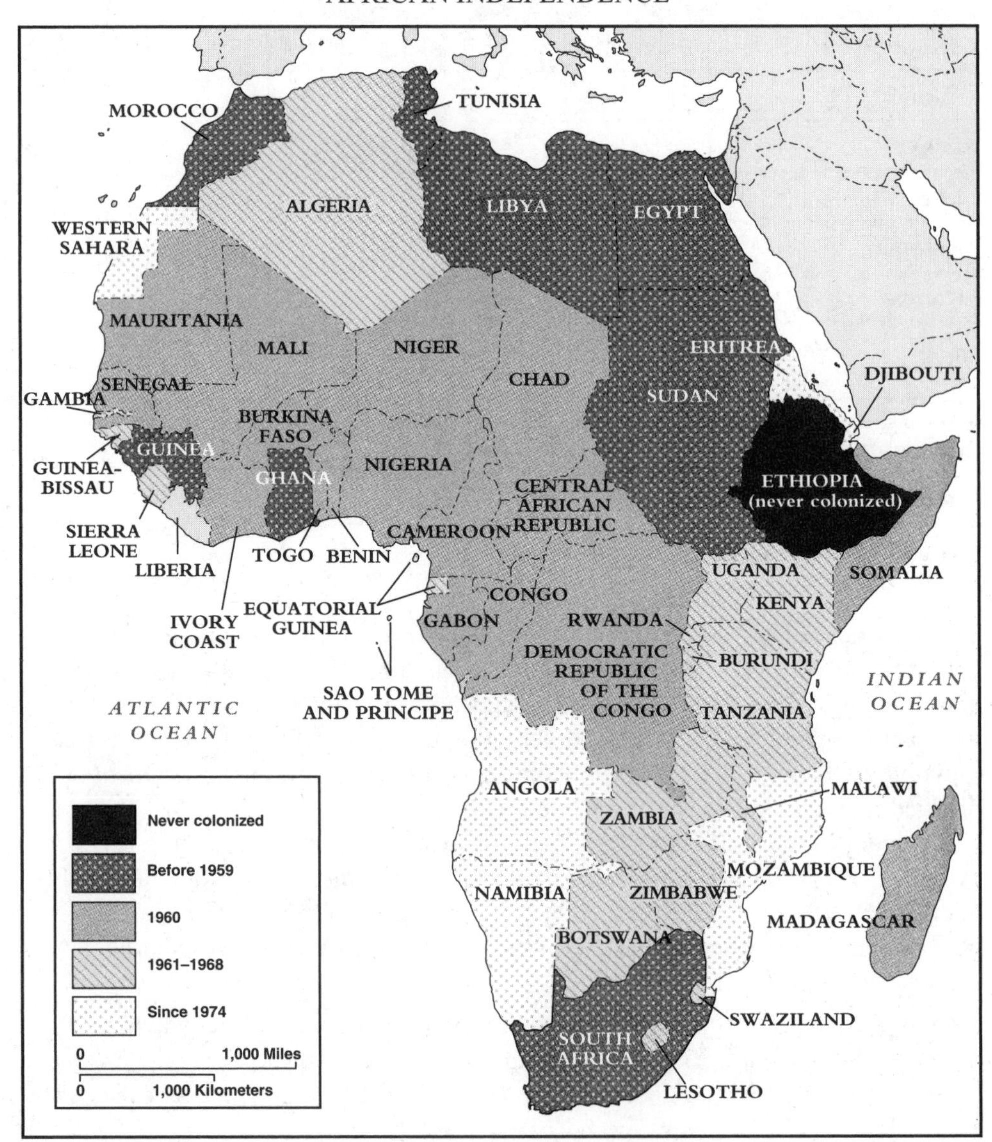

Application

Read the excerpt and answer the questions that follow it.

Kwame Nkrumah, Africa's Future, 1961

> All we ask of the former colonial powers is their goodwill and co-operation to remedy past mistakes and injustices and to grant independence to the colonies in Africa.
>
> It is clear that we must find an African solution to our problems, and that this can only be found in African unity. Divided we are weak; united, Africa could become one of the greatest forces for good in the world.
>
> Although most Africans are poor, our continent is potentially extremely rich. Our mineral resources, which are being exploited with foreign capital only to enrich foreign investors, range from gold and diamonds to uranium and petroleum. Our forests contain some of the finest woods to be grown anywhere. Our cash crops include cocoa, coffee, rubber, tobacco and cotton.
>
> **Source:** Kwame Nkrumah, *I Speak of Freedom: A Statement of African Ideology* (London: Heinemann, 1961).

1. Describe Nkrumah's justification for his request of support from former colonial powers.

___

___

___

2. Explain what Nkrumah means with the phrase "African solution."

___

___

___

3. Name the categories of resources that Nkrumah identifies Africa as being rich in.

___

___

___

4. Identify for which post-World War II movement Nkrumah is advocating.

___

___

___

Lesson 3 *Nationalism in the Middle East*

Conceptual Understanding 10.7c Nationalism in the Middle East was often influenced by factors such as religious beliefs and secularism.

Source: *New York State Grades 9–12 Social Studies Framework.*

One distinctive example of the spread of nationalism in the 1800s was among a group of people who lived scattered throughout Europe, the Middle East, and the rest of the world: Jews. Theodor Herzl was the most powerful advocate for creating a Jewish-led country in the Middle East.

Analyze a Primary Source

Theodor Herzl, *A Jewish State: An Attempt at a Modern Solution of the Jewish Question*, 1904

Read Closely: Evidence
To support their claim, writers often use evidence that they think their readers will accept as accurate. For example, when Herzl refers to "the misery of the Jews," he knows that many readers will agree that Jews have suffered from discrimination and intolerance.

Read Closely: Repetition
Note how writers repeat words to make their point clearly. *Underline the repetition in the excerpt that is intended to make a strong point about Jewish suffering.*

Read Closely: Point of View
Note how Herzl tries to appeal to readers for support by arguing that Zionists are asking for little, just some land. *Circle the phrase in which Herzl suggests that Jews will then be able to take care of themselves.*

The idea which I have developed in this pamphlet is a very old one: the restoration of the Jewish State. The world resounds with outcries against the Jews, and these outcries have awakened the slumbering idea. . . .

Everything depends on our propelling force. And what is our propelling force? The misery of the Jews. . . .

We are a people—one people.

We have honestly endeavored everywhere to merge ourselves in the social life of surrounding communities and to preserve only the faith of our fathers. It has not been permitted to us. In vain are we loyal patriots, our loyalty in some places running to extremes; in vain do we make the same sacrifices of life and property as our fellow citizens; in vain do we strive to increase the fame of our native land in science and art, or her wealth by trade and commerce. In countries where we have lived for centuries we are still cried down as strangers. . . .

Let the sovereignty be granted us over a portion of the globe large enough to satisfy the reasonable requirements of a nation; the rest we shall manage for ourselves.

Source: Theodor Herzl, *A Jewish State: An Attempt at a Modern Solution of the Jewish Question*, 1904, pages 16–25.

Political Change in the Middle East

The breakup of the Ottoman Empire after World War I resulted in several new countries in the Middle East. Competition for control of one small territory would develop into a deadly conflict that would continue for decades.

Zionism

Jews had battled anti-Semitism for centuries. Particularly in the empire of Russia, they faced pogroms, organized efforts to violently attack Jews, often approved of by the government. In a pogrom in the city of Kishinev in 1905, reports stated that more than 100 Jews were murdered. Many Jews had concluded that to be safe, Jews needed to control their own land. The desire of Jewish people to reestablish an independent homeland where their ancestors had lived in the Middle East is know as **Zionism**.

Zionism in the late 19th century gained strength as a reaction to the **Dreyfus Affair**. In 1894 in France, Alfred Dreyfus, a French military officer who was a Jew, was convicted of treason against the French government. However, when people discovered that the conviction had been based on forged documents, it became clear that anti-Semitism was at the core of the accusations. The Dreyfus Affair inspired a worldwide outcry, especially after the French novelist Émile Zola took up Dreyfus's cause. Dreyfus was ultimately pardoned after a time in prison, but the case illustrated just how widespread anti-Semitism was, even in France, one of the countries where Jewish people seemed least oppressed.

Deuxième Année. — Numéro 87

Cinq Centimes

JEUDI 13 JANVIER 1898

Directeur
ERNEST VAUGHAN
ABONNEMENTS

POUR LA RÉDACTION
S'adresser à M. A. BERTHIER
Secrétaire de la Rédaction

ADRESSE TÉLÉGRAPHIQUE : AURORE-PARIS

L'AURORE
Littéraire, Artistique, Sociale

Directeur
ERNEST VAUGHAN
LES ANNONCES SONT REÇUES :
142 — Rue Montmartre — 142
AUX BUREAUX DU JOURNAL

Adresser lettres et mandats :
à M. A. BOUIT, Administrateur
Téléphone : 102-88

J'Accuse...!
LETTRE AU PRÉSIDENT DE LA RÉPUBLIQUE
Par ÉMILE ZOLA

LETTRE
A M. FÉLIX FAURE
Président de la République

Source: Wikipedia Commons

Emile Zola's accusation of anti-Semitism in the Dreyfus Affair, "J'Accuse . . . !" symbolized the increasing role of artists and writers in politics.

Reading Closely: Causation
Rarely does a historical event have a single cause. To help you understand the complexity of an event, pay attention to the multiple causes of it. Identify multiple causes for the Zionist movement.

Theodor Herzl, a well-known Hungarian Jewish intellectual and journalist, used the affair as evidence that assimilation into European society was a failure. At the First Zionist Congress in 1897, he urged the creation of a separate Jewish state. Zionism promoted a close relationship between an individual's Jewish identity and his or her relationship with the state of Israel.

Britain and the Balfour Declaration

Zionists wanted their new state established in Palestine because that was where their ancestors had lived. In modern times, Palestine was part of the Ottoman Empire, and most of its inhabitants were Arabs who practiced Islam. In a new state, Zionists argued, Jews could be free of persecution. In 1917, in the midst of World War I, the British foreign secretary Arthur James Balfour issued the **Balfour Declaration**, which favored the establishment in Palestine of a "national home" for the Jewish people: "His Majesty's Government view with [favor] the establishment in Palestine of a national home for the Jewish people, and will use their best endeavors to facilitate the achievement of this object, it being clearly understood that nothing shall be done which may prejudice the civil and religious rights of existing non-Jewish communities in Palestine or the rights and political status enjoyed by Jews in any other country."

The situation was complicated further because also during World War I, a British officer, T. E. Lawrence, known as Lawrence of Arabia, promised certain Arabs an independent state as well. The British Foreign Office hoped these Arabs would rise up against the Ottoman Empire, which would make it easier for the Allies to help them.

Source: Shutterstock

T. E. Lawrence, whose image was carved into a rock in Arabia, supported the cause of Arab nationalism.

Developments After World War I

The end of World War I brought a number of changes to Palestine and the surrounding Arab countries. However, these changes were often controversial.

An Enduring Issue: Power
The mandate system reflected the continued power of Europeans over other lands. Every society faces the issue of who has power and who does not.

The Mandate System In the peace talks that ended World War I, the Allied powers reduced the Ottoman Empire to the country of Turkey. They could have allowed the people freed from Ottoman rule to form independent states. This would have honored the promise Lawrence had made to the Arabs and the policy of "self-determination" followed for people in eastern Europe. Instead, the victors created a **mandate system**, in which they controlled Middle Eastern lands:

- Britain controlled Iraq, Transjordan (today, Jordan), and Palestine
- France controlled Lebanon and Syria

These new Arab states were essentially colonies of Britain and France. This infuriated the Arabs who lived in these lands.

Pan-Arabism The mandate system infuriated many Arabs. It set the stage for a nationalist movement known as Pan-Arabism, a movement to increase cultural and political unity of all Arabs in Southwest Asia and North Africa. Two organizations led the effort to spread Pan-Arabism:

- The Ba'th (or Ba'ath) Party was formed in 1943 in several countries. It gained ruling power in Syria in 1963 and in Iraq from the 1960s to 2003, ultimately under the leadership of Saddam Hussein.
- The Arab League was organized in 1945 by Egypt, Syria, Lebanon, Iraq, Transjordan, Saudi Arabia, and Yemen. They agreed to support Arab cooperation in politics, culture, economics, social programs, and defense.

In 1952, General Gamal Abdel Nasser, a strong supporter of Pan-Arabism, along with Muhammad Naguib, overthrew Egypt's king and established the Republic of Egypt. Naguib became the republic's first president and was succeeded by the charismatic Nasser. Nasser strengthened the cause of Pan-Arabism by refusing to align Egypt with either the United States or the Soviet Union. Instead of taking a side in the Cold War, Nasser chose to focus on Egyptian sovereignty.

Reading Closely: States
Comparing similar historical trends will help you understand how and why events occur. How do states created by Western imperialism in the 19th century compare to the states created under the mandate system after World War I?

Zionist Migration Increases Britain's control of Palestine, coupled with the Balfour Declaration, sent a signal to Zionists. Soon, Jews from Europe and from other parts of the Middle East began to immigrate to Palestine. As immigration increased, the Arabs in the area protested their loss of land and traditional Islamic way of life.

World War II changed the context for Zionism. The death of six million Jews in the Holocaust caused many Jews to want control over their own country. This provided yet another impetus for Jewish immigration. The fate of European Jews bought worldwide sympathy for the survivors.

Britain, trying to hold the line on Jewish immigration in the face of Arab opposition, turned the matter over to the UN General Assembly. In 1948, after the UN divided Palestine into Jewish and Arab sections, the Jewish section declared itself to be a new country: Israel.

Repeated Wars War broke out immediately between Israel and Palestine, who was supported by neighboring Arab countries. Arab forces from Egypt, Syria, Jordan, Lebanon, and Iraq invaded Israel. After several cease-fires, the Israeli army had gained the upper hand and brokered armistice agreements with each of its neighbors. Immediately following the truce, about 400,000 Palestinians became refugees, living in camps near the Israeli border. Three other Israeli-Arab wars followed:

- In 1956, Israel, with support from Great Britain and France, invaded Egypt's Sinai Peninsula, in part to take back foreign control of the Suez Canal, which had been nationalized by the Egyptian government. Following international protests, Israel and its allies were forced to withdraw from Egypt.
- In the 1967 war, also known as the Six-Day War, Israel fought on three fronts against Egypt, Jordan, and Syria, gaining the Gaza Strip from Egypt, the West Bank and East Jerusalem from Jordan, and the Golan Heights from Syria.
- In the 1973 war, also known as the Yom Kippur War, Israel repelled a surprise invasion by Egypt and Syria.

Reading Closely: Exceptions
Paying attention to patterns in history will help you appreciate when something is not ordinary. Unusual events often have long-lasting consequences. What is significant about how Israel was created?

Peace and Conflict

After 30 years of conflict between Israel and its Arab neighbors, U.S. President Jimmy Carter mediated the **Camp David Accords**, a peace agreement between Egypt and Israel in 1979. While this was a step toward peace in the region, the conflict between the Israelis and the Palestinians continued.

Hoping to build on the progress made at Camp David, the Palestinian Liberation Organization (PLO), a group representing many but not all Palestinians, and Israel began secret negotiations in Oslo, Norway, in 1993. These negotiations resulted in agreements in 1993 and 1995 known as the Oslo Accords. In them, the PLO recognized the right of Israel to exist. In exchange, Israel recognized the PLO as a legitmate representative of the Palestinians.

The Oslo Accords indicated that negotiations could lead to a two-state solution to the problems in the region. One state would be primarily Jewish. The other would be primarily Palestinian Arabs. However, efforts to expand the peace process failed. Thousands of people died in violence in the following decades. Even when violence was low, tensions remained high.

The Israeli-Palestinian conflict was one of three causes of conflict in the Middle East. Another conflict was based on ethnic differences between Arabs, Turks, Kurds, and Persians. The third was rooted in the religous differences between Sunni Muslims and Shia Muslims.

THE MIDDLE EAST—POPULATIONS AND RELIGIOUS GROUPS

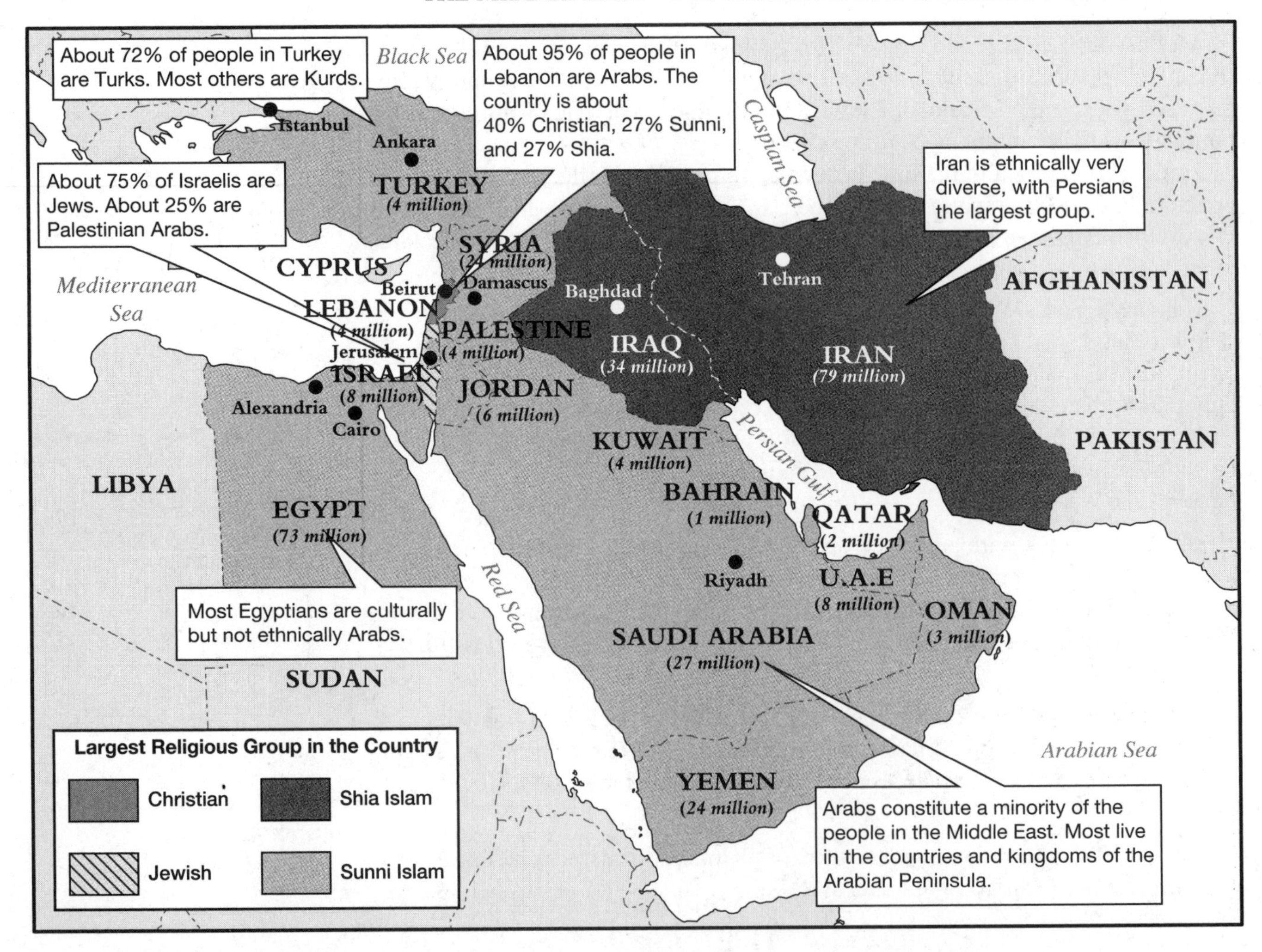

Application

Read the excerpt and answer the questions that follow it.

Letter from Sir Henry McMahon, the British high commissioner in Egypt, letter to Ali ibn Hussein, the sherif of Mecca, October 24, 1915

> As for those regions lying within those frontiers wherein Great Britain is free to act without detriment to the interests of her ally, France, I am empowered in the name of the Government of Great Britain to give the following assurances [pledges] . . . and make the following reply to your letter:
>
> (1) Subject to the above modifications, Great Britain is prepared to recognize and support the independence of the Arabs in all the regions within the limits demanded by the Sherif of Mecca [the leader of the region that included Mecca and Medina].
>
> (2) Great Britain will guarantee the Holy Places against all external aggression and will recognize their inviolability.
>
> (3) When the situation admits, Great Britain will give to the Arabs her advice and will assist them to establish what may appear to be the most suitable forms of government [in] those various territories.
>
> (4) On the other hand, it is understood that the Arabs have decided to seek the advice and guidance of Great Britain only, and that such European advisers and officials as may be required for the formation of a sound form of administration will be British. . . .
>
> I am convinced that this declaration will assure you beyond all possible doubt of the sympathy of Great Britain towards the aspirations of her friends the Arabs and will result in a firm and lasting alliance, the immediate results of which will be the expulsion of the Turks from the Arab countries and the freeing of the Arab peoples from the Turkish yoke, which for so many years has pressed heavily upon them.
>
> **Source:** https://wwi.lib.byu.edu/index.php/Letters_between_Hussein_Ibn_Ali_and_Sir_Henry_McMahon

1. Explain the historical context for the British policies stated by McMahon.

____

____

2. Identify a quote from the excerpt that indicates Britain's intentions regarding its relationship with Arab countries.

____

____

3. Identify a continuity or a change in British policy toward regions outside of Europe seen in the letter.

____

____

Lesson 4 *Nationalism in China*

Conceptual Understanding 10.7d Nationalism in China influenced the removal of the imperial regime, led to numerous conflicts, and resulted in the formation of the communist People's Republic of China.

Source: *New York State Grades 9–12 Social Studies Framework.*

The forces of nationalism and anti-colonialism spread to China. One of the Chinese leaders who emerged was Sun Yat-sen. He was among the many Asian leaders who were impressed by Japan for its success in resisting European domination.

Analyze a Primary Source

Sun Yat-sen, speech in Kobe, Japan, November 28, 1924.

Now, what is the problem that underlies Pan-Asianism, the Principle of Greater Asia, which we are discussing here today?

Briefly, it is a cultural problem, a problem of comparison and conflict between the Oriental [Eastern or Asian] and Occidental [Western or European] culture and civilization. Oriental civilization is the rule of Right; Occidental civilization is the rule of Might.

The rule of Right respects benevolence and virtue, while the rule of Might only respects force and utilitarianism. The rule of Right always influences people with justice and reason, while the rule of Might always oppresses people with brute force and military measures. People who are influenced by justice and virtue will never forget their superior State, even if that country has become weak. So Nepal even now willingly respects China as a superior State.

People who are oppressed by force never submit entirely to the oppressor State. The relations of Great Britain with Egypt and India form a typical example. Although under British rule, Egypt and India have always entertained the thought of independence and separation from Great Britain. If, Great Britain becomes weaker some day, Egypt and India will overthrow British rule and regain their independence within five years. You should now realize which is the superior civilization, the Oriental or the Occidental?

Source: Sun Yat-sen, *China and Japan: Natural Friends–Unnatural Enemies*, (Shanghai: 1941).

Read Closely: Bias
In this excerpt, Sun generalizes about the differences between European and Asian culture. Read such broad statements with caution.
Circle an example of bias toward the West that is shown by Sun.

Read Closely: Point of View
When a writer presents the viewpoint of another group of people, consider whether the people in that group would agree. For example, would the people of Nepal view China as a superior state?

Read Closely: Predictions
If a writer makes predictions, one way to evaluate the insights of the writer is to see if the predictions come true.
Circle one prediction Sun makes that comes true.

Nationalism in China

The Qing Dynasty had ruled China since 1644. However, since the Qing leaders were ethnically Manchus, they were never popular in China. Then their inability to defend China against Western powers in the first Opium War (1839–1842) and the Boxer Rebellion (1899–1901) weakened support for them even more.

Upheaval in China

In 1911, the Qing Dynasty was overthrown. This began a period of instability and hardship in China that lasted for decades.

The Immediate Aftermath In 1912, **Sun Yat-sen (Sun Yixian)** became the first leader of the Chinese republic. But the central government was so weak that regional warlords ruled China. Without a strong national government to control the warlords, violence and crime were widespread. Sun quickly gave up his position to a warlord in a failed attempt to bring stability and order to China.

Source: Shutterstock.

Abraham Lincoln and Sun Yat-sen each attempted to unite a divided country under a strong central government.

Reading Closely: Context
Use what you know about past events to provide context that help you understand new information. Based on knowledge of past events, why did the decision to award Chinese territory to Japan cause conflict?

In 1919, after the end of World War I, many in China had high hopes the Paris Peace Conference would end foreign control over their land. While the leading powers in Paris granted "self-determination" to Eastern Europeans, they did not do the same for China. Instead, they transferred the lands controlled by Germany before the war to Japan. China remained weak.

When news of the Paris treaty reached China, the cities revolted. Though college students and elite youth led what became known as the May Fourth Movement, all social classes in urban areas participated in the protests.

Communists and Nationalists In the wake of the May Fourth Movement, two main groups jockeyed for power. One group was the **Chinese Communist Party (CCP)** led by **Mao Zedong.** He was the son of a prosperous peasant and was inspired by the Communist revolution in Russia. Mao was not like traditional Marxists. They believed that the urban working class would lead a revolution. In contrast, Mao believed that China's Communist revolution could be based on the revolt of peasants, who made up the vast majority of China's population.

The Nationalists The second group was the Chinese Nationalist Party, or Kuomintang, led by Sun Yat-sen. Sun Yat-sen was devoted to full independence and allied with Mao's forces to free China from foreign domination and to overthrow the warlords.

Following Sun Yat-sen's death in 1925, **Chiang Kai-shek (Jiang Jieshi)** took control of the Nationalist Party. Chiang Kai-shek was conservative, and he had a deep-seated distrust of communism. Compared to Mao, he was more at home in urban culture and he had better relationships with Westerners. In 1927, Chiang Kai-shek's forces attacked and nearly wiped out Mao's forces. This marked the start of the Chinese Civil War.

The Long March Mao and what was left of the Chinese Communist Party retreated into China's interior. For several years, they trained in hiding. In 1934, Chiang Kai-shek's army again attacked Mao's. Mao's forces began what is now known as the **Long March**. This trek, which covered about 6,000 miles and took an entire year, traversed some of the world's most treacherous mountains, deepest marshes, and driest deserts. Of the 80,000 or more who began the march, only 10,000 remained to assemble in 1935 in northern China.

Reading Closely: Personal Traits
To understand what motivates historical leaders, consider their personal traits. Mao survived a march to northern China, even though he had to travel 6,000 miles and lost 70,000 troops. What does the Long March indicate about Mao's personality?

However, the Long March gave Mao's army a strong connection with the peasants of the country. Early in the march, the Communists redistributed land from the wealthy to the peasants. More generally, peasants admired the army's stamina and dedication. The Long March became legendary.

Communists and Nationalists Join Forces Meanwhile, the Nationalist Kuomintang continued to rule much of China during the 1930s. However, Chiang Kai-shek was out of touch with the diverse needs of the Chinese people. He advocated Confucianism at a time when the old traditions were no longer popular. When criticism from opponents threatened his power, he suppressed free speech. Corruption was rampant in the Nationalist government as well. These factors alienated China's urban intellectuals.

China's situation was made worse by Japan's invasion of China in the 1930s. In 1935, the Nationalists and Communists suspended their civil war to unite against Japan. Mao's peasant army proved very effective in fighting the Japanese.

The Civil War Resumes In 1945, with the defeat of the Japanese as part of the end of World War II, the Communists and Nationalists once again resumed their war for control of the country. But by that point, Chiang Kai-shek had further lost the support of the people. They felt the Nationalists favored the landlords and the factory owners over the peasants and the workers. The Communists had the support of the peasants. When the Communists took over an area, they reinforced this support by executing landowners and distributing their property among the local farmers.

Communist China

In 1949, the Communists defeated the Nationalists. The Nationalist forces escaped to Taiwan, a large island off the southeast coast of China. There, Chiang Kai-shek reestablished a Nationalist government.

Mao and the Chinese Communist Party called their new country the People's Republic of China. They nationalized the country's industries and created five-year plans on the Soviet model. As the Soviets had done in the 1930s, the Chinese planned to emphasize heavy industry at the expense of consumer goods. They hoped to return China to its former position as a global economic leader.

Great Leap Forward In 1958, Mao attempted to reform the economy dramatically in a short period. His plan was called the **Great Leap Forward**. It affected both rural and urban areas:

- Peasant lands were organized into communes—large agricultural communities where land was held by the state rather than by private owners. The communes were similar to the collectives in the Soviet Union.
- The government tried to increase industrial production, particularly of steel. They forced peasants to go to work in factories and required factories to increase their production.

An Enduring Issue: Scarcity
The tremendous costs of the Great Leap Forward demonstrated the difficult issue of scarcity. China did not have enough workers to both grow crops and work in factories. Every society has limited resources, so decisions on how to use them are always debated.

The Great Leap Forward failed, with terrible consequences. People who protested against the policy were imprisoned in "reeducation camps" or killed. So many workers had been transferred to work in factories that farms had too few workers to harvest crops.

Further, a combination of a drought in some areas and flooding in others ruined some crops. Since local leaders feared punishment if they did not meet production goals, they reported far higher production than was actually occurring. As a result, China continued to transfer food from rural to urban areas and to export grain, even as starvation spread through the countryside. Some 20 million Chinese died from the resulting famines.

Impact of the Great Leap Forward

Year	Total Population (in millions)	Crude Birth Rate (number per 1,000 people)	Crude Death Rate (number per 1,000 people)
1958	660	29	12
1959	672	25	15
1960	662	21	25
1961	659	18	14
1962	673	37	10

Source: Adapted from figures from the National Bureau of Statistics (China), *China Statistical Yearbook* 2000.

Reading Closely: Goals
As you read, note the goals of leaders and their methods for reaching them. This can help you evaluate the leader's effectiveness. What was Mao's goal in launching the Cultural Revolution?

Cultural Revolution In 1966, Mao tried to return to his original principles of communism through the **Cultural Revolution**. Like Stalin's purges, the Cultural Revolution attempted to silence critics and strengthen the ruler's hold on power. Leading the movement were the Red Guards, groups of students and young adults inspired to impose Mao's ideology strictly.

Mao order the Red Guards to seize political leaders, government workers, school teachers, and other well-educated individuals. These people were sent to live and work in the Chinese countryside. The official goal was to reeducate them about the lives of peasants and workers. In reality, they were treated harshly, both physically and emotionally. So many people died or were silenced by fear that China suffered from a "lost generation" of leaders.

Relations with the Soviets Although China and the Soviet Union were both Communist states, they were often rivals, particularly after 1961. The two countries skirmished over their border and competed for influence around the world. For example, Albania, a Soviet satellite country, took advantage of the split by taking China's side against the Soviet Union, thereby receiving additional financial aid from China and more autonomy.

Reading Closely: Changes in Direction
Historians focus more attention on leaders who change a country's direction. How did Deng Xiaoping undo some of Mao's influences?

Reform Under Deng Xiaoping Mao died in 1976. In 1978, **Deng Xiaoping** became the Chinese leader. He was more flexible on ideology than Mao, saying, "It does not matter if the cat is black or white as long as it catches mice." His reform program, the Four Modernizations, focused on four areas:

- science and technology
- agriculture
- industry
- national defense

In agriculture, the government allowed people to farm in small family units, decide which crops to grow, and sell some of them in markets. Under this more liberal system, food production increased by more than 50 percent in six years.

In industry, the government permitted Western manufacturers to open factories in China in special economic zones on the coast. Because wages in China were much lower than in Western countries, goods could be produced significantly more cheaply in China. The sale of Chinese-produced consumer goods around the world gave a substantial boost to China's economy.

In the retail sector, the government allowed people to open small businesses more easily. Restaurants and retail shops began to appear widely.

Under Deng, China remained officially Communist, but it adopted aspects of capitalism. The reforms significantly increased the income, job opportunities, and level of material wealth for millions of people in China, particularly in cities.

Tiananmen Square and Beyond Some Chinese thought that these economic reforms should be accompanied by political reforms, such as freedom of speech and the press and the end of the Communist Party's monopoly on political power. Indeed, political discussions did become somewhat freer than in the past. However, in 1989, a large but peaceful demonstration in **Tiananmen Square** in Beijing led by students and labor leaders was met with force from the government. Soldiers using guns and tanks broke up the demonstrations, killing hundreds of people and injuring thousands. (The government's suppression of information about the incident makes it impossible to determine exact casualty figures.) Thousands of suspected dissidents were arrested in the period that followed.

The democratic nations condemned this violation of human rights. To justify the actions to the Chinese, Deng and his associates claimed that the demonstrators had been plotting to destroy national unity. To convince people that he had their welfare at heart, Deng bolstered economic reforms. China's economic prosperity continued. At the same time, however, he tightened restrictions on political expression and continued to mistreat political prisoners.

The United States threatened to revoke China's special trading privileges if the human rights of government opponents were not observed. To avoid losing their markets in the United States, the Chinese government promised reforms. However, these reforms did not occur. Deng died in 1997, but China generally continued on the path he set: more economic flexibility, but continued political repression.

Application

Read the excerpt and answer the questions that follow it.

Shao Jiang on the Tiananmen Square Protest in 1989

As the days passed, more and more people joined us [in the protest]. We pitched tents in the square and some students began a hunger strike.

On May 19th, the government declared martial law. The military were called in, but we had sheer numbers on our side. Our protest resonated with people from all walks of life, and millions blocked the tanks with makeshift barricades. We felt we had reached a historic moment and started to believe the impossible might be within our grasp.

By the evening of June 3rd, Beijing was a people's city: there were no running buses and all street police had been removed, but the people had organized themselves and the city felt safe. We had no idea of the carnage we were about to witness.

That night, news reached us of troops opening fire on West Chang'an Street, a main road leading to Tiananmen Square. Some friends and I ran towards the street to find out what was happening. Soldiers were shooting at civilians and more followed the tanks on foot, also firing. People were lying wounded on the road and we tried to move them to safety. I hope I never see as many dead bodies as I saw that night. For years afterwards, I was traumatized by what I had seen and suffered nightmares.

In shock, I turned around and started running back to Tiananmen Square to warn my fellow students of what was coming. I remember reaching one of the main crossings and seeing a man in a white coat heading towards a wounded man. He put up his hand, shouting, "Don't shoot, I'm a doctor." They shot him anyway. As I passed one of the main road junctions, people were shouting, "Fascists!" "Murderers!" and some were shot.

Source: Shao Jiang, "I Survived Tiananmen Square," *The Guardian*, May 22, 2009. https://www.theguardian.com/lifeandstyle/2009/may/23/tiananmen-square

1. Explain the point of view from which Shao Jiang remembers the events of 1989.

____

____

2. Describe how the events written about by Shao Jiang show continuity with previous events in China's history.

____

____

3. Compare Shao Jiang's description of government actions with an example of a government response to a protest in another country.

____

____

Chapter 7 Review

Multiple-Choice Questions

Directions (1–6): For each statement or question, choose the number of the word or expression that, of those given, best completes the statement or answers the question.

Base your answer to questions 1 and 2 on the map below and your knowledge of social studies.

THE DIVISION OF BRITISH INDIA 1947

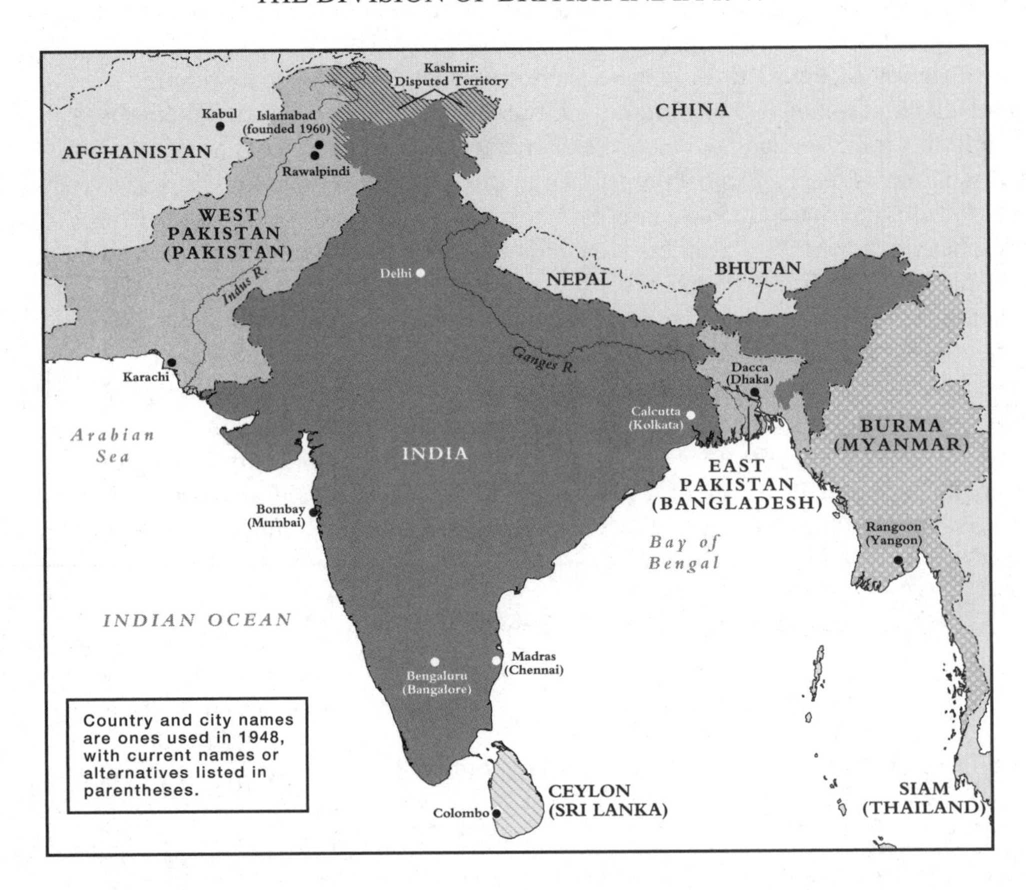

1. What was the primary reason for dividing British India as shown on the map?
   (1) geographic features such as rivers, mountains, and deserts
   (2) religious differences between people
   (3) ethnic division after the Cold War
   (4) political differences resulting from World War II

2. Which was an immediate result of the divisions shown in the map?
   (1) Several million people migrated between India and Pakistan.
   (2) The Soviet Union intervened in the region.
   (3) Gandhi was elected president of India.
   (4) India became part of the British Empire.

Base your answer to questions 3 and 4 on the image below and your knowledge of social studies.

Source: Getty Images. Indian followers of Gandhi sitting with pots of seawater, 1930.

3. What is the goal of the people in this photo?
   (1) to call for peace between people in all lands touched by the oceans
   (2) to highlight one difference between Hindus and Muslims
   (3) to protest against British control over India
   (4) to demonstrate support for the leadership of Gandhi

4. What political idea does this picture best represent?
   (1) communism
   (2) civil disobedience
   (3) peaceful coexistence
   (4) nonalignment

Tips for Answering Multiple-Choice Questions

When viewing a photograph or picture as a primary source, read the caption. It often provides important information about the subject of the photograph or the context in which it was taken. In question 4, the caption states the year the photo was taken, something about the people in the photo, and the contents of the jars. With a familiarity of important events in India's history, a reader can easily identify what they are doing.

Base your answer to questions 5 and 6 on the passage below and your knowledge of social studies.

The Balfour Declaration, issued by the British government, November 2, 1917

> His Majesty's Government view with favor the establishment in Palestine of a national home for the Jewish people, and will use their best endeavors to facilitate the achievement of this object, it being clearly understood that nothing shall be done which may prejudice the civil and religious rights of existing non-Jewish communities in Palestine, or the rights and political status enjoyed by Jews in any other country.
>
> **Source:** http://www.bbc.com/news/world-middle-east-41765892

5. What movement is associated with the statement above?
   (1) Zionism
   (2) the Diaspora
   (3) jihad
   (4) collective security

6. Which was the most important part of the context in which the British government issued the Balfour Declaration?
   (1) Britain was fighting in World War I.
   (2) Britain was trying to establish new colonies.
   (3) Britain wanted to reduce tension with the Ottoman Empire.
   (4) Britain wanted to form a closer alliance with the United States.

Tips for Answering Multiple-Choice Questions

In questions that include references to a geographical location, such as questions 5 and 6, it is helpful to have a good "mental map" of a region. For these questions, it would be helpful to have a mental map of the Middle East. To create a good mental map, practice drawing a world map from memory:

- Sketch a map of the world, outlining and labeling the continents.
- Add and identify large geographic features such as oceans, mountain ranges, and rivers.
- Add more details, such as boundaries and labels for countries and locations of cities.

Creating a world map from memory will highlight regions that you need to learn more about.

Short-Answer Questions

CRQ Directions (7–9): Analyze the documents and answer the short-answer questions that follow each document in the space provided.

Base your answer to question 7 on Document 1 below and on your knowledge of social studies.

Document 1

This excerpt is from writings of Mohandas Gandhi on war and violence.

1. Science of war leads one to dictatorship pure and simple. Science of nonviolence can alone lead one to pure democracy.
2. Democracy and violence can ill go together. The State that are today nominally democratic have either to become frankly totalitarian, or if they are to become truly democratic, they must become courageously nonviolent.
3. Holding the view that, without the recognition of nonviolence on a national scale, there is no such thing as a constitutional or democratic government, I devote my energy to the propagation of nonviolence as the law of our life, individual, social, political, national and international.

Source: www.mkgandhi.org/nonviolence/phil5.htm

7. Describe the historical context for Gandhi's writing.

____

____

____

____

Tips for Answering Short-Answer Questions

To help identify the historical context for an event, consider seeing it in both a global and a regional perspective.

- To focus on the global context, imagine seeing the event from the moon. As the earth revolved, an observer would see what was happening around the entire globe. For example, in the mid-20th century, one would see the rise of Ho Chi Minh in Vietnam and Kwame Nkrumah in Ghana. Both were responding to Western colonization.
- To focus on the region, imagine seeing the event from a drone. From there, an observer could see the importance of the local geography and particular culture in shaping the event. For example, in Vietnam, the success of the Viet Minh was partially because the dense jungles made their guerrilla tactics more effective. In addition, the long struggle of the Vietnamese against domination by China made the desire for self-determination strong.

Base your answer to question 8 on Document 2 below and on your knowledge of social studies.

Document 2

Ho Chi Minh is speaking to the people of Indochina in 1946.

Wage Resistance War!

Compatriots throughout the country! Out of love for peace we have made concessions. But the more concessions we made, the further the French colonialists went because they are resolved to invade our country once again.

No!

We would rather sacrifice everything than lose our country, than return to slavery.

Compatriots! Rise up!

Men and women, old and young, regardless of creeds, political parties, or nationalities, all the Vietnamese must stand up to fight the French colonialists to save the Fatherland. Those who have rifles will use their rifles. Those who have swords will use their swords. Those who have no swords will use their spades, hoes, and sticks. Everyone must endeavor to oppose the colonialists and save his country.

Soldiers, self-defense guards, militiamen!

The hour of national liberation has struck! We must sacrifice to our last drop of blood to save our country. Whatever hardships we must endure, we are ready to endure them. With the determination to sacrifice, victory will be ours!

Long live an independent and unified Viet Nam!

Long live the victorious resistance!

Source: https://www.marxists.org/reference/archive/ho-chi-minh/works/1946/december/19.htm

8. Using this excerpt, identify Ho Chi Minh's purpose in writing this message.

____

____

____

____

____

Base your answer to question 9 on both Documents 1 and 2 and on your knowledge of social studies.

Similarity—tells how something is alike or the same as something else.

Difference—tells how something is not alike or not the same as something else.

9. a) Identify a similarity or a difference in the ideas about decolonization expressed by Gandhi and Ho.
   b) Explain the similarity or difference you identified using evidence from both documents.

____

____

____

____

____

____

Speaking and Listening: Reflect on the Key Idea

Working with a partner, make a Venn diagram comparing nonviolent resistance and armed struggle. Identify at least three distinctive traits of each and at least three traits they share.

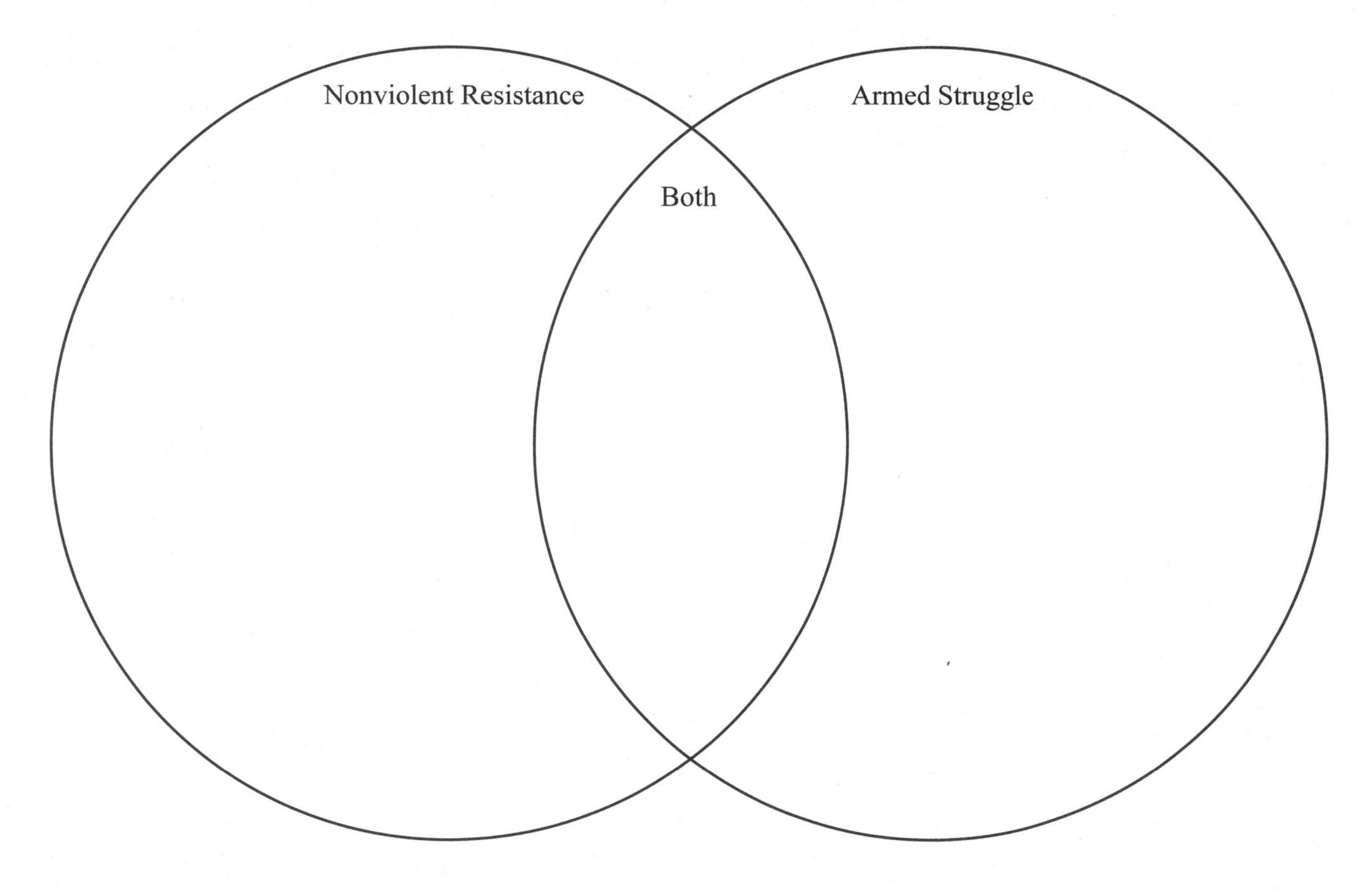

Period 3 *Enduring Issues Extended Essays*

Extended Essay A

Directions

An enduring issue is an issue that exists across time. It is one that many societies have attempted to address with varying degrees of success. Read the following documents and take notes in the margin identifying at least two themes in each one. Then use these notes and the Planning Page to prepare to write the essay. Finally, on a separate sheet of paper or on a computer, write your extended essay.

In your essay:

Identify the issue based on a historically accurate interpretation of **three** documents.

Define the issue using evidence from three documents.

Argue that this is a significant issue that has endured by showing:

- How the issue has affected people or been affected by people.
- How the issue has continued to be an issue or changed over time.

Include outside information from your knowledge of social studies and evidence from the documents.

Keep in mind these terms:

Identify—means to put a name or to name

Define—means to explain features of a thing or concept so that it can be understood

Argue—means to provide a series of statements that provide evidence and reasons to support a conclusion

Topics to consider for your essay: (See page xvii.)

Conflict

Cooperation

Power

Inequality

Innovation

Interconnectedness

Ideas and Beliefs

Environmental Issues

Scarcity

Document 1

A constitution for Europe, proposed in 2004 but not ratified.

DRAWING INSPIRATION from the cultural, religious and humanist inheritance of Europe, from which have developed the universal values of the inviolable and inalienable rights of the human person, freedom, democracy, equality and the rule of law. . . .

III. 133.1. Workers shall have the right to move freely within the Union.

III. 133.2. Any discrimination based on nationality between workers of the Member States as regards employment, remuneration and other conditions of work and employment shall be prohibited.

III. 133.3. Workers shall have the right, subject to limitations justified on grounds of public policy, public security, or public health: (a) to accept offers of employment actually made; (b) to move freely within the territory of Member States for this purpose. . . .

III. 214.1. Each Member State shall ensure that the principle of equal pay for female and male workers for equal work . . . is applied.

Source: https://europa.eu.

Document 2

The Universal Declaration of Human Rights was written by the United Nations soon after World War II ended, 1948.

Article 1. All human beings are born free and equal in dignity and rights. They are endowed with reason and conscience and should act towards one another in a spirit of brotherhood.

Article 2. Everyone is entitled to all the rights and freedoms set forth in this Declaration, without distinction of any kind, such as race, colour [color], sex, language, religion, political or other opinion, national or social origin, property, birth or other status. . . .

Article 3. Everyone has the right to life, liberty and security of person.

Article 4. No one shall be held in slavery or servitude; slavery and the slave trade shall be prohibited in all their forms.

Article 23. (1) Everyone has the right to work, to free choice of employment, to just and favourable [favorable] conditions of work and to protection against unemployment. (2) Everyone, without any discrimination, has the right to equal pay for equal work. (3) Everyone who works has the right to just and favourable remuneration ensuring for himself and his family an existence worthy of human dignity, and supplemented, if necessary, by other means of social protection. (4) Everyone has the right to form and to join trade unions for the protection of his interests.

Source: http://www.un.org/en/universal-declaration-human-rights/

Document 3

By the beginning of the 20th century, most of Africa had been colonized by European powers. The excerpt is from Edward Morel, *The Black Man's Burden*, 1903.

> It is [the Africans] who carry the 'Black man's burden'. . . . What the partial occupation of his soil by the white man has failed to do; what the mapping out of European political 'spheres of influence' has failed to do; what the [gun] . . . , the slave gang, labour [labor] in the bowels of the earth and the lash, have failed to do; what imported measles, smallpox and syphilis have failed to do; whatever the overseas slave trade failed to do, the power of modern capitalistic exploitation, assisted by modern engines of destruction, may yet succeed in accomplishing.
>
> For from the evils of the latter, scientifically applied and enforced, there is no escape for the African. Its destructive effects are not spasmodic: they are permanent. In its permanence resides its fatal consequences. It kills not the body merely, but the soul. It breaks the spirit. It attacks the African at every turn, from every point of vantage. It wrecks his polity, uproots him from the land, invades his family life, destroys his natural pursuits and occupations, claims his whole time, enslaves him in his own home. . . .
>
> To reduce all the varied and picturesque and stimulating episodes in savage life to a dull routine of endless toil for uncomprehended ends, to dislocate social ties and disrupt social institutions; to stifle nascent desires and crush mental development; to graft upon primitive passions the annihilating evils of scientific slavery, and the bestial imaginings of civilized man, unrestrained by convention or law; in fine, to kill the soul in a people-this is a crime which transcends physical murder.
>
> **Source:** E. D. Morel, *The Black Man's Burden,* in Louis L. Snyder, *The Imperialism Reader* (Princeton, N.J.: Van Nostrand, 1962), pp. 163–164. First published in 1920 in Great Britain.

Document 4

Source: CartoonStock.com

Document 5

Cecil Rhodes was an Englishman who lead the way in developing diamond and gold industries in Africa during the colonization of the continent. The excerpt is from, *Need for Imperialism*, 1895

> I. . . attended a meeting of the unemployed [in London] I listened to the wild speeches, which were just a cry for "bread! bread!" and on my way home I pondered over the scene and I became more than ever convinced of the importance of imperialism. . . . My cherished idea is a solution for the social problem, i.e., in order to save the 40,000,000 inhabitants of the United Kingdom from a bloody civil war, we colonial statesmen must acquire new lands to settle the surplus population, to provide new markets for the goods produced in the factories and mines. The Empire, as I have always said, is a bread and butter question. If you want to avoid civil war, you must become imperialists.
>
> **Source:** Quoted in V. I. Lenin, *Imperialism* (1917). Marxist Internet Archive.

Preparing to Write

MY ENDURING ISSUE IS: ____

You may use the Enduring Issues Planning Page organizer to prepare to write your essay. Writing on this Planning Page will NOT count toward your final score.

You may also choose to prepare to write the Enduring Issues Essay by creating an outline or graphic organizer on your own sheet of paper.

ENDURING ISSUES PLANNING PAGE

Essay Requirements	Yes	Circle documents that apply	One or two possible ideas for outside info
Is this an issue supported by at least three documents? Which documents support this issue?		1 2 3 4 5	
Which documents can be used to develop the definition for this issue?		1 2 3 4 5	
Has this issue significantly affected people or been affected by people?		1 2 3 4 5	
Has this issue endured across time or changed over time? In which document or documents do you see this?		1 2 3 4 5	

Extended Essay B

Directions

An enduring issue is an issue that exists across time. It is one that many societies have attempted to address with varying degrees of success. Read the following documents and take notes in the margin identifying at least two themes in each one. Then use these notes to develop an outline or graphic organizer for an essay. Finally, on a separate sheet of paper or on a computer, write an extended essay.

In your essay:

Identify the issue based on a historically accurate interpretation of **three** documents.

Define the issue using evidence from three documents.

Argue that this is a significant issue that has endured by showing:

- How the issue has affected people or been affected by people.
- How the issue has continued to be an issue or changed over time.

Include outside information from your knowledge of social studies and evidence from the documents.

Keep in mind these terms:

Identify—means to put a name or to name

Define—means to explain features of a thing or concept so that it can be understood

Argue—means to provide a series of statements that provide evidence and reasons to support a conclusion

Topics to consider for your essay: (See page xvii.)

- Conflict
- Coperation
- Power
- Inequality
- Innovation
- Interconnectedness
- Ideas and Beliefs
- Environmental Issues
- Scarcity

Document 1

The textile industry grew rapidly as the ability to spin yarn and weave cloth during industrialization. This is an anonymous pamphlet on the impact of mechanized spinning, 1794.

Many things combine to make the hand ppinning of wool, the most desirable work for the cottager's wife and children. A wooden wheel costing 2s. [2 shillings] for each person, with one reel costing 3s. [3 shillings] set up the family. The wool-man either supplies them with wool by the pound or more at a time . . . No stock is required, and when they carry back their pound of wool spun, they have no further concern in it. Children from five years old can run at the wheel, it is a very wholesome employment for them, keeps them in constant exercise, and upright: persons can work at it till a very advanced age.

But from the establishment of the spinning machines in many counties where I was last summer, no hand work could be had, the consequence of which is the whole maintenance of the family devolves on the father, and instead of six or seven shillings a week, which a wife and four children could add by their wheels, his weekly pay is all they have to depend upon.

Source: Anonymous, "Observation on the Detriment which is Supposed must Arise to the Family of every Cottage throughout the Kingdom from the Loss of Woollen Spinning by the Introduction of Machinery in that Worrk," (London, 1794). Pamphlet.

Document 2

Captain Manfred Freiherr von Richthofen, air warfare in World War I.

In Russia our battle squadron did a great deal of bomb throwing. Our occupation consisted of annoying the Russians. We dropped our eggs on their finest railway establishments. One day our whole squadron went out to bomb a very important railway station. The place was called Manjewicze and was situated about twenty miles behind the Front. That was not very far. The Russians had planned an attack and the station was absolutely crammed with colossal trains. Trains stood close to one another. Miles of rails were covered with them. One could easily see that from above. There was an object for bombing that was worthwhile. One can become enthusiastic over anything. For a time I was delighted with bomb throwing. It gave me a tremendous pleasure to bomb those fellows from above. Frequently I took part in two expeditions on a single day.

Source: Captain von Richthofen, *The Red Battle Flyer* (New York: McBride Co., 1918), pp. 99–102, 131–133.

Document 3

Fidel Castro led an overthrow of the Fulgencio Batista dictatorship in Cuba. The excerpt is a speech from Castro to a congress of peasants on February 24, 1959.

> Let us not speak about promises but about realities. The peasants had always lived under terror, they did not have faith because they had been deceived, they did not have hope. . . .
>
> While the enemy [the troops supporting Batista] took away everything, stole everything, and did not pay for what they took, in spite of the many millions they had, the Rebel Army did the opposite. Nothing stopped Batista's Army from stealing personal belongings from the peasants, which were sold later. When they did not find anything to take, they just burned the houses. How little they thought about the efforts that had been needed to build them! How easily they burned houses! How easily they murdered people!
>
> The conduct of the Rebel Army gained little by little the peasants' confidence, their love, and gave them faith in the final victory. We never took anything from the peasants without paying for it, we never invaded their houses. The Rebel Army never took anything that had not been spontaneously offered. Never a rebel soldier humiliated a peasant.
>
> **Source:** http://lanic.utexas.edu/project/castro/db/1959/19590224.html

Document 4

The excerpt is from Richard Dannatt on the drone attacks in contemporary war.

> We need to be very realistic about the use of drones – unmanned aerial vehicles (UAVs), to give them their proper name.
>
> At first glance, the use of a drone – controlled by an operator thousands of miles away in the safety of an air-conditioned cabin on a secure airfield – to kill someone, seems to suggest something that is not quite right – not quite fair. It seems more akin to a computer video game than the deadly business of modern warfare. But we must put such action into its proper context.
>
> The current threats to our security both at home and abroad emanate from groups of people who have torn up the long-established rule book of armed conflict and are using extreme and shocking violence, broadcast worldwide, to achieve their objectives through fear and intimidation. To defeat groups such as Isil, al-Shabaab, Boko Haram, and al Qaeda while remaining within an accepted moral envelope ourselves, we have to be inventive, determined, and highly focused. Drone attacks are an important part of this new way of warfare.
>
> **Source:** http://www.telegraph.co.uk/news/worldnews/islamic-state/11994792/Drone-attacks-are-a-vital-part-of-modern-warfare.html

Document 5

Countries with the Most Deaths from Terrorist Attacks, 2016.

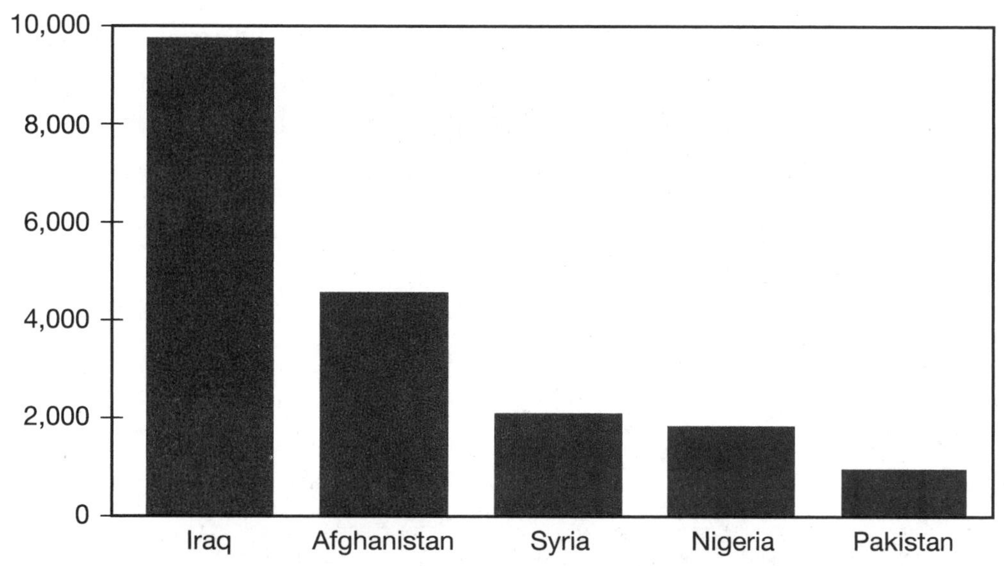

Source: National Consortium for the Study of Terrorism and Responses to Terrorism, U.S. Department of State.

Preparing to Write

MY ENDURING ISSUE IS: ____

You may use the Enduring Issues Planning Page organizer to prepare to write your essay. Writing on this Planning Page will NOT count toward your final score.

You may also choose to prepare to write the Enduring Issues Essay by creating an outline or graphic organizer on your own sheet of paper.

ENDURING ISSUES PLANNING PAGE

Essay Requirements	Yes	Circle documents that apply	One or two possible ideas for outside info
Is this an issue supported by at least three documents? Which documents support this issue?		1 2 3 4 5	
Which documents can be used to develop the definition for this issue?		1 2 3 4 5	
Has this issue significantly affected people or been affected by people?		1 2 3 4 5	
Has this issue endured across time or changed over time? In which document or documents do you see this?		1 2 3 4 5	

Period 4 Contemporary Issues

The world map changed dramatically in the 70 years following the end of World War II in 1945. The number of states increased from about 75 to over 200, even as the world was becoming more integrated economically.

Chapter 8
Tradition and Modernization

Chapter 9
Globalization

Chapter 10
Growing Demands for Human Rights

Map Notes

A

Mexico's population doubled between 1950 and 1975. It doubled again between 1975 and 2015.

B

In Brazil, in the early 1960s, a typical household included about eight people. Today, it is a little more than three.

C

UN Universal Declaration of Human Rights was signed by 48 countries in Paris in 1948. It has prompted people to pass treaties and laws to promote equality and freedom.

D

In 2016, the world GDP per capita was four times larger than in was in 1981. In East Asia and the Pacific, it was eight times larger.

E

Cambodia was the worst example of state-run terrorism since the end of World War II. Under the government of the Khmer Rouge, probably 2 to 3 million people died.

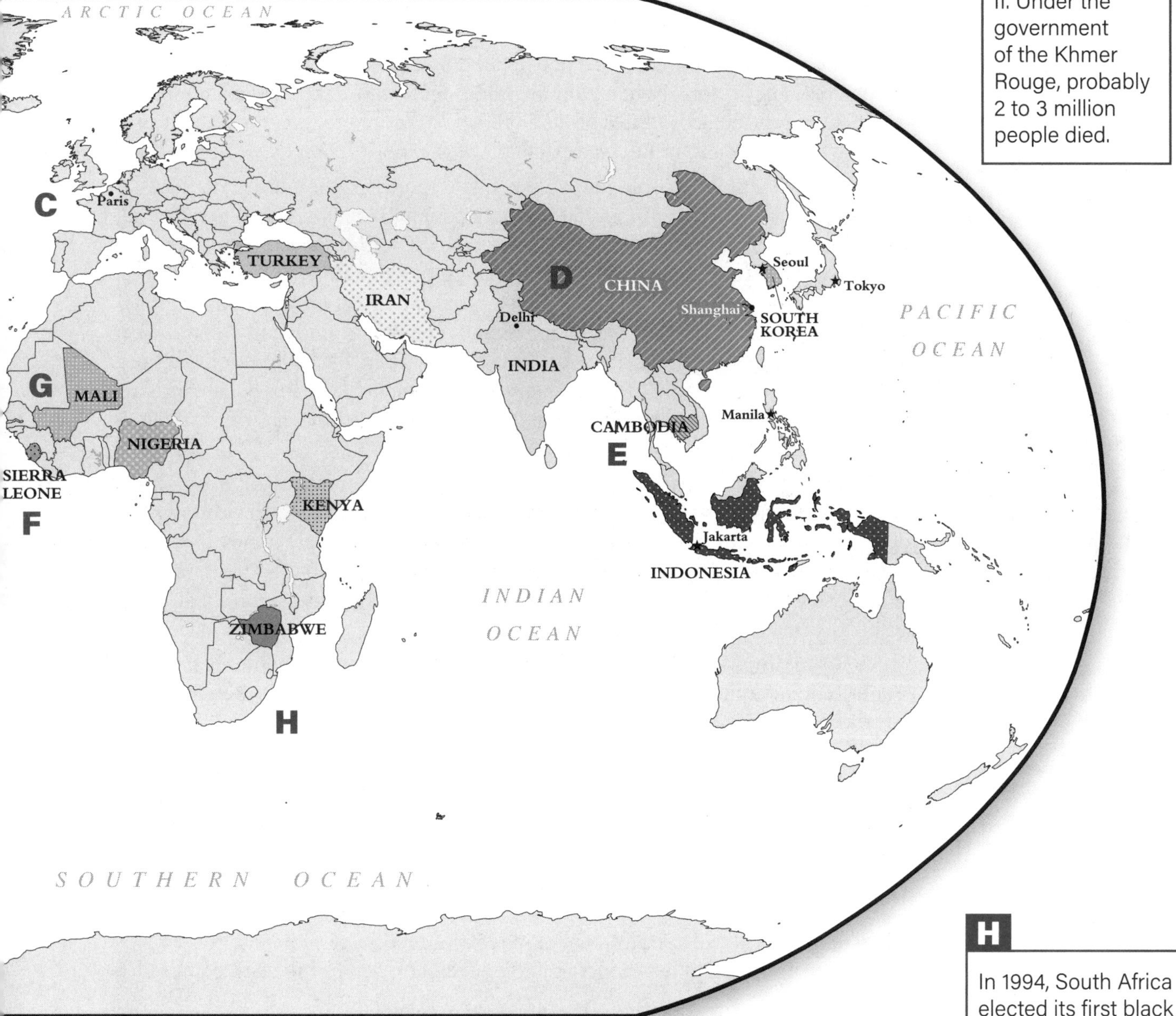

H

In 1994, South Africa elected its first black president, Nelson Mandela. He had led the successful movement to end extreme racial segregation in South Africa.

F

UN troops completed more than 50 peacekeeping missions before 2018. In Sierra Leone they disarmed 75,000 soldiers and destroyed 72,000 weapons.

G

Starting in the late 1900s, deserts expanded in the western United States, the southern edge of the Sahara, and southwestern Asia.

CHAPTER 8

Tensions Between Traditional Cultures and Modernization

Chapter Overview

Forces for modernization included new technologies and ambitious political movements. They often clashed with the traditional culture they were attempting to change or replace. In cultures around the world, people felt strongly about both adopting new ideas and protecting existing practices.

Social Institutions People judged aspects of modernization based on how they affected their lives. In most states, many people traded their traditional rural, agrarian culture for a more urbanized, industrial way of life. Some people saw this as a step forward. Others viewed the change as a threat.

Urbanization and industrialization had a profound effect on social institutions. Family, religion, education, and government all changed significantly. Families worked in different locations and were consistently apart for long periods of time. It also affected how people grew up, learned, and worshiped. These changes had the most significant impact on people in the least developed nations around the world.

Technology Changes in technology spurred socioeconomic changes as well. Communication and transportation were especially significant, as they brought together people who were previously unconnected. For example, many citizens gained a much stronger sense of their country because, for the first time, trains helped them see all of it. These updates in technology contributed to robust nationalist trends in the 19th and 20th centuries.

An Enduring Issue: Tradition One enduring issue in this chapter is how people kept, modified, or gave up the ways of life of their parents. As people moved from rural to urban areas, they changed from working in agriculture to working in a factory or an office. These shifts in where they lived and how they earned money caused other changes. They had to decided what to keep and what not to keep from the culture they grew up in. Many reconsidered their religious beliefs, their ideas about gender roles, and their attitudes about having children.

New York Social Studies Framework: **10.8**

Tensions exist between traditional cultures and agents of modernization. Reactions for and against modernization depend on perspective and context.

Source: *New York State Grades 9–12 Social Studies Framework.*

1. Rewrite Key Idea 10.8 in your own words.

____

____

Identify Enduring Issues

As you identify enduring issues, look for additional examples of them. Below is a list of enduring issues from previous chapters. Add one more to each row under "Examples from Previous Chapters." Then, as you read this chapter, add entries under "Examples from this Chapter."

Support for Enduring Issues		
Enduring Issue	**Examples from the Previous Chapters**	**Examples from this Chapter**
The consequences of the movement of people from place to place	▪ Cities grew rapidly after the Industrial Revolution ▪	1.
The roles of women and men in families	▪ Mary Wollstonecraft advocated for gender equality ▪	2.
Impact of technology on how people think and act	▪ Improvements in plows made farmers more productive ▪	3.

Key Terms and Names

Identity

Westernization (p. 248)

Movement

sharia (p. 253)
secular (p. 254)

Geography

urbanization (p. 247)
total fertility rate (p. 249)
metropolitan (p. 249)
favela (p. 249)
infant mortality rate (p. 250)

Social Structures

modernization (p. 247)
family planning (p. 250)
life expectancy (p. 250)

Governance

Reza Khan (p. 253)
Mohammad Reza Pahlavi (p. 253)
shah (p. 253)
Mohammad Mosaddegh (p. 253)
Ayatollah Ruhollah Khomeini (p. 253)
Mustafa Kemal (p. 254)
Atatürk (p. 254)

Economics

industrialization (p. 247)
gross domestic product (p. 249)

Lesson 1 *Differing Views of Modernization*

Conceptual Understanding
10.8a Cultures and countries experience and view modernization differently. For some, it is a change from a traditional rural, agrarian condition to a secular, urban, industrial condition. Some see modernization as a potential threat and others as an opportunity to be met.

Source: *New York State Grades 9–12 Framework.*

Industrialization and modernization have caused changes in family life throughout the world. In the West African country of Ghana, these changes have been dramatic and recent.

Analyze a Primary Source

Nana Kwaku Kurankye Kwatei, The Ghanaian Family, 2009

The extended family is responsible for the "Right de Passage"—the initiation into adulthood/womanhood, i.e. "Bragoro", "Puberty Rights" of the Akans (Asantes) of Ghana into womanhood and the "Dipo", of the Krobos also of Ghana. . . .

The extended family served as a conduit pipe –to establishing standards and clan identification. Also, one's socio-cultural development starts from the extended/nuclear family; it molds one's character/training to fit into society; shapes one's belief in witchcraft, juju, voodoo, etc.

Before, the family was responsible for the major upbringing and responsibilities of its members as already discussed. However, now we have well-defined agencies undertaking some or all of these tasks; education, sanctions and social control mechanisms have shifted from the family to the educational institutions—from the kindergarten to the university, and the law courts control people's behaviors.

In the modern industrialized and technological environments especially in this era of computer and Internet, the state has taken over more of the functions of the family. Now emphasis has been placed on the globalization concept as the world struggles to become a "Global Village."

Source: https://www.ghanaweb.com/GhanaHomePage/features/The-Ghanaian-African-Extended-Family-system-159990. April 4, 2009.

Read Closely: Unfamiliar Words
As you read, be ready to look up words or phrases you do not fully understand. For example, you will understand this passage better if you know the meaning of extended family and nuclear family.

Read Closely: Controversies
Factual statements often describe ideas or trends on which people disagree sharply. For example, in the third paragraph, the phrase "we have well-defined agencies undertaking some or all of these tasks" focuses on what is happening, not what people think about it.
Circle a phrase in the last paragraph that describes but does not take a position on a topic on which people are likely to disagree.

Read Closely: Rationale
Kwatei believes that the family doesn't have as much responsibility in developing individuals as it once did.
Underline the names of institutions that are mentioned in the excerpt as now having those responsibilities.

Differing Views of Modernization

Modernization is defined as the shift of a society from a mainly traditional, rural, agricultural mode to one that is predominantly urban and industrial. As with any such fundamental change, the move toward modernization can bring serious upheaval that has both positive and negative elements.

Effects of Modernization

Few areas of the world have escaped the effects of **modernization** since 1960. Rapid and large-scale advancements in transportation, communication, and manufacturing, in addition to the overall digital revolution, accelerated the existing trend toward **urbanization** and **industrialization** throughout the world. But how did urbanization and industrialization affect people's lives? What impacts did moving to a city and working in an industrial setting have on people's families, religious observances, and education? The modernization of the developing world lagged somewhat behind that of Europe and North America. Therefore, recent examples from Africa, South America, and Asia provided insights into these questions.

Read Closely: Changes
Many historical terms, such as *industrialization, democracy,* and *totalitarianism*, describe general concepts. To understand them, focus on the specific elements that are part of them. What elements of modernization are noted in this paragraph?

Modernization in Nigeria

Urbanization became a growing reality in Nigeria in the late 20th and early 21st centuries. In 2017, about 50 percent of Nigeria's 191 million people lived in cities. By 2050, about 71 percent of nearly 280 million peple will. The population of Lagos, Nigeria's largest city, numbered about one quarter of a million in the 1860s when Nigeria became an official British colony. By 2015, the population of Lagos proper had topped 9 million, reaching over 13 million with surrounding areas included.

Oil Drove Urbanization in Nigeria Nigeria's urban growth was different from many other countries. Because Nigeria's economy relied for so long on oil income, the country's urbanization was a product of its wealth, rather than the principal driver of it. In other words, people did not necessarily go to cities to participate in industrial work, which then drove the production of the country's wealth. Rather, the oil industry produced the country's wealth and urbanization followed as people moved to cities to try to earn a share of the wealth.

However, in the beginning of the 21st century, Nigerians attempted to diversify their economy. In part this was a response to periodic decreases in oil prices. Efforts to promote manufacturing were hindered by a poor business environment. In the World Bank's 2014 "Doing Business" rankings, Nigeria ranked 175th out of 189 countries. Many problems faced people in urban areas running businesses:

- The electrical supply was not dependable. Urban firms averaged 8 hours of power outage per day.
- Traffic was very congested. This made receiving and shipping products difficult.
- Purchasing land was complicated. The process was expensive and time-consuming.

Read Closely: Stakeholders
Stakeholders are people, or groups of people, who are affected by important developments in a place or event. Some stakeholders are local, such as citizens of a city. Others are not, such as foreign businesses who have financial interest in a city's economy. Who are stakeholders in the oil industry in Nigeria?

Urban Living Conditions As a result of these conditions, living standards for Nigeria's urban dwellers were quite low. Most people lived in informal housing. These were unplanned developments of houses that people built themselves. The houses generally lacked basic services water and sanitary services. As a result, over 60 percent of the people in Nigeria's cities lived in poor housing. .

Living in slum conditions caused serious problems. People were exposed to disease, suffered from violence, and lacked lacked educational opportunities. Children living in Nigerian slums were 35 percent less likely to attend school. About 27 percent of female slum-dwellers left school early, as compared to 16 percent for those not living in slums. However, in spite of these problems, overall literacy rates for urban children (45 percent) were markedly higher than those for rural children (19 percent).

URBANIZATION IN THE CONTEMPORARY WORLD

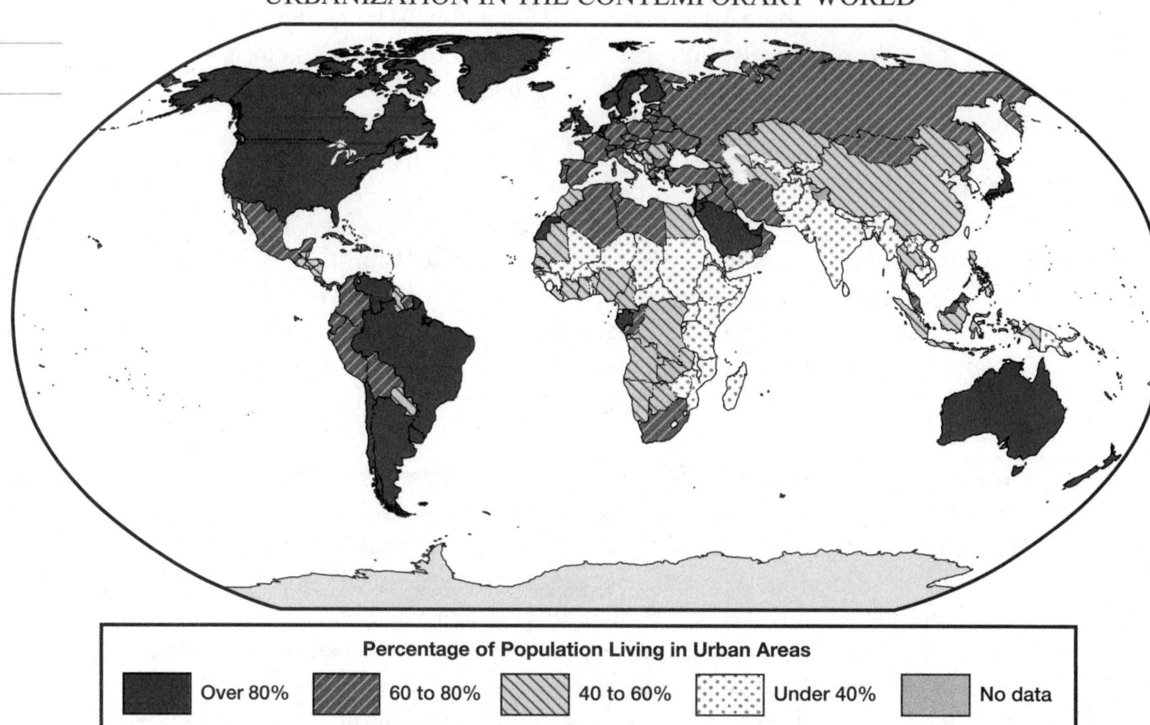

Percentage of Population Living in Urban Areas				
Over 80%	60 to 80%	40 to 60%	Under 40%	No data

Read Closely: Trends
Comparing the effect of similar changes across civilizations will give you a clearer context for understanding historical trends. How do the effects of urbanization in Nigeria compare to the effects of earlier urbanization in England?

Changes to Family Structure Urbanization has had a significant impact on family structure in Nigeria. In traditional rural settings, families lived in households that included not only the nuclear family (mother, father, and children) but also extended family (grandparents, aunts and uncles, their children, and so on). Different parts of the family group had their own areas within a larger compound.

However, in urban Nigeria, land was limited. The increased numbers of people did not necessarily improve the overall family economy, as they might have in a farming setting. Therefore, it was more common for urban family structures to include only a single nuclear family.

Changes to Religion Changes in religion also occurred as Nigeria modernized. About 50 percent of the population was Muslim and 40 percent was Christian. About 10 percent followed traditional beliefs, although people often combined traditional beliefs with Islam or Christianity. Modernizing Nigeria saw the rise of the militant Islamic group Boko Haram, which sought to get ride of the influence of **Westernization** in Nigeria. This group and its actions have heightened tensions between the Muslim northeast of the country and the Christian west.

Modernization in Brazil

The move to cities in Brazil began earlier than it did in Nigeria. In 1960, 46 percent of Brazilians lived in cities; by 2010, that number had become 84 percent, a huge percentage for such a geographically large country. Much of this urbanization was driven by the movement of people from rural areas as agriculture became increasingly mechanized. Many of these people sought manufacturing work in large cities such as São Paulo and Rio de Janeiro. Manufacturing was responsible for about 20 percent of Brazil's **gross domestic product.** São Paulo's manufacturing sector alone accounted for 40 percent of the country's manufacturing output.

An Enduring Issue: Urbanization
Brazil is one example of the global trend of urbanization. When people move to cities, they often hope to find a better life, but often housing is poor and education is hard to obtain.

Changes to the Family During the period from 1960 to 2010, as the percentage of urban dwellers in Brazil nearly doubled, the Brazilian family became dramatically smaller. In that 50-year period, the **total fertility rate** (the total number of children born to an average woman in a given place) for Brazilian women dropped from 6.3 children to 1.9 children. Although other factors contributed to this decline, urbanization was a major factor.

Urban Housing Conditions Brazil had seeral very large cities, including seven cities with more than 2 million people each. About 12 million people resided in its largest city, São Paulo, whose **metropolitan** area was home to about 20 million. The competition for space in Brazil's cities caused land values to increase. Therefore, middle-class citizens were forced into substandard dwellings—tiny apartments in massive high-rise buildings.

As was the case in Nigeria, new arrivals in Brazil's enormous urban centers struggled to find adequate, affordable housing. The poorest residents clustered in collections of informal dwellings called **favelas,** which were shantytowns often made of cardboard, plywood, or other found materials. These slums were on the outskirts of the cities and had few services or utilities.

Read Closely: Modifications
Pay attention to key phrases such as "in spite of." That phrase usually indicates the next sentences will say something readers might not expect because it contradicts or modifies earlier statements. How is "in spite of" used in paragraph about education in Brazil?

Urbanization and Education In spite of the challenges they faced, Brazil's urban poor experienced increasing access to education over the period of rapid urbanization from 1960 to the present. However, the gap in quality of education between the *favela* dwellers and higher-income Brazilians remained wide. Richer Brazilians received a better quality education and were much more likely to attend secondary school and some level of college.

Modernization in South Korea

Like Kenya and Brazil, South Korea experienced rapid urbanization in the mid-20th century. Rural poverty drove migrants to South Korean cities, mainly to the capital, Seoul. Between 1960 and 1970, the population of the city more than doubled, reaching roughly 5.5 million. Fully 50 percent of the city's population in 1970 were recent migrants.

The concentration of urban dwellers primarily in Seoul declined slightly after 1970. Growth occurred more in other cities, such as Pusan, Inchon, and Taegu. As of 2014, the population of South Korea was about 84 percent urban, slightly higher than in the United States. In 2016, the city of Seoul included over 10 million people. The entire Seoul metropolitan region was 26 million people. This made it the second largest metropolitan region in the world. One in every two South Koreans lived in this metropolitan area.

Industrialization and Urbanization After 1960, South Korea developed into an industrial powerhouse. This industrial rise was abetted by the authoritarian

Source: Getty Images

The landscape and level of wealth in Seoul, South Korea, changed dramatically from the 1960s (left) to the early 21st century (right).

government of Park Chung Hee, who was president from 1963 until his death in 1979. The government pursued an industrial policy that focused on exports. It invested in schools and transportation, used tariffs to protect industries, and provided financial support to corporations. Working conditions were poor and the country lacked democracy, but the economy grew. As it did, labor unions became more powerful and people demanded political reforms. By the early 21st century, South Korea was more prosperous than most countries in eastern and southern Europe. Further, it was democratic. It had competitive political parties, a free press, and strong labor unions.

Read Closely: Comparisons
To understand why countries develop as they do, consider how they are similar and different than other countries How was South Korea both like and unlike Brazil?

South Korea tremendous success resulted from several factors. Some of these were its emphasis on intense education, strong leadership, and pragmatism. One theory is that these values reflected the country's Confucian heritage. According to this view, Korea's traditions worked with, not against, modernization.

Changes to the Family As in other countries, South Korea saw the average size of families decrease with modernization and urbanization. Between 1960 and 1995, the average family size in South Korea declined from 5.5 people to 3.3. But in South Korea, the government also was a significant factor in supporting **family planning**, or birth control. As **infant mortality rates** declined and **life expectancy** rose, people choose to have fewer children.

Application

Read the excerpt and answer the questions that follow it.

Michael Schuman on Korea's Rise

> Over the past decade, however, Korea has reinvented itself — it's an Asian miracle again. Korea has become an innovator, an economy that doesn't just make stuff, but designs and develops products, infuses them with the latest technology, and then brands and markets them worldwide, with style and smarts. Samsung and LG, not the Japanese electronics giants, are dominating the hot new LCD-TV business. In 4G phone technology, Samsung is poised to become a leading force, while Hyundai Motor, an industry joke a decade ago, is a top-five automaker, its rising market share fueled by quality cars and nifty marketing. "'Made in Korea' used to be synonymous with cheap and imitative," says Bernie Cho, president of DFSB Kollective, a start-up that markets Korean pop music internationally. "Now it's become premium and innovative."
>
> New industries, from online games to pop music, have emerged as powerhouses. Politically as well, Korea is stepping out of Washington's shadow and becoming an influential voice in its own right. Symbolic of that new role, Seoul is hosting the G-20 summit [a meeting of the leaders of 20 of the world's most influential countries] on Nov. 11 and 12, the first Asian country to do so. This nation is a global leader-in-waiting.
>
> **Source:** Michael Schuman, "Asia's Latest Miracle," *Time,* November 15, 2010.

1. Identify either continuity or change in Korea shown in the excerpt.

____

____

____

____

____

____

2. Explain the cause for the continuity or change identified in the excerpt.

____

____

____

____

____

____

Lesson 2 *Tradition and Modernization*

Conceptual Understanding 10.8b Tensions between agents of modernization and traditional cultures have resulted in ongoing debates within affected societies regarding social norms, gender roles, and the role of authorities and institutions.

Source: *New York State Grades 9–12 Framework.*

The Turkish leader Kemal Atatürk successfully pushed through many reforms. Some of these changed the role of women in the country.

Analyze a Primary Source

Women in the New Turkey

"Everything we see in the world is the creative work of women."

With abiding faith in the vital importance of women in society, Atatürk launched many reforms to give Turkish women equal rights and opportunities. The new Civil Code, adopted in 1926, abolished polygamy and recognized the equal rights of women in divorce, custody, and inheritance. The entire educational system from the grade school to the university became co-educational. Atatürk greatly admired the support that the national liberation struggle received from women and praised their many contributions: "In Turkish society, women have not lagged behind men in science, scholarship, and culture. Perhaps they have even gone further ahead."

He gave women the same opportunities as men, including full political rights. In the mid-1930s, 18 women, among them a villager, were elected to the national parliament. Later, Turkey had the world's first female Supreme Court justice.

In all walks of life, Atatürk's Turkey has produced tens of thousands of well-educated women who participate in national life as doctors, lawyers, engineers, teachers, writers, administrators, executives, and creative artists.

Source: http://www.columbia.edu/~sss31/Turkiye/ata/hayati.html#reforms

Read Closely: Context
To understand the significance of Atatürk's support for gender equality, consider the status of women in other countries. *Underline one statement in this passage that presents a development in Turkey in the context of events outside the country.*

Read Closely: Order of Examples
To help you understand the examples used to support a claim, note the order in which they are listed. The most significant examples often appear either first or last in the list.
Circle the list of examples to support the claim that women in Turkey have had many occupations open to them.

Modernization and Cultural Change

The tension between modernizing influences and those that maintained strictly traditional ways was not new. During the 20th century, this tension played out in highly visible ways in two countries, Iran and Turkey. They followed different paths that led to different countries by the early 21st century. Changes in technology further influenced the interaction between citizens and those in authority in these countries and throughout the world.

Modernization and Retrenchment in Iran

In 1921, an army officer named **Reza Khan** helped carry out a successful coup in Iran. His goal was to end the period of chaos and foreign domination by Britain and Russia that had plagued the country.

Iran Under the Pahlavis At first Reza Khan installed himself as head of only the armed forces and as the minister of war. However, within a few years, he declared himself **shah**, or hereditary ruler. He modernized the country's infrastructure. He abolished extraterritoriality (foreigners' immunity to local laws). He tried to curb the power of the *mullahs*, experts in Islamic law who held most of the official posts in the overwhelmingly Muslim country. The shah flirted with Hitler's Nazi regime during World War II, prompting Russia and Britain to invade Iran in 1941. The two countries forced the shah to abdicate power to his young son, **Mohammad Reza Pahlavi**. They kept their forces in Iran until the war ended.

Iranian nationalists viewed the new shah as a puppet of Western powers, particularly of the United States. In 1951, under direction from the nationalist prime minister, **Mohammad Mosaddegh**, the Iranian parliament voted to nationalize the oil industry, which was controlled by a British-owned oil company. Mohammad Reza was forced to flee Iran when it was discovered that he had asked the CIA to replace Mosaddegh in a failed coup. In 1953, the United States orchestrated the removal of Mosaddegh, and Muhammad Reza returned to power. He instituted several progressive reforms, such as giving women the right to vote, creating a social welfare system, and modernizing the educational system. However, he ran an authoritarian and oppressive regime, making extensive use of secret police. By 1979, he had lost the support of both religious conservatives and advocates for greater democracy.

Read Closely: Examples
One way to appreciate historical patterns is to see how they still exist in your lifetime. For example, new technology has often caused changes to traditional culture. What are examples of how technology has made your life different from those who lived 25 years ago?

The Iranian Revolution In 1979, a revolution toppled the shah, rejecting his **secular**, less religious, worldview. The new government was a theocracy, a form of government in which religion is the supreme authority. The Shia cleric **Ayatollah Ruhollah Khomeini** became the Supreme Leader. The new government established a Guardian Council, a body of civil and religious legal experts who were responsible for interpreting the constitution and making sure all laws complied with **sharia** (Islamic law). The clergy had the right to approve or disapprove of anyone who ran for office. Iran's government became strongly anti-Western. In particular, it was anti-American and anti-Israel.

The Iranian Hostage Crisis The shah fled Iran because of the revolution. In October 1979, he came to the United States for medical treatment. Many Iranians had remained angry at the United States for overthrowing the Mosaddegh government and installing the shah over two decades earlier. In 1979, they were furious at the United States for taking in the shah. Iran's prime minister guaranteed the safety of the U.S. embassy in Iran. But, on November 4, about 3,000 Iranian militants occupied the embassy and took 63 Americans hostage. Three more American diplomats were captured at Iran's foreign ministry.

An Enduring Issue: Modernization
In Iran, the shah pushed Western ideas, often brutally. Conservatives rallied around religious leaders to oppose him. This battle made Iran one of the clearest examples of the widespread conflict between modern and traditional cultures.

Initial attempts at negotiating the release of the hostages—by international and U.S. groups—failed. The militants demanded the extradition of the shah to Iran for trial. Further, Iran's foreign minister demanded an end to U.S. interference in Iran and a declaration that the shah's possessions were stolen property. The United States responded that U.S. courts and international commissions could resolve such complaints, but only after the release of the hostages.

World opinion, supported by United Nations resolutions and a ruling from the International Court of Justice, was critical of the hostage-takers. In addition, the United States halted purchase of Iranian oil and froze all Iranian assets in the United States. In November 1979, Khomeini released 13 hostages, all women or African Americans, who he believed were unlikely to be U.S. spies. In July 1980, another hostage was released for medical reasons, leaving the total at 52.

Read Closely: Problems
To appreciate why people support or oppose a government, connect other elements of culture with politics. People might support a theocracy because it supports their religious beliefs. What problems resulted from Iran's theocracy?

The stalemate continued after a failed U.S. military rescue attempt, an economic embargo against Iran, and the death of the shah. Then the Iran-Iraq War broke out in September 1980. Iran's leaders realized they could not expect international help in the war unless they ended the hostage situation. Renewed negotiations brought the release of the hostages on January 20, 1981.

The conflict beween Iran and the United States continued into the 21st century. In 2015, the United States, its European allies, Russia, and China signed a deal to restrict Iran's development of nucelar weapons. However, in 2018, under President Donald Trump, the United States withdrew from that agreement.

Turkey Under Atatürk

In 1923, after four years of armed struggle against Ottomans, the victorious forces of General **Mustafa Kemal** took control of Turkey. Years later, he adopted the name **Atatürk**, which means "father of the Turks."

Source: Getty Images

Kemal Atatürk ruled Turkey (flag on the left) and was inspired by Japan (flag on the right). Like many nationalist leaders in Asia, he admired Japan's ability to adopt elements of European culture and yet keep many of its traditions.

New Government Atatürk called himself the president of Turkey and proclaimed it a republic. More accurately, he was a dictator. He set up a one-party system and made reforms without putting them to a vote. He refused to allow ethnic minorities, such as the Kurds and the Armenians, to set up their own states.

Nonetheless, Atatürk established a solid framework for a future democratic-style government. He achieved this by separating religion and the state. This change meant that the legal system was based on European, rather than Islamic, law. The state took over the schools and allowed them to teach the same subjects that were taught in modern European schools. Women no longer had to stay in the seclusion as required by some intepretations of Islamic law. Wome were allowed to vote. European civil law rather than Islamic code governed marriage. Men could have only one wife. Women could sue for divorce.

Cultural Changes Atatürk also brought Turkey nearer to the West in everyday life:

- He ordered people to wear Western-style clothes.
- He replaced Arabic script with a new Turkish alphabet based on Roman letters.
- Most important, his government sponsored industrialization, which brought higher employment, larger cities, and a new spirit of progress and independence to Turkey.

Some Turks opposed Atatürk's efforts to reduce Islam's influence in Turkey. Many Muslims wanted their country to be ruled by Islamic tradition and law. They formed an Islamic party and worked against secularization.

After Atatürk After Atatürk's death in 1938, the army took on the role of protecting the Turkish government's status as a secular republic. In 1960, 1971, and 1980, the army temporarily took control of the government when it felt it needed to protect this heritage. Turkey joined NATO in 1952, and became an associate member of the European Union in 1963. Tensions between Islamists and secularists increased in the early 21st century.

Read Closely: Controversies
Cultural changes are usually controversial at the time they occur, even if they are widely praised later. So when you read about them, think about why they caused disagreements among people in the time and place they occurred. Who supported and who opposed changes made by Atatürk?

Technology Affected Communication

In the 21st century, the increasing use of the Internet, social media sites, and smartphones changed how people and governments communicated. These changes brought new opportunities for better communication. They also brought new risks:

- Some governments allowed citizens to engage in policy discussions online. For example, beginning in 2011, the American government sponsored a "We the People" website. A citizen could launch a petition on the site. If it received 100,000 signatures within 30 days, a response from the White House was required. However, presidents have been inconsistent in their responsiveness to these petitions.
- Some governments have been accused of using the Internet and social media to tamper with other countries' elections. For example, Russian operatives with ties to that country's government used the Internet to spread fake and divisive news stories in several countries, including France and the United States.
- Some people used social media to organize protests and other types of resistance to their governments. In the first decade of the 21st century, the "Arab Spring" movement against authoritarian regimes in Egypt, Tunisia,

Libya, Bahrain, and elsewhere made great use of several social media platforms to organize and broadcast protests. This made people in the world at large aware of repression of their movements.

- Some groups used the Internet and social media to recruit followers to their causes. Terrorist groups such as Al Qaeda and ISIS actively used social media to push their anti-Western agenda and recruit fighters to join them.
- Some governments heavily censored the Internet to bolster their own power and limit dissent. For example, China limited what its citizens could read and say online.
- Some countries used computer viruses to attack the networks of rival nations. In 2017, the United States accused North Korea of being directly responsible for a computer virus that locked hundreds of thousands of computers in 150 countries.

As new technologies developed, interactions between citizens, governments, and other groups evolved. Attacks on one country by another became known as cyberwar.

Source: Getty Images

In the Arab Spring, protesters organized using cell phones and social media.

Application

Read the excerpt and answer the questions that follow it.

Iranian Supreme Leader Ayatollah Khamenei and Equality, March 2017

> Today, Western thinkers and those who pursue issues such as gender equality regret the corruption which it has brought about.
>
> Khamenei claimed that men and women are equal in the "ascendance of spiritual positions, the power of leadership, and the capability to lead humankind", but that some tasks for women "collapse and humiliate" their primary roles as housewives and mothers.
>
> A report by the government-controlled Mehr News Agency said the Supreme Leader "expressed hope that views of those who raised similar [gender equality] issues inside Iran were not based on the Western misconception".
>
> Iranian women are heavily restricted in their personal and public lives, including with state-enforced dress codes, curbs on higher education courses, jobs and sporting activities open to them, and freedom of movement under controls requiring a husband's signature to leave the country.
>
> **Source:** http://www.independent.co.uk/news/world/middle-east/iran-supreme-leader-ayatollah-khamenei-gender-equality-women-zionist-plot-society-role-islamic-a7641041.html

1. Identify the movement in Iranian history that is reflected in this excerpt.

____

____

____

____

____

____

____

2. Explain how the excerpt represents a major change in the way of life in Iran before 1979.

____

____

____

____

____

____

____

Chapter 8 *Review*

Multiple-Choice Questions

Directions (1–6): For each statement or question, choose the number of the word or expression that, of those given, best completes the statement or answers the question.

Base your answers to questions 1 and 2 on the passage below and your knowledge of social studies.

The Economic Power of Cities

> As world population continues to grow, an increasing number of people are moving to cities in hope of securing better living conditions, higher quality educations and greater economic opportunities. For the first time in human history, half of the world's population lived in towns and cities in 2008.
>
> Africa is currently the least urbanized continent, but its urbanization rate of 3.5 percent per year is the fastest in the world. In 1980, only 28 percent of Africans lived in urban areas. Today, the number of Africans living in cities is 40 percent, and is projected to grow to 50 percent by 2030. The McKinsey Global Institute projects that by 2016, over 500 million Africans will live in urban areas, and 65 African cities will have populations of over 1 million.
>
> By 2030, the 18 largest cities in Africa will have a combined spending power of $1.3 trillion, presenting a promising new market for international investors.
>
> **Source:** McKinsey Global Institute, "Urban World: Mapping the Economic Power of Cities," March 2011.

1. What would be the best title for this passage?
   (1) Africa Faces an Uphill Climb
   (2) Africa Falls Farther Behind
   (3) The High Cost of African Urbanization
   (4) Africa Is Becoming a Continent of Cities

2. According to the passage, one positive impact of urbanization on Africa is that it
   (1) will be as urbanized as the rest of the world after 2016
   (2) will be increasingly attractive to foreign investors
   (3) will have the fastest rate of urbanization among any continent
   (4) will be able to house many new migrants in its growing cities

Base your answers to questions 3 and 4 on the cartoon below and on your knowledge of social studies.

Source: Harley Schwadron. CartoonStock.com

3. Which statement best describes the context in which this cartoon was drawn?
   (1) The United States was reducing its military involvment in the world.
   (2) Countries outside the United States were recruiting America's most skilled computer scientists.
   (3) The U.S. military wanted to recruit people to work for private companies
   (4) Developments in technology provided new challenges for national security.

4. Which country was most directly involved in the issues addressed in this cartoon?
   (1) Iran
   (2) Turkey
   (3) Egypt
   (4) Russia

Base your answer to questions 5 and 6 on the passage below and your knowledge of social studies

> Almost a year after Tunisia had erupted in mass demonstrations [2010], the central Cairo [Egypt] protests triggered further waves of change across the Middle East and North Africa, in what became known as the Arab Spring.
>
> But while the nature of each pro-democracy uprising, and their ultimate success, varied wildly from country to country, they had one defining characteristic in common: social media.
>
> At times during 2011, the term Arab Spring became interchangeable with "Twitter uprising" or "Facebook revolution," as global media tried to make sense of what was going on.
>
> But despite the Western media's love affair with the idea, the uprisings didn't happen because of social media. Instead, the platforms provided opportunities for organization and protest that traditional methods couldn't.
>
> In the words of one protester, Fawaz Rashed: "We use Facebook to schedule the protests, Twitter to coordinate, and YouTube to tell the world."
>
> **Source:** https://www.theguardian.com/world/2016/jan/25/egypt-5-years-on-was-it-ever-a-social-media-revolution

5. According to the article, what purpose did social media have in the Arab Spring?
   (1) to provide the government with a list of grievances
   (2) to gain support for pro-government counter-protests
   (3) to schedule and coordinate the pro-democracy protests
   (4) to use social media as the main form of protest

6. The best use of this passage would be to support a claim that
   (1) changes in technology change the how people and their government interact
   (2) social media will make democracy more difficult to achieve
   (3) the success of a protest movement can be measured through its use of social media
   (4) technology provides a way for people to protest safely

Tips for Answering Multiple-Choice Questions

Political cartoons, such as the one used in Questions 3 and 4, usually rely on satire or humor to make a political, economic, or social statement. Therefore the use of puns, double meanings, symbols (example: Uncle Sam), and juxtapositions are effective means to convey a bigger message. In the case of the cartoon above, the use of the term "untouchable" has two meanings. It refers to both the people known as the Dalit who were formerly called "untouchables," and to the idea that discussing discrimination against this group is so controversial that no politician wants to be part of it.

Short-Answer Questions

CRQ Directions (7–9): Analyze the documents and answer the short-answer questions that follow each document in the space provided.

Base your answer to question 7 on Document 1 below and on your knowledge of social studies.

Document 1

An analysis of South Korean economic growth and development, 2010.

> Korea's development experience over the past half-century has been a source of inspiration for other developing countries. Indeed, Korea may be the face of hope "for all those countries who want to radically transform the social and economic conditions of their people in the course of a single generation." Even among successful countries characterized by sustained high growth, Korea stands out with its impressive industrial upgrading and ability to recover quickly from shocks.
>
> **Source:** Wonhyuk Lim, "Lessons from the Korean Experience," Presentation at the Korea-World Bank High Level Conference on Post-Crisis Growth and Development, June 3–4, 2010.

7. Describe the historical context in which this presentation was given.

Base your answer to question 8 on Document 2 below and on your knowledge of social studies.

Document 2

The excerpt is from Elsje Fourie, Assistant Professor of Globalization and Development at the University of Maastricht, on modernization in Africa.

> [How] to explain the results of the research I carried out in Ethiopia and Kenya last year? Despite the vast historical differences between the two countries, leaders in both were remarkably eager to imitate other nations they saw as successful. Moreover, both groups looked to one region in particular: east Asia.
>
> "In my head, I've got practically everything mapped out – if you give me 10 years, I will give you South Korea," proclaimed one Kenyan technocrat.
>
> "We are 20 years behind China," said an Ethiopian bureaucrat, "and we're trying to do what they did to get where they are." . . .
>
> Kenya and Ethiopia look at east Asia, and see the need for a strong and unifying national leadership that can transform and unite traditional communities into a new nation of "modern" citizens. This leadership is responsible for using the country's resources to build large and ambitious infrastructure projects, such as Ethiopia's controversial Gibe III dam. It oversees but does not control the economy, intervening directly where necessary to create globally competitive industries and sectors. It relies on advanced technology and double-digit economic growth to solve most of the country's problems.
>
> So important is this economic growth, in fact, that democracy is hardly possible without it; countries develop in stages, they point out, and cannot be expected to become democratic overnight. All of these lessons are a far cry from both the market-led approach of the Washington consensus, and from the participatory, flexible and community-led route advocated by its critics.
>
> **Source:** Elsje Fourie, "Africa Looks to Learn from East Asia's Development Experiences," *The Guardian,* September 28, 2011.

8. Identify Fourie's point of view expressed in this article.

____

____

____

____

____

____

Base your answer to question 9 on both Documents 1 and 2 and on your knowledge of social studies.

Cause—refers to something that contributes to the occurrence of an event, the rise of an idea, or the bringing about of a development.

Effect—refers to what happens as a consequence (result, impact, outcome) of an event, an idea, or a development.

9. Identify and explain a cause-and-effect relationship associated with the historical developments in Documents 1 and 2. Be sure to use evidence from both Documents 1 and 2 in your response.

Speaking and Listening: Reflect on the Key Idea

Working with a partner, write the dialogue for a scene in a play about the tension between two individuals, one who defends traditional culture and one who supports modernization. Make clear the time and place the scene occurs and the relationship between the two individuals.

CHAPTER 9

Globalization and Environmental Change

Chapter Overview

Technological advances made the people of the world more interconnected. In some cases, these changes helped countries cooperate for their mutual benefit. International organizations, such as United Nations (UN), enabled countries to work together to solve problems. However, globalization and massive population growth have led to environmental strain and numerous global tensions.

Technological Advances Technology has been advancing more rapidly than ever. Ideas can cross the globe in an instant, and this ability has spurred innovation and improvement in transportation, communication, and medicine. Businesses can adapt to consumers demands more quickly. Governments can respond to crises more effectively. Protesters can organize more powerfully.

Globalization Closer connections among people meant stronger diplomatic ties among countries and greater trade. Increasing exports created new jobs and economic growth. Increasing imports provided consumers more choices of products and lower prices.

However, globalization came with costs. For example, huge multinational corporations wielded tremendous power to influence economies and governments. Businesses that could not compete with the new technology and lower wages used in other countries lost out. Countries that had weak regulations to protect workers and the environment often prospered.

Limited Resources Globalization also placed strains on the environment. Growing food and providing clean water became more difficult, particularly as the world population grew.

An Enduring Issue: Environment One enduring issue in this chapter is the relationship between people and the earth. The more intensely people used minerals, soil, water, and other natural resources, the greater stress they placed on the environment.

New York Social Studies Framework: **Key Idea 10.9**

Technological changes have resulted in a more interconnected world, affecting economic and political relations and in some cases leading to conflict and in others efforts to cooperate. Globalization and population pressures have led to strains on the environment.

Source: *New York State Grades 9–12 Social Studies Framework.*

1. Rewrite Key Idea 10.9 in your own words.

____

____

Identify Enduring Issues

One way to identify issues that endure is to organize them in a chart. In the title row for the chart below, list an enduring issue. Then, select two regions of the world, such as Africa or Asia, and list examples of that issue for each time period.

Enduring Issue:		
Period	**1. Region:**	**6. Region:**
1750 to 1848	2.	7.
1848 to 1914	3.	8.
1914 to 1992	4.	9.
1992 to Present	5.	10.

Key Terms and Names

Geography

overpopulation (p. 275)
deforestation (p. 278)
desertification (p. 278)

Governance

peacekeeping (p. 281)
European Union (p. 283)
Al Qaeda (p. 285)

Economics

sustainable development (p. 270)
multinational corporation (p. 271)
World Trade Organization (WTO) (p. 272)

Technology

information system (p. 267)
public health (p. 268)
Zika virus (p. 269)
Centers for Disease Control and Prevention (CDC) (p. 269)
Green Revolution (p. 277)

Exchange

Internet (p. 267)
World Health Organization (WHO) (p. 269)
globalization (p. 270)
nongovernmental organization (NGO) (p. 272)
World Bank (p. 272)
International Monetary Fund (IMF) (p. 272)
Kyoto Protocol (p. 284)

Lesson 1 *Advances in Technology*

Conceptual Understanding 10.9a Technological changes in communication and transportation systems allow for instantaneous interconnections and new networks of exchange between people and places that have lessened the effects of time and distance.

Conceptual Understanding 10.9b Globalization is contentious, supported by some and criticized by others.

Source: *New York State Grades 9–12 Framework.*

This excerpt is taken from the Pew Research Center's polls on global attitudes and trends conducted in 2014. Results for the survey are based on telephone and face-to-face interviews conducted under the direction of Princeton Survey Research Associates International. The survey covered seven African countries and the United States. Pew Research is considered by many to be one of the most reliable sources of information on personal interest, attitudes, and trends.

Analyze a Primary Source

Cell Phones in Africa

More people in Africa's poorest countries have mobile phones than have bank accounts. That reality is spurring mobile service companies to explore how they can capture a share of the potential banking market by enabling migrants from these countries to transfer funds back home to their families.

Sending such remittances [money sent by migrants to family in their home country] by mobile phone can be a cheap, efficient and safe alternative to the usual channels of employing money transfer companies or acquaintances traveling to the home country. People can send money to even remote rural areas quickly, so long as the recipient has cell phone access or can go to a participating business that pays out cash.

The market is a potentially lucrative one, said Pieter Verkade, an executive at the MTN telecommunications company, in an interview with Africa Renewal. Such transfers already are "a well-beaten track, with a lot of migrant remittance money coming into Africa for some time through other channels."

While mobile networks in sub-Saharan Africa have spread rapidly, landline penetration in the seven countries surveyed is close to zero. A median of only 2 percent across these nations say they have a working landline telephone in their house, with a median of 97 percent saying they do not have one. There is little variation across the countries on landline ownership. Landlines are simply rare on the continent. By contrast, 60 percent of Americans have a landline telephone in their household. (However, the share of wireless-only households in the United States has been growing rapidly during the past decade as landline ownership falls.)

Source: http://www.pewglobal.org/2015/04/15/cell-phones-in-africa-communication-lifeline/

Read Closely: Sources
As a reader, develop the habit of questioning the source of data. Even reputable sources can have difficulty collecting accurate information.
Circle a claim in the excerpt that might be difficult to verify in an underdeveloped area of Africa.

Read Closely: Quotations
One way to support a claim is with direct quotations from participants or experts. These are comments that are the exact words of someone, so they are enclosed in quotation marks.

Read Closely: Comparisons
Comparisons are useful, but explaining similarities and differences is difficult. Many factors can make a comparison less reliable.
Underline a comparison made in the excerpt that might include so many variables that the comparison is not useful.
riables involved

The Power of Knowledge

The present era of globalized information sharing and commerce is a direct result of technological changes that affect how information is accessed, exchanged, and controlled. These changes had an impact on all aspects of life in the late 20th and early 21st centuries, including commerce, transportation, and medicine.

The Importance of Information

As technology allows the world to become more interconnected, access to information becomes increasingly important. The ability to share information easily is vital in bringing far-flung parts of the world closer to one another. Individuals and organizations need access to accurate and up-to-date information to make knowledgeable decisions of all kinds.

Information Systems Defined An **information system** is an interconnected structure of hardware, software, and networking systems for collecting, processing, exchanging, and controlling data. Computer scientists created and regulated these networks so people could handle interoffice communications, accounting and human resource management. These networks also helped carry out order processing, customer service and supplier communication, and well as marketing and advertising.

Information systems have transformed the way people buy and sell goods and services. A business that exists solely on the **Internet** and deals in electronic products is basically a giant information system that includes a group of people to help it run smoothly. Other organizations that exists online or includes both an online and brick-and-mortar presence combine their information systems with varying amounts of physical locations and goods. Information systems also help individuals to perform a variety of activities such as consuming news, conducting research, keeping in touch with friends and family, paying bills, and shopping.

Read Closely: Examples
When you learn about new concepts in your reading, connect them with concepts you already know. This will help you understand the new material more easily. What are examples of information systems you know of?

Elements of an Information System Though no two information systems are precisely the same, each one uses similar elements:

- The **hardware**, the parts of any information system that one can physically touch, including computers, tablets, or other devices; servers; and keyboards; was the same.
- The **software**, the part of the information system that could not be touched physically, was the same. Software is essentially a list of instructions that tells the hardware what to do. The two main categories of software are operating system software, which allows users to operate hardware, and application software, which performs a certain useful task. Examples of operating systems software included the Apple iOS, Microsoft Windows, and Google Android. Word processing, spreadsheet, and presentation programs were examples of application software. Smartphone apps also are examples of application software.
- The **networking systems**, the parts of the information technology that enable computers to communicate with each other, are the same. In today's globalized world, it is not much use to have stand-alone systems of hardware and software.

- The **data**, the collection of facts that could be used or analyzed, is collected and either shared or sold. A single piece of data when brought together with other related data and properly organized, becomes quite useful. People use hardware, software, and telecommunications systems to manage and move data.
- The **procedures**, the steps followed to arrive at a desired outcome, evolve as new technology developed. They have to be continually improved in order to use an information system to its full potential.
- The people, such as software engineers, tech support personnel, and database administrators, are key elements to making an information system efficient.

Polio Eradication

One type of information comes from scientific research. In medicine, research combined with aggressive public health efforts dramatically reduce the danger from many diseases. Polio is one of the best examples of the progress in this area. After vaccines were developed in the 1950s, the combined efforts of governments and nonprofit organizations led to the steady elimination of the disease around the world.

PROGRESS AGAINST POLIIO

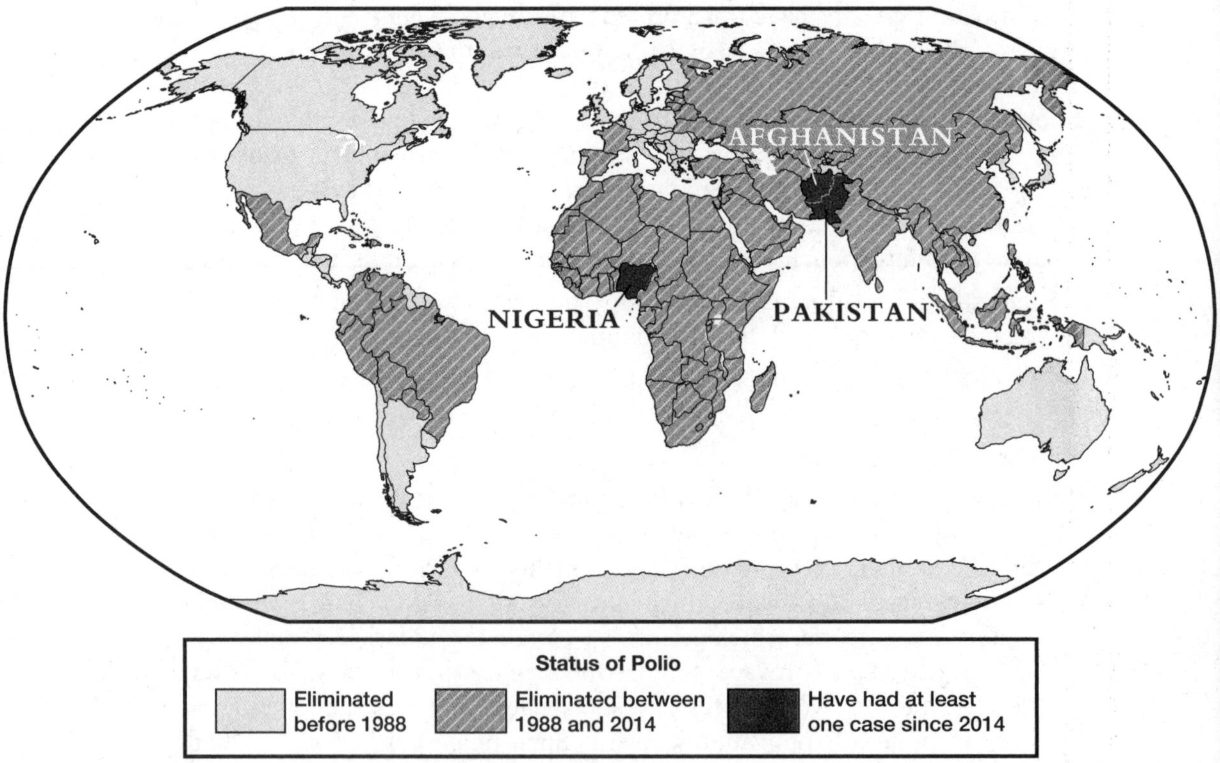

Status of Polio

Eliminated before 1988 | Eliminated between 1988 and 2014 | Have had at least one case since 2014

Source: Data based on information from the World Health Organization.

The Zika Virus

The gathering and sharing of data has always been important in helping public health agencies manage infectious diseases. The growth of sophisticated information systems beginning in the later 20th century gave public health officials new tools for managing and treating such diseases. The outbreak of the Zika virus in the Americas in 2015 provides a recent case study.

History of the Zika Virus The Zika virus was first identified in 1947 in a monkey in the Zika Forest in the central African country of Uganda. Researchers determined that the virus was carried by certain types of mosquitoes. The first human case of Zika fever appeared in Uganda in 1952. In most humans, Zika passed without symptoms. Some people suffered fever, rash, headache, and muscular and/or joint pain for up to a week.

However, the disease could cause severe problems, particularly in newborn children. Some babies were born with microcephaly, an abnormal smallness of the head. They had smaller brains, which could lead to serious conditions such as seizures, poor balance, hearing loss, and extreme learning disabilities.

Until 2007, only 14 cases had been identified. That year, the first widespread outbreak in humans occurred. It happened on the island of Yap located several hundred miles off the coast of southeast Asia. Almost three-quarters of the island residents were infected. Outbreaks then began occurring throughout the world.

Read Closely: Context
You can use the dates given in a text to help you understand the context for an event. Picture a timeline in your head to help you keep track of events that occured about the same time. How does the year the Zika virus was identified fit among world events?

Zika in the Americas In spring 2015, Brazilian health authorities confirmed the presence of the virus in the country. The number of infants born with microcephaly increased. In November 2015, Brazil declared a national public health emergency.

Outbreaks of Zika were reported to the **World Health Organization (WHO)**, which collected data and shared it with public health officials everywhere. In February 2016, the WHO declared the threat of microcephaly and other neurological disorders resulting from Zika virus infection to be a worldwide public health emergency. The WHO indicated that the virus was present in 60 countries around the world, including 39 in the Americas.

Information Supported Diagnosis and Treatment The WHO's information systems provides data to public health agencies around the world, including the **Centers for Disease Control and Prevention** (CDC) in the United States. Togther, the WHO, the CDC, and other agencies provided information to fight Zika. For example, the public health network funded research on new diagnostic tests and possible vaccines. Through websites they shared information:

- They educated individuals on how to prevent transmission of the virus by providing tips on how to avoid mosquito bites.
- They advised women who were pregnant or who were planning to become pregnant to avoid traveling to areas where the virus was prevalent.
- They compiled databases of pregnancies and births among women who had been exposed to the virus or tested positive for it so that they could be tracked and early intervention could be provided for babies with problems.

Read Closely: Shift in Tone
When writers use words such as "however," they often indicate a change in tone is coming. The change might be from something positive to something negative, or the reverse. What does "however" indicate in the second paragraph on this page?

In November 2016, the WHO declared an end to the public health emergency related to Zika. However, the organization also said that it would support countries and organizations in managing the threat from Zika on a long-term basis as they would other infectious diseases. Systems run by public health agencies that collected, analyzed, and applied lessons from information would continue to be an important part of this ongoing strategy.

The WHO and HIV/AIDS

The WHO also took a leading role in combatting the spread of the human immodeficency virus (HIV) and of acquired immune deficency syndrome (AIDS). As with Zika, the WHO coordinated efforts of national public health agencies. New HIV infectiond decline by one-third between 2000 and 2017.

Economic and Social Changes

Read Closely: Word Parts
To help you define a term, identify parts of it that are similar to parts of words you know. For example, break *globalization* into two parts: *global* and *-ization*. What are other words or phrases that use each of these parts?

The spread of Zika and the international efforts to combat it show how interconnected the world has become. These interconnections in economics and social issues are known as **globalization**.

Globalization Controversies

Some experts focus on the positive effects of globalization. They argue that it brings people around the world together. However, critics have expressed many concerns about the changes that are part of globalization.

Decline of the Nation-State Starting in the 19th century, Europeans and others throughout the world struggled to divide sprawling multiethnic empires into smaller nation-states in which everyone shared the same culture. By the mid-20th century, most governments in Europe were nation-states. This remains true today. For example, most people in Poland identify with Polish culture.

However, the rise of international organizations, international standards, and international business took away some of the power of nation-states. Many people resented the loss of control over their own nation-state. In the early 21st century, many European countries experienced a rise in political parties that emphasized nationalism rather than internationalism.

At the same time that the power of international organizations were growing, so was a demand for local control. Reformers argued that cities and states could govern themselves more effectively than could the the national or central government. As a result, nation-states grew weaker as they lost power to local or regional layers of government.

Global vs. Local One fundamental idea of globalization was encouraging trade among countries. This allowed, for example, a person in Russia to buy furniture from a global Swedish retail chain, which obtained the wood to make the furniture from South America, which was then sent to a factory in Bangladesh for assembly. Consumers got inexpensive goods, the owners of each company received profits, and workers in several countries had jobs. These benefits led some to conclude that globalization was positive.

However, critics of globalism and promoters of local, **sustainable development**, raised concerns:

- One concern was environmental damage. The shipping of raw materials and finished products all over the world produced carbon dioxide or CO_2 emissions that polluted the air. Climate scientists found a link between these emissions and global climate changes that harmed the environment.
- Another concern was exploitation of workers. The competition among companies meant that operated on very tight margins. To make a profit so they could stay in business, they had to squeeze every penny out of every transaction. The loggers and factory workers had jobs, but were they paid a living wage? Were their working conditions safe? Did they have access to health care?
- A third concern was capital flight. When consumers bought a piece of furniture from a company based halfway across the world, where did their money go? What happened to companies in local communities that sold furniture? When people spent money on locally made products, they were investing in their own communities. Instead of supporting foreign conglomerates, consumers supported neighbors and provided jobs, revenue, and tax dollars locally.

China's Role in the Global Economy Ever since China began its rise as a global economic power in the late 1970s, many criticized the way that its economy functioned. China embraced capitalism to some degree. However, the country's Communist central government still was vitally involved in planning and finance. Critics complained that the Communists used unfair tactics to give their companies unfair advantages:

- China has long been charged with manipulating the value of its currency—lessening its value to make the country's exports less expensive and thereby more attractive to consumers than goods from other countries. Only the Chinese government had the power to manipulate the country's currency.
- The Chinese government also was accused of supporting overproduction of products such as steel and textiles. These products were then "dumped" on foreign markets at prices often below cost—prices that competitors couldn't hope to match.
- Critics said that the Chinese government's control of its financial system kept unprofitable ventures alive by allowing them to forego debt repayment. This practice gave these enterprises an unfair advantage over their global competitors that operated in free and unsupported marketplaces.

Defenders of China pointed out it was following the pattern set by other countries. Earlier in history, businesses in Europe, the United States, and other countries also benefitted from government support to get established.

Read Closely: Connections
Look for connections between what you are reading about and your everyday life. Examining how these concepts have affected you will help you understand them. How does China's rise in manufacturing and trade impact how you live?

Multinational Corporations Companies that operate internationally have existed since at least the 17th century. Organizations such as the Dutch East India Company operated a chain of trading outposts around the world. However, globalization has spurred an explosion in huge, **multinational corporations**. With markets and suppliers on multiple continents, multinationals grew in size and influence throughout the 20th century. These huge corporations provided jobs and a greater variety of goods for people around the world. Their large size enabled them to become very efficient producers.

However, by the mid-20th century, critics argued that some of these corporations were becoming so large and powerful that they were hard to regulate. They could use their economic clout to persuade governments not to enforce rules designed to protect the environment and worker safety. If a country tried to have high standards, companies could move their factories elsewhere.

In addition, critics pointed out that multinationals made large profits from using natural resources and workers in poor countries. However, these profits flowed to the investors who usually lived in Europe and the United States. The result was the multinationals acted to redistribute wealth from the world's poor to world's wealthy.

Read Closely: Motivations
When you are reading about the actions of individuals or organizations, consider how motivations shape these actions. What motivations shape the actions of the World Trade Organization?

Diversity vs. Homogenization Globalization promoted commerce and employment. In some ways it also promoted promote cultural homogenization, making things the same everywhere. For example, a century ago, in most major cities of the world, most restuarants served local food. Restuarants in Rome served Italian food. Restaurants in Tokyo served Japanese food. Today, some of these restuarants have been replaced by chains that provide the same food, such as hamburgers, everywhere. A similar process of homogenization occurred in fashion, music, movies, architecture, and other areas. A single global style often, though not always, replaced the traits that made each society distintinctive.

International Financial NGOs

Several nongovernmental organizations (NGOs) work closely with the United Nations on economic issues. Each is independent and has been controversial.

An Enduring Issue: Globalization
The creation of the World Bank, IMF, and WTO reflected how interconnected people had become economically. The financial integration of the world had a wide impact on jobs, wages, and the environment.

The World Bank The **World Bank** was created in 1944 to fight poverty by providing loans to countries. It first focused on projects such as dams and roads that boosted long-term development. It later expanded its mission to also finance social projects such as education and disease prevention.

Critics charged that the World Bank often ignored how its projects damaged the environment and local culture. For example, a dam might permanently flood many farm. A highway might promote growth, but the resulting profits might all go to investors overseas rather than people living in the region.

The International Monetary Fund The **International Monetary Fund** (IMF) was created in 1945 to stabilize a country's economy by promoting stable currency exchange rates. It focused on making short-term loans and providing economic advice to countries. Some economists argued that conditions on IMF loans were so strict they failed to take into account each country's individual needs. Loans were too influenced by large, wealthy nations. The IMF acted on their behalf, even while it claimed to help developing nations.

World Trade Organization The **World Trade Organization** (WTO) was created in 1995 to promote trade worldwide. It tried to reduce restrictions on trade and to resolve trade disputes.Some people charged that WTO-backed free trade policies benefited consumers in wealthy countries but kept producers in poor countries poor. In addition, the WTO undercut efforts by countries to pass laws to protect their environment.

The Interconnected Global Economy

Globalization and international NGOs made the economy more interconnected then ever before. Any economic change now affects people everywhere.

OPEC In industrial economies, oil became so important that the countries that produced it had great power. Several of these formed the Organization of Petroleum Exporting Countries (OPEC). During the 1973 Arab-Israeli War, Arab members of OPEC imposed an embargo against the United States, the Netherlands, Portugal, and South Africa.The embargo was retaliation against countries that supported Israel.

Economic Growth National economies often rise and fall together. For example, when unemployment rose in the United States in the 2008 recession, the impact was felt around the world. China sold fewer exports. Europe had fewer American tourists. Fewer migrants from Latin American entered the United States. When the U.S. economy rebounded, other countries benefited.

Development and Inequality The interconnections in the global economy can promote equality. Globally, severe poverty has declined sharply in the past two decades. However, they can also promote inequality. Poor countries export crops and natural resources based on what they can sell rather than using those products to improve the lives of people in their own country.

Migration and Labor One result of the mobility of work is that workers around the world compete with each other for jobs. This creates jobs for some and pushes down wages for others. However, modern transportation also enables workers to move to where work is more easily than in the past. Further, jobs done online or by phone enable people to find work without having to move.

Application

Study the cartoon below and answer the questions that follow it.

Source: Larry Lambert, CartoonStock.com

1. Identify the historical context in which this cartoon was created.

____

____

2. Identify the geographical context in which this cartoon was created.

____

____

3. Explain the cartoonist's point of view on mechanization.

____

____

____

____

Lesson 2 Strains on the Environment

Conceptual Understanding 10.9c Population pressures, industrialization, and urbanization have increased demands for limited natural resources and food resources, often straining the environment.

Source: *New York State Grades 9–12 Framework.*

Analyze a Primary Source

J. Van Bavel, University of Leuven in Belgium, The Global Population Explosion, 2013

In the year 1900, Belgium and the Philippines had more or less the same population, around 7 million people. By the year 2000, the population of the Western European monarchy had grown to 10 million citizens, while the Southeast Asian republic at the turn of the century already counted 76 million citizens. The population of Belgium has since then exceeded 11 million citizens, but it is unlikely that this number will rise to 12 million by the year 2050. The population of the Philippines on the other hand will continue to grow to a staggering 127 million citizens by 2050, according to the demographic projections of the United Nations (UN 2013).

The demographic growth rate of the Philippines around the turn of the century (2% a year) has already created enormous challenges and is clearly unsustainable in the long term. . . .Even the rather modest Belgian demographic growth rate around the turn of this century (0.46%) is not sustainable in the long term. In any case, it exceeds by far the average growth rate of the human species (*homo sapiens*) that arose in Africa some 200,000 years ago. . . .

The point of this story is that the current growth numbers are historically very exceptional and untenable in the long term. The demographic growth rates are indeed on the decline worldwide and this paper will attempt to explain some of the mechanisms behind that process. That doesn't change the fact, however, that the growth remains extraordinarily high and the decline in some regions very slow. This is especially the case in Sub Saharan Africa. In absolute numbers, the world population will continue to grow anyway for quite some time as a result of demographic inertia.

Source: https://www.ncbi.nlm.nih.gov/pmc/articles/PMC3987379/

Read Closely: Claim
Writers can choose to present the evidence first and build up to their claim or state their claim and follow it with evidence.
Underline the author's claim about world population.

Read Closely: Averages
Recognize how an average can hide enormous variation.
Circle a statistic or an average that doesn't follow the pattern of the others.

Read Closely: Context
The author uses the phrase "That doesn't change the fact" to remind readers of the context for what he is writing about. He is focusing on what is causing growth rates to decline, but the larger picture is that population growth remains high by historic standards.

Problems of Growth

The issues of **overpopulation**, (the growth of population in a region high enough to cause serious problems social or environemental problems), urbanization, and industrialization affected each other. They created strains on the natural environment and human welfare.

Rampant Population Increase

Human population has been growing at an exponential rate, raising the risk of famine and refugee crises. However, this growth is not equally distributed, It has caused more problems in some areas of the globe more in others.

Population Growth to 1900 From the beginning of humanity, the hunting and gathering way of life naturally limited population growth. With the advent of agriculture, human societies became more settled and capable of sustaining larger numbers of people. At the beginning of the Common Era, Earth's population was between 200 and 300 million people. By the year 1600, that figure had at least doubled, hitting an estimated 600 million.

When the Industrial Revolution began in the 1700s, many people's living standards increased. Humans began to develop new crops and new agricultural methods that significantly increased the amount of food available. By around 1800, the world's population had increased to about 1 billion, and by 1900 it was about 1.6 billion.

Population Growth Since 1900 The 20th and 21st centuries have seen world population increase at an even faster pace. This increase could be attributed to continually rising living standards for a broader range of people, as well as advancements in sanitation and improvements in medical care that became available to more people. Infant mortality rates continue to decrease while life expectancies continued to rise. Between 1900 and the mid-1960s, the world's population doubled, rising above 3 billion. By 2004, it had doubled again, hitting 6.4 billion. In 2018, the figure had reached 7.6 billion. Projections suggest that growth will reach 11.2 billion in 2100.:

An Enduring Issue: Population
As the number of people in a region increased, the problems in that region changed. Population growth in the past century created crowded cities and new demands on natural resources.

Birth and Death Rates by Level of Development

Country	Level of Development	Birth Rate (per 1,000 people)	Infant Mortality Rate (per 1,000 live births)	Death Rate (per 1,000 people)
Niger	Less developed	48	51	10
Bangladesh	Less developed	19	28	5
Mexico	Moderate	18	13	5
Australia	More developed	13	3	7
France	More developed	12	3	9
World	-----	19	31	8

Source: The World Bank.

This enormous growth in human population during the past 100 years was not evenly distributed. Most of it occurred in less-developed countries, where the tradition of having large families remained strong. In the 47 least-developed countries in the world, the fertility rate is 4.3 births per woman. In contrast, the fertility rate in more developed countries in Europe and North America, along with Japan, New Zealand, and Australia, is below 2.0. In some countries, the fertility rate is low enough that the population will decline if the country does not invite immigration. The rapid population growth in the countries least prepared to deal with it puts pressure natural resources, including land, food, and water. However, globally, most resources are consumed in prosperous countries.

WORLD POPULATION DISTRIBUTION

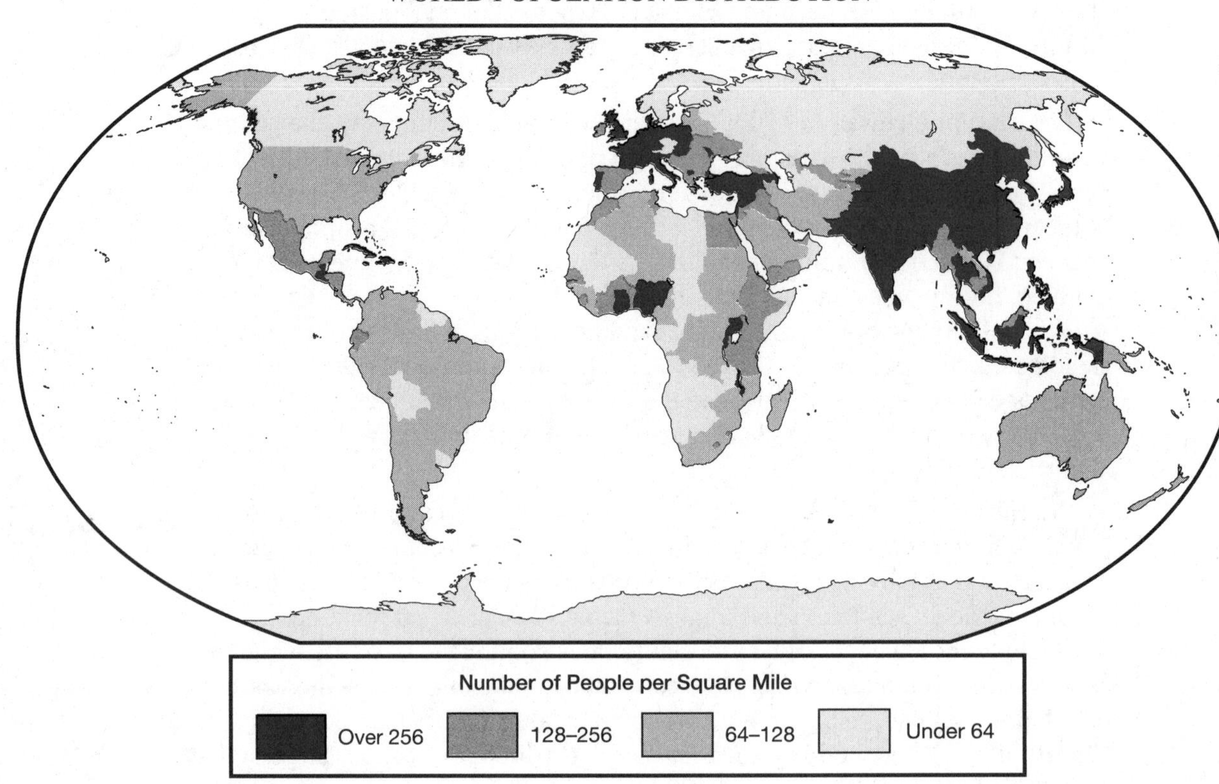

Source: Data based on information from the United Nations.

Efforts to Increase Food Production

> **Read Closely: Geography**
> Note how location shapes actions. Germany relied heavily on imported fertilizer and food from the Americas. Fearful that a British blockade could cut off this supply, the government invested in research to create artificial fertilizers. How did geography make Germans fearful of a British blockade?

To feed the world's growing population, people have developed innovative ways of increasing and intensifying food production.

Fertilizers Use of natural fertilizers is likely almost as old as agriculture itself. A recent study concluded that European farmers were using animal manure to fertilize their crops as long as 8,000 years ago. This was the main form of fertilizer for thousands of years.

In the 18th century, however, people discovered that ground-up bones improved plant health and production, though they were not sure why. Small improvements such as this and the use of bird guano, often found in huge deposits on islands where seabirds nested, helped revitalize soil and boost crop production.

In the late 19th century, scientific researchers identified nitrogen (N), phosphorus (P), and potassium (K)—elements abundantly present in seabird guano—as essential nutrients for crop production. Further research and experimentation, particularly in Germany, developed the processes by which NPK fertilizers could be produced on an industrial scale. Their use was limited by their price and by issues surrounding application amounts and methods.

World War II changed the situation for producing fertilizer significantly. Because nitrogen was an essential component of explosives, production of it skyrocketed. By producing it in large quantities, it became less expensive. This made nitrogen fertilizers easy to purchase.

In addition, researchers developed new and improved equipment for applying chemical fertilizers. By applying fertilizers more efficiently, farmers could make use of them.

Together, making fertilizer less expensive and easier to use set the stage for a dramatic increase in food production. In turn, the increase in food made possible a large growth in the population.

The Green Revolution In the mid-20th century, the **Green Revolution** emerged as a possible long-term solution to food shortages for growing populations. Scientists developed new varieties of wheat, rice, and other grains that had higher yields and greater resistance to pests, diseases, and drought. The new varieties were first developed by cross-breeding, breeding two varieties of a plant to create a hybrid. These hybrids grew particularly well in the climates and soils of India and Bangladesh.

More recently, scientists have used genetic engineering, manipulating genes within an organism to change its basic characteristics. Farmers also began using more irrigation, chemical fertilizers, and pesticides. In Brazil and elsewhere, forests were burned down and the land was plowed for agriculture. Acreage devoted to crops increased dramatically worldwide. Grain production increased sharply.

Read Closely: Motivation
Always consider a person's point of view. If you know what motivated a person to act a certain way, it will be easier to understand why historical events happened they way they did. What motivated mid-20th century scientists to pursue the Green Revolution?

Average Output of Grain Crops in Pounds per Acre

Region	1961 to 1963	1991 to 1993
Africa	803	981
Latin America	1,115	2,052
Asia	1,071	2,632
Middle East	981	1,606
Developed Countries	1,517	2,721

Source: Adapted from data compiled by the Food and Agricultural Organization of the United Nations.

Green Revolution solutions were not free of problems. These problems were economic, social, and environmental:

- Many small farmers could not afford the new fertilizers or pesticides, reducing their ability to compete with large landowners. Many of these small farmers were then forced to sell their land, increasing the holdings of large landowners even more.
- Since many of the techniques developed in the Green Revolution involved the use of mechanized equipment, fewer jobs were available for farm laborers.
- A genetic modification designed to give a plant resistance to insects might cause a decline in the population of pollinating insects, such as bees.
- The loss of old seed varieties as new genetically engineered plants were adopted might cause the loss of plants that could be valuable in the future.

Environmental Issues

Industrialization and new technology helped feed and care for the world's ballooning population. However, they have been costly for the environment. Chemicals used in agriculture and industry have polluted soil and water. Fossil fuels such as coal, oil, and natural gas have harmed air and water quality. Environmental scientists have concluded that the burning of fossil fuels has contributed to global climate change. Together, these changes have caused the extinction of of many species of plants and animals. In addition, land development, deforestation, and desertification threatened wildlife.

Read Closely: Main Concept
After you read a section, you should be able to summarize the individual points into one overall message. Uniting smaller ideas into one underlying concept will help you make sure you understand what you have read. What is the concept in this section?

Acid Rain and Deforestation Acid rain, which is a combination of moisture and airborne chemicals from factories and cars, has damaged the forests of industrialized nations. Even more harm has been done by **deforestation**, the clearing of forests for their timber or so the land could be used in other ways. Deforestation occurs all over the world. The most dramatic example is the destruction of the Amazon rain forest. Its 5 million square kilometers comprises the largest continuous expanse of tropical rain forest remaining in the world. Though such forests cover only 7 percent of the planet's land surface, they contain approximately 50 percent of the plants and animals found on the globe. Thousands of species face extinction as a result of forest destruction.

Desertification Drought, overgrazing, and excess removal of trees and bushes caused **desertification**, the process by which farmland or grassland becomes desert. The roots of trees and bushes held down the topsoil so that it could not be blown away. This problem is common in Africa, where the Sahara expanded at an alarming rate into the Sahel, a grassland on its southern border.

ENERGY CONSUMPTION AROUND THE WORLD

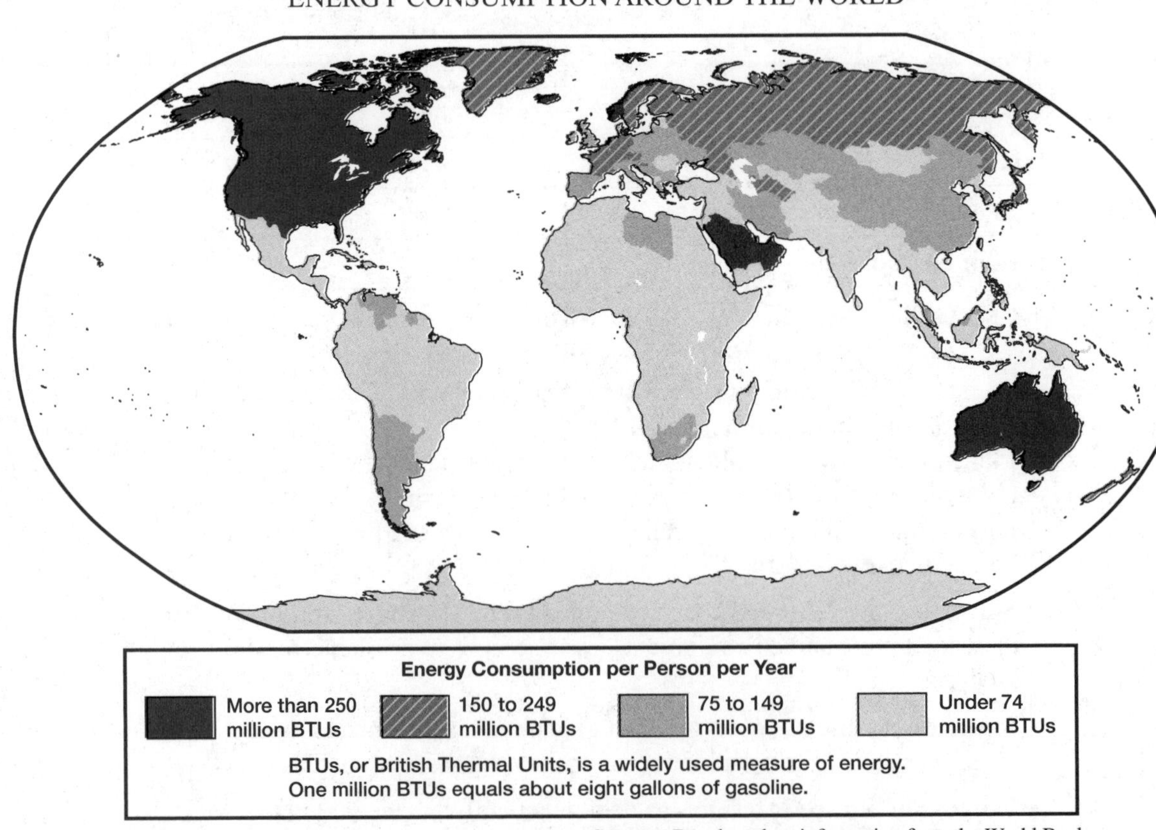

Source: Data based on information from the World Bank.

Application

Study the chart and answer the questions that follow it.

Global Population in 2009 and Projected for 2050			
Year	**More Developed Countries**	**Less Developed Countries**	**Total Global Population**
2009	1.2 billion	5.6 billion	6.8 billion
2050 (projection)	1.2 billion	7.9 billion	9.1 billion

Source: "World Population Prospects, the 2008 Revision," United Nations Department of Economic and Social Affairs, Population Division. http://www.un.org/en/development/desa/population/publications/trends/population-prospects.shtml

1. Identify the projected to be the total global population by 2050.

____

____

____

2. Analyze how will the distribution of the global population change by 2050.

____

____

____

____

____

3. Suggest three likely results of the shift in global population by 2050.

____

____

____

____

____

____

____

Lesson 3 *International Relationships*

Conceptual Understanding
10.9d Globalization has created new possibilities for international cooperation and for international conflict.

Source: *New York State Grades 9–12 Framework.*

People around the world recognized how human demands on the environment posed dangers to everyone. In a 1992 agreement reached in Rio de Janiero, Brazil, countries vowed to cut pollution and combat climate change.

Analyze a Primary Source

Principles of the Rio Declaration, 1992

Read Closely: Context
Note the historical context of events. For example, the Rio negotiations took place as the Soviet Union was breaking apart. The end of the Cold War reduced international tensions, which made reaching global agreements easier.

Read Closely: Audience
Recognizing the tone of a source can help you identify its audience. More formal sounding words and phrases might mean this is intended for governments or international agencies.
Circle words that show this document was intended for formal organizations.

Read Closely: Point of View
When reading a political document, consider who might agree with it and who might not.
Underline a phrase in the final paragraph that suggests why developed countries might oppose the agreement.

1. Human beings are at the centre [center] of concerns for sustainable development. They are entitled to a healthy and productive life in harmony with nature.

2. States have . . . the sovereign right to exploit their own resources pursuant to their own environmental and developmental policies, and the responsibility to ensure that activities within their jurisdiction or control do not cause damage to the environment of other States or of areas beyond the limits of national jurisdiction.

3. The right to development must be fulfilled so as to equitably meet developmental and environmental needs of present and future generations.

4. In order to achieve sustainable development, environmental protection shall constitute an integral part of the development process. . . .

5. All States and all people shall cooperate in the essential task of eradicating poverty as an indispensable requirement for sustainable development. . . .

6. The special situation and needs of developing countries, particularly the least developed and those most environmentally vulnerable, shall be given special priority. . . .

7. States shall cooperate . . . to conserve, protect and restore the health and integrity of the Earths ecosystem. In view of the different contributions to global environmental degradation, States have common but differentiated responsibilities. The developed countries acknowledge the responsibility that they bear in the international pursuit of sustainable development in view of the pressures their societies place on the global environment and of the technologies and financial resources they command.

Source: http://www.un.org/documents/ga/conf151/aconf15126-1annex1.htm

Global Issues and Global Responses

Globalization has created new economic opportunities, but these opportunities have come at a price, including some notable, negative side effects. In a similar way, in the area of international relations, globalization has created new opportunities for both cooperation and conflict.

The United Nations Promotes Cooperation

The Cold War came to an end in the early 1990s. However, the calmer relations among the world's superpowers did not bring about global security. Power struggles continued throughout the developing world; in parts of Eastern Europe, long-smoldering conflicts erupted into violence. Often when these eruptions occurred, the UN was called on to help restore order.

The Peacekeeping Role of the United Nations The UN's **peacekeeping** role expanded greatly in the early 1990s. In 1988, the UN had only five active peacekeeping operations. By 1993, it had 28. Individual countries supplied soldiers to form UN peacekeeping forces. They came from dozens of countries—including Canada, Venezuela, Ukraine, Egypt, and Bangladesh. The soldiers were usually lightly armed and instructed to return fire only if attacked.

In the 1990s, the United Nations sent peacekeeping missions to the hotspots of the world in Africa, Central America, the Caribbean, and Southeast Asia. In Africa, UN troops kept peace while Namibia changed from a South African colony to an independent state. Peacekeeping troops helped end devastating civil wars in Mozambique, El Salvador, and Cambodia. In Haiti, they maintained peace while a democratic government replaced a military dictatorship.

Some UN peacekeeping efforts failed. In 1994, they could not prevent the massacres in the African country of Rwanda. Around 800,000 Rwandans were killed. In 1995, UN forces withdrew from Somalia while that country's civil war still raged. The struggle to bring order to Bosnia in the former Yugoslavia also took years and had mixed results. As one UN officer in Bosnia observed, "It's much easier to come in and keep peace when there's some peace around."

Challenges for Peacekeeping Missions One problem faced by UN peacekeepers has their slow response. By the time countries agree on the UN mission and send forces, the war might have grown and become hard to control.

A second problem occurs when people expect peacekeepers to be more than than their names says. They are expected to stop the fighting instead of simply monitoring a truce, running free elections, and providing supplies to civilian populations. In Rwanda, Somalia, and Bosnia, the peacekeepers arrived in the midst of ongoing wars. At times, they actually took part in the fighting.

By 2018, the United Nations was involved in fewer but larger peacekeeping missions. The number of missions had dropped to 15, but the number of troops involved had increased.

Number of UN Peacekeepers Deployed

Year	Number
2000	30,000
2007	80,000
2014	95,000

Source: http://peaceoperationsreview.org/stratsum/

Read Closely: History
Focusing on a person's youth can help you understand how he or she acts as an adult. Similarly, focusing on the formation of an organization can help explain its later actions. How did the formation of the United Nation affect its role in the Cold War?

Read Closely: Key Words
Pay close attention to key words that describe essential content when you read. When discussing UN operations, a key term is "peacekeepers." What are peacekeepers, and how do they represent the mission of the UN?

NATO in Transition

The North Atlantic Treaty Organization (NATO) was created in 1949 to provide mutual defense to Western Europe and North America against attack by the Soviet Union. When the Soviet Union dissolved in 1991, NATO leaders began to rethink the purpose of the alliance.

Read Closely: Comparisons
Noting how the structure and goals of two organizations are distinctive even as they share some traits can help you understand how they act. NATO and the UN were both created after World War II and shaped by the United States. How are those organizations different?

New Strategies and Organization In November 1991, the leaders of the NATO countries met in Rome to reorganize NATO's military forces. Though the Cold War was over, new problems had arisen, for which new approaches were needed. The alliance's 16 member nations focused on three troubled areas:

- In **Eastern Europe**, several of the former Soviet satellite nations wanted to join NATO for protection from Russia. NATO promised to defend them should the need arise.
- In the **Balkans**, national, ethnic, and religious rivalries were simmering in the former Yugoslavia. NATO feared that these conflicts would spread throughout the region.
- In the **Middle East**, multiple problems existed. Iraqi dictator Saddam Hussein threatened the region's security. Iran was identified as a supporter of terrorist organizations. Tension continued between Israel and its neighbors. Controlling hostilities in this region was especially important to NATO members because it contained much of the world's oil reserves.

To deal with the new dangers, NATO leaders took a number of steps. Formerly, they had massed most of their forces in Germany to meet threats from Eastern Europe and the Soviet Union. Since many new conflicts were now arising in southern areas of the globe, they had to adopt a more flexible strategy. Therefore, they divided their forces into smaller units, backed by highly mobile reserves. Troops from the United States, however, would not leave Europe altogether.

Expansion of NATO To better respond to the intricate security problems that faced the post–Cold War world, the leaders of NATO reached out to the countries of Eastern Europe. The Partnership for Peace was established in 1994 to give these nonmember nations an opportunity to increase their political and military cooperation with NATO. In 1995, Russia became one of the 27 countries to join the Partnership for Peace.

Expansion of NATO became a reality in March 1999 when Poland, Hungary, and the Czech Republic became full members. Seven more Eastern European states—Bulgaria, Estonia, Latvia, Lithuania, Romania, Slovakia, and Slovenia—were invited to join NATO in 2004. In 2009, Croatia and Albania also joined.

NATO in the 21st Century Al Qaeda's attacks against the United States on September 11, 2001, again caused NATO members to rethink the organization's role. Fighting terrorism became a higher priority. In addition, countries considered whether NATO should take military action beyond Europe.

- The Afghan government had been sheltering Al Qaeda's leadership. In the response, the United States organized an attack on Afghanistan. All 28 member nations of NATO contributed troops to the effort. This was the first NATO action taken outside of Europe.
- The United States, in 2003, then invaded Iraq. NATO members were divided on this decision. Two powerful NATO countries, France and Germany, opposed it. They argued that Iraq had not been involved in the September 11 attacks, so the invasion was not justified.

The European Union

The interdependence of the world's nations led to what in the recent past must have seemed unthinkable to many—a united Europe. In 2018, the European Union had 28 member states, and it had greatly improved international relations in that once-volatile continent.

Origin of the European Union The **European Union** (EU) traced its roots back to 1957, when six nations organized the European Community (EC), or Common Market. The Common Market's goal was to encourage economic cooperation among the major non-Communist industrial countries of the region. They wanted to form a single market by eliminating trade barriers.

The EC slowly moved beyond the status of a common market. In 1992, the members signed a treaty in the Dutch city of Maastricht that changed the EC into the European Union in 1994. The Maastricht Treaty removed almost all barriers to the movement of people, goods, and services across national borders in Western Europe. The treaty also committed members to establish a single European currency, the euro, and to coordinate foreign and defense policies.

Source: Getty Images

The euro coin symbolized the breakdown of many of the economic and political barriers separating European countries.

Read Closely: Point of View
Understand how actions reflect underlying points of view. How people act shows how they view a situation. How did the British response to joining the European Union reveal the point of view of many of its citizens?

Pros and Cons of the EU The creation of a single market not only strengthened Western Europe economically, but it also set the stage for greater political unity. Many people viewed the Maastricht Treaty as an important step toward a federal Europe. It increased the powers of EU institutions, such as its executive offices in Brussels, Belgium.

Other Europeans feared such a development. They continued to feel a strong nationalism. They worried that stronger EU institutions would threaten individual nations. The United Kingdom and several other countries opposed giving the European Union too much power. Britons' skepticism about the EU never went away; in 2016, Britain voted to exit the EU, a move that became known as "Brexit."

Britons were not alone in their "Euroskepticism." This feeling was fed by a massive migrant crisis. In 2015, civil war and instability in the Middle East and North Africa motivated a great number of people to seek asylum in Europe. The arrival of these migrants, many of whom were Muslims, frightened many on the continent. Migrants were forced to shelter in refugee camps, and countries on the forefront of the crisis began to shut down borders and turn people away. Conservative leaders in many countries used the situation to boost their support, claiming connections between migrants, crime, and terrorism.

International Efforts to Preserve the Environment

Because of the challenges to the environment brought about by population growth, industrialization, and urbanization, a number of international efforts and organizations have arisen to attempt solutions.

Kyoto Agreement On December 1, 1997, delegates from more than 150 nations arrived in Kyoto, Japan, to attend the Conference of the Parties to the United Nations Framework Convention on Climate Change. They met to devise the first international treaty on ways to reduce the emission of carbon dioxide, methane, and other detrimental greenhouse gases into the atmosphere. In the atmosphere, greenhouse gases acted as a sort of one-way windowpane, like the glass in a greenhouse. They trap heat and raise temperatures across the planet.

At the Kyoto convention, the delegates reached an agreement, known as the **Kyoto Protocol**, in which a specific strategy was developed to combat climate change. This strategy required 38 industrialized nations to reduce their combined greenhouse-gas emissions to more than 5 percent below their 1990 levels. Developing nations, which emitted fewer greenhouse gases into the atmosphere, could set their own limits on such emissions.

> ***An Enduring Issue: The Environment***
> The Kyoto Protocol demonstrated that people recognized how climate change had an impact on humans. It is one example of responding to the impact of the environment on people.

The Kyoto Protocol was signed by 178 nations in 2001. However, it was rejected by the United States. Opponents of the treaty argued that to cut the use of fuels that produced emissions of carbon dioxide to the extent that the treaty required could cause energy prices to soar and would damage the U.S. economy. This action by the United States discouraged some developing nations from limiting their carbon emissions.

In the end, almost no countries met the established targets. Some would argue that the agreement had little impact because the world's two biggest greenhouse-gas emitters, China, considered a developing country, and the United States, were not bound by the protocol. Though the Kyoto Protocol expired in 2012, efforts to internationally legislate greenhouse gas emissions continued.

> **Read Closely: Priorities**
> People's decisions are based on their priorities. Everyone has an order in which they value different ideas. What actions by Greenpeace revealed their priorities?

Greenpeace Several nonprofit organizations formed to advocate for the environment. Among these was Greenpeace. It was founded in 1971 and grew into a multinational agency with offices in 40 countries. It battles deforestation, desertification, global climate change, the killing of whales, and overfishing. Greenpeace engages in lobbying and education but is most famous for its direct actions, such as confronting whaling boats on the ocean, occupying coal-fired power plants, and exposing the dumping of toxic waste at sea.

Global Security Issues

In the post–Cold War era, large-scale conflicts between sovereign states are rare. Terrorism, however, has grown as a real threat to public safety throughout the world. Larger-scale conflicts between countries, especially in the developing world, should never be ruled out—especially considering the booming worldwide business in arms sales.

The Growth of Terrorism Terrorist groups and campaigns are nothing new. Many existed around the world before the end of the Cold War:

- The **Irish Republican Army (IRA)** led a decades-long campaign of bombings and shootings in an attempt to achieve its goal of a free, united Ireland. Fighting between the IRA and its adversaries, including British soldiers and Protestant Loyalist paramilitaries, led to the deaths of more than 2,000 people between the beginning of "The Troubles" in 1969 and their end in 1998. The end came with a negotiated settlement.

- A longstanding campaign for independence for the Basque people, whose homeland straddles the borders of Spain and France, morphed into a terrorist military struggle waged by the group known as **Euskadi Ta Askatasuna (ETA)**. Between 1968 and 2010, more than 800 people were killed and thousands more wounded. ETA declared an end to armed activity in 2011 and surrendered its remaining weapons in 2018.

Al Qaeda One of the best-known terrorist organizations is **Al Qaeda.** It bases its actions on a radical interpretation of Islam that is condemned by most Muslims. The organization was led and partly financed by Osama bin Laden from Saudi Arabia. It carried out a number of bombings against U.S. targets throughout the 1990s and beyond.

On September 11, 2001, it carried out a series of devastating attacks that had grave ripple effects around the world. In these coordinated attacks, terrorists killed more than 3,000 people by hijacking and crashing two planes into the World Trade Center in New York City, and a third plane into the Pentagon near Washington, D.C. Passengers and crew aboard a fourth plane attacked the hijackers and caused the plane to crash in a field in rural Pennsylvania before it could reach another high-profile target. Most of the world rallied to condemn Al Qaeda and support the United States.

In the years that followed the September 11 attacks, Al Qaeda and groups with similar agendas, such as ISIS and Boko Haram, carried out additional bombings and executions that killed thousands. While high-profile attacks occurred in Madrid, London, and Paris, most victims of these terrorist organizations were Muslims living in rural communities in countries such as Yemen and Nigeria.

Read Closely: Causation
Some words clearly indicate a cause and effect relationship: *because, as a result, therefore.* As you read, identify causes and effects that are implied by the writing. What phrases in the text indicate the impact of Al Qaeda?

Cyber Warfare In this high-tech form of attack, countries or terrorist groups disrupted, disabled, or spied on the computer systems of another. They could also attack the computer systems of large businesses that were based in a certain country. Several kinds of cyber attacks emerged:

- Hacking was the penetration of computer systems of governments or businesses for the purpose of stealing data.
- Ransomware locked up computers or systems until a ransom was paid to the perpetrator.
- Malware and viruses could disable critical government, military, and commercial systems.
- Denial-of-service attacks flooded a website's servers with so much information that the site was disabled, keeping legitimate users from gaining access.

One of the best-known examples of cyber warfare occured during the 2016 presidential election in the United States. According to the intelligencne agencies of the U.S. government, Russians wanted to discredit American democracy and to support their preferred candidate, Donald Trump. They used several tactics:

- spreading consistently negative information about one of the candidates through a government-sponsored news website, radio station, and television network
- hiring and directing the activities of an entity that employed hundreds of "trolls" to post malicious, divisive, and false comments and news stories on social media platforms such as Facebook

International Trade in Arms

When Rwandan rebels and government forces clashed in the early 1990s, each side had a large stash of weapons. These weapons included mortars from France, assault rifles from Romania and Russia, and machine guns and grenades from South Africa. Each year, buyers from many countries spend tens of billions of dollars for weapons sold on the world arms market.

Leaders in the Arms Industry Many nations had arms-exporting industries. China led in the production of light arms, such as rifles and hand grenades; it also sold missiles. Sweden sold everything from fighter planes to submarines. But the United States outsold almost everyone.

While the world's leaders often denounced the arms trade, they also encouraged it. Many presidential administrations in the United States have actively assisted U.S. corporations in winning arms contracts from allied nations. After the Cold War ended, the U.S. government cut back its purchases from U.S. arms manufacturers. These cutbacks led to layoffs of workers, decreases in research, and mergers among arms manufacturers. The arms industry was on the verge of collapse. To prevent further economic hardship, the government stepped up the promotion of sales to other countries.

Attempts to Limit Arms Sales The major nations tried to put limits on the sale of certain especially destructive weapons, such as missiles and their associated technology. The Missile Technology Control Regime (MTCR) helped coordinate these efforts. The United States, Canada, France, Germany, Italy, Japan, and the United Kingdom started this organization in 1987. Several other nations have since signed on. The MTCR limited exports of all but the shortest-range ballistic and cruise missiles. A separate agreement restricted sales of arms and military technology to states they viewed as uncooperative, such as Iran and North Korea.

Read Closely: Problems
To better comprehend a person or nation's actions, consider the problems facing them when they decided. Why do you think China broke its agreement regarding the sale of missile technology?

Though China did not sign the MTCR, it did agree to observe the controls. Nevertheless, Beijing sold missile technology to Pakistan in the 1990s. China also purchased advanced military technology from Israel. To stop such activities, the United States has occasionally cut off exports of high-tech goods to China.

Source: Shutterstock

In Great Britain, protesters objected to arms sales to Saudi Arabia and the United Arab Emirates.

Application

Read the excerpt and answer the questions that follow it.

The Guardian, a British newspaper, on EU Membership 2012

At a time when Europe seems on the brink of falling apart, when Europeans are taking to the streets to express their wrath towards other partners in the union and when mainstream politicians in the UK are looking for a way out of the club, a decision by a group of Norwegian intellectuals [prompts] the question: what has the EU done for us? We take a look at some of the more positive impacts the EU has had on our lives.

Peace: The origins of peace in Europe lie in the alliance made between France and Germany that gave birth to the European Coal and Steel Community, a forerunner of the EU. The ECSC was first conceived by Robert Schuman, the French foreign minister in 1950 "to make war not only unthinkable but materially impossible." The continent has indeed enjoyed lasting peace. International security remains one of the EU's top priorities, not just in Europe but the rest of the world.

Single Market: The single market is probably the EU's single biggest achievement after peace, though it's arguably hard to separate the two. It guarantees the free movement of people, goods, services and capital. Apart from the unifying effect of this set-up on European citizens, it has provided the opportunity for them to travel, live, work, study and do business across the union, and to enjoy a wide range of competitively priced services and goods.

Single Currency: . . . Most Europeans see the benefits it brings to them as travelers—not having to convert money while away on holiday or business. But its main practical benefit has to do with economic growth. It has helped to strengthen the EU's international standing and improve integration within the union itself.

Democracy and Human Rights: Brussels sets standards of human rights, democracy and the rule of law to which countries must adhere if they want to be part of the European Union. In practical terms these guidelines have had a particular impact on the countries of southern, central and eastern Europe, which joined after they emerged from dictatorships with often underdeveloped civil societies.

Source: https://www.theguardian.com/world/2012/oct/12/europe-nobel-peace-prize-10-things

1. Specify the intended audience for this excerpt.

____

____

2. Describe how has peace been established since the 1950s, according to the excerpt.

____

____

3. Detail the economic benefits that have been provided by the EU.

____

____

Chapter 9 *Review*

Multiple-Choice Questions

Directions (1–6): For each statement or question, choose the number of the word or expression that, of those given, best completes the statement or answers the question.

Base your answers to questions 1 and 2 on the chart below and your knowledge of social studies.

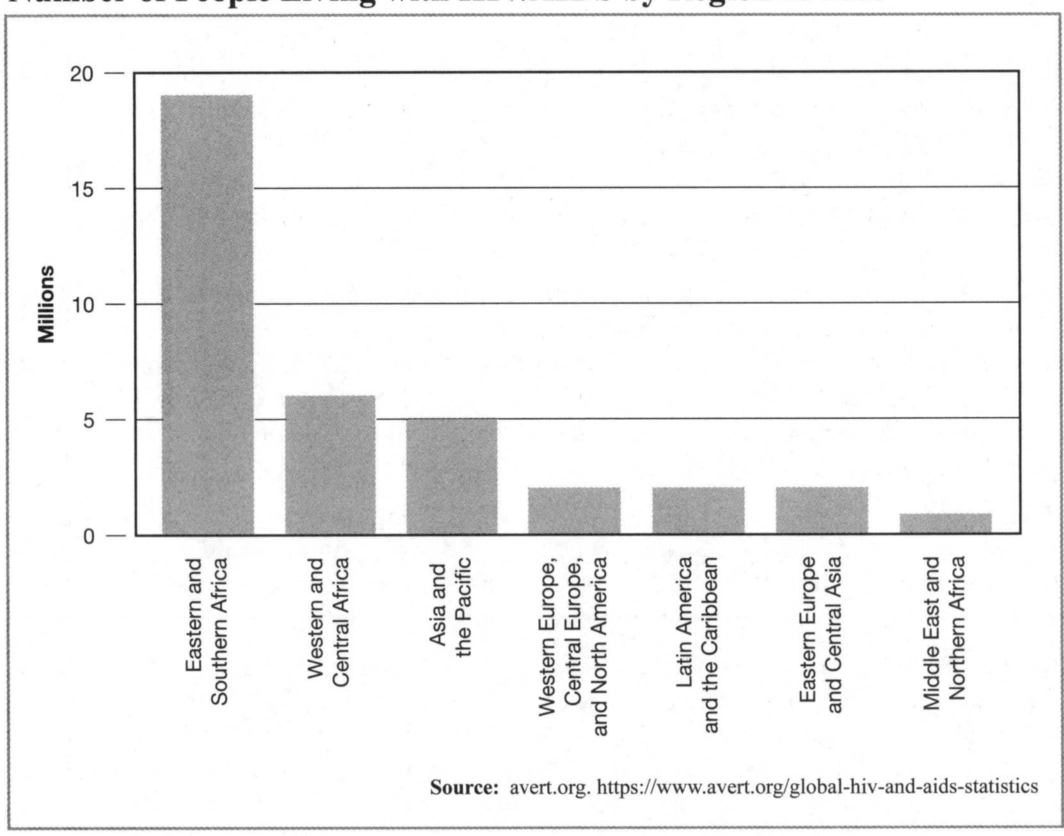

1. Which conclusion does this chart most clearly support?
   (1) Fewer people live in Asia and the Pacific than in Western and Central Africa.
   (2) Fewer people contract HIV/AIDS today than in the past.
   (3) HIV/AIDS has become a limited problem.
   (4) Africa has the highest number of HIV/AIDS cases in the world.

2. How has the international community tried to deal with the HIV/AIDS epidemic?
   (1) The World Health Organization and other international groups have monitored and raised awareness of the epidemic in order to prevent its spread.
   (2) Several countries have placed travel bans on countries that have high rates of HIV/AIDS.
   (3) International agencies have sent peacekeeping forces into areas to enforce laws banning risky behaviors.
   (4) Researchers have studied the effectiveness of oral contraceptives in slowing the spread of the disease.

Base your answers to questions 3 and 4 on the cartoon below and on your knowledge of social studies.

Source: CartoonStock.com

3. What is the main idea behind this cartoon?
   (1) Europe is an old area that can no longer defend itself from outsiders.
   (2) Many Europeans want to move out of the continent to other parts of the world.
   (3) Europe is trying to keep immigrants out of the area.
   (4) The number of immigrants is small compared to the native-born population of Europe.

4. What set of international events motivated the cartoonist to create this image?
   (1) mass immigration from the Middle East and Africa after the Arab Spring and civil wars
   (2) the genocide in the former Yugoslavia against Muslims
   (3) the failure to protect ethnic minorities after the fall of the Berlin Wall
   (4) the mass migration of Holocaust survivors heading to Israel

Tips for Answering Multiple-Choice Questions

Reading charts and graphs as part of as assessment is similar to reading an excerpt from a written source. One difference is that charts and graphs tend to use numbers, statistics, and images to convey information about a topic. Start with the title of the chart or graph. Find out what topic the information addresses. Then try to determine what cause or effect is being demonstrated or how regions/areas/people addressed by the graph or chart compare. What you notice is likely to be addressed by one of the questions.

Base your answers to questions 5 and 6 on the passage below and your knowledge of social studies.

> State policies to encourage economic development, such as road and railway expansion projects, have caused significant, unintentional deforestation in the Amazon and Central America. Agricultural subsidies and tax breaks, as well as timber concessions, have encouraged forest clearing as well. Global economic factors such as a country's foreign debt, expanding global markets for rainforest timber and pulpwood, or low domestic costs of land, labor, and fuel can encourage deforestation over more sustainable land use.
>
> **Source:** https://earthobservatory.nasa.gov/Features/Deforestation/deforestation_update3.php

5. Which is the most accurate title for the above passage?
   (1) "Rainforest destruction leads to global warming"
   (2) "Misguided government policies add to the destruction of forests"
   (3) "Deforestation helps the rich get richer"
   (4) "Central America exports deforestation to the Amazon"

6. Which claim is most strongly supported by this passage?
   (1) Sustainable land use is a high priority for governments in dealing with deforestation.
   (2) Deforestation is one of the most damaging economic practices.
   (3) Ignorance of the impact of deforestation leads to more deforestation.
   (4) Government action often causes unintended consequences such as deforestation.

Tips for Answering Multiple-Choice Questions

Some questions have two or more plausible answers. The question writer is likely trying to make you think critically about these two possible answers. You must determine out of the two or more possibilities the ones that have errors, omissions, or less of a relation to the information contained in the stimulus or in your broader knowledge of history.

Short-Answer Questions

CRQ Directions (7-9): Analyze the documents and answer the short-answer questions that follow each document in the space provided.

Base your answer to question 7 on Document 1 below and on your knowledge of social studies.

Document 1

The following statistics are from Daniel Workman and show Chinese exports to nations around the globe in 2016 (The report was released November 24, 2017).

> The world's largest exporter, China shipped US$2.119 trillion worth of products around the globe in 2016. That figure represents roughly 13.1% of overall global exports estimated at $16.236 trillion one year earlier in 2015.
>
> From a continental perspective, half (49.8%) of China's total exports by value in 2016 were delivered to other Asian trade partners.
>
> North American importers purchased 21.2% of Chinese shipments while 18.5% worth [of shipments] arrived in European countries.
>
> At 4.4%, a much smaller portion of Chinese exports were bought by importers in Africa.
>
> 1. United States: US$388.1 billion (18.3% of total Chinese exports)
> 2. Hong Kong: $292.2 billion (13.8%)
> 3. Japan: $129.5 billion (6.1%)
> 4. South Korea: $94.7 billion (4.5%)
> 5. Germany: $65.8 billion (3.1%)
> 6. Vietnam: $61.6 billion (2.9%)
> 7. India: $58.9 billion (2.8%)
> 8. Netherlands: $57.7 billion (2.7%)
> 9. United Kingdom: $56.3 billion (2.7%)
> 10. Singapore: $45.8 billion (2.2%)
> 11. Taiwan: $40.4 billion (1.9%)
> 12. Malaysia: $38.5 billion (1.8%)
> 13. Thailand: $37.7 billion (1.8%)
> 14. Australia: $37.6 billion (1.8%)
> 15. Russia: $37.5 billion (1.8%)

7. Describe the statistics in the document in context of how Chinese trade has changed.

___

___

___

___

___

Base your answer to question 8 on Document 2 below and on your knowledge of social studies.

Document 2

"Well, Santa may live at the North Pole, but these labels say his workshop is in China."

Source: https://globaltraderelations.com/2017/05/15/new-us-china-trade-understanding-not-much-substance-better-than-nothing/

8. Using this cartoon, identify the cartoonist's bias.

Base your answer to question 9 on both Documents 1 and 2 and on your knowledge of social studies.

Similarity—tells how something is alike or the same as something else.
Difference—tells how something is not alike or not the same as something else.

9. Identify and explain a similarity in the ideas expressed in Documents 1 and 2. Use evidence from both Documents 1 and 2 in your response.

Speaking and Listening: Reflect on the Key Idea

Working with a small group, draw a sketch of a world map showing the continents and several countries. On each continent list a connection someone has with that continent. The connection might be a product they own, a famous entertainer or sports star they like, a food they eat, or something else.

CHAPTER 10

Growing Demand for Human Rights

Chapter Overview

In response to the Holocaust, people around the world began paying closer attention to human rights violations. Scholars wrote the United Nations Universal Declaration of Human Rights to provide a set of principles for the fight against human rights abuses.

Multinational Treaties and Courts Multinational treaties bound countries to adhere to human rights principles and defend them when necessary. When these treaties were violated, nations convened special courts to judge the perpetrators.

Historical Events Historians often look at past events to evaluate instances of oppression using the UN Declaration. The atrocities of Augusto Pinochet in Chile, Deng Xiaoping in China, and Slobodan Milošević in the former Yugoslavia are important examples. In addition, genocides in Cambodia, Rwanda, and Darfur prompted people to ask what the international community could do to protect people when their own government did not.

After the fall of apartheid in South Africa, blacks and whites tried to confront their country's past. They created Truth and Reconciliation Committees that followed UN Universal Declaration of Human Rights principles as a guideline. Nelson Mandela led the effort in South Africa while other leaders, such as Aung San Suu Kyi in Myanmar (Burma) and the Mothers of the Plaza de Mayo in Argentina exemplified the principles in the ways they handled persecution.

An Enduring Issue: Human Rights One enduring issue in this chapter is the debate about human rights. The outrages that occurred during World War II, particularly the Holocaust, caused many people to support the idea that all people deserve basic protections. The stronger sense of internationalism that emerged after the war created a climate in which countries were willing to cooperate. As a result, countries agreed that the international community, not just individual countries, could hold trials for people accused of terrible acts.

New York Social Studies Framework: **Key Idea 10.10**

Since the Holocaust, human rights violations have generated worldwide attention and concern. The United Nations Universal Declaration of Human Rights has provided a set of principles to guide efforts to protect threatened groups and has served as a lens through which historical occurrences of oppression can be evaluated.

Source: *New York State Grades 9–12 Social Studies Framework.*

1. Rewrite Key Idea 10.10 in your own words.

____

____

Identify Enduring Issues

Based on your study of global history and geography, make a list of four enduring issues and provide two examples for each of them. Examples can come from earlier chapters or this chapter.

Identifying Examples of Enduring Issues		
Enduring Issue	**Example 1**	**Example 2**
1.		
2.		
3.		
4.		

Key Terms and Names

Geography

The Hague (p. 304)
Darfur (p. 311)
Rwanda (p. 311)

Social Structures

Hutu (p. 311)
Tutsi (p. 311)

Governance

International Criminal Tribunal for the Former Yugoslavia (ICTY) (p. 304)
Deng Xiaoping (p. 309)
General Augusto Pinochet (p. 309)
Salvador Allende (p. 309)
Khmer Rouge (p. 310)
Pol Pot (p. 310)
Slobodan Milosevic (p. 310)
apartheid (p. 311)
Desmond Tutu (p. 312)
Nelson Mandela (p. 313)
Mother Theresa (p. 313)
Aung San Suu Kyi (p. 313)
Mothers of the Plaza de Mayo (p. 314)
Dirty War (p. 314)

Civics

crimes against humanity (p. 297)
crimes against peace (p. 297)
Nuremberg Charter (p. 297)
war crimes (p. 297)
United Nations Universal Declaration of Human Rights (p. 298)
American Convention on Human Rights (p. 303)
European Convention on Human Rights (p. 303)
European Court of Human Rights (ECHR) (p. 303)

Lesson 1 *Declaration of Human Rights*

Conceptual Understanding 10.10a Following World War II, the United Nations Universal Declaration of Human Rights (1948) was written. This provides a set of principles to guide efforts to protect threatened groups.

Source: *New York State Grades 9–12 Framework.*

Throughout most of history, people had rights because of their wealth or their position in society or status as a citizen. The idea that all people have basic rights simply because they are humans is a modern one the emerged during the Enlightenment. By the 1940s, this idea was accepted widely enough that the victorious powers in World War II were able to set up courts, called tribunals, to punish people who had violated these fundamental human rights.

Analyze a Primary Source

Charter of the International Military Tribunal

The International Military Tribunal (IMT) is composed of judges from the United States, Great Britain, France and the Soviet Union. Leading Nazi officials will be indicted and placed on trial in Nuremberg, Germany, under Article 6 of the IMT's Charter for the following crimes: (1) Conspiracy to commit charges 2, 3, and 4, which are listed here; (2) crimes against peace—defined as participation in the planning and waging of a war of aggression in violation of numerous international treaties; (3) war crimes—defined as violations of the internationally agreed upon rules for waging war; and (4) crimes against humanity—namely, murder, extermination, enslavement, deportation, and other inhumane acts committed against any civilian population, before or during the war; or persecution on political, racial, or religious grounds in execution of or in connection with any crime within the jurisdiction of the Tribunal, whether or not in violation of domestic law of the country where perpetrated."

Verdict at Nuremberg The International Military Tribunal (IMT) announces its verdicts. It imposes the death sentence on 12 defendants. . . . Three are sentenced to life imprisonment. . . . Four receive prison terms ranging from 10 to 20 years. . . . The court acquits three defendants. . . . The death sentences are carried out on October 16, 1946, with two exceptions: Goering committed suicide shortly before his scheduled execution, and Bormann remained missing. The other 10 defendants are hanged, their bodies cremated, and the ashes deposited in the Iser River. The seven major war criminals sentenced to prison terms are remanded [sent] to the Spandau Prison in Berlin.

Source: https://www.ushmm.org/outreach/en/article.php?ModuleId=10007722

Read Closely: Generalizations
Look for general patterns among details by identifying connections among them. *Underline the names of the four home countries of the judges on the IMT. Note that all of these countries were allies during World War II.*

Read Closely: Change
One controversial change represented by the IMT was that it claimed its legitimacy to punish came from the people of the world, rather than from the laws of any specific country.
Circle the phrase in the first paragraph where the court states this power.

Read Closely: Larger Trends
Consider whether a specific event was part of a larger historical trend. For example, the IMT was one of many international institutions created after World War II, including the United Nations and NATO.

Global Efforts to Protect Rights

The actions of the Nazis in World War II made defending universal human rights a global issue. These rights were formally listed in 1948 in the Universal Declaration of Human Rights. One task of the United Nations and other international bodies was to stand up for them.

Evolving Ideas about Human Rights

Before the Enlightenment began in the 18th century, most Europeans assumed that people were born possessing different rights. Kings had more rights from commoners. Men had more rights from women. Citizens of one state had different rights from those of another.

However, these ideas changed as the writings of philosophers such as John Locke and Jean-Jacques Rousseau won supporters. People modified how they viewed rights. People began to believe that every individual is born possessing basic rights. A government might ignore or violate these rights, but they could never be taken away.

Revolutions and Reforms Belief in universal human rights inspired revolutionaries in the United States, France, and Latin America. For example, the American Declaration of Independence declared that all people were born with inalienable rights to life, liberty, and happiness.

During the 19th and early 20th centuries, the idea of human rights continued to spread. This belief shaped reform movements to end slavery, allow women to vote, and regulate child labor.

Rights and Colonies The issue of human rights was important in the debates about colonization. Defenders of colonization argued that Europeans defended these rights in their colonies. For example, in India, Great Britain supported laws that granted women more equality than was traditional in that region. However, opponents of colonization disagreed. Gandhi and others asserted that colonization violated the right of people to self-government.

Human Rights after World War II

Even before defeating the Axis Powers, the Allies made plans to prosecute Germans and Japanese for committing atrocities. The Allies argued they had the right to punish people for violating universal standards, even if those people could not be convicted under the law of any single state. Once the war was over, the Allies established International Military Tribunals, one in Germany and the other in Japan, to conduct the trials.

Read Closely: Turning Points Look for events that mark a major shift in how people think or act. Recognizing them will help you understand how history changes over time. How are the post-World War II military tribunals a turning point?

The Nuremberg Trials The trials in Germany were held in Nuremberg. They followed provisions stated in the **Nuremberg Charter** for conducting the trials of Nazi war criminals. Article 6 of the Nuremberg Charter specifically identified the three types of crimes that would fall within the jurisdiction of the tribunal:

- **crimes against peace,** such as planning or starting a war of aggression or a war that violates international treaties
- **war crimes,** such as murdering or mistreating civilians in an occupied territory, mistreatment of prisoners, destruction of communities not required by military necessity, or other violations of the customs of war
- **crimes against humanity,** such as murdering or enslaving people before or during a war or persecuting people based on political, racial, or religious grounds, even if the acts are not illegal in the country where they occurred

Read Closely: Motivation
One way to understand the motives of people is to look at the results of their actions. The trials in Nuremberg and Tokyo, resulted in a variety of sentences. What does this variety suggest about the motives of the people who conducted the trials?

The initial trial of the 23 highest-level defendants, including Herman Goring, in Nuremberg yielded three acquittals, seven lengthy prison sentences (three of life in prison), and 12 sentences of death. One prisoner was ruled unfit to stand trial. Another killed himself with poison before he could be executed.

The Tokyo Trials The International Military Tribunal for the Far East was conducted by the U.S. Army. It followed procedures outlined in the Tokyo Charter, which was closely modeled on the Nuremberg Charter. In the Tokyo Trials, 25 people were indicted, and all were convicted. Two received short prison terms. Sixteen were given life sentences.Seven people were sentenced to death.

Evaluating the Trials Defenders of the trials in Nuremberg and Tokyo saw them as a step towards international recognition of universal human rights. The trials set standards for the actions of countries and individuals that could be used in all times and all places.

However, critics of the post-war trials charged they were unfair. The trials focused on the actions of only the Axis countries. According to critics, the leaders of the Allies should have been tried for the extensive bombings of German cities such as Dresden, the use of atomic weapons on Hiroshima and Nagasaki, and the deaths of hundreds of thousands of civilians.To these critics, the trials marked continuity with the past, when winners of a war punished those who had lost.

The UN Promotes Universal Human Rights

The charters and trials that brought people to justice for committing atrocities contributed to the development of the **UN Universal Declaration of Human Rights**. In particular, the clause in the Nuremberg Charter citing crimes against humanity cemented the idea that those who committed atrocities should be accountable for their actions. The standard for judging them would be a universal one rather than just the laws of one particular country.

The preamble to the UN Universal Declaration of Human Rights began by explaining why the belief existed that the declaration was necessary. Note that the atrocities of World War II were referred to as a principal cause of the declaration.

Read Closely: Comparison
Comparing similar events, people, or items from different time periods in your reading can help you understand how the world has changed, as well as how people view the past. How is the UN Universal Declaration of Human Rights similar to the United States Declaration of Independence?

Whereas recognition of the inherent dignity and of the equal and inalienable rights of all members of the human family is the foundation of freedom, justice and peace in the world,

Whereas disregard and contempt for human rights have resulted in barbarous acts which have outraged the conscience of mankind, and the advent of a world in which human beings shall enjoy freedom of speech and belief and freedom from fear and want has been proclaimed as the highest aspiration of the common people,

Whereas it is essential, if man is not to be compelled to have recourse, as a last resort, to rebellion against tyranny and oppression, that human rights should be protected by the rule of law,

Whereas it is essential to promote the development of friendly relations between nations,

Whereas the peoples of the United Nations have in the Charter reaffirmed their faith in fundamental human rights, in the dignity and worth of the human person and in the equal rights of men and women and have determined to promote social progress and better standards of life in larger freedom . . .

Source: Designed by Freepik

Poster representing International Human Rights Day.

An Enduring Issue: Equity
One aspect of human rights is equality of access for all people to basic needs of life. Issues around access to adequate food, clean water, and a job that pays a living wage appear in countries around the world.

Following the preamble, Articles 1 and 2 expressed the basic human rights all should expect to be granted in broad terms:

Article 1.
All human beings are born free and equal in dignity and rights. They are endowed with reason and conscience and should act toward one another in a spirit of brotherhood.

Article 2.
Everyone is entitled to all the rights and freedoms set forth in this Declaration, without distinction of any kind, such as race, color, sex, language, religion, political or other opinion, national or social origin, property, birth or other status. Furthermore, no distinction shall be made on the basis of the political, jurisdictional or international status of the country or territory to which a person belongs, whether it be independent, trust, non-self-governing or under any other limitation of sovereignty.

The following 20 articles fell into two categories. People have a right to basic actions or conditions:

- life, liberty, and security
- recognition as a person before the law
- equal protection before the law, without discrimination
- a presumption of innocence until guilt is proven
- freedom of movement and the right to leave any country
- the ability to marry without limitations due to race, nationality, or religion
- freedom of thought, conscience, and religion

- freedom of opinion and expression
- peaceful assembly and association
- the ability to work and choose one's own employment
- equal pay for equal work and the right to join trade unions
- access to education
- full participation in the cultural life of one's community
- a social and international order in which the rights and freedoms of the declaration can be fully realized

Read Closely: Negatives
Historical accounts often focus on the main purpose or result of a development. While that purpose or result might be positive, note the possibilities for negatives as well, such as weaknesses, problems, or bad results. What is one negative about the UN Declaration of Human Rights?

In addition, no one should be subjected to certain actions or conditions that were particularly harmful. Among those listed were slavery, torture, arbitrary arrest, arbitrary interference with one's privacy, deprivation of one's nationality, and unjustified loss of property.

The declaration was not legally binding, but it stated the principles that people could use to evaluate violations of human rights. For example, it has been cited as a way to put pressure on abusive regimes in Sudan and Cambodia

One group of people that the United Nations wanted to protect were refugees, people driven from their home and into another country by war or fear of persecution. The UN High Commissioner for Refugees was established in 1950 to help Europeans uprooted by World War II. Since then, it has worked around the world. It now serves both refugees as well as people forced from their homes but who remain within their countries.

.

Source: National Archives

Eleanor Roosevelt holding the United Nations Declaration of Human Rights.

Application

Read the excerpt and answer the questions that follow it.

Preamble to the Universal Declaration of Human Rights, 1948

Whereas recognition of the inherent dignity and of the equal and inalienable rights of all members of the human family is the foundation of freedom, justice and peace in the world,

Whereas disregard and contempt for human rights have resulted in barbarous acts which have outraged the conscience of mankind, and the advent of a world in which human beings shall enjoy freedom of speech and belief and freedom from fear and want has been proclaimed as the highest aspiration of the common people,

Whereas it is essential, if man is not to be compelled to have recourse, as a last resort, to rebellion against tyranny and oppression, that human rights should be protected by the rule of law,

Whereas it is essential to promote the development of friendly relations between nations,

Whereas the peoples of the United Nations have in the Charter reaffirmed their faith in fundamental human rights, in the dignity and worth of the human person and in the equal rights of men and women and have determined to promote social progress and better standards of life in larger freedom,

Whereas Member States have pledged themselves to achieve, in co-operation with the United Nations, the promotion of universal respect for and observance of human rights and fundamental freedoms,

Whereas a common understanding of these rights and freedoms is of the greatest importance for the full realization of this pledge,

Now, therefore THE GENERAL ASSEMBLY proclaims THIS UNIVERSAL DECLARATION OF HUMAN RIGHTS as a common standard of achievement for all peoples and all nations, to the end that every individual and every organ of society, keeping this Declaration constantly in mind, shall strive by teaching and education to promote respect for these rights and freedoms and by progressive measures, national and international, to secure their universal and effective recognition and observance, both among the peoples of Member States themselves and among the peoples of territories under their jurisdiction.

Source: http://www.un.org/en/universal-declaration-human-rights/

1. Identify the historical context for this excerpt.

____

____

2. Explain the purpose for the creation of this document.

____

____

3. Identify the "barbarous acts" the excerpt refer to in the second paragraph.

____

____

Lesson 2 *Responding to Atrocities*

Conceptual Understanding 10.10b Governments, groups, and individuals have responded in various ways to the human atrocities committed in the 20th and 21st centuries.

Source: *New York State Grades 9–12 Framework.*

The International Criminal Tribunal for Rwanda (ICTR) was established by the United Nations Security Council on November 8, 1994, and formally closed on December 31, 2015. The Tribunal had a mandate to prosecute persons bearing great responsibility for genocide and other serious violations of international humanitarian law committed in Rwanda between January 1, and December 31, 1994.

Analyze a Primary Source

The International Criminal Tribunal for Rwanda

The first trial started in January 1997, and by December 2012, the Tribunal had completed the trial phase of its mandate. During its two decades of work in Arusha, Tanzania, the ICTR sentenced 61 people to terms of up to life imprisonment for their roles in the massacres. Fourteen accused were acquitted and 10 others referred to national courts. The ICTR held 5,800 days of proceedings, indicted 93 people, issued 55 first-instance and 45 appeal judgments, and heard the "powerful accounts of more than 3,000 witnesses who bravely recounted some of the most traumatic events imaginable during ICTR trials," ICTR President Judge Vagn Joensen told the UN Security Council in December 2015.

The Mechanism for International Criminal Tribunals (MICT), set up by the Security Council in December 2010, took over the remaining tasks of the ICTR—and of the International Criminal Tribunal for the former Yugoslavia (ICTY). The Mechanism plays an essential role in ensuring that the ICTR's closure does not leave the door open to impunity for the remaining fugitives. The ICTR branch of the Mechanism began to function on July 1, 2012.

The Tribunal has issued several landmark judgments, including:

In the first judgment by an international court on genocide, a former mayor, Jean-Paul Akayesu, was convicted in 1998 of nine counts of genocide and crimes against humanity. The judgment was also the first to conclude that rape and sexual assault constituted acts of genocide in so far as they were committed with the intent to destroy, in whole or in part, a targeted group.

The conviction of the prime minister during the genocide, Jean Kambanda, to life in prison in 1998 was the first time a head of government was convicted for the crime of genocide.

The Tribunal's "Media Case" in 2003 was the first judgment since the conviction of Julius Streicher at Nuremberg after World War II to examine the role of the media in the context of international criminal justice.

Source: http://www.un.org/en/preventgenocide/rwanda/about/bgjustice.shtml

Close Reading: Modifiers
Notice how people use modifiers that reflect their judgments about facts. *Underline three modifiers in the quotation from Judge Vagn Joensen.*

Read Closely: Clarifications
Readers often confuse terms that are new to them and somewhat similar. For example, the ICTR and the IMT both resulted from international efforts to prosecute criminals. Yet they were created in different eras, for accused people from different countries, and with different punishments.

Read Closely: Firsts
Note carefully the conditions under which a document labels an action a "first." *Circle the judgments that are "firsts" as described in the excerpt.*

Multinational Agreements and Organizations

In response to the violent 20th century, several governments, organizations, and individuals took steps to support the victims of injustice. They identified and investigated human rights abuses and tried to hold the perpetrators accountable.

Agreements Supporting Human Rights

In the more than 70 years that have passed since the end of World War II, the nations of the world have made a number of international agreements and conventions, some supported by judicial bodies, that focus on human rights. The following are just a few examples.

European Convention on Human Rights The European Convention on Human Rights went into effect late in 1953. Its articles were similar to those of the UN Universal Declaration of Human Rights, in that they guaranteed the right to life, liberty, and security; a fair trial; respect for the family; freedom of conscience, religion, expression, and assembly; and marriage. The convention also prohibited torture, slavery and forced labor, punishment without law, and discrimination.

The European Convention on Human Rights also had an enforcement mechanism, the **European Court of Human Rights** (ECHR), which was established in 1959. When an individual believed his or her rights had been violated and this violation had not been fairly dealt with in the person's national courts, he or she might petition to have the case heard before the ECHR.

In addition to individuals, the court could hear cases brought by states. For example, in 1976, Ireland brought a case against the United Kingdom regarding interrogation techniques used against suspected members of the Irish Republican Army (IRA) that Ireland regarded as torture. The court ruled that the techniques were inhuman but not torture. The decisions of the court were binding in regard to all 47 members of the Council of Europe.

American Convention on Human Rights This 1969 convention, a result of the Pact of San José, Costa Rica, asserted in its preamble that its aim was "to consolidate in this hemisphere, within the framework of democratic institutions, a system of personal liberty and social justice based on respect for the essential rights of man." It covered much of the same ground as the UN Universal Declaration of Human Rights and that of the European convention. As in Europe, there was an enforcement arm of the convention: the Inter-American Court of Human Rights. The court's decisions were binding upon all member countries.

However, the American and European conventions differed in how widely they were supported. Almost all countries in Europe supported the European convention. In contrast, only about two-thirds of countries in the Americans have supported the American convention.

The reasons some countries did not support the American convention demonstrated how complicated human rights issues can be. Canada refused to sign the convention because it defined life as beginning "in general, from the moment of conception." This definition reflected the viewpoint of people who opposed abortion in most or all circumstances. Canada's position was that abortion was a women's health issue. In that context, it should be decided between a woman and her doctor.

The United States signed the convention, but the U.S. Senate never ratified it, as all international treaties must be. As was the case with the League of Nations more than 50 years earlier, U.S. lawmakers expressed concern about potential

An Enduring Issue: Human Rights
After World War II, countries worked together to stop human rights violations. The cooperation was new, but problems such as discrimination and massacres had existed for centuries.

Read Closely: Context
Always pay attention to the context of an event. That includes both place and time. Think about what was going on during and around that event. What was the context when European nations created the European Convention on Human Rights?

> **Read Closely: Causes**
> As you read, distinguish between more and less important causes. While reading, pay attention to all causes for an event, not just the obvious. Every event has numerous causes, some more significant than others. What are two causes for the United States Senate not ratifying the American Convention on Human Rights?

infringement on national sovereignty. This concern had to do with the binding nature of the decisions reached by the Inter-American Court of Human Rights. This loss of control over the issue of human rights was deemed unacceptable.

The International Criminal Tribunal for the Former Yugoslavia (ICTY) Established by the UN in 1993 and convened at **The Hague** in the Netherlands, this tribunal has been likened to the Nuremberg Trials. It was convened for a specific purpose: to indict and try war criminals from the conflict that grew out of the breakup of the former Yugoslavia between 1992 and 1995. In some ways the tribunal was very successful. It showed that war could not function as a cover for illegal activity, regardless of a person's rank. Those who committed war crimes, genocide, and crimes against humanity would face justice, whether they were the president of a country or a local militia commander.

The tribunal also gave hope to victims who previously had no voice. However, justice was often slow. During its 24-year existence, the ICTY brought about 161 high-level indictments. One was against former Yugoslav president Slobodan Milošević, who died while on trial. Another was against Bosnian Serb leader Radovan Karadžić, who was found guilty of genocide and sentenced to 40 years in prison. Overall, 90 individuals were sentenced for genocide, crimes against humanity, and other crimes before the tribunal completed its work in December 2017.

Source: Getty Images

The International Criminal Tribunal for the Former Yugoslavia met in The Hague, which is located in the Netherlands.

Organizations Promoting Human Rights

It was not only multinational agreements that promoted people's health, human rights, well-being, and dignity. A network of organizations was created to protect people from the perils of the modern world and the threats posed by oppressive governments. The following are just a few examples.

Amnesty International (AI) Founded in London in 1961, this nongovernmental organization (NGO) has grown into a sophisticated worldwide entity, with offices in 50 countries and three million members. "Through our detailed research and determined campaigning," the organization said, "we help fight abuses of human rights worldwide. We bring torturers to justice, change oppressive laws, and free people jailed just for voicing their opinion." Amnesty International's areas of concern included many issues:

- arms control
- corporate accountability
- elimination of the death penalty
- politically motivated disappearances
- freedom of expression
- rights of indigenous peoples
- torture

Read Closely: Quotations
When a text includes a quotation, consider the original audience for the statement. This will help you put the quotation in context and understand it accurately. Who was the original audience for the quotation from Amnesty International?

A sampling of issues AI was publicizing and working on in 2018 showed the breadth and depth of the organization's work in the human rights realm:

- women's rights in Poland
- repression against antidiscrimination activists in Mauritania
- Internet privacy in China
- freedom of expression and assembly in Zambia
- capital punishment in Iraq
- violence against women online

Médecins Sans Frontières (MSF)/Doctors Without Borders Founded in 1971 by a group of doctors and journalists, MSF established offices in 21 countries all over the world. On any given day, more than 30,000 volunteers and employees of MSF—doctors, nurses, administrators, and others—are at work helping people in more than 60 countries. A recent statement from MSF described the organization's purpose and unique role in protecting human rights. "Doctors Without Borders/Médecins Sans Frontières (MSF) provides emergency medical care to millions of people caught in crises in more than 60 countries around the world. MSF provides assistance when catastrophic events—such as armed conflict, epidemics, malnutrition, or natural disasters—overwhelm local health systems. MSF also assists people who face discrimination or neglect from their local health systems or when populations are otherwise excluded from health care."

Read Closely: Distinctions
Phrases such as "in contrast" highlight important distinctions. While the Red Cross and MSF are both aid organizations, what is one key difference between them?

Another well-known organization that provides emergency medical care is the Red Cross. Both MSF and the Red Cross try to remain neutral in conflict zones so that they can provide aid. However, they apply this principal differently. The Red Cross does not publicize human rights issues in countries where they are providing assistance. However, MSF has somtimes spoken out against severe human rights abuses or when military or police actions have led to medical crises.

Human Rights Organizations	
Organization	**Mission Statement**
Amnesty International	"Amnesty International's vision is of a world in which every person enjoys all of the human rights enshrined in the Universal Declaration of Human Rights and other international human rights instruments. In pursuit of this vision, Amnesty International's mission is to undertake research and action focused on preventing and ending grave abuses of these rights."
Human Rights Watch	"Human Rights Watch defends the rights of people worldwide. We scrupulously investigate abuses, expose the facts widely, and pressure those with power to respect rights and secure justice. Human Rights Watch is an independent, international organization that works as part of a vibrant movement to uphold human dignity and advance the cause of human rights for all."
The United Nations High Commissioner for Refugees (UNHCR)	"The United Nations High Commissioner for Refugees' primary purpose is to safeguard the rights and well-being of refugees. UNHCR strives to ensure that everyone can exercise the right to seek asylum and find safe refuge in another state, or to return home voluntarily. By assisting refugees to return to their own country or to settle in another country, UNHCR also seeks lasting solutions to their plight."
Norwegian Refugee Council	"We stand up for people forced to flee. NRC is a determined advocate for displaced people. When we witness injustices, we alert the world. We promote and defend displaced people's rights and dignity in local communities, with national governments and in the international arena. NRC's Internal Displacement Monitoring Center in Geneva is a global leader in monitoring, reporting on, and advocating for people displaced within their own country."
International Crisis Group	"The International Crisis Group is an independent organization working to prevent wars and shape policies that will build a more peaceful world. Crisis Group sounds the alarm to prevent deadly conflict. We build support for the good governance and inclusive politics that enable societies to flourish. We engage directly with a range of conflict actors to seek and share information, and to encourage intelligent action for peace."

International Peace Bureau (IPB) The International Peace Bureau was founded in 1891–1892. It started when members of groups called peace societies from many countries decided they needed a permanent office to coordinate their activities and yearly meetings, the Universal Peace Congresses. These congresses had been meeting from the end of the Napoleonic Wars onward. In its early days, the IPB emphasized disarmament, the development of international law, and the peaceful settlement of conflicts. The IPB also promoted the establishment of a league of nations and an international court. However, the organization lost some of its importance amid the war-plagued years from 1914 to 1945.

Read Closely: Comparison
Making comparisons between different groups' goals can help you clarify what each is looking for. When you read, think about how different people confront the same situation. How does the International Peace Bureau compare to Amnesty International?

Beginning in the 1960s, the IPB rebounded. It was involved in protesting wars, supporting people who refused to serve in the military for reasons of personal conscience, restricting the arms trade, and stopping the spread of nuclear weapons.

In the 21st century, the IPB began to focus on reallocating military expenditures. "We believe that by reducing funding for the military sector, significant amounts of money could be released for social projects, domestically or abroad, which could lead to the fulfillment of real human needs and the protection of the environment. At the same time, we support a range of disarmament campaigns and supply data on the economic dimensions of weapons and conflicts."

The IPB established 300 member organizations in 70 countries. These organizations worked with individual members to form a global network to partner with other similarly minded organizations to help prevent, limit, and end conflict and build peaceful societies.

Application

Read the excerpt and answer the questions that follow it.

The History of Amnesty International

> In 1961, British lawyer Peter Benenson was outraged when two Portuguese students were jailed just for raising a toast to freedom. He wrote an article in *The Observer* newspaper and launched a campaign that provoked an incredible response. Reprinted in newspapers across the world, his call to action sparked the idea that people everywhere can unite in solidarity for justice and freedom.
>
> This inspiring moment didn't just give birth to an extraordinary movement, it was the start of extraordinary social change.
>
> "Only when the last prisoner of conscience has been freed, when the last torture chamber has been closed, when the United Nations Universal Declaration of Human Rights is a reality for the world's people, will our work be done." said Peter Benenson, Amnesty International founder.
>
> Over the years, human rights have moved from the fringes to center stage in world affairs.
>
> Amnesty has grown from seeking the release of political prisoners to upholding the whole spectrum of human rights. Our work protects and empowers people—from abolishing the death penalty to protecting sexual and reproductive rights, and from combatting discrimination to defending refugees' and migrants' rights. We speak out for anyone and everyone whose freedom and dignity are under threat.
>
> **Source:** https://www.amnesty.org/en/who-we-are/

1. Identify the historical context for the start of Amnesty International.

____

____

2. Explain how Amnesty International has changed since its beginning.

____

____

3. Explain how the efforts of Amnesty International and the United Nations to protect human rights differ.

____

____

Lesson 3 *Evaluating Human Rights Violations*

Conceptual Understanding
10.10c Historical and contemporary violations of human rights can be evaluated, using the principles and articles established within the UN Universal Declaration of Human Rights.

Source: *New York State Grades 9–12 Framework.*

The events of the spring of 1989 in Tiananmen Square in Beijing, China, are depicted in these two photographs from that period. Protests by students and workers had begun in April. Events unfolded throughout the next two months, culminating in the actions taken by Deng Xiaoping's government on June 4.

Read Closely: Symbolism
Look for symbolism in visual information. Painters, sculptors, and street protestors all use symbols as a way to communicate with their intended audience. The Goddess of Democracy uses the symbolism of the American Statue of Liberty.

Read Closely: Context
To understand the meaning of each of these images, consider the historical context in which they were each used.
Circle parts of each image that give clues to the context in which the photos were taken.

Read Closely: Comparison
Each of the visuals is a case study in the fight for human rights. They represent the actions of individuals in specific conflict with their government. In comparison, a document such as the UN Declaration of Human Rights sets out general principles.

Analyze a Primary Source

Source: Getty Images

Source: Getty Images

Attacks on Basic Rights

In the last 30 years of the 20th century and into the 21st, several extreme, large-scale violations of human rights took place in around the globe. These violations could be evaluated using the principles and articles of the UN Universal Declaration of Human Rights.

> **Read Closely: Theme**
> Always use introductory sections to help frame the next section. This will help you understand the overall context for what you are reading, and focus on the theme of the lesson. What are the theme and context for this lesson?

Late 20th-Century Human Rights Violations

In the late 20th century, several authoritarian rulers committed widely-reported violations of human rights. Three of these were particularly well-known.

Augusto Pinochet in Chile For decades in Chile during the 1900s, the government alternated between liberal and conservative governments and policies. However, people in the political center always moderated the actions of each side's more radical supporters. The country remained peaceful. Other countries praised Chile's democratic institutions as a model for the nations of South America.

By 1970, that balance in the political system was gone. A series of liberal and socialist reforms, including seizures of land and redistribution of it to peasants in the countryside, raised the expectations of Chile's poor and landless and frightened the wealthy landowners and business people. These reforms were championed by what began as a centrist government. The election of the socialist candidate **Salvador Allende** as president in 1970 further alarmed the conservatives. Allende and his Popular Unity party began to implement their program to redistribute land and wealth in Chile. As part of this, they wanted to break the grip of foreign companies, mainly from the United States, on the country's mining wealth.

On September 11, 1973, military leaders backed by the United States took over the government. President Allende died in the military's assault on the presidential palace. **General Augusto Pinochet** declared himself Chile's ruler. The Chilean Congress was broken up and left-wing parties were outlawed.

A brutal crackdown on supporters of Allende followed. The government denied people legal due process. Thousands of people were imprisoned and tortured. Pinochet's operatives even went beyond Chile's borders. They assassinated prominent exiled Chilean opposition leaders in Buenos Aires, Rome, and Washington, D.C. During Pinochet's 16-year reign, nearly 3,200 Chileans and others who opposed his rule were killed.

Deng Xiaoping in China In spring 1989, pro-democracy activists organized a public event mourning the death of a sympathetic high official. The protesters demanded a chance to speak with Chinese leaders about freedom of the press and other reforms. After the Chinese government refused to meet with the activists, citizens in more than 400 Chinese cities staged sit-ins, refused to attend classes, and began hunger strikes. Hundreds of thousands of students, professors, and urban workers staged a massive protest in Beijing's Tiananmen Square. After seven weeks of protests, Deng Xiaoping's government decided to end the protest. It declared martial law and sent troops armed with tanks and assault weapons into Beijing. Citizens responded by setting up barricades to block the troops.

> ***An Enduring Issue: Security***
> China's crackdown on dissidents at Tiananmen Square reflected the government's concern about security. This concern is an ongoing issue found in many countries.

On June 4, 1989, the army arrived in Tiananmen Square and attacked the unarmed protesters. The Chinese government claimed that nobody died in Tiananmen Square that day. No mention of the event was included in school textbooks, and all websites that discussed the incident and the human rights abuses committed there were blocked. However, estimates by Amnesty International, the International Red Cross, and the *New York Times* indicated that

> **Read Closely: Statistics**
> Many statistics are estimates, and they often differ. When you read a range of estimates, consider reasons why they might vary. What made counting deaths at Tiananmen Square difficult?

anywhere from several hundred to a few thousand civilians were killed. Tens of thousands were arrested in the crackdown that immediately followed and continued in subsequent years.

Slobodan Milošević and the Former Yugoslavia After World War II and the horrors of the Holocaust, the global community said "never again" to genocide. However, another genocide occurred in Europe less than 50 years later.

Ethnic conflict drove the genocide in Bosnia. The end of World War I brought with it the creation of several new nations in Eastern Europe, including Yugoslavia. That country was home to Serbians, who were Eastern Orthodox Christians; Croats and Slovenes, who were Catholic; and Bosniaks, many of whom were Muslims. Marshall Tito led Communist Yugoslavia from the end of World War II until his death in 1980. During his rule, the dictatorial Tito managed to suppress ethnic, religious, and separatist impulses among Yugoslavia's different regions and peoples.

After the Soviet Union collapsed in 1991, so did Yugoslavia. Slovenia, Croatia, and Serbia each went their separate ways and defined citizenship in terms of ethnic background and religion.

Serbian nationalists led by the Slobodan Milošević were particularly emphatic about ethnic purity.They attempted to create a "greater Serbia" that included regions of Croatia and Bosnia and Herzegovina where many Serbs lived. The Serbs committed murder and rape against Croats and Muslim Bosniaks. Their violations of the Universal Declaration of Human Rights shocked people around the world. In 1995 and again in 1999, NATO forces, used bombing campaigns to successfully halt Serbian aggression.

As fighting continued, casualties mounted. More than 300,000 people in the region perished over the course of Yugoslavia's disintegration.

Human Rights Violations and International Inaction

Some of the largest violations of human rights reflected a failure of the international community to act quickly and efficiently.

> **Read Closely: Statistics**
> Note that estimate for the number of deaths under the Khmer Rouge is very general and that the causes of death are also broad. Suggest reasons that the information is vague.

Cambodia The war in Vietnam created turmoil throuhgough southweat Asia. In 1975, Cambodia's capital, Phnom Penh, was seized by the forces of the Communist **Khmer Rouge,** led by **Pol Pot.** In this new order, the peasantry was elevated to an exalted status, while intellectuals, ethnic minorities, such as the Vietnamese, and city dwellers were seen as potential enemies. Many thousands of them were murdered.

Khmer Rouge soon began emptying the nation's cities, forcing their inhabitants into the countryside. Here, they essentially worked as slave laborers in agricultural camps. Over the following four years, between 1.5 and 2.5 million Cambodians, about one-fourth of the total population, died from violence, starvation, overwork, or disease.

Although Cambodia was closed off to foreigners at this time, news of slaughter and starvation on a massive scale reached the outside. However, with their defeat in Vietnam so fresh in their memories, American policymakers were unwilling to involve themselves in another conflict in Southeast Asia. Similarly, other Western powers chose not to intervene.

Another powerful nation in the region was China. Like the Western powers, it also refused to step in to end the massacre. Instead, China was the source of 90 percent of the Khmer Rouge's foreign assistance. It provided construction equipment, arms, and some food.

The people of Cambodia were left in a virtual human rights void until late 1978. At that time, Vietnam invaded the country after years of mutual border raids and skirmishes. The Vietnamese quickly overthrew the Khmer Rouge and took control of Cambodia for roughly 10 years.

Rwanda One of the smallest countries in Africa, **Rwanda** was the site of one of the worst genocides in modern history. Ethnic rivalry and hatred going back to the colonial era were behind the slaughter. Belgian colonizers had treated the minority **Tutsi** people better than the majority **Hutu** people. The Hutus resented all the power that the Tutsis enjoyed.

When Rwanda won independence from Belgium in 1962, the Hutu majority easily won control of the government and took revenge on the Tutsis by discriminating against them. In response, tens of thousands of Tutsis fled the country and formed a rebel army.

In 1993, Tutsi and Hutu representatives in Rwanda began negotiations for a coalition government in which both ethnic groups would share power. The negotiations were cut short in 1994 when Rwanda's president, a Hutu, was killed in an airplane crash, supposedly shot down by rebel forces. The incident lit the fuse of genocide. Over the next three months or so, as many as one million civilians, mostly Tutsis and some moderate Hutus, were killed. Some sources estimate that casualties were even higher.

International responses ranged from insufficient to callous. United Nations peacekeepers were instructed not to use force to restore order. There were also too few peacekeepers to make any real impact on the situation. Individual countries, including the United States, evacuated their personnel from the country after Belgian peacekeepers were killed. UN peacekeepers and individual nations failed to evacuate any Rwandans.

The Rwandan genocide focused attention on the lack of leadership in the international community. It became clear that the United Nations needed to think seriously about its role in violent conflicts if it wanted to effectively protect human lives and human rights.

Read Closely: Indirect Effects
Events have both direct and indirect effects. Considering the indirect effects of world events will help you understand their importance. What are major indirect effects of the Rwandan genocide?

Darfur In 2003 another incidence of genocide took place in **Darfur,** a region located in western Sudan. The people involved were all Muslims, but some were nomads of Arab descent, while others were non-Arab farmers. The government of Sudan was controlled by Arab Muslims. Two Darfur rebel groups composed of non-Arabs took up arms against the Sudanese government in response to attacks from nomads.

In response, the Sudanese government unleashed Arab fighters known as the Janjaweed on the region. Together with Sudanese government forces, the Janjaweed attacked and destroyed hundreds of villages throughout Darfur, slaughtering more than 200,000 people, mostly non-Arab Muslim Africans. More than one million people were displaced, creating a refugee crisis that spilled into neighboring Chad. Charges of war crimes were brought against Sudan's president by the International Criminal Court.

South Africa's Apartheid Regime

Unlike most African nations, post-independence South Africa was ruled by a white minority. Until 1994, its government put severe economic and political restrictions on the black majority through a policy called **apartheid**—which is the Afrikaans word for "apartness." Afrikaans, a form of Dutch brought to South Africa by colonists, was one of the country's official languages.

Source: Getty Images

Nelson Mandela

Source: Shutterstock

Desmond Tutu

Apartheid in Practice This policy maintained strict separation of the races. Laws required all blacks to carry passes, prevented them from voting, and made them subject to arrest at any time. South Africa's large South Asian population also suffered from discrimination.

Read Closely: Compare
Comparing similar world events across time and location is a good strategy when you read. It helps you connect what you are learning with what you already know. How did South African apartheid compare with forms of racial or class discrimination in other countries?

In the 1980s, moderate groups in South Africa tried to find an acceptable and peaceful way to let black people participate fully in the government. Protest demonstrations became common in black areas. **Desmond Tutu,** a black archbishop in the South African Anglican Church, led many of these protests. He followed the teachings of Mohandas Gandhi, who had lived in South Africa as a young lawyer before World War I and fought against its racial policies. Tutu urged his followers to use nonviolent tactics. He was awarded the 1984 Nobel Peace Prize for his work.

Sanctions The white South African government responded harshly to black African resistance. Many Western nations became indignant at its disregard for black Africans' human rights. To discourage this abuse of human rights, several countries placed trade sanctions on South Africa. Sanctions are laws prohibiting a nation's businesses from trading with a country that violates international law.

As poverty in South Africa increased, so did violence between blacks and whites. Foreign business people lost confidence in South Africa's economy and withdrew their investments. By 1990, a more moderate leadership began to respond to foreign pressure and the demands of black leaders by reducing the level of discrimination in South Africa.

Then in 1992, a majority of white South Africans voted to end apartheid and minority rule. Following the writing of a new constitution, multiracial elections were held for the first time in April 1994.

The African National Congress The struggle by the black majority to achieve equality and political power was led by the African National Congress

(ANC). The South African government of President F.W. de Klerk recognized the ANC in 1990 and cooperated with its leader, Nelson Mandela. Mandela had been serving a life sentence for sabotage since 1962; President de Klerk released Mandela from prison in 1990. However, violent clashes between rival black groups and attacks on blacks by white extremists made reform difficult.

Nelson Mandela As a result of the 1994 elections, Nelson Mandela became South Africa's president. De Klerk became one of two vice-presidents in the new multiracial government. The new government's primary concern was to improve the lives of black South Africans without losing the support of other groups.

One of the government's first steps in stabilizing South Africa was to repair its damaged economy. Mandela promised to preserve its system of free enterprise. With the ending of economic sanctions, trade with other nations resumed, and the economy soon improved. Mandela continued as president until 1999. He remained a visible leader until his death in December 2013. Since then, he has become one of the most honored figures around the world.

While South Africa ended apartheid, it continued to suffer from its legacy. Racial tension and economic inequality remained as problems.

Read Closely: Results
Writers use key phrases, such as "as a result," to indicate a cause and effect relationship. The first section is the cause, and the "as a result" section is the effect. How does this apply to Nelson Mandela's election?

Women Confront Human Rights Violations

Many people from diverse backgrounds have fought and continue to address and confront human rights violations. The following women led the way in this area, setting an example for other people and groups worldwide.

Mother Teresa Born in 1910 in the Balkan country of Macedonia, Mother Teresa moved to Ireland at age 18 to join a Roman Catholic religious order. Soon afterward she set sail for India to teach in the city of Calcutta, now Kolkata. After teaching there for 17 years, Mother Teresa felt the calling to devote herself to the scores of sick and desperately poor people she saw daily. She devoted the rest of her life to this ministry. Eventually she founded her own religious order, the Order of the Missionaries of Charity. Mother Teresa and her devoted nuns ministered to the blind, the terminally ill, and the disabled. They founded a leper colony near Calcutta. In 1979, in recognition of her tireless work on behalf of the human rights of Calcutta's poor, Mother Teresa won the Nobel Peace Prize.

Aung San Suu Kyi In the 1940s, a man named Aung San led Burma's successful attempt to gain independence form Great Britain. However, he was assassinated in 1947. His daughter, **Aung San Suu Kyi** was only two years old a that time. She grew up in Burma and then India, where her mother was a diplomat. She then studied at the University of Oxford in the United Kingdom. In 1988 she returned to Burma to care for her infirm mother. She began to speak out for human rights. In particular, she criticized the mistreatment of people protesting against the country's military rulers.

Read Closely: Turning Point
Words such as "finally" can indicate a turning point in history. How was life for Suu Kyi different before and after 2012?

In response to Aung San Suu Kyi's public campaign in support of political prisoners and a return to civilian rule, the government confined her to house arrest. She remained under house arrest off and on for the next 20 years, during which time she won the Nobel Peace Prize, in 1991.

Finally in 2012, Suu Kyi's house arrest restrictions were relaxed. She was allowed to meet with domestic allies and foreign dignitaries. She could even run for office. Her continued work to liberalize the political system in Myanmar paid off when the country finally held unrestricted parliamentary elections. Her party won a majority of seats. One of her close allies became the country's president. However, she served as Myanmar's de facto (in practice) leader starting in 2016.

The Mothers of the Plaza de Mayo In 1976 the military in Argentina overthrew the country's elected government. This coup was similar to General Augusto Pinochet's rise to power in Chile. The military junta in Argentina also unleashed a deadly campaign of kidnappings, torture, disappearances, and murders against leftists and other adversaries, both real and imagined. Some captives were drugged and taken aboard military cargo planes for flights over the frigid South Atlantic Ocean from which they never returned. Victims' children were taken by the government and handed over to be raised by families loyal to the junta.

This period from 1976 to 1983 in Argentina became known as the **Dirty War.** Approximately 30,000 people were killed. Many thousands more were detained and tortured.

In spite of the very real danger they faced, a group of women whose children and grandchildren had disappeared began to hold weekly vigils in the Plaza de Mayo, which faced the presidential palace. These women became known as the Mothers of the Plaza de Mayo. They continued to hold their weekly vigils 40 years after they first took on the people who violated their relatives' and fellow citizens' human rights. Their campaign brought results. By 2016 more than 700 of the authors of the Dirty War had been tried and convicted for their crimes.

Source: Getty Images

The persistence of the Mothers of the Plaza de Mayo kept the issue of Argentina's mistreatment of its citizens in the public eye for four decades.

Application

Use the images to answer the questions that follow them. The first is from Cambodia about deaths in the 1970s. The second is from Bosnia-Herzegovina about deaths in 1995.

Source: Shutterstock

1. Describe the historical context for the memorial from Cambodia.

____

____

2. Describe the historical context for the memorial from Bosnia-Herzegovina.

____

____

3. Detail how the two memorials are similar.

____

____

4. Interpret what the memorials say about the people who erected them.

____

____

Chapter 10 *Review*

Multiple-Choice Questions

Directions (1–6): For each statement or question, choose the number of the word or expression that, of those given, best completes the statement or answers the question.

Base your answers to questions 1 and 2 on the passage below and your knowledge of social studies.

Solomon Radasky, a survivor of the Holocaust

> I am from Warsaw. I lived in Praga, which is the part of the city across the Vistula River. I had a nice life there; I had my own shop where I used to make fur coats. In Warsaw when a Jewish holiday came we used to know it was a holiday. All the stores were closed, and the people were in the synagogues.
>
> Out of the 78 people in my family, I am the only one to survive. My parents had 3 boys and 3 girls: My parents were Jacob and Toby; my brothers were Moishe and Baruch, and my sisters were Sarah, Rivka and Leah. They were all killed. . . .
>
> My father was killed in April 1942. He went to buy bread from the children who were smuggling food into the ghetto. The children brought bread, potatoes, and cabbages across the wall into the ghetto. A Jewish policeman pointed out my father to a German and told him that he saw my father take . . . bread from a boy at the wall. The German shot my father in the back.
>
> **Source:** http://www.holocaustsurvivors.org/data.show.php?di=record&da=survivors&ke=7

1. Which development from the World War II era does the passage describe?
   (1) the division of Germany following the war
   (2) the persecution of Jews
   (3) the turning point in the war that occurred in 1942
   (4) the origins of the Solidarity movement

2. Which was a major cause of the event described in the passage?
   (1) the invasion of Poland by Germany
   (2) the D-Day invasion
   (3) the Treaty of Versailles
   (4) the rise of the Weimar Republic

Base your answer to questions 3 and 4 on the passage below and your knowledge of social studies.

Peter Benenson, Amnesty International founder, 2001

> "Only when the last prisoner of conscience has been freed, when the last torture chamber has been closed, when the United Nations Universal Declaration of Human Rights is a reality for the world's people, will our work be done."
>
> **Source:** https://www.amnesty.org/en/who-we-are/

3. Which action is most likely to be taken by the group Amnesty International?
   (1) stop unlawful whaling in the Pacific Ocean
   (2) write letters on behalf of a jailed dissident in Myanmar
   (3) call for UN troops to intervene in a border dispute
   (4) encourage the United States to increase its commitment to NATO

4. The United Nations Universal Declaration of Human Rights mentioned in the excerpt was written in the context of
   (1) the influenza outbreak of 1918–1919
   (2) the Vietnam War
   (3) World War II
   (4) the rise of Islamic fundamentalism

Tips for Answering Multiple-Choice Questions

In order to answer Question 4 above, it is necessary to have a good chronological understanding of history. On your exam, you might have been able to determine the chronological basis for this question using the clues from earlier or later questions. For instance, questions 1 and 2 were based on a primary source describing the Holocaust. A question about the Declaration of Human Rights would fit within the context of a question about genocide.

Base your answer to questions 5 and 6 on the table below and your knowledge of social studies.

Countries Hosting the Most Refugees, 2017			
Country	**Number of Refugees**	**Location**	**Host Country's Wealth per Capita**
Turkey	2,900,000	Middle East	$26,500
Pakistan	1,400,000	South Asia	$5,400
Lebanon	1,000,000	Middle East	$19,500
Iran	979,000	Middle East	$20,000
Uganda	940,000	East Africa	$2,400
Ethiopia	792,000	East Africa	$2,100
World	22,500,000	-----	$12,800

Source: United Nations High Commissioner for Refugees: World Factbook

5. Which headline best fits a story that would include the chart?

   (1) REFUGEES FLOOD WEALTHY COUNTRIES FOR BENEFITS

   (2) UN RESETTLES REFUGEES EQUALLY AROUND GLOBE

   (3) MIDEAST AND NEIGHBORS ABSORB MOST REFUGEES

   (4) UNITED STATES HIT HARDEST BY REFUGEE CRISIS

6. Since refugees often flee to nearby lands, from which country did most refugees probably come?

   (1) Kashmir

   (2) North Korea

   (3) Syria

   (4) Serbia

Short-Answer Questions

CRQ Directions (7-9): Analyze the documents and answer the short-answer questions that follow each document in the space provided.

Base your answer to question 7 on Document 1 below and on your knowledge of social studies.

Document 1

Signs commonly seen in South Africa prior to the 1990s.

Source: Shutterstock. Apartheid signs

7. Explain the historical situation in South Africa that is pictured in Document 1.

____

____

____

____

____

____

Base your answer to question 8 on Document 2 below and on your knowledge of social studies.

Document 2

The photo below was taken in South Africa after the nation's presidential election in 1994.

Source: Alamy

8. Based on the moment that the photo was taken, what message might the photographer have been trying to capture?

____

____

____

____

____

Base your answer to question 9 on both Documents 1 and 2 and on your knowledge of social studies.

Cause—refers to something that contributes to the occurrence of an event, the rise of an idea, or the bringing about of a development.

Effect—refers to what happens as a consequence (result, impact, outcome) of an event, an idea, or a development.

9. Identify and explain the cause-and-effect relationship between the documents regarding the changes that took place in South Africa in the last half of the 20th century. Use evidence from both Documents 1 and 2 in your response.

Speaking and Listening: Reflect on the Key Idea

Working with a partner or a small group, write a summary of the United Nations Universal Declaration of Human Rights and a list of actions that have either violated it or supported it.

Period 4 *Enduring Issues Extended Essays*

Extended Essay A

Directions

An enduring issue is an issue that exists across time. It is one that many societies have attempted to address with varying degrees of success. Read the following documents and take notes in the margin identifying at least two themes in each one. Then use these notes and the Planning Page to prepare to write the essay. Finally, on a separate sheet of paper or on a computer, write your extended essay.

In your essay:

Identify the issue based on a historically accurate interpretation of **three** documents.

Define the issue using evidence from three documents.

Argue that this is a significant issue that has endured by showing:

- How the issue has affected people or been affected by people.
- How the issue has continued to be an issue or changed over time.

Include outside information from your knowledge of social studies and evidence from the documents.

Keep in mind these terms:

Identify—means to put a name or to name

Define—means to explain features of a thing or concept so that it can be understood

Argue—means to provide a series of statements that provide evidence and reasons to support a conclusion

Topics to consider for your essay: (See page xvii.)

- Conflict
- Coperation
- Power
- Inequality
- Innovation
- Interconnectedness
- Ideas and Beliefs
- Environmental Issues
- Scarcity

Document 1

Kristallnacht, November 9–10, 1938

Source: Bridgeman Art

Document 2

The Italian unification grew in strength in the mid-1800s and continued to grow under Count Cavour. He was named prime minister and the excerpt is from his speech to the Piedmont Chamber of Deputies, 1858.

> After the disaster of Novara and the Peace of Milan [1849], two courses were open to us. We could, bowing to adverse fate, renounce all the aspirations which had guided King Carlo Alberto during the last years of his reign, seal ourselves up within our frontiers, think only of the material and moral interests of this country [Piedmont-Sardinia]. . . . On the other hand, we could, while accepting all the hardships imposed by accomplished facts, keep alive the faith that inspired the great actions of King Carlo Alberto, and, while declaring our firm intention to respect treaties, maintain in the political sphere the enterprise which was defeated in the military sphere [Italian unification]. . . . In recent years, therefore, we have tried to do away with the last hindrances to our country, and we have lost no occasion to act as the spokesman and defender of the other peoples of Italy. This policy found one such occasion in the Crimean War. . .Our hopes were not disappointed in regard to the credit that Piedmont would acquire. As for the defense of the rights of Italy, that was our task in the course of the Congress of Paris . . . it was an outstanding fact that the cause of Italy was for the first time supported by an Italian power.
>
> **Source:** D. Zanichelli, ed., *The Writings of Count Cavour* (Bologna, 1892), II: pp. 4–50; *The Annual Register or a View of the History and Politics of the Year, 1858* (London, 1859), pp. 186–188; Count C. Arrivabene, *Italy under Victor Emmanuel* (London, 1862)

Document 3

Ali Jinnah was the president of the Muslim League in the 1930s and 1940s. This excerpt was from Jinnah on December 6, 1945.

I wish His Majesty's Government, who by now ought to be in full possession of the facts regarding the quintessence of the Indian problem, would apply their mind to the real issue. Sir Stafford Cripps made it clear in his statement after the breakdown of the Simla Conference on July 15th, 1945, when he said there will be no agreement possible till the Pakistan issue is solved. When His Majesty's Government and the Secretary of State for India, Lord Pethick-Lawrence, boldly and frankly come out and expedite a permanent settlement on the basis of Pakistan, which is the major issue and the only solution of India's constitutional problem, the deadlock will resolve itself. I therefore earnestly commend to His Majesty's Government to declare their resolute resignation to the establishment of Pakistan in India. Muslim India will never accept any method of framing the Constitution of India by means of one Constitution-making body for all India, in which the [Muslims] will be in a hopeless minority and the conclusions are foregone in such an assembly. Nor will they agree to any united India Constitution, federal or otherwise, with one Centre, in which, again, they will be in a hopeless minority, and will be at the mercy of the perennial Hindu majority domination. Further, any attempt to set up a Provisional Government at the Centre, which would in any way prejudice or militate against the Pakistan demand, will not be acceptable to us, as the thin end of the wedge, as it is sought by Hindu India under the term of the Provisional "National" Government of India.

Source: http://www.nationalarchives.gov.uk/education/resources/the-road-to-partition/jinnah-calls-pakistan/

Document 4

Theodor Herzl was a Hungarian Jewish writer and intellect who wanted the creation of a separate Jewish state. The excerpt is from his book, ***The Jewish State***, 1896.

The idea I have developed in this pamphlet is an ancient one: It is the restoration of the Jewish State. . . . The decisive factor is our propelling force. And what is that force? The plight of the Jews. . . . I am profoundly convinced that I am right, though I doubt whether I shall live to see myself proved so. Those who today inaugurate this movement are unlikely to live to see its glorious culmination. But the very inauguration is enough to inspire in them a high pride and the joy of an inner liberation of their existence . . .

The plan would seem mad enough if a single individual were to undertake it; but if many Jews simultaneously agree on it, it is entirely reasonable, and its achievement presents no difficulties worth mentioning. The idea depends only on the number of its adherents. Perhaps our ambitious young men, to whom every road of advancement is now closed, and for whom the Jewish state throws open a bright prospect of freedom, happiness, and honor, perhaps they will see to it that this idea is spread . . .

It depends on the Jews themselves whether this political document remains for the present a political romance. If this generation is too dull to understand it rightly, a future finer, more advanced generation will arise to comprehend it. The Jews who will try it shall achieve their State; and they will deserve it . . .

I consider the Jewish question neither a social nor a religious one, even though it sometimes takes these and other forms. It is a national question, and to solve it we must first of all establish it as an international political problem to be discussed and settled by the civilized nations of the world in council.

We are a people—one people.

Source: http://www.jewishvirtuallibrary.org/excerpts-from-quot-the-jewish-state-quot

Document 5

For many years Sudan has dealt with religious conflicts between Muslim and non-Muslim groups. The excerpt is from Francis M. Deng about the conflict in the Sudan, 2001

> The great challenge for Christianity in the Sudan, especially in the southern part of the country, is closely linked to the civil war between Sudan's North and South. This war has raged intermittently since 1955, making it possibly the longest civil conflict in the world. . . . Religion is the pivotal factor in the conflict. The North, with roughly two-thirds of Sudan's land and population, is Muslim and Arabic-speaking; the Northern identity is an inseparable amalgamation of Islam and the Arabic language. The South is more indigenously African in race, culture, and religion; its identity is indigenously African, with Christian influences and a Western orientation.
>
> **Source:** Francis M. Deng, "Sudan–Civil War and Genocide," *Middle East Quarterly*, Winter 2001, pp. 13–21. http://www.meforum.org/22/sudan-civil-war-and-genocide

Preparing to Write

MY ENDURING ISSUE IS: ______________________________

You may use the Enduring Issues Planning Page organizer to prepare to write your essay. Writing on this Planning Page will NOT count toward your final score.

You may also choose to prepare to write the Enduring Issues Essay by creating an outline or graphic organizer on your own sheet of paper.

ENDURING ISSUES PLANNING PAGE

Essay Requirements	Yes	Circle documents that apply	One or two possible ideas for outside info
Is this an issue supported by at least three docu-ments? Which documents sup-port this issue?		1 2 3 4 5	
Which documents can be used to develop the definition for this issue?		1 2 3 4 5	
Has this issue significant-ly affected people or been affected by people?		1 2 3 4 5	
Has this issue endured across time or changed over time? In which document or documents do you see this?		1 2 3 4 5	

Extended Essay B

Directions

An enduring issue is an issue that exists across time. It is one that many societies have attempted to address with varying degrees of success. Read the following documents and take notes in the margin identifying at least two themes in each one. Then use these notes to develop an outline or graphic organizer for an essay. Finally, on a separate sheet of paper or on a computer, write an extended essay.

In your essay:

Identify the issue based on a historically accurate interpretation of **three** documents.

Define the issue using evidence from three documents.

Argue that this is a significant issue that has endured by showing:

- How the issue has affected people or been affected by people.
- How the issue has continued to be an issue or changed over time.

Include outside information from your knowledge of social studies and evidence from the documents.

Keep in mind these terms:

Identify—means to put a name or to name

Define—means to explain features of a thing or concept so that it can be understood

Argue—means to provide a series of statements that provide evidence and reasons to support a conclusion

Topics to consider for your essay: (See page xvii.)

Conflict

Coperation

Power

Inequality

Innovation

Interconnectedness

Ideas and Beliefs

Environmental Issues

Scarcity

Document 1

Chiagozie Udeh, Climate Change and Crisis in Nigeria, January 19, 2018

Climate change is not ranked among the five top causes of conflict in Nigeria, namely, tribalism, resource control, religion, land and trade. But that reality has been altered. The past 36 months has been fiercely violent for several Nigerian States that experienced rampaging Fulani herdsmen killing many subsistence farmers, who defend their farms from grazing herds. . .

The Fulani herdsmen are nomadic and habitually migratory. They move from North to South annually, with their cattle in search of grazing fields. The movement is seasonal. Now with climate change, the movement pattern has been markedly altered. Due to expansive desertification, drought and unchecked deforestation in northern Nigeria, the herdsmen naturally seek greener pasture southward. As the resultant migration has intensified, so too has violent clashes over grazing lands between local farmers in the South and pastoral herdsmen, whom the former accuse of wanton destruction of their crops and forceful appropriation of their lands. The emerging conflict is compounded further by the shrinking of Lake Chad from 45,000km to 3000km in less than three decades. The consequence, according to the United Nations, is the displacement of about 10.5 million people. It's a combination of these factors that have pushed herders from the north-eastern Nigeria, the region closest to Lake Chad, to the southern parts of the country.

Source https://newtelegraphonline.com/2018/01/climate-change-herdsmen-crisis-nigeria/

Document 2

Asma Khan Lone, "How Can Climate Change Trigger Conflict in South Asia?" November 20, 2015

Boasting a trans-national drainage system, the Tibetan Plateau is the main source of water for the region. It is the point of origin for the region's major rivers – Indus, Ganges, Yangtze, Mekong, and Brahmaputra, catering to 40 percent of the world's population. In fact shared waters, and the contests they conjure lie at the heart of the region's most disparaging conflicts.

The conflict symbolizing this phenomenon in the most stark manner is the Kashmir dispute between India and Pakistan. Premised on the right of self-determination of the Kashmiri people, it also overlaps with Pakistan's pursuit of water security. With all of Pakistan's major rivers flowing from the Indian administered part of Kashmir, the issue has always been of intrinsic importance for Pakistan, amply emphasized by its first Foreign Minister Sir Zafarullah Khan, who sanctified Kashmir as a lifeline and key element of Pakistan's security construct. Rivers originating from Kashmir are Pakistan's main source of irrigation, driving its primarily agriculture based economy. Over time the issue has acquired greater national security significance.

Source: http://foreignpolicy.com/2015/11/20/how-can-climate-change-trigger-conflict-in-south-asia/

Document 3

Elizabeth Warn and Susana B. Adamo, "The Impact of Climate Change: Migration and Cities in South America"

Cities—particularly megacities—are becoming focal points for climate change impacts. Rapid urbanization, accelerating demand for housing, resource supplies and social and health services, place pressure on already stretched physical, social and regulatory infrastructure, heightening risks and vulnerability. In South America, internal migration flows—as well as immigration—are mostly to cities. Migrants, notably those of low socioeconomic status, are often particularly vulnerable as they are more likely to reside in areas at risk of environmental hazards. They are also likely to lack local knowledge, networks and assets, and are, therefore, less prepared to cope with, and avoid, the impacts of these hazards. . .

South America and the Caribbean is the most urbanized of the developing regions and one of the most urbanized in the world. In 2010, 83% of the population of South America resided in cities—it will be 86% by 2020. While the Southern cone has some of the lowest population densities in the world, a high proportion live in one or two very large cities per country. . .

Migration patterns are modified or exacerbated by climate events and trends rather than solely caused by them, making the impact of environmental or climate change dynamics hard to predict. Urban areas and cities are affected by slow-onset events, changes in water availability and the general scarcity of natural resources, which may also be linked with potential migration.

Source https://public.wmo.int/en/resources/bulletin/impact-of-climate-change-migration-and-cities-south-america

Document 4

Source: CartoonStock.com

Document 5

As India gained its freedom from Britain, Muslims feared a Hindu dominated nation. Ultimately, two nations were created, India for Hindus and Pakistan for Muslims.

> [The year] 1947 signaled the end of British rule when British India was divided into two states, India and Pakistan. The Punjab and Bengal were split between the two countries. This meant that millions of Hindus, Muslims, and Sikhs who had shared neighborhoods for generations suddenly found themselves on the wrong side of the newly created borders.
>
> As many celebrated independence, over 14 million people attempted to cross hastily drawn borders in what became the largest migration in history. Hindus and Sikhs fled to India, and Muslims to Pakistan. The Grand Trunk Road and the railway built alongside it became the major routes along which millions of refugees travelled. They were also the scenes of some of the worst violence—in the Punjab alone, hundreds of thousands of people were murdered. Vast refugee camps sprung up along the road as people gathered together for protection or found themselves homeless in a new country.
>
> **Source:** Adapted from http://www.mylearning.org/migration-from-india-and-pakistan/p-3202/.

Preparing to Write

MY ENDURING ISSUE IS: ____

You may use the Enduring Issues Planning Page organizer to prepare to write your essay. Writing on this Planning Page will NOT count toward your final score.

You may also choose to prepare to write the Enduring Issues Essay by creating an outline or graphic organizer on your own sheet of paper.

ENDURING ISSUES PLANNING PAGE

Essay Requirements	Yes	Circle documents that apply	One or two possible ideas for outside info
Is this an issue supported by at least three documents? Which documents support this issue?		1 2 3 4 5	
Which documents can be used to develop the definition for this issue?		1 2 3 4 5	
Has this issue significant-ly affected people or been affected by people?		1 2 3 4 5	
Has this issue endured across time or changed over time? In which document or documents do you see this?		1 2 3 4 5	

New York Global History and Geography Practice Exam

Part 1: Multiple-Choice Questions

Directions (1–30): For each statement or question, choose the number of the word or expression that, of those given, best completes the statement or answers the question.

Base your answers to questions 1 and 2 on the table below and your knowledge of social studies.

Traits of Mughal India and Bourbon Frances		
Category	**Bourbon France**	**Mughal India**
Religion	• Mostly Roman Catholic Christian • Many Protestant Christians in some regions	• Mostly Sunni Muslim and Hindu • Tolerance under Akbar
Taxes	• Mostly on peasants	• Mostly on peasants • Special taxes on non-Muslims, except under Akbar
Trade	• Primarily overland trade before 1500	• Heavy overland trade
Military	• Under the command of the king • Frequently at war	• Independent of the central government • Small navy

1. In which category would Tokugawa Japan be most similar to the empires listed in this chart?

    (1) Religion
    (2) Taxes
    (3) Trade
    (4) Military

2. How did the Ottoman Empire compare to the Mughal and Bourbon Empires?

    (1) Its overland trade network was always much weaker than the Bourbon's.
    (2) It restricted trade far more than did the other two empires.
    (3) Its military was also under the control of the central government.
    (4) It relied more on a strong navy than did the Mughal Empire.

Base your answers to questions 3 and 4 on the passage below and your knowledge of social studies.

A. SEVEN YEARS' WAR TREATY MAKES CANADA A BRITISH COLONY
B. BRITISH EAST INDIA COMPANY WINS BATTLE OF PLASSEY
C. DAIMYOS EXPEL THOUSANDS OF FOREIGNERS AND SHUT PORTS
D. JAVA REBELS ATTACK DUTCH EAST INDIA COMPANY

3. Which of the following statements is supported by these headlines?
   (1) European states followed isolationist policies in the 18th century.
   (2) The expansion of European power caused conflicts and often violence.
   (3) Religion was more important than trade in shaping 18th century events.
   (4) Countries responded to European advances in similar ways.

4. The main theme of the historical period described by these headlines is
   (1) technological advancement
   (2) international cooperation
   (3) imperialism
   (4) mercantilism

Base your answers to questions 5 and 6 on the passage below and your knowledge of social studies.

> Women! . . . The liberty of a people has for its basis good morals and education, and you are its guardians and first dispensers. . . . Appear in the midst of our national festivals with all the brilliance of your virtues and your charms! When the voice of the public acclaims the heroism and wisdom of a young citizen, then a mother rises and leads her young, beautiful and modest daughter to the tribunal where crowns are distributed. . . .
>
> **Source:** Louis-Marie Prudhomme, "On the Influence of the Revolution on Women," 1791. http://chnm.gmu.edu/revolution/d/483/

5. This passage expresses the writer's support for
   (1) the humanitarian ideals of the Enlightenment era
   (2) the importance of universal suffrage
   (3) the important role for women in politics
   (4) the superiority of the domestic cottage labor over the factory system

6. The author wrote this passage during the French Revolution, when he could have witnessed
   (1) women trying to prevent men from forcing the king back to Paris from Versailles
   (2) women refusing to host salons for Enlightenment intellectuals
   (3) women voting in a national referendum
   (4) women marching to protest taxes on salt and bread

Base your answers to questions 7 and 8 on the passage below and your knowledge of social studies.

> Children were occupied in factories for twelve, fifteen, twenty and sometimes even thirty hours successively, in an overheated and moist atmosphere, and without any relaxation, but a scanty allowance of time for their meals. This was a vicious system in the extreme, and if the victims to it ever survived, it could only be with diminished health, and the utter absence of mental improvement.
>
> **Source:** House of Commons Debates, the Labour of Children in Factories, 1832. https://api.parliament.uk/historic-hansard/commons/1832/feb/01/labour-of-children-in-factories#S3V0009P0_18320201_HOC_9

7. This passage is describing conditions caused by the
   (1) Scientific Revolution
   (2) Agricultural Revolution
   (3) French Revolution
   (4) Industrial Revolution

8. Which of the following was a response to the problem highlighted in this passage?
   (1) restrictions on education
   (2) rise of dictatorships
   (3) greater interest in socialism
   (4) increases in market competition

Base your answers to questions 9 and 10 on the passage below and your knowledge of social studies.

> I contend that we are the finest race in the world and that the more of the world we inhabit the better it is for the human race . . . Africa is still lying ready for us it is our duty to take it. It is our duty to seize every opportunity of acquiring more territory and we should keep this one idea steadily before our eyes that more territory simply means more of the Anglo-Saxon race more of the best the most human, most honourable race the world possesses.
>
> **Source:** Cecil Rhodes, "Confession of Faith," 1877. http://pages.uoregon.edu/kimball/Rhodes-Confession.htm

9. Which of the following would someone who agreed with this author most likely support?

    (1) the Boxers in the Boxer Rebellion
    (2) the British in the Boer War
    (3) the indigenous Kenyans in the Mau Mau rebellion
    (4) the Indians in the 1857 rebellion

10. Which of the following best describes an idea that the author might use to justify the actions he recommends?

    (1) a belief in British superiority
    (2) a belief in the doctrine of appeasement
    (3) a desire to spread Christianity
    (4) a desire for natural resources and low-wage labor

Base your answers to questions 11 and 12 on the passage below and your knowledge of social studies.

> The German economic system as it existed before the war depended on three main factors: I. Overseas commerce as represented by her mercantile marine, her colonies, her foreign investments, her exports, and the overseas connections of her merchants; II. The exploitation of her coal and iron and the industries built upon them; III. Her transport and tariff system. . . . The Treaty aims at the systematic destruction of all three. . . .
>
> **Source:** John Maynard Keynes, *The Economic Consequences of the Peace,* 1920. http://oll.libertyfund.org/titles/keynes-the-economic-consequences-of-the-peace

11. Which war is the author writing about?

(1) Franco-Prussian War
(2) World War I
(3) World War II
(4) Cold War

12. Which was a result of the treaty described by the author?

(1) Germany gained territory.
(2) The League of Nations was established.
(3) A wall was built to divide the city of Berlin.
(4) Poland was divided among the victors in the war.

Base your answers to questions 13 and 14 on the passage below and your knowledge of social studies.

> All Chinese without exception must lean either to the side of imperialism or to the side of socialism. Sitting on the fence will not do, nor is there a third road.
>
> **Source:** Mao Zedong, "On the People's Democratic Dictatorship," 1949. https://www.marxists.org/reference/archive/mao/selected-works/volume-4/mswv4_65.htm

13. This quotation shows China in the midst of a transition from
    (1) Buddhism to Confucianism
    (2) nationalism to capitalism
    (3) warlordism to communism
    (4) empire to democracy

14. Which statement best describes the relationship between this passage and the Cultural Revolution?
    (1) Both led to better relations beween China and the United States.
    (2) Both resulted from a growing closeness between China and the Soviet Union.
    (3) Both showed Mao's willingness to try new approaches to solve old problems.
    (4) Both reflected Mao's rejection of moderation when faced with a difficult situation.

Base your answers to questions 15 and 16 on the passage below and your knowledge of social studies.

> We spent a few days like this and were dispatched with all possible speed to Ypres, here we went in to support the Canadians and spent a most unpleasant eight days, during which time we lost several hundred men, nearly all my friends who came out in the same draft and were killed or wounded, we had to retire, the best part being that the Germans did not find this out until two days after when we were more or less safely bivouacking in a very pretty wood. We stayed here for about a week; then we got to work again, digging reserve trenches just behind the front line, building up parapets which had been demolished by the enemy's high explosive shells and such like, working all night and getting what sleep we could in the daytime.
>
> One morning we were awakened by the most awful din, it seemed as though hell had broken loose, shells were falling like summer rain. And people have often told me in the course of conversation it was raining shells and I admit I took it with a grain of salt, could not be possible I thought, but such I was surprised to find was possible and actually taking place there about 3:30 a.m. This bombardment started and about half an hour later, I, with three others, were ordered to start reinforcing. We went up in fours, it being considered safer that way, half a mile over open ground we had to do, this being swept continually with shells, to give you a slight idea I can say the previous night, just in front of our reserve trenches was a beautifully green field, and the next morning it was as much as one could do to see any grass at all, simply one mass of craters, varying in diameter from ten to twelve paces.
>
> **Source:** Private Edward Henry Cecil Stewart, letter, undated, France. He died on 1 July 1916. http://www.nationalarchives.gov.uk/education/resources/letters-first-world-war-1915/trenches-swept-continually-shells/

15. What significant characteristic of World War I is described in the above passage?
    (1) air warfare
    (2) cavalry warfare
    (3) trench warfare
    (4) submarine warfare

16. Which change in military technology made the style of fighting described in the passage so deadly?
    (1) radar
    (2) machine gun
    (3) cluster bomb
    (4) atomic weapons

Base your answers to questions 17 and 18 on the table below and your knowledge of social studies.

The Fall of Communism in the Eastern Bloc		
1989	**June**	Poland elects a non-communist government.
	September	Hungary opens its border with Austria.
	October	Hungary allows non-communist parties in its elections.
	November	East Germany allows citizens to go from East Berlin to West Berlin.
	November	Czechoslovakian government gives up power.
	December	Romanians overthrow their dictator.
1990	**February**	Bulgarian government steps down.
	July	Soviets agree to allow East Germany and West Germany to unite.
1991	**July**	The Warsaw Pact is ended.
	December	The Soviet Union is dissolved.

17. A symbol of the Cold War that was destroyed as part of the events listed above was the
    (1) Kremlin
    (2) Warsaw Ghetto
    (3) Berlin Wall
    (4) Hungarian Parliament

18. One reason the events listed above occurred was because of the
    (1) implementation of perestroika and glasnost
    (2) suppression of student dissent in China
    (3) success of command economy in increasing agricultural production
    (4) failure of Polish Solidarity Party

Base your answers to questions 19 and 20 on the passage below and your knowledge of social studies.

> Non-violence is a matchless weapon, which can help everyone. I know we have not done much by way of non-violence and therefore, if such changes come about, I will take it that it is the result of our labors during the last twenty-two years and that God has helped us to achieve it.
>
> When I raised the slogan "Quit India" the people in India, who were then feeling despondent, felt that I had placed before them a new thing. If you want real freedom, you will have to come together, and such a coming together will create true democracy—the like of which has not so far been witnessed or attempted.
>
> I have read a good deal about the French Revolution. . . . and Jawaharlal has told me all about the Russian Revolution.
>
> But I hold that though theirs was a fight for the people it was not a fight for real democracy, which I envisage. My democracy means that everyone is his own master. I have read sufficient history, and I have not seen such an experiment on such a large scale for the establishment of democracy by non-violence. Once you understand these things you will forget the differences between the Hindus and Moslems. . . .
>
> There are people who may call me a visionary, but I am a real bania [shrewd business man] and my business is to obtain swaraj [home rule]. . . .
>
> I want you to adopt non-violence as a matter of policy. With me it is a creed, but so far as you are concerned I want you to accept it as policy. As disciplined soldiers you must accept it in toto, and stick to it when you join the struggle.
>
> **Source:** Mohandas Gandhi, speech to the All-India Congress, August 7, 1942. http://www.ibiblio.org/pha/policy/1942/420807a.html

19. Where else were the policies described in the document used?
    (1) Vietnam
    (2) South Africa
    (3) Rwanda
    (4) Korea

20. The above passage is best understood as part of what global movement?
    (1) expansion of the Communist revolution
    (2) reaction to authoritarian dictatorships
    (3) alliance of capitalism and imperialism
    (4) decolonization of international empires

Base your answers to questions 21 and 22 on the passage below and your knowledge of social studies.

> As the online world has become a fundamental part of Arab and Iranian societies, leaders are waking up to the "dangers" of social media and placing new restrictions on what can be read or posted online. . . .
>
> Conditions in Egypt—where social media played a fundamental role in mobilising protesters and documenting police brutality—continued to decline over the past year. In only the first six months of Mohammad Morsi's term, more citizens were prosecuted for "insulting the office of the president" than under Hosni Mubarak's entire 30-year reign. Cases have now been brought against the same bloggers and activists that were instrumental in rallying the masses to protest against Mubarak (and later Morsi) in Tahrir Square, while countless others were tortured by Muslim Brotherhood thugs or state security forces. . . .
>
> If governments are beginning to pay attention, it is because online tools for social mobilisation and individual expression are having a profound impact. Social media accounts were set up for every candidate in Iran's 2013 presidential elections, despite the fact that Twitter, Facebook, and YouTube are all blocked within the country. In Saudi Arabia—which now boasts the highest Twitter and YouTube usage per capita of any country in the world—social media has been used to promote campaigns for women's right to drive, to highlight the mistreatment of migrant workers, and to debate sensitive subjects such as child molestation. Citizen journalism was vital in documenting chemical weapons use in Syria, and a new online platform alerts local residents of incoming scud missiles. Nonetheless, Iran, Saudi Arabia, and Syria rank as some of the least free countries in the world in terms of internet freedom. . . .
>
> **Source:** Adrian Shabaz, "Three years after Arab Spring officials thwart digital dissent," *Index on Censorship*, Jan 21, 2014. https://www.indexoncensorship.org/2014/01/three-years-arab-spring-officials-thwart-digital-dissent/

21. According to the above passage, what is the post-Arab Spring role of social media in the Arab world?
    (1) Social media have been completely shut down by authoritarian governments.
    (2) Social media continue to function freely and openly.
    (3) Social media have been effectively used in promoting social justice issues.
    (4) Social media have lost popularity as a result of the dangers of use.

22. What are ways that the effective use of social media in the Arab world can be seen as contradictory, according to the above passage?
    (1) Social media accounts are blocked in Iran, but accounts were set up for electoral candidates.
    (2) Social media users have not been prosecuted in Egypt, but the use of social media for protest is decreasing.
    (3) Syria has allowed documentation of chemical warfare on social media but prevented the notice of bombing attacks.
    (4) Although Saudi Arabia is one of the smallest social media markets in the Middle East, it still has heavy government censorship.

Base your answers to questions 23 and 24 on the passage below and your knowledge of social studies.

> Understanding drivers of deforestation and degradation is fundamental for the development of policies and measures that aim to alter current trends in forest activities toward a more climate and biodiversity friendly outcome. . . . The study analyzed national data . . . on drivers of deforestation and forest degradation. . . .
>
> The results highlight that commercial agriculture is the most prevalent deforestation driver, accounting for 40% of deforestation. . . . The other important land use is local/subsistence agriculture, which is related to 33% of deforestation. Other drivers are of less importance, with mining accounting for 7%, infrastructure for 10% and urban expansion for 10% of the total. Thus, according to this study, agriculture alone causes 73% of all deforestation. . . . For decades the common view was that growing populations of shifting cultivators and smallholders were the main driver of forest changes. More recently, it has been argued that commercial actors play an increasingly larger role in the expansion of agriculture into the forest. . . . Looking at the development of deforestation drivers through time . . . the contribution of commercial agriculture increases. Currently, deforestation in Africa is still largely driven by small-scale subsistence activities . . . but this might change in the coming years. . . .
>
> Regarding forest degradation, timber extraction and logging are related to about 52%, fuelwood collection and charcoal production 31%, uncontrolled fire 9% and livestock grazing 7% of forest degradation. . . . [L]ocal small-scale activities . . . are the most relevant in large parts of Africa, while in the majority of the other country cases forest degradation is dominated by commercial wood extraction. The importance of the fuelwood/charcoal driver decreases in the post-transition phase. This can be explained by urbanization tied to economic development, and a progressing reliance on other energy resources.
>
> **Source:** Noriko Hosonuma et al., "An assessment of deforestation and forest degradation drivers in developing countries," *Environmental Research Letters,* October 2012. http://iopscience.iop.org/article/10.1088/1748-9326/7/4/044009

23. According to the above passage, what role does subsistence farming play in deforestation?

(1) Its role is increasing over time.

(2) It is being replaced by commercial agriculture.

(3) It causes 73 percent of all deforestation.

(4) Its role is least important in Africa.

24. What explains the decrease in fuelwood collection as a cause of forest degradation?

(1) change in the availability of a variety of energy sources

(2) change in use of new building materials

(3) change in timber harvesting practices

(4) change in awareness of pollution from burning wood

Base your answers to questions 25 and 26 on the passage below and your knowledge of social studies.

> Reports of gross violations of human rights in Chile, which had nearly ceased earlier this year, are again on the rise. . . . [T]he Pinochet government is reverting to the practices that have jeopardized its international standing since the 1973 coup . . .
>
> Chile's National Intelligence Directorate is apparently behind the recent increase in torture, illegal detentions, and unexplained "disappearances." The Directorate's chief, Colonel Manuel Contreras, is a close confidant of Pinochet, who acclaimed the organization in a recent press interview for its "decisive role" in bringing extremism under control. Contreras answers directly to the President, and it is unlikely that he would act without the knowledge and approval of his superior. . . .
>
> The Directorate's detention facility at Cuatro Alamos is said to be in operation again. This site was largely abandoned after a decree in January 1976 empowered the Supreme Court president and the interior minister to inspect—without prior notice—areas suspected of being used for torture. Neither official appears to have exercised this authority since last year.
>
> Pinochet stated this week that the emergency measures in effect under the state of siege will be enforced as long as necessary "to repress drastically any attempt that might become a threat to internal security or domestic peace." Following his recent crackdown on former president Frei's Christian Democratic Party and on outspoken democratic labor leaders, Pinochet has made clear that he will move harshly against anyone who runs afoul of his government.
>
> The President may believe that the cutoff in US aid has removed Washington's leverage against his regimes on the human rights issue. . . . In any case, reports of increased repression are sure to leak out, refueling the human rights controversy.
>
> **Source:** United States Central Intelligence Agency, "Latin America Regional and Political Analysis," May 24, 1977. Released June 11, 1999. https://nsarchive.gwu.edu/NSAEBB/NSAEBB212/19770524%20Violations%20of%20human%20rights.pdf

25. According to the above passage, how could the use of torture in Chile be linked to President Pinochet?

    (1) Pinochet said that torture is a necessary emergency measure.

    (2) The colonel behind the torture normally acted with Pinochet's approval.

    (3) Pinochet was directly in charge of the facility used for torture.

    (4) The colonel in charge of torture was a friend of Pinochet.

26. What document most powerfully opposed Pinochet's policies?

    (1) United Nations Declaration on the Rights of Indigenous Peoples

    (2) Convention on the Rights of Persons with Disabilities

    (3) Universal Declaration of Human Rights

    (4) United Nations Standard Minimum Rules for the Treatment of Prisoners

Base your answers to questions 27 and 28 on the passage below and your knowledge of social studies.

White House statement on the international deal on Iran's use of nuclear energy, 2016

> On January 16, 2016, the International Atomic Energy Agency verified that Iran has completed the necessary steps under the Iran deal that will ensure Iran's nuclear program is and remains exclusively peaceful.
>
> Before this agreement, Iran's breakout time—or the time it would have taken for Iran to gather enough fissile material to build a weapon—was only two to three months. Today, because of the Iran deal, it would take Iran 12 months or more. And with the unprecedented monitoring and access this deal puts in place, if Iran tries, we will know and sanctions will snap back into place.
>
> Here's how we got to this point. Since October, Iran has:
>
> - Shipped 25,000 pounds of enriched uranium out of the country
> - Dismantled and removed two-thirds of its centrifugesw
> - Removed the calandria [a tank that is part of a nuclear reactor] from its heavy water reactor and filled it with concrete
> - Provided unprecedented access to its nuclear facilities and supply chain
>
> Because Iran has completed these steps, the U.S. and international community can begin the next phase under the JCPOA (Joint Comprehensive Plan of Action), which means the U.S. will begin lifting its nuclear-related sanctions on Iran. However, a number of U.S. sanctions authorities and designations will continue to remain in place.
>
> **Source:** https://obamawhitehouse.archives.gov/node/328996

27. Which was the major reason that the world powers, including the United States, negotiated the agreement described above?

    (1) to help the Iranian people gain more control over their own defense

    (2) to help maintain the balance of power in the Middle East

    (3) to promote Iran as a balance to the power of Sunni countries

    (4) to limit the ability of Iran to develop and produce nuclear weapons

28. Which agreement is most similar to the one described above in its approach to solving problems?

    (1) the Nuclear Non-Proliferation Treaty

    (2) the Kyoto Protocol

    (3) the Camp David Accords

    (4) the Paris Agreement

Base your answers to questions 29 and 30 on the passage below and your knowledge of social studies.

Protesters in Beijing, June 1989

Source: Getty Images

29. What was the main goal of the people shown in the photograph?
    (1) to promote the spread of capitalism in China
    (2) to resist growing corporate power in China's economy
    (3) to demand democratic reforms in China
    (4) to protest against foreign interference in Chinese affairs

30. Which best explains why the protesters carried signs written in both Chinese and English?
    (1) Protesters wanted to get their message to people outside of China.
    (2) English was a common second language for people in China.
    (3) Many of the protesters had learned English while attending school in the United States.
    (4) Many government officials did not read the type of Chinese spoken by the protesters.

Part 2: Short-Answer Questions

CRQ Directions (7-9): Analyze the documents and answer the short-answer questions that follow each document in the space provided.

Set 1: Read the two documents and answer the questions that follow them on a separate sheet of paper. Base your answer to each question on the document and on your knowledge of social studies.

Document 1

This excerpt is from P. F. Siebold, a German physician who lived in Japan wrote about Japanese culture, 1852.

> [The women of Japan are] kept in a state of tutelage: that is, of complete dependence on their husbands, sons, or other relatives. They have no legal rights, and their evidence is not admitted in a court of justice. . . . [The husband] also has the power of divorce, which may be considered unlimited. . . . At home, the wife is the mistress of the family; but in other respects she is treated rather as a toy for her husband's amusement, than as the rational, confidential partner of his life.
>
> **Source:** P. F. Siebold, *Manners and Customs of the Japanese, in the Nineteenth Century*, 1852.

1. Identify the historical context in which Siebold made his observations.

Document 2

This excerpt is from Baron Kikuchi, a minister in the Japanese government, on the education of women in Japan, 1907

> Our female education, then, is based on the assumption that women marry, and that its object is to fit girls to become good wives and wise mothers. . . .The house was, and still is . . . the unit of society, not the individual. . . . The object . . . of female education—in a word, to fit girls to be good wives and mothers, proper helpmates and worthy companions of the men of the Meiji, and noble mothers to bring up future generations of Japanese.
>
> **Source:** Baron Kikuchi, minister in the Japanese government, 1907.

2. Explain Kikuchi's point of view about the role of female education in Japan.

3. Identify and explain a similarity or difference between Documents 1 and 2. Be sure to use evidence from both Documents 1 and 2 in your response.

Set 2: Read the two documents and answer the questions that follow them on a separate sheet of paper. Base your answer to each question on the document and on your knowledge of social studies.

Document 1

U.S. General Lucius Clay, telephone conversation with U.S. Chief of Staff Omar Bradly about the Soviet blockade of Berlin, April 10, 1948.

> I do not believe anything will come from protest to Moscow except rejection accompanied by legal argumentation. Nethertheless, I believe that for the record a protest at Moscow is desireable, particularly if it can be given concurrently with similar protests from British and French Governments. Both of latter are weakening and apt to give in to Soviet position. This is particularly true in case of French who really lack means to support their Berlin contingent by air. An approach to British and French Governments by our Government relative to protest might at least serve to hold their positions for time being.
>
> **Source:** *The Papers of General Lucius D. Clay: Germany, 1945–1949,* vol. 2 (Bloomington: Indiana University Press, 1974). Jean Edward Smith, ed.

1. Explain the geographic context of the issue described by Clay.

Document 2

This excerpt is from Andrei Vyshinsky, speech to the UN Security Council, October 4, 1948.

> Beyond any dispute, the question of the Berlin situation is closely connected with the question of Germany as a whole, and the separation of the Berlin problem from the German problem as a whole would be utterly artificial and could result only in wrong decisions not in conformity with the real state of affairs. The placing of the Berlin problem before the Security Council would constitute a direct violation of Article 107 of the [UN] Charter which says that "Nothing in the present charter shall invalidate or preclude action in relation to any state which during the second World War has been an enemy of any signatory to the present charter, taken or authorized as a result of that war by the governments having responsibility for such action.".
>
> **Source:** *The USSR and World Peace: Andrei Y. Vyshinsky,* ed. Jessica Smith (New York: International Publishers, 1949), 41–46.

2. Idenitfy the intended audience of Vyshinsky in this excerpt.

3. Explain how the conflict over Berlin in 1948 was a turning point in international affairs. Be sure to use evidence from Documents 1 and 2 in your response.

Part 3: Enduring Issues Extended Essay

Directions

An enduring issue is an issue that exists across time. It is one that many societies have attempted to address with varying degrees of success. Read the following documents and take notes in the margin identifying at least two themes in each one. Then use these notes and the Planning Page to prepare to write the essay. Finally, on a separate sheet of paper or on a computer, write your extended essay.

In your essay:

Identify the issue based on a historically accurate interpretation of **three** documents.

Define the issue using evidence from three documents.

Argue that this is a significant issue that has endured by showing:

- How the issue has affected people or been affected by people.
- How the issue has continued to be an issue or changed over time.

Include outside information from your knowledge of social studies and evidence from the documents.

Keep in mind these terms:

Identify—means to put a name or to name

Define—means to explain features of a thing or concept so that it can be understood

Argue—means to provide a series of statements that provide evidence and reasons to support a conclusion.

Document 1

In the wake of the Boxer Rebellion, the Qing Dynasty saw a need for fundamental reforms. The excerpt is the Qing Reform Edict, January 29, 1901.

> We have now received Her Majesty's decree to devote ourselves fully to China's revitalization, to suppress vigorously the use of the terms *new* and *old,* and to blend together the best of what is Chinese and what is foreign. The root of China's weakness lies in harmful habits too firmly entrenched, in rules and regulations too minutely drawn, in the overabundance of inept and mediocre officials and in the paucity of truly outstanding ones, in petty bureaucrats who hide behind the written word and in clerks and yamen runners [administrative clerks] who use the written word as a talismans [an object that brings good luck] to acquire personal fortunes, in the mountains of correspondence between government offices that have no relationship to reality, and in the seniority system and associated practices that block the way of men of real talent.
>
> **Source:** *Sources of Chinese Tradition: From 1600 Through the Twentieth Century,* edited Wm. Theodore de Bary and Richard Lufrano (New York: Columbia University Press, 2000), volume 2, 286.

Document 2

This excerpt is from Sukarno, leader of Indonesia, speaking at the Bandung Conference, 1955. The conference saw representatives from Asian and African nations meet to discuss economic development and decolonization.

> All of us, I am certain, are united by more important things than those which superficially divide us. We are united, for instance, by a common detestation of colonialism in whatever form it appears. We are united by a common detestation of [racism]. And we are united by a common determination to preserve and stabilize peace in the world. . . .
>
> We are often told, "Colonialism is dead." Let us not be deceived or even soothed by that. I say to you, colonialism is not yet dead. How can we say it is dead, so long as vast areas of Asia and Africa are unfree?
>
> And, I beg of you, do not think of colonialism as only in the classic form which we of Indonesia, and our brothers in different parts of Asia and Africa, knew. Colonialism has also its modern dress, in the form of economic control, intellectual control, actual physical control by a small but alien community within a nation. It is a skillful and determined enemy, and it appears in many guises. It does not give up its loot easily. Wherever, whenever and however it appears, colonialism is an evil thing, and one which must be eradicated from the earth.
>
> **Source:** *Africa-Asia Speaks from Bandung* (Djakarta: Indonesian Ministry of Foreign Affairs, 1955).

Document 3

This excerpt is from the Declaration of the Non-Aligned Movement Conference, Belgrade, Yugoslavia, 1961. Meeting during the Cold War, this conference defined the intentions of nations to not ally with either superpower.

> Imperialism is weakening. Colonial empires and other forms of foreign oppression of peoples in Asia, Africa, and Latin America are gradually disappearing from the stage of history. Great successes have been achieved in the struggle of many peoples for national independence and equality. . . .
>
> The Governments of countries participating in the Conference resolutely reject the view that war, including the "cold war," is inevitable as this view reflects a sense both of helplessness and hopelessness and is contrary to the progress of the world. They affirm their unwavering faith that the international community is able to organize its life without resorting to means which actually belong to a past epoch of human history.
>
> **Source:** "Text of the Final Declaration of the Belgrade Conference of Non-Aligned Nations," *New York Times,* September 7, 1961.

Document 4

This excerpt is from Jean-Bertrand Aristide, 1990. He had just been the first democratically elected president of the nation in nearly 200 years.

What happens to poor countries when they embrace free trade? In Haiti in 1986 we imported just 7,000 tons of rice, the main staple food of the country. The vast majority was grown in Haiti. In the late 1980s Haiti [accepted] . . . free-trade policies [backed] by the international lending agencies and lifted tariffs on rice imports. Cheaper rice immediately flooded in from the United States where the rice industry is subsidized [supported by the government]. . . . Haiti's peasant farmers could not possibly compete. By 1996 Haiti was importing 196,000 tons of foreign rice at the cost of $100 million a year. Haitian rice production [almost stopped]. Once the dependence on foreign rice was complete, import prices began to rise, leaving Haiti's population, particularly the urban poor, completely at the whim of rising world grain prices. And the prices continue to rise. . . .

The dilemma [problem] is, I believe, the classic dilemma of the poor; a choice between death and death. Either we enter a global economic system, in which we know we cannot survive, or, we refuse, and face death by slow starvation. With choices like these, the urgency of finding a third way is clear.

Source: Jean-Bertrand Aristide, *Eyes of the Heart: Seeking a Path for the Poor in the Age of Globalization* (Monroe, Maine: Common Courage Press, 2000).

Document 5

Growth in Exports by World Region, 1960 to 2016

Region	Exports as Percentage of the Total Economy in 1960	Exports as Percentage of the Total Economy in 2016
World	12	29
North America	6	14
South Asia	6	18
Latin America and the Caribbean	11	21
East Asia and Pacific	8	25
Sub-Saharan Africa	21	28
Europe	19	44

Source: Adapted from the World Bank. https://data.worldbank.org/indicator/NE.EXP.GNFS.ZS

Index

C

D

E

F

G

H

I

J

K

L

M

N

O

P

Q

R

S

Y

Z